THE BEST SHORT PLAYS 1977

Chilton Book Company

RADNOR, PENNSYLVANIA

THE
BEST
SHORT
PLAYS *1977*

edited and with an introduction by

STANLEY RICHARDS

Best Short Plays Series

Copyright © 1977 by Stanley Richards
First Edition
All Rights Reserved
Published in Radnor, Pa., by Chilton Book Company and simultaneously in Don Mills, Ontario, Canada, by Thomas Nelson & Sons, Ltd.

Library of Congress Catalog Card No: 38-8006
ISBN: 0-8019-6515-2
ISSN: 0067-6284

Manufactured in the United States of America

for Ella Gerber

BOOKS AND PLAYS *by Stanley Richards*

B O O K S:

The Best Short Plays 1976
The Best Short Plays 1975
The Best Short Plays 1974
The Best Short Plays 1973
The Best Short Plays 1972
The Best Short Plays 1971
The Best Short Plays 1970
The Best Short Plays 1969
The Best Short Plays 1968
Great Musicals of the American Theatre: Volume One
Great Musicals of the American Theatre: Volume Two
America on Stage: Ten Great Plays of American History
The Tony Winners
Best Mystery and Suspense Plays of the Modern Theatre
10 Classic Mystery and Suspense Plays of the Modern Theatre
Best Plays of the Sixties
Best Short Plays of the World Theatre: 1968–1973
Best Short Plays of the World Theatre: 1958–1967
Modern Short Comedies from Broadway and London
Canada on Stage

P L A Y S :

Through a Glass, Darkly
August Heat
Sun Deck
Tunnel of Love
Journey to Bahia
O Distant Land
Mood Piece
Mr. Bell's Creation
The Proud Age
Once to Every Boy
Half-Hour, Please
Know Your Neighbor
Gin and Bitterness
The Hills of Bataan
District of Columbia

CONTENTS

INTRODUCTION

With the publication of *The Best Short Plays 1977,* the series, under my editorship, enters its tenth year of publication. Since anniversaries customarily are a time for reflection and a restatement of values, if I may, I should like to offer a few comments within these pages.

For a decade now, each volume has juxtaposed established writers with talented unknowns. In other words, what I have endeavored to do is provide an annual collection of discovery, a discovery of eminently playable, entertaining and enlightening plays whether by name writers or heretofore untapped talents.

Incidentally, upon occasion I have been asked how I decide on the order of presenting the plays in the book. Let me hasten to add now, that it is not a matter of the authors' previous track-records, nor is it a matter of personal preference, but rather an attempt to present a well-balanced collection to my readers.

Within the span of ten years, we have published 129 plays in *The Best Short Plays* series and, to paraphrase what I wrote in the fifth anniversary edition, almost eighty percent of them received their first publication in these pages. The list of contributors includes some of our foremost international dramatists, yet there is an almost equal representation of new and outstanding young writers, a number of whom have since gone on to their own prominence.

Plays from these collections have been widely produced on professional and amateur stages, in colleges and universities, regional, community, and stock theatres, and on public and network television.

Many have successfully survived sea changes by being effectively produced in distant areas of the world and this, to me, is one of the most significant tasks of an editor—the ability to select plays that can appeal widely and to various cultures.

Naturally, and quite justifiably, the question arises: just how is this accomplished? The answers, of course, are numerous and dependent upon those questioned. Yet, a basic factor remains steadfast in spite of all the advances of theatrical techniques and increasing experimentation. Drama is deeply rooted in humanity and, consequently, for a play to have audience appeal it must revolve about that most essential element, characterization; vivid, vibrant people from whom all else springs dramatically. To quote once again from my earlier introduction, when the legendary Sarah Siddons was queried about what she was looking for in plays, whether new or old, she is reported to have replied, "truth to nature." She did not mean naturalism *per se* but rather that the situations and the emotions expressed by the *characters* should be credible ones which both she and her audiences could accept as true to human nature, however extravagantly or in whatever form they might be expressed.

In addition to selecting plays, it often is the duty of an editor to work closely with an author, to guide him as he develops his play to its most polished and effective state possible. Frequently, a writer—regardless of the degree of his experience—requires this editorial hand just as an actor benefits from the guidance of a perceptive director.

Too often, in my reading of manuscripts, I have noted that the author is prone to overwrite, particularly in the earliest drafts of his work. By encumbering his creation with too much explanatory or extraneous matter he negates its dramatic effectiveness. It is at this point that he benefits from a judicious eye, whether it be that of a director or editor, who steps in to guide and assist him, or at least advise, on the efficacy of pruning and sharpening and, accordingly, generating a heightened perspective to characterizations and scenes.

As dramatist Robert E. Lee (co-author with Jerome Lawrence of *Inherit the Wind* and many other plays) wrote in the American College Theatre Festival's *Playwriting Awards Newsletter:* "Plays do not flow only from the point of a pencil; sometimes they must be written with an eraser. A gifted young man or woman wants to pour out the cornucopia of his (or her) imagination. Picking the best and scissoring out the clutter is often the hardest trick in the whole discipline of writing.

"Emlyn Williams observed (after helping Oscar Hammerstein peel *South Pacific* down to size): 'If there's something that you rather like, take it out!' A play, unlike a novel, is such a highly distilled essence—the minutes one has to share with the audience are so fragile and few—that there is no room for anything which dilutes the piece."

In the same vein, the late Sir Noël Coward, after cutting more than half an hour out of a play, declared: "It is a distressing experience and a bitter lesson for an author to find that cutting his work improves it."

This, then, is one of the major tasks of a creative editor embarking on a collection of mainly new works. There are many other duties, to be sure, but it is in the overseeing of the fulfillment of a creative work that undeniably provides the most rewarding moments.

The time is appropriate for me to once again express my deepest gratitude to the contributing authors in the series, the reviewers who have helped spark the way, and, of course, to my readers and those myriad groups and theatres who, in the past ten years, have found in these annuals new material to produce and new theatrical territories to explore.

STANLEY RICHARDS
New York, N.Y.

David Mamet

THE DUCK
VARIATIONS

David Mamet

Undeniably one of the most acclaimed new playwrights of recent years, David Mamet was born on November 30, 1947, and grew up in the environs of Chicago, which he still considers "home."

After receiving his B.A. in English Literature from Goddard College, Vermont, in 1969, Mr. Mamet spent the following years teaching acting and playwriting at Marlboro College, Goddard, the University of Chicago, and at the St. Nicholas Theatre Company in Chicago which he helped found.

According to a press interview, the author began writing while a student at Goddard. Mark Ryder, the dancer and choreographer taught there, and Mr. Mamet showed him some of his plays. "I'd say they don't look like plays to me," Mr. Mamet said. Ryder replied: "That's not your responsibility, you teach yourself to write, write it down and then it's a play. Let your critics worry about that."

There was no cause for alarm. The first of his plays to be commercially produced in New York were *Sexual Perversity in Chicago* and *The Duck Variations,* the latter included in this anthology. Originally, the double bill opened at the Off-Off-Broadway St. Clement's Theatre and such was its impact and success that it subsequently was transferred to the Off-Broadway Cherry Lane Theatre where it continues to be a major success of the season. Both short plays, as well as his full-length comedy, *American Buffalo,* brought him an "Obie" award for the "best new American plays of 1975-76."

As of this writing, *American Buffalo* now is scheduled for Broadway presentation. Director Ulu Grosbard who will stage the play has described Mamet as "a totally fresh voice in the American theatre," an opinion documented by many other sources who have written that he unquestionably "is a playwright to watch and listen to . . . what we watch for is his future; what we listen to is his present."

When the double bill of *Sexual Perversity in Chicago* and *The Duck Variations* opened at the Cherry Lane, the reviewers trotted out their most expansive adjectives declaring that it was "wild and hilarious . . . flawless . . . superb and brilliant."

The idea for *The Duck Variations,* Mr. Mamet has admitted, "came from listening to a lot of old Jewish men all my life, particularly my grandfather." As John Simon wrote in *The New Leader:* "Something larger looms beyond its facade. Two old men, strangers, occupy the same lake-front bench in a Chicago park. In very Jewish constructions and cadences, they start talking; the conversation takes off from and keeps returning to what is in front of them: ducks. All the verbal flotsam spouted by trivial old people, bored with the past and afraid of the future or its lack, is there: pitiable platitudes, pontifications, half-remembered newspaper and magazine items, fantasies propounded as gospel truth, nuggets of fact mixed in with quicksands of fiction. It is meant to sound interesting, knowledgeable, even profound—to earn a little recognition and prestige before loneliness and death close in . . . Talk is the last, precarious hold on active life; what matters is not making sense, but hanging in."

The author, who recently was chosen to receive a CBS Fellowship in Creative Writing at the Yale School of Drama, also has written *Squirrels; The Woods;* and *The Poet and the Rent,* all produced by the St. Nicholas Theatre Company in Chicago, and *The Revenge of the Space Pandas,* commissioned by and written for the New York State Council on the Arts under a "plays for younger audiences" grant.

Characters:

EMIL VAREC
GEORGE S. ARONOVITZ } two gentlemen in their sixties

Scene:

A park on the edge of a big city on a lake. An afternoon around Easter.

First Variation:
It's Nice, the Park Is Nice

EMIL: It's nice.

GEORGE: The park is nice.

EMIL: You forget . . .

GEORGE: . . . You remember.

EMIL: I don't know . . .

GEORGE: What's to know? There's a boat!

EMIL: So early?

GEORGE: I suppose so. . . . Because there it is.

EMIL: I wonder if it's cold out there.

GEORGE: There, here, it's like it is today. How it is *today*, that's how it is.

EMIL: But the boat is moving . . .

GEORGE: So it's colder in relation to how fast the boat is going.

EMIL: The water is colder than the land.

GEORGE: So it's cold in relation to the water.

EMIL: So it's a different temperature on the boat than on a bench.

GEORGE: They probably got sweaters.

EMIL: There's more than one in the boat?

GEORGE: Wait 'til they come round again.

EMIL: Where did they go?

GEORGE: Over there, behind the pier, where could they go?

EMIL: Not far . . . it's expensive a boat.

GEORGE: They care?

EMIL: No.

GEORGE: If they got the money for a *boat*, they can afford it.

EMIL: It's not cheap.

GEORGE: I said it was cheap?

EMIL: Even a small boat.

GEORGE: I know it's not cheap.

EMIL: Even a very small boat is expensive.

GEORGE: Many times a small boat is even *more* expensive.

EMIL: Ah.

GEORGE: Depending . . .

EMIL: Mmm.

GEORGE: On many factors.

EMIL: Mmm.

GEORGE: . . . The size of the boat . . .

EMIL: Yes.

GEORGE: . . . The engine.

EMIL: Yes. The *size* of the engine.

GEORGE: Certainly, certainly.

EMIL: The speed of the engine.

GEORGE: Many factors.

EMIL: The speed of the *boat*.

GEORGE: That. None of it's cheap. It's all very intricate.

EMIL: Cars.

GEORGE: Boats, cars . . . air travel. The military. It was never cheap.

EMIL: Housing.

GEORGE: *(Looks)* There's two of them in the boat.

EMIL: It's the same boat?

GEORGE: How many boats have we seen today?

EMIL: That's what I'm asking.

GEORGE: One.

EMIL: *(Looks)* Another boat!

GEORGE: One, two . . .

EMIL: A real clipper, too.

GEORGE: Where?

EMIL: Look at *her,* will ya!

GEORGE: That?

EMIL: What else? Go, sister!

GEORGE: That?

EMIL: Sure as shooting.

GEORGE: That's the water pump.

EMIL: That?

GEORGE: Yes.

EMIL: That?

GEORGE: Yes.

EMIL: The pump house?

GEORGE: Yes.

EMIL: She's the water pump?

GEORGE: Yes.

EMIL: . . . Look at her float.

GEORGE: Mmm.

EMIL: Look at her . . . just sit there.

GEORGE: Mmm.

EMIL: All year 'round.

GEORGE: I'll give you that.

EMIL: What a life.

GEORGE: Ducks!

EMIL: Where?

GEORGE: Where I'm pointing.

EMIL: Ahh.

GEORGE: A sure sign of spring.

EMIL: Autumn, too.

GEORGE: Uh huh.

EMIL: . . . You see them . . .

GEORGE: Yes.

EMIL: They go south . . .

GEORGE: Um.

EMIL: They come back . . .

GEORGE: Ummm.

EMIL: They live . . .

GEORGE: They go . . .

EMIL: Ahhh.

GEORGE: Ducks like to go . . .

EMIL: . . . Yes?

GEORGE: Where it's *nice* . . .

EMIL: Ehhh?

GEORGE: *At that time!*

EMIL: Of course.

GEORGE: And they're made so they just *go.*
Something inside says it's getting a little cold .   a
little too cold . . .

EMIL: Like humans, they don't like cold.

GEORGE: And there they go.

EMIL: There they go.

GEORGE: And the same when it's warm.

EMIL: They come back.

GEORGE: They got a leader. A lead duck. He starts . . . he's a
duck. But he stays with the pack. Many times. He comes, he goes.
He learns the route. Maybe he's got a little more on the ball.

EMIL: All this time there is another lead duck.

GEORGE: Of course. But *he,* he goes, he lives, maybe he finds a
mate . . .

EMIL: Yes.

GEORGE: And he *waits* . . . The *lead* duck . . . who knows?

EMIL: He dies.

GEORGE: One day, yes. He dies. He gets lost . .

EMIL: And our duck moves up.

GEORGE: *He* is now the leader. It is *he* who guides them from one home to the next. They all know the way. Each of them has it in him to know when the time is to move . . . but *he* . . . He will be in charge until . . .

EMIL: Yes.

GEORGE: Just like the other one . . .

EMIL: There's no shame in that.

GEORGE: Just like the previous duck . . .

EMIL: It happened to *him,* it's got to happen to *him.*

GEORGE: The time comes to step down.

EMIL: He dies.

GEORGE: He dies, he leaves . . . something. . . . And another duck moves on up.

EMIL: And *someday.*

GEORGE: Yes.

EMIL: Someone will take *his* place.

GEORGE: Until . . .

EMIL: It's boring just to think about it.

Second Variation:
The Duck's Life

GEORGE: You know, the duck's life is not all hearts and flowers.
He's got his worries, too.
He's got fleas and lice and diseases of the body.
Delusions.
Wing problems.
Sexual difficulties.
Many things.

EMIL: It's not an easy life.

GEORGE: Only the beginning.
The duck is at the mercy of any elements in the vicinity.
Sunspots.
Miscarriage.
Inappropriate changes in the weather.

EMIL: Yes.

GEORGE: Hunters. Blight. Tornadoes.
Traps. Any number of airplanes.
EMIL: Small vicious children.
GEORGE: Chain stores. And, of course, the Blue Heron.
EMIL: Blue Heron?
GEORGE: The hereditary Enemy of the Duck.
EMIL: Yeah?
GEORGE: It's what they call symbiosis. They both live to insure the happiness of each other. The Blue Herons eat ducks, and the duck . . .
EMIL: Yes?
GEORGE: The duck's part of the bargain . . .
EMIL: Is to be eaten by the Heron?
GEORGE: Is to. Well, it slips me for the moment, but it's not as one-sided as it might appear.
Nature has given the duck speed and endurance and the art of concealment. She has made the Heron large and unwieldy and *blue* to be able to spot at a distance. On the other hand he has the benefits of size and occasional camouflage, should he come against something blue.
EMIL: And shaped like a bird.
GEORGE: Not always necessary.
The battle between the two is as old as time.
The ducks propagating, the Herons eating them. The Herons multiplying and losing great numbers to exhaustion in the never-ending chase of the duck.
Each keeping the other in check, down through history, until a bond of unspoken friendship and respect unites them, even in the embrace of death.
EMIL: So why do they continue to fight?
GEORGE: Survival of the fittest. The never-ending struggle between heredity and environment. The urge to combat.
Old as the oceans. Instilled in us all. Who can say to what purpose?
EMIL: Who?
GEORGE: We do not know.
But this much we *do* know. As long as the duck exists, he will battle day and night, sick and well with the Heron, for so is it writ. And as long as the sky is made dark with the wing of the Monster Bird, the Heron will feast on duck.

Third Variation:
Also They Got Barnyard Ducks

EMIL: Also they got barnyard ducks.
GEORGE: Yeah. I know.
EMIL: That they raise for Easter and Thanksgiving.
GEORGE: You're thinking of turkeys.
EMIL: Also ducks.
GEORGE: They keep 'em? In captivity?
EMIL: Yeah. In the barnyard. They clip their wings.
GEORGE: Uh.
EMIL: Yeah.
What? You can't put 'em on their honor?!
GEORGE: Times have changed.
EMIL: Vandalism . . . . . .
They fat 'em up.
They feed 'em, the farmers, on special mixtures.
Corn, and maybe an oat. And they got special injections they give
'em. To keep 'em happy.
GEORGE: And they can't fly.
EMIL: No.
GEORGE: All the wildness is gone.
EMIL: Just walking around the farm all day. Eating.
GEORGE: They're allowed to mate?
EMIL: This we do not know.
GEORGE: Eh?
EMIL: Only a few farmers know this.
GEORGE: Yeah?
EMIL: The mating of ducks is a private matter between the duck
in question and his mate.
GEORGE: Yeah?
EMIL: It is a thing which very few white men have witnessed.
. . .
And those who claim to have seen it . . .
Strangely do not wish to speak.
GEORGE: There are things we're better off not to know.
EMIL: If you don't know, you never can be forced to tell.
GEORGE: Yeah.
EMIL: They don't got those beaks for nothing.
GEORGE: Too true.
EMIL: Everything has a purpose.
GEORGE: True.

EMIL: Every blessed thing.

GEORGE: Oh, yes.

EMIL: That lives has got a purpose.

GEORGE: Ducks . . .

EMIL: Sweat glands . . .

GEORGE: Yeah.

EMIL: We don't sweat for nothing, you know.

GEORGE: I know it.

EMIL: Everything that lives must sweat.

GEORGE: It's all got a purpose.

EMIL: It's all got a rhyme *and* a reason.

GEORGE: The purpose of sweat is, in itself, not clear.

EMIL: Yes . . .

GEORGE: But . . . There it is.

EMIL: A purpose and a reason. Even those we, at this time, do not clearly understand.

GEORGE: Sure as shooting.

EMIL: The yearly migration of the duck, to mate and take a little rest . . .

GEORGE: Purpose.

EMIL: Sweat . . .

GEORGE: Purpose.

EMIL: There's nothing you could possibly name that doesn't have a purpose.

. . .

. . .

Don't even bother to try.

Don't waste your time.

GEORGE: I'm in no hurry.

EMIL: It's all got a purpose. The very fact that you are sitting here right now on this bench has got a purpose.

GEORGE: And so, by process of elimination, does the bench.

EMIL: Now you're talking sense.

GEORGE: Darn tootin'.

EMIL: The law of the universe is a law unto itself.

GEORGE: Yes. Yes.

EMIL: And woe be to the man who fools around.

GEORGE: You can't get away with *nothing*.

EMIL: And if you *could* it would have a purpose.

GEORGE: Nobody knows that better than me.

EMIL: . . .

Well put.

Fourth Variation:
The Duck Is Not Like Us

EMIL: The duck is not like us, you know.
GEORGE: How so?
EMIL: The duck is an egg-bearing creature.
GEORGE: And we're not, I suppose?
EMIL: I didn't say that.
The young of the duck at birth are already trained to do things most humans learn only much later.
Swim.
Follow their mother.
GEORGE: Fly.
EMIL: No. I don't believe they can fly until later in life.
GEORGE: But it's possible.
EMIL: It's possible, but you're wrong.
GEORGE: . . .
As a matter of fact I do remember reading somewhere that many small ducks *do* possess the ability to fly at birth.
EMIL: I do think you are mistaken.
GEORGE: No. It could be . . . But no.
EMIL: Yes. I believe you're sadly wrong.
GEORGE: No. I wouldn't *swear* to it . . .
EMIL: No.
GEORGE: But I'd almost *swear* I've read that *somewhere* . . .
EMIL: Yes, I'm fairly sure you're wrong on that one point.
GEORGE: Some little-known group of ducks.
EMIL: No. All my knowledge of nature tells me I must say no.
GEORGE: A very small group of ducks.
EMIL: I can not let that by.
GEORGE: But I think . . .
EMIL: It's possible you *misread* the . . .
GEORGE: Possible, but . . .
EMIL: No, no. No. I must still stick to my saying no.
No.
GEORGE: . . .
Perhaps I misread it.
What a thing, however, To be able to fly. In later life.
EMIL: Swimming ain't so bad either.
GEORGE: But any fool who knows how to swim can swim.
It takes a *bird* to fly.
EMIL: Insects also fly.

GEORGE: But not in the same category.
EMIL: Insects . . . birds and insects and . . .
. . .
. . .
I *could* be wrong, but . . .
GEORGE: You *are* wrong. Nothing else flies.

Fifth Variation: Did You Know What I Was Reading

GEORGE: Did you know what I was reading somewhere?
EMIL: Don't start.
GEORGE: About the stratosphere.
The stratosphere, particularly the lower stratosphere, is becoming messy with gook.
EMIL: Eh?
GEORGE: According to the weatherman.
EMIL: *Our* stratosphere?
GEORGE: Everybody's. Because it's all the same thing.
EMIL: Eh?
GEORGE: As if you drop a pebble in a pond and the ripples spread you-know-not-where . . .
EMIL: Yes?
GEORGE: So, when you stick shit up in the stratosphere . . .
EMIL: Yes?
GEORGE: You got the same problem.
EMIL: What kind of gook?
GEORGE: All kinds.
Dirt . . .
EMIL: Yes.
GEORGE: Gook . .
EMIL: No good.
GEORGE: Automotive . .
EMIL: Yeah.
GEORGE: Cigarette smoke. It's all up there. It's not going anywhere.
EMIL: Yeah.
GEORGE: They're finding out many things about the world we live in from the air.
EMIL: Yes.

GEORGE: For, in many ways . . . the air is more a part of our world than we would like to admit.
Think about it.

EMIL: I will.

GEORGE: Planes that come down, they got to wash 'em right away.
They go up clean, they come down filthy.

EMIL: Yes.

GEORGE: But creatures with no choice: insects, ducks

EMIL: Gliders

GEORGE: It's a shame. They should be shot.

EMIL: Some of them are shot.

GEORGE: No, *them,* the ones responsible.
Ducks!
They're finding ducks with lung cancer.
I was reading about this hunter in the forest and he shot a bunch of ducks that were laying down . . .

EMIL: Yes.

GEORGE: And he missed.
But! As he was walking away he heard this hacking, and he went back to investigate.
And there were these five or six stunted ducks sitting in a clearing hacking their guts out.

EMIL: No!

GEORGE: Coughing and sneezing. Runny noses . . . and they'd flap their wings and go maybe two flaps and fall down coughing.

EMIL: It's no good for you.

GEORGE: And he says instead of running off they all came up and huddled around his feet with these rheumy, runny eyes.
Looking quite pathetic.
And he says he couldn't get it out of his mind . . .

EMIL: What?

GEORGE: I'll feel silly to say it.

EMIL: Tell me.

GEORGE: That they looked like they were trying to bum a smoke.

EMIL: . .
. . .
That's ridiculous.

GEORGE: I know it.

EMIL: I think someone is putting you on.

GEORGE: Very likely.

EMIL: You aren't even *supposed* to smoke in a forest.

GEORGE: Go fight City Hall.

Sixth Variation:
What Kind of a World Is it

GEORGE: What kind of a world is it that can't even keep its streets clean?

EMIL: A self-destructive world.

GEORGE: You said it.

EMIL: A cruel world.

GEORGE: A dirty world.
Yeh. I'm getting old.

EMIL: Nobody's getting any younger.

GEORGE: Almost makes a feller want to stop trying.

EMIL: Stop trying what?

GEORGE: You know, life is a lot simpler than many people would like us to believe.

EMIL: How so?

GEORGE: Take the duck.

EMIL: Alright.

GEORGE: Of what does his life consist?

EMIL: Well, flying . . .

GEORGE: Yes.

EMIL: Eating.

GEORGE: Yes.

EMIL: Sleeping.

GEORGE: Yes.

EMIL: Washing himself.

GEORGE: Yes.

EMIL: Mating.

GEORGE: Yes.

EMIL: And perhaps getting himself shot by some jerk in a red hat.

GEORGE: Or "Death."

EMIL: Should we include that as one of the activities of life?

GEORGE: Well, you can't die in a vacuum.

EMIL: That's true.

GEORGE: So there we have it: the duck, too, is doomed to death . . .

EMIL: As are we all.

GEORGE: But his life prior to that point is so much more simple. He is born. He learns his trade: to fly. He flies, he eats, he finds a mate, he has young, he flies some more, he dies. A simple, straightforward easy-to-handle life.

EMIL: So what's your point?

GEORGE: Well, lookit:

EMIL: Okay.

GEORGE: On his deathbed what does the duck say if only he could speak?

EMIL: He wants to live some more.

GEORGE: Right. But remorse? Guilt? Other bad feelings? No. No.
He is in tune with nature.

EMIL: He is a part of nature. He is a duck.

GEORGE: Yes, but so is man a part of nature.

EMIL: Speak for yourself.

GEORGE: I am speaking for myself.

EMIL: Then speak to yourself.

GEORGE: Who asked you to listen?

EMIL: Who asked you to talk?

GEORGE: Why are you getting upset?

EMIL: You upset me.

GEORGE: Yeh?

EMIL: With your talk of nature and the duck and death.
Morbid useless talk. You know, it is a good thing to be perceptive,
but you shouldn't let it get in the way.

GEORGE: And that is the point I was trying to make.

Seventh Variation:
Yes, In Many Ways

GEORGE: Yes, in many ways nature is our window to the world.

EMIL: Nature *is* the world.

GEORGE: Which shows you how easy it is to take a good idea and
glop it up.

EMIL: So who do you complain to?

GEORGE: Well, you complain to me.

EMIL: Do you mind?

GEORGE: I'm glad I got the time to listen.

EMIL: A man needs a friend in this life.

GEORGE: In this or any other life.

EMIL: You said it.
Without a friend, life is not . . .

GEORGE: Worth living?

EMIL: No, it's still worth living. I mean, what is worth living if not life? No. But life without a friend is . . .

GEORGE: It's lonely.

EMIL: It sure is. You said it. It's good to have a friend.

GEORGE: It's good to be a friend.

EMIL: It's good to have a friend to talk to.

GEORGE: It's good to talk to a friend.

EMIL: To complain to a friend . . .

GEORGE: It's good to listen . . .

EMIL: Is good.

GEORGE: To a friend.

EMIL: To make life a little less full of pain . . .

GEORGE: I'd try anything.

EMIL: Is good.

GEORGE: For you, or for a friend.

Because it's good to help

EMIL: To help a friend in need is the most that any man can want to do.

GEORGE: And you couldn't ask for more than that.

EMIL: I wouldn't.

GEORGE: Good.

EMIL: Being a loner in this world . . .

GEORGE: Is not my bag of tea.

EMIL: It's no good. No man is an Island to himself.

GEORGE: Or to anyone else.

EMIL: You can't live alone forever.

You can't live forever anyway. But you can't live alone. Nothing that lives can live alone. Flowers. You never find just one flower. Trees. Ducks.

GEORGE: Cactus.

EMIL: Lives alone?

GEORGE: Well, you take the cactus in the waste. It stands alone as far as the eye can tell.

EMIL: But there are other cacti.

GEORGE: Not in that immediate area, no.

EMIL: What are you trying to say?

GEORGE: That the *cactus,* unlike everything else that cannot live alone, *thrives* . . .

EMIL: I don't want to hear it.

GEORGE: But it's true, the cactus . . .

EMIL: I don't want to hear it. If it's false, don't waste my time and if it is true I don't want to know.

GEORGE: It's a proven fact.

EMIL: I can't hear you.
GEORGE: Even the duck sometimes.
EMIL: *(Looks)*

. . .

. . .

Nothing that lives can live alone.

Eighth Variation: Ahh, I Don't Know

EMIL: Ahh, I don't know.
GEORGE: So what?
EMIL: You gotta point.

. . .

. . .

Sometimes I think the park is more trouble than it's worth.
GEORGE: How so?
EMIL: To come and look at the lake and the trees and animals and sun just once in a while and traipse back. Back to . . .
GEORGE: Your apartment
EMIL: Joyless. Cold concrete.
Apartment. Stuff. Linoleum. Imitation.
GEORGE: The park is more real?
EMIL: The park? Yes.
GEORGE: Sitting on benches?
EMIL: Yes.
GEORGE: Visiting tame animals?
EMIL: Taken from wildest captivity.
GEORGE: Watching a lake that's a sewer?
EMIL: At least it's water.
GEORGE: You wanna drink it?
EMIL: I drink it everyday.
GEORGE: Yeah. After it's been pured and filtered.
EMIL: A lake just the same. My Inland Sea.
GEORGE: Fulla Inland Shit.
EMIL: It's better than nothing.
GEORGE: Nothing is better than nothing.
EMIL: Well, it's a close second.
GEORGE: But why does it hurt you to come to the park?
EMIL: I sit home, I can come to the park. At the park the only place I have to go is home.

GEORGE: Better not to have a park?

EMIL: I don't know.

GEORGE: Better not to have a zoo? We should forget what a turtle is?

EMIL: Aaaaah.

GEORGE: Our children should never know the joy of watching some animal . . . behaving?

EMIL: I don't know.

GEORGE: They should stay home and know only guppies eating their young?

EMIL: Let 'em go to the country. Nature's playground.
The country.
The Land that Time Forgot.
Mallards in formation.
Individual barnyard noises.
Horses.
Rusty gates.
An ancient tractor.
Hay, barley.
Mushrooms.
Rye.
Stuffed full of abundance.
Enough to feed the nations of the world.

GEORGE: We'll have 'em over. We don't get enough riffraff.

EMIL: Enough to gorge the countless cows of South America.

GEORGE: Did you make that up?

EMIL: Yes.

GEORGE: I take my hat off to you.

EMIL: Thank you.

GEORGE: "Feed the many" . . . how does it go?

EMIL: Um. Stuff the nameless . . .
It'll come to me.

GEORGE: When you get it, tell me.

Ninth Variation:
At the Zoo They Got Ducks

EMIL: At the zoo they got ducks.
They got. What do you call it? . . .
A mallard. They got a mallard and a . . . what is it?
A cantaloupe.

GEORGE: You mean an antelope.
EMIL: No . . . no, it's not cantaloupe. But it's *like* cantaloupe. Uh . . .
GEORGE: Antelope?
EMIL: No! *Antelope* is like an elk. What *I'm* thinking is like a duck.
GEORGE: Goose?
EMIL: No. But it's . . .
What sounds like *cantaloupe,* but it isn't.
GEORGE: . . . . Antelope.
I'm sorry, but that's it.
EMIL: No. Wait! Wait. Ca . . . cala . . . camma . . . grantal . . .
GEORGE: Canadian ducks?
EMIL: No! I've *seen* 'em, the ones I mean. I've seen 'em in the zoo.
GEORGE: Ducks?
EMIL: Yes! Ducks that I'm talking about. By God, I know what I mean . . .
They're called . . .
The only thing that comes up is canta. Pantel. Pandel. Panda . . . Candarolpe . . .
GEORGE: They ain't got no panda.
EMIL: I know it . . . Panna . . .
GEORGE: They *had* a panda at the *other* zoo but it died.
EMIL: Yeah. Nanna . . .
GEORGE: There were two of 'em. Or three. But they were all men and when they died . . . they couldn't have any babies, of course . . .
EMIL: Randspan?
GEORGE: . . . So the pandas . . .
EMIL: . . . Lope . . .
GEORGE: Died.
EMIL: Lo . . . Lopa? LooLa . . .
GEORGE: Not swans?
EMIL: No. Please. I know swans. I'm talking about ducks.
GEORGE: I know it.
EMIL: Can . . .
GEORGE: Those pandas were something.
EMIL: Yeah.
GEORGE: Giant pandas.
EMIL: Yeah.
GEORGE: *Big* things.

EMIL: I've seen 'em.
GEORGE: Not lately you haven't.
EMIL: No.
GEORGE: 'Cause they been dead.
EMIL: I know it.
GEORGE: From the Orient. Pandas from the Far East. There for all to see.
EMIL: Mantalope?
GEORGE: Black and White.
EMIL: Palapope . . .
GEORGE: Together.
EMIL: Maaaa . . .
GEORGE: The giant panda.
EMIL: Fanna . . .
GEORGE: Over two stories tall.
EMIL: Raaa?
GEORGE: It got too expensive to feed it. They had to put 'em to sleep.

Tenth Variation:
It's a Crying Shame

EMIL: It's a crying shame.
GEORGE: Eh?
EMIL: A crying piss-laden shame.
A blot on our time.
Gook on the scutcheon.
Oil slicks from here to Africa.
GEORGE: Huh?
EMIL: They allow no smoking on ocean liners. One spark over-board and the whole ocean goes.
GEORGE: Yeah?
EMIL: Oil-bearing ducks floating up dead on the beaches.
Beaches closing. No place to swim. The surface of the sea is solid dying wildlife. In Australia . . . they're finding fish, they're going blind from lack of sun.
New scary species are developing. They eat nothing but dead birds.
GEORGE: Yeah?
EMIL: Catfish.
GEORGE: . . .

I think that's something different.
EMIL: Nevermore. Thrushes.
No more the duck.
Bluejays.
Cardinals. Making the dead ocean their last home.
GEORGE: When I was young . . .
EMIL: Floating up dead on the beaches.
GEORGE: Around my house . . .
EMIL: Their lungs a sodden pulp of gasoline.
They're made for something better than that.
GEORGE: In the springtime we used to . . .
EMIL: Can't even burn leaves in the fall. We have to wrap them in plastic. Next we'll have to wrap each leaf individually.
Little envelopes for each leaf, it shouldn't contaminate us with the vapors. Little numbered packets.
GEORGE: Our lawn was.
EMIL: What?
GEORGE: Eh?
EMIL: What was your lawn?
GEORGE: I forget.
EMIL: Can you imagine, being the last man alive to have seen a Blue Heron? Or a wild buffalo?
GEORGE: No man can live in the path of a wild buffalo.
EMIL: Alright. A regular buffalo, then.
GEORGE: They got 'em at the zoo.
EMIL: Buffalos?
GEORGE: Yeah, they got plenty of 'em.
EMIL: But that's in captivity.
GEORGE: I should hope so.
EMIL: Well, in any case, you see my point.
GEORGE: Yes . . .
EMIL: Well, that's the point I was trying to make.

Eleventh Variation:
You Know, I Remember

GEORGE: You know, I remember reading somewhere .
EMIL: Please.
GEORGE: Alright.
EMIL: I hurt your feelings.

GEORGE: Yes.

EMIL: I'm sorry.

GEORGE: I know.

EMIL: There is no excuse for that.

GEORGE: It's alright.

EMIL: What were you gonna say?

GEORGE: About the balance of nature.

EMIL: Yes?

GEORGE: Being dependent on one of the Professional Spectator Sports.

EMIL: You're fulla shit.

GEORGE: For its continuation.

EMIL: What made you think of that?

GEORGE: I'm not sure.

EMIL: Some sport?

GEORGE: I don't know.

EMIL: Nature?

GEORGE: Perhaps.

EMIL: Do you remember which sport?

GEORGE: I . . . no, I wouldn't want to go on record as remembering.
One of the Major League Sports.

EMIL: Where did you read it?

GEORGE: I don't know. The *Readers' Digest* . . .

EMIL: Eh?

GEORGE: Also they've found a use for cancer.

EMIL: Knock wood.

GEORGE: It's about time. All the millions we spend on research, cigarettes . . .

EMIL: Wildlife.

GEORGE: Nothing wrong with spending money on wildlife.

EMIL: It's all take, take, take.

GEORGE: Nature gives it back many times over.

EMIL: Yeah?

GEORGE: A Blue Heron at sunset.

EMIL: They're all dead.

GEORGE: A whiff of breeze from the lake . . .

EMIL: Or hiding.

GEORGE: A flight of ducks.

EMIL: The duck is, after all, only a bird.

GEORGE: But what a bird.

EMIL: A pigeon, too, is a bird.

GEORGE: There's no comparison.

EMIL: What is the difference between a duck and a pigeon?

GEORGE: Basically, a lack of comparison.

EMIL: Aside from that?

GEORGE: It is a difference of . . . self-respect. You can't argue with that.

EMIL: I won't begin.

GEORGE: It wouldn't get you anywhere.

EMIL: Ha. Ha.

GEORGE: Big talk.

EMIL: I'm ready to back it up.

GEORGE: Oh yeah?

EMIL: Yeah.

GEORGE: Alright.

EMIL: . . . Anytime you're ready.

GEORGE: I'm ready.

EMIL: Alright, then.

GEORGE: Are you ready?

EMIL: You betcha, Red Ryder.

GEORGE: Good.

EMIL: . . .

. . .

Hey! What? Grownups squabbling about birds?

GEORGE: You started it.

EMIL: I beg to differ.

GEORGE: Go right ahead.

EMIL: Alright, I *do* differ.

GEORGE: It makes no difference. I was holding an intelligent conversation and then you came along . . .

EMIL: And simply pointed out that you were turning something into a thing which it is not.

GEORGE: What is more noble than a duck?

EMIL: Depends on the duck.

GEORGE: Is a pigeon more noble than a duck?

EMIL: Are you saying that just because the duck is wild and has no rules . . .

GEORGE: No rules? No rules? No rules but the sun and the moon!

No rules but the law of the seasons and when to go where at what specific times? No rules but to find a mate and cleave into her until death does him part?

EMIL: Is that true?

GEORGE: It surely is.

EMIL: That I didn't know.

GEORGE: Well, learn from your mistakes.
EMIL: I will.
GEORGE: No rules!
EMIL: Alright.
GEORGE: One of the most rigid creatures.
EMIL: I'm sorry.
GEORGE: Did you know that many human societies are modeled on those of our animal friends?
EMIL: Pish.
GEORGE: I beg to differ about it.
EMIL: Pish foo.
GEORGE: The French, for example.
EMIL: Are modeled on animals?
GEORGE: Historically, yes.
EMIL: Where did you get that?
GEORGE: Some guide to France.
EMIL: I don't believe it.
GEORGE: I got it somewhere, I'll show you.
EMIL: You do that.
GEORGE: I will.
EMIL: You just do that.
GEORGE: Don't push me.
EMIL: I won't.
GEORGE: Alright.
EMIL: Darn tooting.

Twelfth Variation:
Whenever I Think of Wild Flying Things

EMIL: Whenever I think of wild flying things I wonder.
GEORGE: Yes?
EMIL: If, in the city, as we are
GEORGE: Yes?
EMIL: We maybe . . .
GEORGE: Yes?
EMIL: Forget it.
GEORGE: Ducks.
EMIL: Ducks.
GEORGE: Ducks. Flying wild.

EMIL: Wild over boundaries.

GEORGE: Lakes, rivers.

EMIL: Imaginary lines . . .

GEORGE: The equator.

EMIL: Never minding . . .
Never stopping . . .

GEORGE: Stopping for no man.

EMIL: High above unmanned terrain.

GEORGE: Barren.

EMIL: Unexplored North Country.

GEORGE: Naked. Strange.

EMIL: Here and there a Mountie.

GEORGE: Cold.

EMIL: No where to rest.

GEORGE: What a life.

EMIL: Sleeping on the fly.

GEORGE: Blown by storms.

EMIL: You know, that is not a laughing matter . .

GEORGE: Who's laughing?

EMIL: Much wildlife is, I am about to tell you, killed each year in
storms and similar . . . things where they have a lot of wind.

GEORGE: Don't I know it.

EMIL: Another countless danger for the duck.

GEORGE: Frost, too.

EMIL: Hail.

GEORGE: Uh.

EMIL: Can you imagine it?

GEORGE: . . .
Hail . . .

EMIL: Pelting the poor creature. Alone in the sky. Many feet in
the air. He can't go right, he can't go left . . . .

GEORGE: Nowhere to go.

EMIL: Hail all over. Hitting him. Pelting him. Making ribbons of
his wings. Creaming him out of the sky.

GEORGE: The Law of Life.

EMIL: That's what you say *now*.

GEORGE: Some must die so others can live.

EMIL: But they must die, too.

GEORGE: So some must die so others can live a little longer.
That's implied.

EMIL: And then *they* die.

GEORGE: Of course.
So that others can live. It makes sense if you think about it.

Thirteenth Variation: They Stuff Them

EMIL: They stuff them.

GEORGE: Eh?

EMIL: They stuff them. They shoot them and they stuff them.

GEORGE: So long as they're dead.

EMIL: Sawdust. And they tack 'em on the wall.

GEORGE: Also they stuff 'em for the oven.

EMIL: That, too.

GEORGE: Yeah.

EMIL: But to kill for no reason . . . without rhyme or reason . . . to shoot them.
What a waste.

GEORGE: Yes.

EMIL: What a waste in the life of a duck.
To be shot.
And not even eaten. Shot.
Shot down like some animal.

GEORGE: At least they shoot 'em in the air.

EMIL: Huh?

GEORGE: Yeah! What do you think? You can't shoot 'em on foot?
What!?

EMIL: Yeah?

GEORGE: They got *laws.* Seasons. Didn't you ever hear of Duck Season?

EMIL: Of course.

GEORGE: Well, duck season is when you can kill 'em. Legally.

EMIL: And when is it?

GEORGE: Duck season?

EMIL: Yeah.

GEORGE: Uh, the spring. Several weeks . . . The fall, several weeks.

EMIL: . . . Whenever the ducks *is around!*

GEORGE: No, it's . . .

EMIL: Eh?

GEORGE: No, I . . .

EMIL: *Eh?*

GEORGE: Well,

EMIL: *EH?*

GEORGE: . . . Yeah!

EMIL: They got the season so the only time it's not legal to shoot
'em is when they *ain't here*.
. . . Yeah.
EMIL: They're no dummies.
GEORGE: Yeah.
EMIL: Influence . . . strings.
GEORGE: It ain't cheap to hunt ducks.
EMIL: Are you kidding me?
GEORGE: No.
You need land.
EMIL: You need a *lot* of land.
GEORGE: At least a mile. And you need . .
EMIL: Guns.
GEORGE: One gun only.
EMIL: And a spare.
GEORGE: And some ammo to put *in* the gun.
EMIL: Telescope.
GEORGE: And those hats.
EMIL: A blatter to call them.
GEORGE: Not always necessary.
EMIL: But good to have in an emergency.
. . .
A bag to put them in.
GEORGE: Big boots.
EMIL: A raincoat.
GEORGE: A radio.
EMIL: You gotta take lunch.
GEORGE: You need a lotta things.
EMIL: A license.
GEORGE: And a *lot* of luck.
EMIL: Oh, yes.
GEORGE: It's easy to pick out a little wobbling duck from miles
in a clear blue sky?
EMIL: No.
GEORGE: A *LOT* of luck.
EMIL: And practice.
GEORGE: Who's got the time?
EMIL: Every day. A half-hour anyway. Practicing . . .
GEORGE: . . . Is where they separate the men from the boys.
At that moment there is no turning back.
You're committed.
You've been blatting around and searching the sky and crouching
'til your back hurts. From dawn on.

EMIL: Yes.

GEORGE: Lying on the cold earth, trying not to look like anything.

Hoping. Praying for that ONE DUCK . . .

EMIL: A low flying duck . . .

GEORGE: That one chance to show what *dreams* are made of.

Until . . .

EMIL: Yes?

GEORGE: Off in the distance, *beyond* the horizon, 'til you don't even know what it is is a honking.

The honking comes closer. Closer and louder. You see a far-off blur.

The blur becomes a speck. The speck gets bigger. It's a big speck. It's a dot. The dot is advancing and it's honking and the honking is louder and becomes clear and precise. You can just make it out. Flapping. Flying straight in a line to join its comrades.

Frantic. Lost. Dangerous. Vicious: A DUCK.

. . . And on he comes. You quietly raise from the ground.

One knee . . . two knees. You lift the gun, you put the gun on your shoulder and point it at the duck.

It's you and him. You and the duck on the marsh.

He wants to go home and you want to kill him for it.

So you fire the gun. Once, again. Again. Again.

Your ears are ringing. Your eyes are covered in spots.

You cannot see. You are quivering and you gotta sit down.

. . . your heart is going fast. . . .

EMIL: Where's the duck?

GEORGE: . . . Slowly. Slowly you lower yourself to the earth.

Your joints creak . . .

EMIL: *Where's the duck?*

GEORGE: . . . With the weight of your body. Your shoulder aches from pounding, and your . . .

EMIL: WHERE'S THE DUCK?

GEORGE: The duck is dying.

EMIL: Out in the marsh.

GEORGE: Out in the marsh.

EMIL: Oh, no.

GEORGE: In a flock of feathers and blood.

Full of bullets. Quiet, so as not to make a sound.

Dying.

EMIL: Living his last.

GEORGE: Dying.

EMIL: Leaving the earth and sky.

GEORGE: Dying.
EMIL: Lying on the ground.
GEORGE: Dying.
EMIL: Fluttering.
GEORGE: Dying.
EMIL: Sobbing.
GEORGE: Dying.
EMIL: Quietly bleeding.
GEORGE: Thinking.
EMIL: Dying.
GEORGE: Dying, dying.
EMIL: But wait! This here!
He summons his strength for one last time.
GEORGE: No.
EMIL: Maybe he beats around and tries to make it . .
GEORGE: No.
EMIL: Back in the air?
GEORGE: No.
EMIL: One last . . .
GEORGE: No.
EMIL: A flutter of . . .
GEORGE: No.
EMIL: A little . . .
GEORGE: No.
EMIL: He's dead, isn't he?
(George nods)
EMIL: I knew it.
GEORGE: The Law of Life.

Fourteenth Variation: For Centuries Prior to This Time

EMIL: You know, for centuries prior to this time man has watched birds.
GEORGE: I still watch 'em.
EMIL: To obtain the secret of flight.
GEORGE: We're better off without it.
EMIL: Yeah.
GEORGE: They'll go to their graves with it.
EMIL: The Ancient Greeks used to sit around all day looking at birds.

GEORGE: Yeah?

EMIL: Oh, yes. They'd take a chair and go sit and look at 'em.
Just watch them all day long and wonder.

GEORGE: I, too, would wonder.

A crumbling civilization and they're out in the park looking at
birds.

EMIL: These were the Ancient Greeks. Old. Old men. Incapable
of working.
Of no use to their society.
Just used to watch the birds all day.
First light to last light.
First Light: Go watch birds.
Last Light: Stop watching birds. Go Home.
Swallows. Falcons.
Forerunners of our modern birds.
And the forerunners of our modern States.
Greeks. Birds.
Used to sit out all day long. Sit on a bench and feed them . . .
Give them little bits of . . .

GEORGE: . . . Rice?

EMIL: Rice, yes. History is not completely clear on that point,
but we can imagine rice. For the sake of argument . . .
Rich, sleek birds of prey.

GEORGE: And fat old men.

EMIL: Watching each other.
Each with something to contribute.
That the world might turn another day.
A fitting end.
To some very noble creatures of the sky.
And a lotta Greeks.

Curtain

Corinne Jacker

BITS AND PIECES

Corinne Jacker

When Corinne Jacker's *Bits and Pieces* initially was showcased at the Manhattan Theatre Club, some of New York's leading critics extolled both play and author. Michael Feingold wrote in the *Village Voice* that "Miss Jacker, a gifted writer who obviously knows that old events always require new objective correlatives, has written an up-to-the-minute equivalent of the old legacy drama. In her play, a young man of exceptional intelligence—a classics professor—dies and leaves virtually all his organs to be transplanted. His wife, unsatisfied with the empty funeral rites this leaves her, bribes the doctor for a list of the recipients and sets out to find her husband's many last resting places. . . . But to find the organs is to find the events in her marriage that they remind her of, which come back, like her husband's body, in bits and pieces. The ease with which Miss Jacker manipulates her complex flashback structure to its startling conclusion is one index to her substantial ability.

"The play is a fine piece of work," and "she is emphatically a writer to take note of."

Mel Gussow of *The New York Times* described the play as both "humorous and touching . . . Miss Jacker has observed her people keenly and has a gift for ironic dialogue . . . She is very much a playwright to watch."

A winner of a double "Obie" award for *Bits and Pieces* and *Harry Outside*, the author was educated at Stanford University, and Northwestern University where she took her B.S. and M.A. In 1954, she was named a Lovedale Scholar, and in 1955, a University Scholar.

Her other published and produced plays include: *Harry Outside; Travellers; Night Thoughts; Project Omega: Lillian; Seditious Acts; The Scientific Method; Breakfast, Lunch, and Dinner;* and *Other People's Tables.* Her newest work for the theatre, *My Life,* is scheduled for presentation by the Circle Repertory Company, New York, early in 1977.

Additionally, she has published the following books: *The Biological Revolution; The Black Flag of Anarchy: Antistatism in the United States; A Little History of Cocoa; Window on the Unknown: A History of the Microscope;* and *Man, Memory, and Machines: An Introduction to Cybernetics.*

Miss Jacker also has written extensively for television, notably, *John Adams, President,* acclaimed as one of the most dramatic episodes in the series, *The Adams Chronicles;* and was presented with an Emmy Citation for her participation in the *Benjamin Franklin* series.

Characters:

PHILIP
DOCTOR
TECHNICIAN
IRIS
HELEN
FARLEY
MRS. EBERLY
ANTONIO
MONK

There are many scenes in this play, they happen in a number of places. Before each scene there is a title. The title should be shown to the audience by means of slide or projector. The scenery should be minimal. Most important is that the audience be helped in every way possible to understand when Iris is on her journey and when she has returned to the past life from which she started.

Scene One:
Philip and the Past

Philip is alone on stage. He is holding a picture of an ancient Greek vase.

PHILIP: This vase was twenty-five hundred years old. It was made in Greece, when men knew gods and dark things moved beneath the earth. The painting on it has been evaluated in two ways. Some said it was the work of a master craftsman, one of the finest of the classical period. They pointed to the line of the shoulders, to the almost dancing movement of the figures . . . But others found the execution mediocre, the work of a hack. (*He puts the picture down, picks up a shard, a hunk of a vase*) Unfortunately, while it was on loan to a museum, the vase broke. Only a few shards were left. The state of the art is no longer in question. It has become the work of a master craftsman. And time is standing still now, for the vase, for the man who painted it. And this piece—it's something to pick up in the night when you can't sleep and rub your hands around. A little powder talcums the fingers, and they've become 2,500 years old.

Scene Two:
What Happens After Death?

The Doctor and the Technician are working in a hospital "white room,"
adjacent to an operating room. They are surrounded by Styrofoam boxes
of various sizes. Each box is piled haphazardly on top of another. Each
box contains one human organ, all the organs have been taken from
Philip's body just after his death. He was a donor, and now his parts are
packed up and being made ready for shipment. The Doctor and
Technician have been working all day. They are tired. They have only a
few more boxes to label and record.

DOCTOR: *(He is checking his records. He has lost track of one of the*
organs. He tries to get the attention of the Technician) Hey . . . Hey, did
you see the liver anywhere?

TECHNICIAN: Under the kidney.

DOCTOR: No. It's not there.

TECHNICIAN: Really? I'm sure I put it there. Look again.

DOCTOR: I have looked. Twice. *(She comes over, finds it for him)*
Thanks.

TECHNICIAN: When I label the eyes—the corneas—I mean, do I
put left and right or what?

DOCTOR: Have you ever done this kind of work before?

TECHNICIAN: No. Usually they keep me down in obstetrics. I
like it down there . . . So—do I put left and right, or what?

DOCTOR: It's optional . . . You know, this man—the guy who
donated all this. He was incredible.

TECHNICIAN: All this stuff came from one body? *(The Doctor*
nods) Well, how many more organs do we have to label? . . . I'm
hungry.

DOCTOR: You just ate a *Twinkie.*

TECHNICIAN: Well, we've been locked up in here working for
hours and hours.

DOCTOR: There's never been one like this. I'm sure of it. He
gave away everything. He—you know—he thought about it, and he
made a will, and he arranged to have himself cut up and—dis-
tributed.

TECHNICIAN: If they're going to have many more like this,
there's going to have to be some financial arrangement. I'm
seventeen minutes into overtime.

DOCTOR: Listen . . . The thing is—suddenly—I have this ir-
resistible urge to fuck you.

TECHNICIAN: Now? In the middle of all this?
DOCTOR: Why not?
TECHNICIAN: Forget it. His soul could be here right now. Float-
ing all over his parts, trying to find a new host body. Please. Not
here.
PHILIP: *(He comes on, speaks quite matter-of-factly)* At least death
was instantaneous. It took me completely by surprise. Even though
I'd been lying there, waiting for it.

Scene Three:
Iris: The Mourning Begins

Iris and Helen are in the kitchen of what was Philip and Iris's apartment.
Iris was his wife, Helen, his sister. The two women are sitting at the table.
They both wear dark clothes. They have been at Philip's funeral. Now,
after the people have gone, they are sitting and drinking.

IRIS: He was the most important person in my life. I lived for
him. I thought about him all the time. We were attached to one
another by a thin invisible unbreakable—thing.
(Helen looks at her. Short pause)
HELEN: Go ahead and cry. It would do you good.
IRIS: Would it? . . . We know he didn't give away the penis.
He was very explicit about that.
HELEN: Would you like another drink?
IRIS: Why are you talking to me as if I'm retarded?
HELEN: Funerals are hard.
IRIS: David told me on the phone last night—he didn't want to
come back for the funeral. It was no good he said, if his father
wasn't going to be there. That's pretty good for a nine-year-old
. . . I didn't feel much like being there either . . . There wasn't
anything to bury. A little heap of unwanted stuff. The bones.
There was nothing to do with the bones.
HELEN: Stop it, please.
IRIS: So, when the undertaker called, you know, to ask me what
to do, I said we'll burn it, the remains. Just a few ashes in a little
box, put into a bigger box and buried in the ground. . . . Did you
know that ashes don't rot? He isn't even going to rot.
HELEN: Do you want me to leave, Iris?
IRIS: I will have another drink, thank you . . . I'm not a logical

person, Helen. That's why I can't figure it out. You and Philip were
raised on syllogisms. I grew up with the collected poems of Robert
and Elizabeth Browning.

HELEN: There's nothing difficult about logic.

IRIS: Oh. I think there is. There's a logic attached to all this
death and dying. And I'm going to figure out what it is. I'm going
to be the most logical of us all . . . For instance—more Scotch,
please. I don't think you put any Scotch at all in my last drink. For
instance, take how we got to the cemetery. There we were. Up the
avenue, down the main street, onto the throughway. We were
following the hearse. Until—did you notice when it was we weren't
following the hearse any more? I didn't. But all at once it wasn't
there. But I figured it out. The hearse takes a short cut. Or we take
a long cut—and it gets to the cemetery ahead of us. And the whole
thing is out and on display before the mourners turn up.

HELEN: You're being morbid.

IRIS: That bastard your brother didn't leave me anything to
bury. How could he do that if he loved me? What am I going to do?

HELEN: You'd better go to bed.

IRIS: Don't you try to manage me!

HELEN: I'm trying to be sensible. Philip would want me to be
sensible.

IRIS: Echo, echo—I've got to figure out what he was paying me
back for. Giving himself away like that. Like pieces of a saint . . .
Please. Get the hell out of here, will you? This is no time for sister-
in-laws—sisters-in-law . . . Stay. I'm sorry. Let's have a drink
together.

HELEN: You don't want me here.

IRIS: What do you want to do? Move in?

HELEN: Should I? For a few weeks?

IRIS: No.

HELEN: He was my brother.

IRIS: That's right.

HELEN: I'm very tired.

IRIS: I'm not going to live. I know it. I'm going to develop a
wasting disease and die slowly.

HELEN: We'll talk about that later.

IRIS: I tried turning on the radiator in the living room. There
wasn't any heat. I'm cold.

HELEN: Do you have any aspirin? Or something stronger.

(Iris does not respond. She has been drawn to Philip)

PHILIP: And save the Sunday *Times* till I've read it? . . . And
don't use the business section for the garbage pail.

IRIS: I can't stand it when you're pompous.
PHILIP: You love me when I'm pompous. It makes me sexier.
IRIS: Go to hell.
PHILIP: Go to hell yourself.
IRIS: They don't have double beds in hell.
PHILIP: Then it must be heaven.
IRIS: *(Laughing)* You bastard.
PHILIP: Sexy bastard.
(He leaves, Iris is back with Helen now)
IRIS: Let's stay up all night and talk about love, Helen.
HELEN: You need your sleep.
IRIS: I thought I'd sleep out there. On the sofa.
HELEN: You slept in the bed when he was in the hospital.
IRIS: It's different now.
HELEN: You can't have a nervous breakdown. You have obligations.
IRIS: He's dead. He's gone.
HELEN: I know that.
IRIS: Not like I know it.
HELEN: Let's not argue. I'm trying to help you. *(She takes out a list)*
IRIS: Not now . . . Please. Put me to bed. Stay the night. Just one night more.
HELEN: You don't want me to move in here. You said so.
IRIS: Just as a guest.
HELEN: I have a home of my own. . . . You'll have to pack up the clothes. We should give them to the Salvation Army. It'll be a tax deduction. You can use it next year.
IRIS: Fine. You take care of it.
HELEN: No. You. And the books. You don't read French or German. You might as well give them away, too. Maybe to the university library. In his name . . . Oh, there's one—*A Child's Garden of Verses.* From when we were little. I'd like that, if you don't mind.
IRIS: All right. Go home. Leave me alone.
HELEN: Only a few more things. Did he leave a will?
IRIS: I'll kill myself. I'll jump out a window.
HELEN: Didn't he go over any of this with you?
IRIS: I won't be intimidated when I'm in mourning.
HELEN: Next week will be worse. You'll see.
IRIS: What's so important about the will? You want to know if you're a beneficiary? What shall we do, Helen? Make an agreement now, we'll split it all, fifty-fifty? My God, you want his, and mine,

and the whole family's. Well. The money stops here. I'll be sure you don't get any of it.

HELEN: I thought you were going to kill yourself.

(Iris reaches out to hit Helen, who intercepts her fist and gets in a slap of her own. Iris stands a moment, dazed, and then cries)

IRIS: *(She sits down, talks really to herself)* He never explained that I'd be all alone. Forever. He didn't go into that.

HELEN: I'm going to run a hot tub for you. Bubble bath. And then I'll bring you a hot drink. Tea with rum. And you'll drink it and fall asleep. Tomorrow you'll be thinking of other things.

IRIS: We really shouldn't argue.

HELEN: You'll put cream all over your body. Some good-smelling cream. You'll sleep. You'll see.

(She leaves, for the bathroom, to fix Iris's bath. Philip comes in with a book. He is the young Philip, in the early years of his teaching. Iris has gone to a mirror. She looks carefully at herself)

IRIS: Mirrors are absolutely fascinating. Look. There's something about the eyes. There's something strange about that woman's eyes. . . . Phil! Phil! I need you.

PHILIP: *(Now in the past with her)* Come on! I just need five minutes more. I'll be there in five minutes.

IRIS: *(Directly to Philip)* I was afraid. I looked in the mirror and I was afraid. There was something so odd—and I wanted to go on looking until I figured it out.

PHILIP: *(Into his book again)* We'll talk about it at dinner.

IRIS: Dinner's been ready half an hour.

PHILIP: Heat it up.

IRIS: Why do you have to be such a damn scholar?

PHILIP: Because it's my business. To be a scholar.

IRIS: Well, you can think on your own time. Come eat your supper.

PHILIP: I'll be right there. I just want to finish this page.

IRIS: You just turned a page, you cheating bastard. You have sixty seconds to get to the table. If you don't, I'm picking up the phone and calling Howard Garfield. He's been trying to seduce me for three weeks.

PHILIP: Howard Garfield's a prick.

(She leaves him for the kitchen)

IRIS: *(With her back to him)* You haven't put the book down yet.

PHILIP: How do you know.

IRIS: I'm psychic. Twenty-seven seconds.

PHILIP: Are you at the phone?

IRIS: Come and see.

PHILIP: Howard Garfield? . . . Now I've forgotten why I was reading the damn dialogue.

IRIS: Then come eat your supper. You've got fifteen seconds.

PHILIP: Shit. Have your affair with the bastard then.

IRIS: Phil . . . Phil . . . *(She goes to him)* I don't have a watch with a second hand.

PHILIP: *(He is angry. Then he finds it funny. He laughs)* My God! Think what I'd be like if I had original ideas.

IRIS: Come on. It's roast beef. I got a special price today.

PHILIP: I like my work, but oh you kid. *(He pulls her down onto his lap)*

IRIS: I love you despite your eccentricities.

PHILIP: Let's get married.

IRIS: Not again.

PHILIP: I want to marry you. I want to be the father of your children. Me Tarzan. You Jane.

IRIS: Why do you waste all that energy on books?

PHILIP: There's plenty for other things.

IRIS: I bet you're awful at touch football. The Kennedys are great at it.

PHILIP: They have more money than I do.

IRIS: Not much. I'll be very rich when we get married, won't I?

PHILIP: Very.

IRIS: That's good . . . I said I'd marry you.

PHILIP: I heard you.

IRIS: Good.

PHILIP: Good.

IRIS: I'm an idiot.

PHILIP: You'll be completely happy.

IRIS: Will I?

PHILIP: Now get the hell out of here and let me finish my work. *(He dumps her on the floor and starts to make notes. Iris runs out, back to the apartment area)*

IRIS: I hope the damn roast is burned to a crisp.

PHILIP: I like it that way.

(The Doctor is in the apartment area, sitting on the sofa. Iris hands him a drink)

IRIS: I'm a very rich widow, you know.

DOCTOR: So I've heard. Most donors are—upper middle or upper.

IRIS: I want the names of all the donees. For each organ you gave away.

DOCTOR: I'm afraid not.

IRIS: It isn't like adoption, Doctor. I'm not going to try to get the pieces back.

DOCTOR: It's a question of medical ethics.

IRIS: Doctor, my husband was unique—and while he was dying—the two months it took—he continued to be unusual. I have tapes he made for me. Points of view. Philosophical recollections. He thought they would last me as long as I needed. Keep us connected while I was grieving. They may. *(Iris takes out a cassette machine, puts in a cartridge, turns the machine on)*

PHILIP: *(On the machine)* What Osiris is, you see. He had a powerful magic. He gave the dead a drink of water, and that brought them back to life. Because the soul has to quench its thirst or die.

(Iris turns the tape off)

IRIS: All the tapes are like that. Not one personal remark. Not one intimate memory. When I've finished, I can donate them to a library.

DOCTOR: I was very moved by it.

IRIS: I have to have your list. It's—a kind of mission. It's crucial. He's dead. But his parts aren't. They aren't rotting away in the ground. They weren't burned to ashes. That was a present he gave me. Or a curse. He's somewhere, in someone's body. Alive, with blood running through him. Moving. A hand grasping some other woman's hand. And I could see that hand.

DOCTOR: All right. I'll do it. I'll try to get the list. If I fuck you. Right now. I have this thing, about making it with strangers.

IRIS: I always seem to bring out definitions in people . . . All right, Doctor, let's as you said, fuck. *(She abruptly begins to undress)* I suppose you're blessed in your way. Hermes the messenger. I forget what the Egyptians called him.

PHILIP: Where the hell's my pipe? Did you hide it again?

(Iris turns when he calls her, then she turns back to the Doctor. Philip does not leave the room)

IRIS: *(To the Doctor)* Don't worry, I'm not mad. Or if I am, it's harmless. A death psychosis. Gone in a month or two.

DOCTOR: Don't you have a bedroom?

(Iris leads him into the bedroom. As they are going out of the room, Philip comes down, takes the recorder, turns it on, speaks into it. He is making a recording for her)

PHILIP: I have it now. The clear, bright core. Here in my bed, waiting to die, I see the perfection of my essence. I see myself shining, phosphorescent in the darkness. Clear of mind, only functioning, heart beating, blood moving, fingers curling with my breath and moving out again, air coming in, sweat on my skin. This is what I am. The body living. And all there will be. Well, . . . The one breath that is left is frozen. Suspended. The heart contracted, about to beat. The diaphragm still stretched. The word not spoken. I would say something to her. She would say something. But, tranquil and quiet. The last second is about to flick by. The swelled artery stretched, bursts, and I am dead.

Scene Four:
The Journey Begins. Iris In California

Iris has changed her clothes. It is a week or so later. She is with a young man, Farley. They are in Los Angeles, beside Farley's swimming pool. He is a plain but rather attractive person; Farley is paralyzed from the waist down and in a wheelchair, but although some of his movements are restricted, he is not a passive person. He speaks with an exaggeratedly British accent.

IRIS: I don't know. I thought—just barging in. I had to see you.
FARLEY: My days are very free.
IRIS: *(She has been waiting for him to talk. The pause has become very difficult)* I'm not supposed to be here. I bought your name and address. . . . I don't know how to— *(Another pause)* Helen—my sister-in-law—thinks I'm crazy.
FARLEY: Do you want some tea? . . . I can make some . . . I don't really care for it.
IRIS: I thought you were English.
FARLEY: Canadian. . . . I came here to be in films. For God's sake, sit down. So he's in a variety of pieces, then—your husband.
IRIS: In a variety of places.
FARLEY: That must be unpleasant.
IRIS: Painful.
FARLEY: *(He is having her on)* You loved him.
IRIS: Intensely.
FARLEY: Why the hell didn't you stay home in your nice little house and mourn, like a sensible widow?
IRIS: I couldn't . . . We were very close. Extremely close, Philip and I. And. I really can't stand it, you know, not having him. He gave his parts away for a reason. He wanted me to know something. I'm sure of it. I'm sure I'll have a sense of him again—when I see it. Whatever you have—or touch it—or—that's why I'm here.

FARLEY: To find his little piece in me.

IRIS: I won't hurt you.

FARLEY: Do you know what piece I have, then?

IRIS: No. He just gave me a list.

FARLEY: Organ, organ, who's got the organ . . . I'm sorry.

IRIS: Please—won't you let me see it.

FARLEY: His eardrum? You must be joking.

IRIS: I don't make jokes.

FARLEY: They offered a leg first. It wasn't the first offer. But it has to be a pair of legs. It can't be just one, you see, it's got to be a matched set. But legs don't satisfy me. Not yet . . . But it was essential for me to hear. I needed his eardrum.

IRIS: Hear what?

FARLEY: You should be under guard.

IRIS: Look. I've got a light. Like the doctors use. It won't hurt. You'll turn to one side, and I'll put the light in your ear, and take a look. Just one look. *(She waits for a response)* Do you want money?

FARLEY: Don't try to buy me! I don't need your money! I don't need anything from any of you . . . I collected a great deal for this. *(He means being crippled)* I spend it, too. On books, and liquor, and clothes. I still like to wear good clothes.

IRIS: Please let me see it.

FARLEY: Suppose I showed you the wrong ear?

IRIS: I'd know.

FARLEY: Would you?

IRIS: Would you? *(That is, show the wrong ear)*

FARLEY: You're absolutely bananas. *(He turns, Iris looks, then takes the light and puts it away)*

PHILIP: *(Appearing as Iris looks in Farley's ear)* How do you do. My name is Philip Uberman. I teach assorted subjects at various universities.

FARLEY: Is it all right?

IRIS: *(Happy at Philip's presence)* Were you ever in a movie?

FARLEY: Three. I had no lines in the first two. They cut my scene out of the other one.

IRIS: I'm sorry.

FARLEY: I didn't want to be an actor—just to be in films. I thought it would make me handsome.

PHILIP: I'm a socialist. I inherited it from my father.

IRIS: I guess I'm an anarchist.

FARLEY: Really? I thought it was illegal.

IRIS: No. I'm the nonviolent kind.

PHILIP: There is no such thing as nonviolence.

FARLEY: I did it myself. I ran the bloody machine off the road. I was pissed. Just giving way to another cliche. Like the phony accent. . . . It's all right, being a cripple. It's less demanding.

IRIS: *(To Philip)* Success is crucial to a man, isn't it?

FARLEY: *(Sensing her separateness)* Is it all right? The ear? What did it look like? It feels odd, you know, someone else living in my head.

(Iris does not answer. A Mozart record is playing. It has grown louder as Farley talked, and Iris leaves him, moving to Philip)

PHILIP: We'll play music till dawn, and screw the neighbors.

IRIS: I love you.

PHILIP: Only because my book has been published today. And I will be a full professor and short of moral turpitude or other failing of character our future is secure.

IRIS: *Dionysius and the Moral Temper of the Athenians.* It'll be a best seller.

PHILIP: A first printing of two thousand.

IRIS: And it's so relevant.

PHILIP: Let's dance.

IRIS: To Mozart?

PHILIP: Why not.

IRIS: You're drunk.

PHILIP: Not much. Thanks for the champagne . . . Listen to this part. Right here. It's so damned personal.

IRIS: Mozart?

PHILIP: Why do you keep asking about Mozart?

IRIS: Okay. Let's dance . . . Let's toast the book. And the next one. And the next one.

PHILIP: Let's hope one of them's original.

IRIS: I'll just slip into something more comfortable, as the mummy said to the pharaoh.

(Philip groans)

PHILIP: Did you make that up?

IRIS: I've got a million of them.

PHILIP: Shut up and kiss me.

IRIS: Let's talk. All night. While the Mozart plays . . . Except at the good parts. Tell me about Ricardo's economic principles. Or the decline and fall of the Roman Empire. Anything. I just want to hear you talk.

PHILIP: Like a waterfall, babbling in the distance. Well, in the beginning, God made Karl Marx, and Karl Marx grew. On the first day, he went to God and said, here is my thesis. I've got to publish in order to become famous. On the second day, he went to God the Father and said: Only bullshit and cliches are written down. That's my antithesis.

Scene Five:
A Conversation Between Two Women

Iris and Helen are in Helen's apartment. They have had lunch, now, they are sitting, looking at Helen's photo albums, books of clippings, etc. All of it, mementos of Philip. The two women are just getting to know one another. This is just after Philip and Iris were married.

HELEN: Don't ever tell him I showed it to you.

IRIS: *(Holding up a bronzed baby shoe)* I think it's sweet.

HELEN: He'd kill me. He's forgotten about it, I'm sure.

IRIS: He was so little. Look at that little foot.

HELEN: Not so little. He must have been a year old. He didn't walk till then. And he didn't talk until he was two. I was sure he was retarded. But once he started, he didn't shut up. Sentence after sentence. Talking on and on . . . He loved spaghetti, the canned spaghetti. But he couldn't say it. Pisgetti, he'd say. I'd say it to him, spa-get-ti. And he'd repeat it, spa-get-ti. Okay, spaghetti. Pisgetti. Our father loved to do it with him over and over. *(She laughs with the memory)*

IRIS: Show me some more pictures.

HELEN: There aren't any more. You've seen everything.

IRIS: Tell me something else. Anything. Did you go to the movies together?

HELEN: A lot. When we saw *Hound of the Baskervilles,* we took turns looking at the screen. We were both scared.

IRIS: Tell me about when he was born.

HELEN: I don't remember that. I was so little myself.

IRIS: What did you do when they brought him home from the hospital? Was it sibling rivalry at first sight?

HELEN: He was so quiet. I remember that. He was boring. Sleeping all the time. Just laying there and grinning. He was too good natured to believe . . . Oh, and he liked beer. Dad used to give him little sips of beer.

IRIS: I love it. Go on. I want to pump you dry.

HELEN: . . . I had such a bad complexion when I was a girl. I ate too many starches.

IRIS: When he was in high school—was he a Romeo?

HELEN: . . . He's still my best friend. He always has been.

IRIS: I'm an only child . . .

HELEN: My first year in college. I was home over Christmas. And after breakfast, while I was still drinking my coffee, he called me on the phone. Where are you, I asked. We have to talk this way, he said. I can't tell you this face to face. What can't you tell me? What's so terrible? You tell me everything. I'm having a spiritual crisis, he said. I've become an atheist. So of course, I burst out laughing. God damn you, he said, and hung up on me. He never would talk to me about it after that. Not at all. Right now, I still don't know whether he's an atheist or not. You know, there are these subjects. He gets so stubborn. Nothing's going to move him from A to B. Nothing at all.

Scene Six:
Iris In Wisconsin

Mrs. Eberly's kitchen. There is an old, often-painted table, and three straight-backed chairs. Mrs. Eberly is shelling peas. Iris has just been let in to talk to her.

MRS. EBERLY: I have to go on workin' while we talk. I have my living to earn. You know how to shell peas? *(Iris nods)* Show me. *(Iris takes a pea, shells it)* You have to work faster than that.
IRIS: What do you do with them?
MRS. EBERLY: The shells or the peas? The shells I throw out. I don't keep pigs on my property. *(Pause. They work)* And I don't have any sodas.
IRIS: I'm here because of my husband. He died recently.
MRS. EBERLY: People don't eat right. Not enough roughage.
IRIS: Your address was given to me by a doctor.
MRS. EBERLY: I don't do cures . . . If a doctor can't help you, I'm not going to try. I can tell by lookin' at you though. Your kidneys don't flush proper. Nobody pays attention to that anymore. My father had a glass of hot water with lemon in it every morning of his life. And he died of a stroke, not one of your dirty diseases like cancer. You don't believe me. You think, that's what they all say . . . Things used to be different. When I was a girl, I used to swim all the time. I was going to swim the English channel. First woman ever. I trained and trained. My father had me in the lake water soon as the ice thawed. I swam. For hours a day. The crawl, and the backstroke; my specialty was the butterfly. You know how that goes? Arms and legs together, then you push out. I was good. I had lots of power. And I was ready. My father was sure of it. And then that—bitch—that Gertrude Ederle got greased up and into the water 'fore we'd even left for England. So there was nothing left for me to do. Oh, for years I was a very unhappy person.
IRIS: I'm sorry.

MRS. EBERLY: You'll have to speak up. I don't hear good . . . I'm a medical phenomenon. But I suppose you know that. I was rotting away inside. So they cut it out and put in new stuff.

IRIS: That's what I've come to see you about.

MRS. EBERLY: Last month, God saved me. While I was on the operatin' table, when they were givin' me the ether, he came to me in the form of Gabriel the archangel. And he said, "Gertrude, you will be saved. You will live and be fruitful." Since we was talkin' I asked him about my investments. "Should I buy or sell, God," I said. He paused a minute. Then he said, "Buy industrials and hold." . . . So I did . . . I put all my cash into stocks. Now I'm goin' to be rich. When I die, I'm leavin' the money back to God. He'll know what to do with it.

IRIS: My husband was your donor.

MRS. EBERLY: He gave me his lung? I trust in God. I take his advice. If more people listened to God, there'd be less divorce.

IRIS: I'm sorry, you're confusing me.

MRS. EBERLY: Oh, yes. That's what they all say . . . You want to see the scar? It's seventeen inches long. I charge, though. And then I invest the money. It's small investors like me that keep American business running. Did you know that?

IRIS: Yes. I want to see the scar. He'll come then. He won't leave me alone.

MRS. EBERLY: Jesus Christ the savior is always with us . . . Give me five dollars and I'll open up for you. (*Iris opens her purse, takes out five dollars and puts it onto the table. Mrs. Eberly picks it up, makes sure it's money, and opens her dress. The scar is huge, diagonal across her chest. It is suppurating and very ugly. Iris can't look at it*) You have to kiss it. Because you could be Christ in disguise. There's no point in letting opportunity go by. If it turned out you were, I'd refund your money . . . All right, now. Kiss it, like a good girl. (*It takes a moment, but then Iris does kiss the scar*) No. You aren't God. I thought not. (*Mrs. Eberly closes up the dress, buttons it up again. She is disappointed*) You want your money back? No chance. You're a nice girl, though, you can live here with me if you want. I need someone to strain the fruit. My hands are stiffening up. You want the job?

PHILIP: (*Suddenly appearing*) I don't feel like talking.

IRIS: Did I invent you?

MRS. EBERLY: (*Laughs*) That all depends on how you look at it, don't it, dear. What's your name?

IRIS: Iris.

MRS. EBERLY: You ought to be married.

IRIS: My husband died.

MRS. EBERLY: Good for him.

(Philip has only passed through the stage. Now Mrs. Eberly leaves Iris alone. She hesitates, is lost without Philip. Then, she moves down to his chair as there is the sound of a key in the lock. Iris sits in the chair, afraid and angry. Philip walks into the light. It is eight years before he died. They have been married two years)

IRIS: Phil? Phil? Is that you? . . . Who is it?

PHILIP: It's me. I still have my key . . . I hope I didn't frighten you.

IRIS: Give me the key.

PHILIP: Sure. *(He tosses the key down)* I've got to get to school.

IRIS: What did you come for?

PHILIP: Books. I need some books.

IRIS: Do you want breakfast? I could make some eggs.

PHILIP: I don't like eggs.

IRIS: I've already eaten.

(Short pause. They look warily at one another).

PHILIP: Did you talk to your uncle?

IRIS: Did you see your cousin?

PHILIP: Not yet. I thought I'd let you go first.

IRIS: I've been busy.

PHILIP: Well, I'll come back next week for the rest of my clothes.

IRIS: I'd rather know in advance. So someone else can be here.

PHILIP: Anything you say.

IRIS: I'm trying to make a list. Of what we should each have.

PHILIP: You keep the china, all that stuff.

IRIS: And I suppose you want the *Britannica?*

PHILIP: That's right, Iris.

IRIS: Anything you say, Philip.

PHILIP: Philip?

IRIS: I don't have to call you Phil any more.

PHILIP: Most people do.

IRIS: Phil's a little boy's name. Now that you're getting a divorce, you're a big grown man.

PHILIP: *(He starts to leave)* I'll have a lawyer call you in the morning.

IRIS: I'm sorry. I just get these trolls.

PHILIP: You sure as hell do.

IRIS: I had a migraine this morning when I woke up. About five in the morning. It was all grey and ugly. There was soot on the window sill in the bedroom.

PHILIP: You should see a doctor.

IRIS: I'll call you Phil if you want.

PHILIP: What is this with names? You want me to call you I—J love you I, or give us a kiss, Ris?

IRIS: You made your point.

PHILIP: Damn it! Why did I come back here. I could have sent one of the grad students. Or had my secretary call.

IRIS: *(After a moment)* There's no reason we can't be orderly about this.

PHILIP: Have you been sleeping all right?

IRIS: I'm going to apply to law school.

PHILIP: You look like you were up all night.

IRIS: The fact is, I want the *Britannica,* myself. I'll need it in school.

PHILIP: In law school?

IRIS: I may get my doctorate in English instead. I'm not sure.

PHILIP: Let's toss for it.

IRIS: You can buy another. *(Philip takes out a coin, tosses it)* Tails.

PHILIP: Heads. You have any paper. I'll keep a list.

IRIS: Now the unabridged. *(He tosses again)* Tails.

PHILIP: Heads again.

IRIS: You call the next one.

PHILIP: This is childish.

IRIS: Make it the Grote.

PHILIP: I don't want the Grote. You keep it.

IRIS: All right. You give me the dictionary and I'll take the Grote.

PHILIP: I *need* the dictionary.

IRIS: All right. I'll take the Grote and you take the bar glasses.

PHILIP: I don't want the fucking bar glasses . . . That's the whole thing. You manipulate me. From beginning to end. You're a fucking psychologist. That's what you are. *(He pounds his fist into the table)*

IRIS: You wanted to beat me, didn't you?

PHILIP: All the time. And I should have. You needed it.

IRIS: Hit me now if it helps you.

PHILIP: No.

IRIS: Go ahead. Maybe then we can talk to one another.

PHILIP: Jesus! Manipulation.

IRIS: I'd like to indulge in an act of rage myself. I'd like to take my coffee cup and break it over your head. I'd like to scald you with boiling coffee, all over your face and in your eyes. And rip your clothes apart with my nails. I'd like to take the fucking bar glasses and shatter them and grind the fragments up and feed them to you with a sterling silver spoon, so you'd writhe on the floor with your intestines bleeding . . . I'm not ready to live alone. Not at all.

(Pause)

PHILIP: I'd better leave.

IRIS: *(Going on)* I know. We're not good for one another. We just—it's chemical or something. We fight all the time. You were a fool for marrying me.

PHILIP: I'm a fool to put up with all this nonsense. Come on. Go wash your face and comb your hair. Do what I told you for Christ's sake or I'll start socking you around. *(She looks at him, leaves. He pauses, sits in his chair, lights out)*

Scene Seven:
Another Conversation Between Two Women

Iris's living room. She is with Helen. It is long before Philip's illness.

IRIS: I wish you'd stay. At least till Phil gets home . . . At least for some dinner.

HELEN: No. Thank you.

IRIS: Why just drop in for five minutes at a time, Helen? You could do that on the phone. You should stay with us. Spend time with us.

HELEN: I'm sorry.

IRIS: Have I done something? Are you angry with me?

HELEN: Well then, I'll be going.

IRIS: What's wrong, Helen?

HELEN: Nothing.

IRIS: You sit there and you stare at me. What're you trying to tell me?

HELEN: Philip told me you're going to have a baby.

IRIS: That's right.

HELEN: I'm glad.

IRIS: Good.

HELEN: When?

IRIS: About six months . . . nothing shows yet.

HELEN: *(Brightly)* Do you want a boy or a girl?

IRIS: I don't care. Both . . . Maybe it'll be twins.

HELEN: It's a good thing you're not a career girl like me.

IRIS: Come on, hang around, Helen. We'll have a drink. Maybe some wine. I feel like celebrating . . . Maybe on Saturday we can go shopping, get started with the layette . . . I guess people still buy layettes. *(She laughs)* I'm going to feel so odd, being a mother. *(She hugs Helen)*

HELEN: I'm sure you'll adjust to it.

IRIS: We want you to be part of it—of everything—of—you know, what the hell.

HELEN: I know. *(She smiles)*

IRIS: I like you, Helen.

HELEN: I know.

IRIS: Well? Don't you like me?

HELEN: Of course. Of course I do. You've been good for him, too. For Phil . . . And I'm certainly very happy you're going to have a baby. *(She reaches for a cup of coffee, spills it, starts to cry)* Oh, damn it. Damn it!

IRIS: I'll get something to clean it up.

HELEN: Don't bother. I'm fine. I'm fine. I just—it's all over the floor. *(She gets* Kleenex *out of her purse, sops it up. Iris helps her. Both women are on the floor, they look at one another, then they laugh. Helen laughs even more than Iris)*

IRIS: Hell, we'll regard it as a christening. An early christening. *(Pause. They look at each other. Iris gets a cigarette, lights it)*

HELEN: You know, I'm a shy person.

IRIS: I know that.

HELEN: It's hard for me to express myself.

IRIS: I know that, Helen.

HELEN: Sometimes I would just like to lock my apartment, and double-lock it and never go back. I mean, just take a suitcase and never go back. I could go to—San Francisco, or Peoria, or Rio de Janeiro. I have no obligations. I could go anywhere, and I could be anything. I could go back to school.

IRIS: *(After a moment)* So. Could you stay for supper?

HELEN: *(With a little laugh)* Yes. I'd like that. I'd like to stay.

IRIS: Listen. I've got the vitamin pills, and the calcium pills, all that stuff . . . And I've got morning sickness. *(Helen has not been paying much attention)* Would you rather talk about something else?

HELEN: Well—it's an area of experience I don't know anything about.

IRIS: For God's sake, nobody's a spinster any more!

HELEN: I have had a perfectly adequate sex life. And I'm not in love with my brother. And I'm just not interested in pregnancy, all right? I mean— *(She tries to make a joke)* I mean, rabbits do it all the time. It's not such a big deal. *(Neither of them finds it funny)* You know, Iris, some people just—I really don't want anyone to be my whole life. I really don't.

IRIS: Oh, God, you don't know what you're missing, Helen. I wake up in the morning and I *want* to take his grapefruit and cut it in half and cut up all the little segments very neatly. You know what I mean?

HELEN: It's just not for me . . . I've never met someone I could love wholeheartedly. I used to think there was something wrong with me. People were planning to devote their lives to one another right and left.

IRIS: I have this feeling that if we go on talking like this, it's going to hurt my baby, so will you please shut up, Helen . . . I'm sorry, they say women get very emotional. Well, I'm very emotional, and I want to have nothing but happiness around my baby. For the next six months, I don't plan to have an argument. Or to listen to one.

(Helen looks at her, holds out her arms, Iris goes to her, Helen hugs her, very maternally)

HELEN: You know, if it's a girl, I'd really like you to consider naming her after our mother.

Scene Eight:
Iris In Rome

Iris has a piece of paper with her, a list on which the names of the donors and their addresses appear. She doesn't know how to find her way in this strange neighborhood. This is a slum, in the worst possible section of Rome. All around her is the sound of women shouting, children crying, cats yowling. A man, Antonio, is sitting on the steps of a tenement. He has a bottle of wine and is half drunk already. Iris walks hesitantly up to him. Antonio will only be able to speak in Italian. There should be subtitles to the scene.

IRIS: Prego. Signore Antonio Vivaldi . . . Where do I find him?

ANTONIO: *(In Italian)* I'm Vivaldi, what do you want? (Sono Vivaldi. Cosa volete?)

IRIS: *(Enunciating carefully)* I'm looking for Antonio Vivaldi. *(She fishes in her purse for another piece of paper, looks at it, reads awkwardly from it in Italian)* I'm looking for Antonio Vivaldi.

ANTONIO: *(In Italian)* Damn it! I *am* Vivaldi. (Porce Madonna. Son' *io* Vivaldi.)

IRIS: Do you speak English?

ANTONIO: *(Simultaneouly, in Italian)* Don't you speak Italian? (Non parlate Italiano, voi?)

IRIS: Antonio Vivaldi?

ANTONIO: *(Pointing to himself)* That's me. You want to hire me? I've gone honest. (Ecco mi. Ma che cazzo voleta? Son onestu orami. Cazzo.)

IRIS: Oh. You're Vivaldi. . . . How do you do? Are you related to the composer? *(Antonio stares at her. Iris starts to find her Italian phrase book)*

ANTONIO: Get the hell out of here, will you? I want to drink privately. (Ma va mori' ammasato, va. Hai capito? Non vedi che sto bevando?)

IRIS: The composer. Musica . . . Maestro. Maestro.

ANTONIO: *(He is afraid, ready to run away)* Maestro? How'd you know they call me that? (Maestro? Maestro? Come sai che mi chiammaro cosi?)

IRIS: Don't be afraid. I just want to see—you had an operation. Hospital? . . . How do you say it? Hospitale? Dottore?

ANTONIO: You're sick? I was, too. Lousy doctors. (Sei malatta? Vatene! Disgraziati medici!)

IRIS: You had a transplant . . An organ. Can I see it? *(She points to her eyes)*

ANTONIO: *(He makes the evil eye at her)* You're a witch? You want to curse me? What'd I ever do to you? (Ma sei una strega! Cosa vovi? Vuoi maledirmi?)

(He gets up, she pushes him down)

IRIS: I have to see it. You have to let me see it. I'll find it. I can tell by the scar. *(She starts examining his body, opening his shirt, looking for a clue to the organ. She is quite desperate and really hurting Antonio)* I have to see it. I need him.

ANTONIO: Help! Help! (Aiuto! Aiuto!) *(Antonio tries to beat her off, but Iris is stronger. The fight turns serious. Iris starts to choke him. He breaks away, makes an obscene gesture)* Crazy bitch! (Figlia d'una mignotta.)

IRIS: The hand! He got the hand! *(She makes a grab for it. Philip appears suddenly. Iris is distracted from Antonio)* Phil?

PHILIP: *(In Italian. He will have subtitles to translate his lines, too)* Leave me alone . . . Damn it! You've got to let me have some privacy. (Lasciarmi. Per l'amure di dio, ogni tanto devi lasciarme in pace.)

ANTONIO: Holy Jesus! There's a witch loose. (Porca miseria! Aiuto! Qui c'è una strega.)

(He runs off)

IRIS: I don't understand you. I can't speak Italian. I'm lonely, Phil.

PHILIP: You've never known when to stop. It's time to stop now, Iris. (Non hai mai saputo smettere, Iris. Adesso smetti.)
IRIS: How do I get back to the hotel? *(Philip leaves her. She looks around, truly frightened)* Does anyone here speak English?

Scene Nine:
Knowing How It Is Going To Go
But Going On Anyway

Philip is in a hospital bed. There is a bouquet of flowers, candy, a couple of books. Iris is sitting in a chair very close to the bed. Helen is sitting in another chair, a little removed from the other two.

HELEN: *(To Philip)* It's funny, isn't it? The last few days, I've never felt closer to you.
IRIS: Were you friends—when you were little?
HELEN: Sometimes. Sometimes we hated one another . . . When he was seven, he was all muscle. You know, one of those swaggering boys who play all day at getting dirty. He never read a book. I don't know when he changed. He always had a cut or a scab from falling, or a black eye. Oh, God, he was aggressive. It was hell growing up his sister.
PHILIP: Was it really?
HELEN: When's your next meal?
PHILIP: What difference does it make?
IRIS: It's five-thirty.
HELEN: I think I'll leave when they bring the tray in.
PHILIP: You can leave now. It's all right, Helen. You don't have to spend every day here.
HELEN: Oh. Well, I don't mind. Not at all. I have a vacation coming to me. And they won't take the rest of the time off without paying me. You'll see. I'm never out of the office with a cold or, you know, when my period comes, any of those things. I'm healthy as a horse, actually, so I never use up the sick leave anyway . . . I talk too much. *(She grinds to a slow halt)*
IRIS: Yes.
HELEN: I always did. Especially when there's a chance to say the wrong thing. Remember when I got in that freight elevator at work and whistled Dixie all the way up to my floor. *(She laughs uneasily)* And there was a black operator. Just when the—you know, the civil rights movement was starting up. And when I heard myself, I was

so embarrassed. I didn't know what to do, so I kept on whistling Dixie. *(She laughs again)*

PHILIP: There's something about death that makes people stupid.

HELEN: Stop it, Phil.

PHILIP: I'm dying, Helen.

HELEN: I don't like to hear about it.

PHILIP: Really, you know, it's none of your business.

IRIS: Why don't you go have an early dinner. That way you can have a visit with him while I'm eating.

HELEN: He's spiteful. There's no reason to be spiteful. *(She leaves)*

IRIS: You are.

PHILIP: I've got a right to be.

IRIS: Maybe I'd better take a walk.

PHILIP: No. Please. I don't want to be alone. Not yet.

IRIS: *(She holds his hand)* Can I get you anything?

PHILIP: No.

IRIS: How about the pillow. Does it need any fluffing up.

PHILIP: I'm fine.

IRIS: It's hard to talk to you.

PHILIP: The doctor—that psychiatrist—she says in a while I'll want to be alone. Now—

IRIS: You're afraid.

PHILIP: God damn it! I'm thirsty. Get me something to drink, will you? Some ginger ale.

(He turns away from her. She moves off, encounters the Doctor)

DOCTOR: I'm sorry. It simply isn't operable.

IRIS: I don't believe that. My husband's a strong man. He's perfectly healthy. And he's young.

DOCTOR: We'd do much damage getting to it, Mrs. Uberman.

IRIS: I don't care. Even if he's an invalid. You've got to—

DOCTOR: The aneurism is leaking now . . . You understand? . . . It's a bubble, like a balloon in his artery. And it's growing bigger. When it bursts, suddenly, without any warning, well, that'll be it.

PHILIP: Where the hell are you? I'm thirsty. *(Iris comes back to him)* Didn't they have any ice?

IRIS: Someone's bringing it.

PHILIP: I want to talk to him when he comes on rounds today. I want you to find out what the news is. About it.

IRIS: You know there isn't any, Phil. He told us. There's no way to know. You just have to keep still. The stiller you are the better your chance is.

PHILIP: I moved just now. I tried to crank up the damned bed. Nothing happened.

IRIS: It could. You shouldn't do that. I'll ring for the nurse.

PHILIP: I didn't do any damage . . . You aren't even upset, are you?

IRIS: Of course I am. We've got to be calm. Both of us. Now try to relax.

PHILIP: I suppose the sooner I die the better off you'd be. It's expensive keeping me here.

IRIS: That sounds like Helen. *(She takes his hand again)*

PHILIP: Put your head down, on the bed. Like you did before. *(She does. He strokes it again)* How's the boy?

IRIS: Fine. He wants to come and visit . . . They still won't let me bring him in.

PHILIP: Maybe I'll make it till he's twelve. Only three more years.

IRIS: He's making you a steam engine. It's supposed to be finished next week.

PHILIP: That's fine.

IRIS: I've been trying to figure out a way that you could do some work.

PHILIP: On what?

IRIS: You've got so many unfinished things. I was going through the papers—do you mind? And I sorted them. There are three short articles that just need a little work. A book review. And the book.

PHILIP: The book's out. It's impossible. Too much. And all the research left.

IRIS: Couldn't I do some of that?

PHILIP: Don't sit up. Please.

IRIS: What's the matter?

PHILIP: Lock the door. There's a lock on it, isn't there?

IRIS: We can't. You know what the doctor said.

PHILIP: I want you.

IRIS: I know. *(They kiss)*

PHILIP: Jesus!

IRIS: We have to settle for this.

PHILIP: I can't.

IRIS: Talk to me about it. Tell me about loving me.

PHILIP: I want you.

IRIS: You love me.

PHILIP: What'll you do? When—you know.

IRIS: I don't know.

PHILIP: You won't have to work.

IRIS: Maybe I will anyway.
PHILIP: You'll marry again.
IRIS: I don't know.
PHILIP: You will. You're too fucking sexy not to.
IRIS: Would you mind?
PHILIP: I'll be dead.
IRIS: I don't want to talk about it.
PHILIP: My golf clubs. I'd hate to see you give them away. Maybe the boy could use them when he's old enough.
IRIS: I wouldn't give them away.
PHILIP: Remember? I'm the only professor of the philosophy of literature to win the club's open. In its history.
IRIS: You're the only one who's entered.
PHILIP: It's still a distinction.
IRIS: I won't marry. If you don't want me to.
PHILIP: Don't make stupid promises.
IRIS: I keep thinking there must be something to say and I'm forgetting it. *(She kisses him again)*
PHILIP: Listen. Lock the door. It doesn't matter. An hour more or less. Please.
IRIS: You're sure?
PHILIP: Come to bed, honey.
IRIS: *(She gets on the bed. They lie there for a moment)* No. Be still.
PHILIP: Forget it.
IRIS: We can be careful . . . Come on. We do it my way.
PHILIP: Whoever would've thought it. That dying's an aphrodisiac.

Scene Ten:
Assorted Information

Iris and Philip each at a lectern with scripts.

IRIS: Part 1. The Meeting.
PHILIP: I was walking to work one morning.
IRIS: I was sitting in the library doing my research for a term paper.
PHILIP: And she came toward me, with an open umbrella. It wasn't raining.
IRIS: And he stumbled against the chair.
PHILIP: So I asked her why. I thought it was a joke. A sorority initiation or something.

IRIS: He apologized and asked me to have coffee. But I had a class to get to.

PHILIP: She invited me back to her apartment.

IRIS: We didn't see each other for a few weeks after that.

PHILIP: We went to bed that very night.

IRIS: I loved him then.

PHILIP: Part 2. The Ninth Anniversary.

IRIS: You'll be late for school.

PHILIP: I just decided to retire from teaching.

IRIS: And stay in bed all day?

PHILIP: Stay in bed with you all day.

IRIS: Come home early tonight.

PHILIP: Can't. There's a department meeting.

IRIS: Okay . . . Call the dean and give him your notice. Part 3. Getting Acquainted.

PHILIP: I was a champion marbles player when I was seven.

IRIS: Did you ever play hi-lo? You know with the paddle and the rubber ball?

PHILIP: No. But I played Ping-Pong.

IRIS: Gnip gnop.

PHILIP: Did you win at it?

IRIS: Only once.

PHILIP: Well, then. You were all A's in graduate school.

IRIS: Almost. I got a B in library science.

PHILIP: Part 4. Domestic.

IRIS: You never wash out the bathtub.

PHILIP: I like handkerchiefs not Kleenex.

IRIS: Please, no chicory in the coffee this week.

PHILIP: You'd better go on a diet.

IRIS: You'd better start jogging.

PHILIP: Where's my red tie?

IRIS: I threw it out. Wear the blue striped one.

PHILIP: We're out of toilet paper.

IRIS: Part 5. Phone calls . . . Philip?

PHILIP: Hurry up. I've got to get to my ten o'clock.

IRIS: I went to the doctor today.

PHILIP: What's wrong?

IRIS: He says I'm pregnant.

PHILIP: Are you sure?

IRIS: Well—the rabbit is.

PHILIP: Jesus!

IRIS: Are you glad?

PHILIP: How long?

IRIS: In June. That's six months.
PHILIP: I'll be on sabbatical.
IRIS: Are you glad?
PHILIP: Stunned. I think so. Listen . . .
IRIS: I can't. My dime's up.
PHILIP: I'll call you. What's the number?
IRIS: Just tell me.
PHILIP: Hello. Hello. *(He shrugs. Hangs up the phone. Then he picks it up again. Iris picks hers up)*
IRIS: Hello?
PHILIP: I love you.
IRIS: I'm in labor.
PHILIP: My God. And I'm in London.
IRIS: They're coming every fifteen minutes. How did the paper go?
PHILIP: I'm going to write a book.
IRIS: What shall I call it?
PHILIP: If it's a boy, call him David.
IRIS: And if it's a girl?
PHILIP: You name it.
IRIS: Clara. After your mother.
PHILIP: Swell. Is it fifteen minutes yet?
IRIS: Not quite.
PHILIP: Is Helen there?
IRIS: I have to hang up now, dear.
PHILIP: I'm catching the next plane back.
IRIS: Get some rest . . . Are you there?
PHILIP: Do you need anything?
IRIS: I can't hear you.
PHILIP: I can't hear you. *(He can't hear, hangs up)*
IRIS: Oh, I want you here. I love you.
PHILIP: I love you.
IRIS: Hello. Operator. Operator, I've been disconnected.
PHILIP: Last section.
IRIS: Take an aspirin and come to bed.
PHILIP: You know, about swinging. I don't think I'd like it.
IRIS: Want to try it?
PHILIP: We could spend a few weeks with Masters and Johnson.
IRIS: There's no such thing as a vaginal orgasm.
PHILIP: Who cares?
IRIS: You're drunk.
PHILIP: I want—
IRIS: *(At the same time)* I love—

PHILIP: Why do you put the nightgown on if you're only going to have to take it off?

IRIS: It's sexy.

PHILIP: Did you take the pill?

IRIS: What about vasectomy?

PHILIP: No more kids.

IRIS: I think I'm starting change of life.

PHILIP: They have hormones now.

IRIS: Postscript. Honeymoon.

PHILIP: If anything happens to me, I want you to get married again, you understand?

IRIS: I'll be long gone and you'll be living with a twenty-year-old model.

PHILIP: It's a statistical fact. Men die first.

IRIS: I made a will.

PHILIP: There's a will in the safe deposit box.

IRIS: You won't die. You wouldn't. I insist on it. I'm going first.

PHILIP: I couldn't live without you.

IRIS: I couldn't live without you.

Scene Eleven: Iris On Top Of The World

Iris has a pack on her back, and in the manner of Chinese theatre, she performs a stylized, spiral motion that will indicate that she is climbing a mountain. Philip stands to one side, watching her. As the climb goes on, Iris will grow more tired, there is less oxygen in the air.

PHILIP: There's nothing left but my heart.

IRIS: Nothing.

PHILIP: Has the trip been successful.

IRIS: No. Not yet . . . I'm still hoping, though.

PHILIP: You should rest.

IRIS: The connections are wearing thin. I'm climbing to the top of the world, Phil . . . I thought it would be otherwise.

PHILIP: I expected more from dying, and it's so simple. And I've gone away too quickly. Iris?

IRIS: It's getting cold. I'd better move on.

(Iris goes on in her endless spiral, the lights fading on her completely after a bit. Philip is alone, in his area. It is the moment of his death)

Scene Twelve:
Iris In India

Iris is sitting with a basket of food and wine, she has been eating. A Monk comes in.

IRIS: Good afternoon. I wondered when I'd see someone.
MONK: You found the food though.
IRIS: You speak English?
MONK: Whatever tongue may be necessary.
IRIS: Am I taking someone's meal?
MONK: May I sit with you?
IRIS: I was cold on the way up, but I'm quite comfortable, now. I expect it's the sun through the clouds or something.
MONK: Do you plan to stay here?
IRIS: I was looking for something—someone.
MONK: We leave a meal out every day, for someone who may have come without food.
IRIS: Oh. You get a lot of visitors then?
MONK: No.
IRIS: Are there many people here? I don't see—you know, houses, stores. I didn't even see any farms.
MONK: The soil is not good for growing things.
IRIS: Are you in charge?
MONK: We live in—openings of the mountain. You wouldn't notice them.
IRIS: You don't answer my questions.
MONK: I'm sorry. Ask one.
IRIS: I was trying to find someone. My husband died.
MONK: Yes.
IRIS: And I've been traveling, trying to find him.
MONK: His pieces.
IRIS: Yes. All over. And. They said. His heart. Could anyone do an operation like that up here?
MONK: Operation?
IRIS: A transplant.
MONK: That isn't what we did.
IRIS: I thought there was a mistake.
MONK: No mistake, the heart came here . . . Have you tried some of the wine? It's very good. It's made from spring flowers. *(He reaches in the basket, takes out two glasses, pours the wine)*

IRIS: Thank you. But I don't like wine.

MONK: Cheers.

IRIS: Were you educated in England?

MONK: No. I've never been down this mountain.

IRIS: This is good . . . The wine. May I have some more? *(He pours some)* I'm sorry. I don't want to—intrude. Is this a religious community?

MONK: Yes.

IRIS: You're very handsome. *(Short pause)* I come from Indiana. Originally. I've lived most of my life in New York. In the United States . . . Should I worry about a sunburn? So high up. This is going to be the last stop on my trip. Then I'm going home . . . When I was little, my father gave me a book, about a boy and a girl who traveled all over the world. They had lived on a farm, but they left the farm and they went to Paris, France, and London. They even went to China. And when they came back, all the little girl wanted to do was to go out to the barn to see if her baby calf had grown any. I thought travel was something else. I expected to turn into a new person in each country. But what I've found is, I keep staying more and more the same. And I'm middle-aged . . . I think I'll do what Philip did. Then we'd have a chance, you know. The girl who gets my liver could marry the boy who got his bone marrow. If I die soon enough. Then we'd have more children. It bothers me not to have had more babies.

MONK: You could stay here with me.

IRIS: Do you find me pretty?

MONK: No. But I like you.

IRIS: Was that an eagle? Do they fly this high? I'll have to stay the night, I guess. I'd never get down the mountain by dark. And I stay with you?

MONK: No birds fly up here. It's going to rain. *(He packs up the food that's left, the glasses, etc.)*

IRIS: What happened to Philip's heart? Who got it?

MONK: I did.

IRIS: You seem so healthy.

MONK: I am.

IRIS: You said there was no operation. Is it something new? Something—Eastern?

MONK: I ate it.

Last Scene:
More Conversations Between Two Women

Iris and Helen at Iris's kitchen table. Iris is wearing paint spotted blue jeans.

HELEN: I thought you wouldn't want to be alone all day.

IRIS: I needed the coffee. And I needed a break from the painting. I'm going to be stiff tomorrow.

HELEN: I noticed how healthy the plants were.

IRIS: David's coming home for a few days tonight. I wanted to get his room all ready . . . But I can't put a wet bookcase in there.

HELEN: It's his birthday today, Phil's birthday.

IRIS: I know.

HELEN: I just meant—well, I was surprised to find you painting things today.

IRIS: I thought about painting this table purple. Like eating on an eggplant.

HELEN: Can I take you both out to supper? Pizza. He likes pizza . . . I got the nicest letter from him last week.

IRIS: David likes you.

HELEN: He's just like his father.

IRIS: No. Not really. Not at all.

HELEN: Whatever you say.

IRIS: Oh, come on, Helen.

HELEN: I've enrolled at the New School. Biology. And I'm going to take some math. Statistics . . . Something I can really get involved in . . . I've always felt very connected to science.

IRIS: All right, Helen. Phil's dead. I'm sorry . . . Now I have to go on working.

HELEN: You used to say he was your whole life.

IRIS: He was . . . I mean I thought he was. At that last place. While I was on my trip, Helen. I discovered that I had to make up my mind. To go on, or to stop. Whatever. So today, I decided to paint a bookcase. That's what I'm going to do. Even on my husband's birthday.

HELEN: I have to go to school.

(Helen leaves the kitchen. She goes to another area. She is in a tight light. She picks up a phone. Iris picks up her phone)

IRIS: I just can't go on talking about Phil every time we see one another, Helen.

HELEN: Why not?

IRIS: Because there's no point in it.

HELEN: Ever since you came back, you've been different. Are you in love with someone?

IRIS: Not on the phone, Helen.

HELEN: I'm sorry. It's been worrying me.

IRIS: How's school?

HELEN: I had to stop. All those fluorescent lights. They gave me headaches. And I can't go to school during the daytime. I mean, I don't want to give up my job.

IRIS: All right, Helen. No more about Phil then.

HELEN: David's starting to look just like him. *(They hang up. Then Iris picks hers up, followed by Helen)* Hello?

IRIS: What's all this about your giving a cocktail party?

HELEN: For the victims of the Spanish Civil War.

IRIS: That was 1937.

HELEN: Well, some of them are still alive.

IRIS: All right. I'll come.

HELEN: I've been learning how to crochet.

IRIS: Isn't that hard on the eyes?

HELEN: Do you want me to make you an afghan?

IRIS: If you want to.

HELEN: How's David?

IRIS: He wants to be an engineer.

HELEN: I don't know how to go on, Iris. Really. I don't. *(Helen comes back into the kitchen)* I don't know why. I—no, I wasn't even drunk. And I went home with him.

IRIS: Did you enjoy it?

HELEN: Yes.

IRIS: Well?

HELEN: What about you?

IRIS: I like being alone. For a while.

HELEN: You'll end up making someone else your whole life.

IRIS: Not ever again, Helen. No one.

HELEN: Sometimes I wonder if I'm capable of love.

IRIS: I love you, Helen.

HELEN: I love David. I'm sure of that . . . And you. I love you . . . Lately, for the last few years, I'm always afraid.

IRIS: About going on? *(Helen nods)* I am, too.

HELEN: I'm forty years old.

IRIS: When I was in India, I was on top of a mountain. And— it's not that I saw God—almost the reverse. I had this sure sensation, as firm and as real as a string of beads; mortality. I finally believed in mortality. I finally believed in mortality. Phil's dead. I'm going to die some time. Even my son will. I find that reassuring. *(She hands Helen an envelope)* Here.

HELEN: What is it?

IRIS: The list. Of all the people who got his organs. I think you should take the trip. I think you should quit your job and pack one small suitcase and take the trip . . . I'll take care of your aquarium . . . You'll find out. It's good. Going crazy. I'm really glad I did it. Everything. Even being crazy. And then he'll be dead. For both of us. He'll be dead for the rest of our lives.

Curtain

Curt Dempster

MIMOSA PUDICA

Curt Dempster

Although a gifted playwright, Curt Dempster is perhaps best known in the theatrical world as the founder and artistic director of the noted Off-Off-Broadway Ensemble Studio Theatre. The company, under his energetic and inspiring guidance and in a comparatively short period, has risen to the forefront of New York theatrical organizations dedicated to the spawning and nurturing of promising and/or outstanding new plays by both known and unknown playwrights. As reported in *The New York Times:* "Curt Dempster's Ensemble Studio Theatre is a community of artists—actors, directors, playwrights, designers—who often change roles. Mr. Dempster invests in people. For him, they are a natural resource. In a sense, the company is ecological, reclaiming talent and preserving theatre as well as creating new work . . . the Ensemble Studio Theatre has grown until it has become an essential part of Off-Off-Broadway."

At EST, Mr. Dempster has helped to develop more than forty new plays, and as author, he has seen two of his own works mounted on its premises, *Michigan South* and *Mimosa Pudica,* which is published for the first time in *The Best Short Plays 1977.*

A former assistant to Jerome Robbins and Ulu Grosbard, his many directorial credits include the staging of Frank D. Gilroy's *Present Tense, Sunday Dinner* by Joyce Carol Oates, Chekhov's *The Seagull* and Arthur Miller's *The Crucible.*

As an assistant director he was associated with the long-running Off-Broadway production of Miller's *A View from the Bridge;* the full-length recording of *Death of a Salesman,* starring Lee J. Cobb; and the movie, *Who is Harry Kellerman?*

An instructor as well, he has served as Visiting Professor at Johnson State College, Vermont; as Artist-in-Residence at Smith College; on the staff of the American Musical & Dramatic Academy; and as a consultant for the New York State Council on the Arts.

During the summer of 1976, the Ensemble Studio Theatre was in residence on the Rutgers University campus, with a number of projects, including new plays by Phillip Hayes Dean, Conrad Bromberg and John Ford Noonan. And while the EST specializes in new dramatic works, during its tenure at Rutgers, Mr. Dempster varied things a bit by staging a successful and sold-out workshop production of *Hamlet* with film star Jon Voight in the title role.

Characters:

DIANNE
DAVID

Scene One:

Place: An aging apartment building in New York. Time: The early afternoon of Christmas Eve.

As the lights come up, Dianne, carrying groceries and packages, enters hallway. She is twenty-five, very Italian, basically plain but attractive in a vulnerable and appealing way. She waits a moment, her attention focused down the hall. Then quickly, she approaches her apartment door and fumbles with packages and keys. David enters. He is thirty-two, intense, pre-occupied. She watches as he passes her and reaches the entrance to his apartment. He takes no notice of her and she waits until the last possible instant to speak.

DIANNE: Hello. *(He opens his door)* Hello there!
DAVID: Oh . . . good morning.
DIANNE: I'm Three-G.
DAVID: Pardon me?
DIANNE: We're neighbors. *(Indicates her door)* Would you like some coffee?
DAVID: Coffee?
DIANNE: I mean over here. Have some coffee over here.
DAVID: *(Agitated)* Well . . . I have something I must—
DIANNE: It'll only take a second. I just have to heat it.
DAVID: I don't want to put you to any trouble.
DIANNE: It's no trouble. *(He is off-balance, hesitant. She comes a step closer, smiles)* Your neighbor Dianne Rosemary Francesca Pizzarusso cordially invites—what's your name?
DAVID: *(Involuntarily)* David.
DIANNE: David what?
DAVID: . . .Meyer.
DIANNE: Cordially invites David Meyer to tea this morning in honor of their recent acquaintance and especially in honor of the holiday season! *(Unlocks her door, pushes it open)* Now we know each other and you're formally invited. *(Stands aside for him to enter)* How can you refuse?
DAVID: . . . I'm sorry, I only have a few minutes.
DIANNE: So come for a few minutes. *(Smiles)* After all, what's the worst that could happen in a few minutes?

DAVID: *(Still hesitant)* Well, if you don't mind me leaving right away?

DIANNE: Leave when you have to.

DAVID: *(A beat)* Thank you, I accept. *(He comes closer. She struggles with the large package)* Can I help you with that, Miss—?

DIANNE: Pizzarusso. Yes, thank you. *(He takes package, follows her into the small, one-room apartment. The room is colorful, charming and comfortable. Dianne crosses quickly to the Pullman-kitchen area)* You can put the bag there by the closet and drop your coat on the bed.

DAVID: *(After a moment)* This is very nice.

DIANNE: *(Pleased)* You really think so? I feel like it's really my house, you know? Like it's waiting for me to come home and make it complete. *(She indicates window boxes filled with an array of plant life)* I think my plants make me feel this way. Do you like plants?

(He is unsettled by her familiarity but is gamely trying not to withdraw)

DAVID: Well . . . no, not really. But I think it's nice that you do. It shows you're optimistic.

DIANNE: What do you mean?

DAVID: Growing things—It shows you believe in the future.

DIANNE: That's like my mother.

DAVID: What is?

DIANNE: She's always analyzing everything I do.

DAVID: I'm sorry—

DIANNE: No, it's okay. Like my mother believes in reincarnation. And I love plants, right? So she says I must have been a tree or something in another life. *(She inspects one of the window boxes)* I've got all these new cuttings I just transplanted. Are you sure you wouldn't like a couple of them?

DAVID: No, thanks.

DIANNE: Why not—*(Crosses to stove)* Aren't you an optimist?

DAVID: I guess I think people shouldn't waste affection on plants and animals.

DIANNE: *(Busy with the coffee, turns to him)* Oh, but see, it's not a waste. It helps you with other things, keeps you in practice, you know what I mean? And especially plants. Don't you know about them?

DAVID: Know what about them?

DIANNE: If you give them affection, they grow better.

DAVID: Do you really believe that?

DIANNE: Sure, they're alive, too, you know. Come here, I'll show you something. *(She crosses to window; he follows)* This is my favorite.

DAVID: What is it?

DIANNE: Mim . . . mim . . . Wait, it's hard to say . . . Mimosa Pudica.

DAVID: What?

DIANNE: Mimosa Pudica—that's the what do you call it? . . .

DAVID: Latin?

DIANNE: The Latin name for it. Its other name is the Sensitive Plant. Look. *(She gently touches a slender branch; the tiny, delicate leaves contract)*

DAVID: The leaves closed up—that's amazing!

DIANNE: And when you hold your hand close, they tremble . . . see? *(He watches, fascinated)* Do you want to do it? *(He hesitates)* Go ahead. Just be careful.

(Tentatively and somewhat clumsily, he touches the fragile, wand-like branch. Again, its leaves contract)

DAVID: They're like tiny fingers that close up into fists. It's really incredible.

DIANNE: If you touch the leaves too much, they fall off in self-defense.

DAVID: *(With wonder)* Where did you find this?

DIANNE: At a store in the neighborhood. *(Crosses to window)* That brick wall out there is so horrible I pretend my plants are really the beginning of a forest. If you lean close to the window you can see the top of an honest-to-God tree.

DAVID: *(Looks out)* So you can.

DIANNE: *(Moves to closet)* The coffee will be right up. Excuse me, I want to put these away. Why don't you sit down? *(He does so)*

DAVID: *(Referring to the boxes she removes from a large bag)* Christmas presents?

DIANNE: No, they're empty. I like them that way. *(Holds one aloft)* I love boxes. They have four perfect sides and a bottom. *(Turns box to demonstrate)* And when you put on the top . . . *(She does so)* They fit together all the way around, see? *(She smiles, puts boxes into closet)* The whole closet is full of boxes and things. I save them for the kids. *(She crosses back to the kitchen area)*

DAVID: You have children?

DIANNE: *(Brings him cheese, crackers, etc.)* Sort of. I work in the children's part of the library. Every day at three o'clock I read a fairy tale or something to the kids. And once a week we make things. It's not really part of my job but they let me do it.

DAVID: You must enjoy it.

DIANNE: *(Crosses back to kitchen, turns)* Kids are great. It's like being in another country where you're the stranger and they make you feel at home. *(Serves him coffee)* Would you like some good Italian soup?

DAVID: No, thank you. This is fine.

DIANNE: *(Setting a bowl near him)* Well, I'll just put it here. If you don't want it, don't eat. *(She sits, watches with satisfaction as he tastes the soup)* May I ask you something . . . a personal question?

DAVID: *(Half-joking)* Do I have to answer?

DIANNE: No.

DAVID: Go ahead.

DIANNE: Did it surprise you when I said hello to you? I mean did it seem strange or weird or anything?

DAVID: . . . Well, I suppose . . . sure, a little. It doesn't happen very often.

DIANNE: That's why I do it. I mean you never meet anybody and I just got tired of being around strangers. So I decided to talk to people. Sugar?

DAVID: One.

DIANNE: *(Stirring in sugar)* I don't say hello to just anybody—like creeps and degenerates. I even tried that for a while. At least they answer you. *(Pours herself coffee)*

DAVID: I hope you're careful.

DIANNE: That's the trouble. Everybody's too careful! It was different for a while. Were you here for the power failure?

DAVID: No, but I read about it. I was away, I think.

DIANNE: It was really fantastic. All over the city the lights and TV's and radios and record players and everything all went off—bang! For a long time it was quiet, like in the country. After a while, out in the air shaft you could hear the windows sliding up and people talking in low voices.

DAVID: Weren't you afraid?

DIANNE: A little, at first. But then I got excited, like when I was little and there would be a storm or something. Finally, somebody knocked to see if I was alright. When I opened the door, there were all these people with flashlights and candles milling around, whispering. They looked like giant fireflies.

DAVID: Was there any panic?

DIANNE: Not really. But the three old Puerto Rican ladies from the top floor were huddled on the steps, holding hands and praying. So I brought them in and made them coffee. Then other people came by and pretty soon it was like an open house in a deserted building. *(He laughs)* After that, we all used to visit each other, but that didn't last very long.

DAVID: Do you still see them?

DIANNE: Not really. Now things are back to normal. They just hurry by and nod or mumble something.

DAVID: I know. You can go for months and never meet anyone.

DIANNE: Right. Like when I see you in the hall you never seem to notice anything. And I wanted to meet you. That's why I said hello. My sister doesn't have to do that—she's very pretty.

DAVID: Your sister? Does she live here?

DIANNE: No, she's married.

DAVID: Is she here in New York?

DIANNE: Don't.

DAVID: What?

DIANNE: Ask any more about my sister. I'm jealous of her. I used to think people pretended they liked me just so they could be around her.

DAVID: You can relax. I don't even know her.

DIANNE: That doesn't matter.

DAVID: Okay, you win. I apologize. *(They laugh. Short pause)* Anyway, I'm glad you said hello.

DIANNE: *(Pleased)* Oh, so am I . . . After all, everybody should be more sociable on Christmas Eve. That reminds me. *(Goes to refrigerator)* I got some eggnog! *(Pours two glasses, brings him one)*

DAVID: No, thank you.

DIANNE: Just have a little. You know, in the Yuletide Spirit.

DAVID: I said no thanks! *(Rises, crosses away)*

DIANNE: *(Rises)* What's wrong? Hey, are you all right?

DAVID: *(Takes coat, moves toward door)* I'm okay.

DIANNE: Wait, what did I do?

DAVID: You didn't do anything.

DIANNE: What is it?

DAVID: I don't . . . really celebrate Christmas.

DIANNE: What, are you Jewish?

DAVID: No. But I usually try to ignore the whole thing.

DIANNE: Don't you have any family here?

DAVID: No.

DIANNE: What about your parents?

DAVID: My parents are dead.

DIANNE: Oh, I'm sorry.

DAVID: Don't be. That's not why I told you.

DIANNE: Look, I understand. Everybody feels something like that this time of year. It was even in the paper about how the suicide rate goes up. They call it the Christmas . . .?

DAVID: Syndrome.

DIANNE: Right. I mean I have a big family in Boston with aunts and uncles but there aren't any kids any more so I decided not to go. I'd just get depressed. Besides, I don't want to go home anyway. My father just sits around with his shirt off and looks at my legs and my mother gets nervous and peroxides her hair.

DAVID: I see what you mean.

DIANNE: And . . . I was . . . married. So they give me a bad time about that, too.

DAVID: I'm sorry.

DIANNE: What's to be sorry? Everybody I know is divorced or separated. *(A beat)* So, I'm not going home. Besides, I have to work . . . Hey, I know! We're having a Christmas party at the library for some of the kids this afternoon. Would you like to come?

DAVID: Oh, no thanks, really. I have work to do.

DIANNE: What kind of work?

DAVID: *(Hesitates)* . . . I guess you could say I'm a student.

DIANNE: So what do you study?

DAVID: It's a long story. Look, I really have to go.

DIANNE: You are, too, aren't you?

DAVID: What?

DIANNE: Divorced or separated.

DAVID: *(After a moment)* Yes.

DIANNE: Which?

DAVID: Divorced.

DIANNE: How long?

DAVID: Two months.

DIANNE: I'm sorry.

DAVID: Now we're both sorry. *(Moves to door)* Thanks for the coffee.

DIANNE: *(With a new intensity)* Wait a minute! I've got something I need to ask you.

DAVID: Something wrong?

DIANNE: I need you to help me . . . please.

DAVID: What is it?

DIANNE: Can you come back for just a minute? *(He studies her, then comes back into the room. She goes to bed, sits. He waits)* I know this must seem weird or something. I mean I don't really know you, but there isn't anybody else, you know?

DAVID: Yes.

(Short pause)

DIANNE: . . . I'm getting a divorce. I mean I hope I can hold out. *(An emotion threatens; she resists)* We've been separated three years. I told him never to call me unless he wanted to start over again and I haven't heard from him in three months. He's supposed to go to Mexico in January—I already got the papers.

DAVID: And?

DIANNE: And we always spent Christmas together, even after we got separated. But if I haven't heard from him by now . . . *(She fights back tears)* I started to call him a hundred times but I never did . . . And now I want to call him and just be with him for Christmas even if it's bad . . . Do you know what I mean?

DAVID: . . . I know.

DIANNE: So what should I do?

DAVID: *(Studies her for a long moment)* No one can tell anybody else what to do in a situation like that.

DIANNE: I know—Tell me anyway.

DAVID: What do you think you should do?

DIANNE: I don't want to think about it. So tell me.

DAVID: *(Starts to leave)* I think you picked the wrong neighbor.

DIANNE: No, wait—Please! . . . Please?

(Short pause)

DAVID: I think you should do . . . whatever gives you the most . . . sustenance.

DIANNE: I knew you'd say something like that.

DAVID: *(Starts out)* Sorry I can't be of more help.

DIANNE: Wait! Can I ask you something else?

DAVID: *(Stops)* Sure.

DIANNE: Why don't we have a Christmas party tonight? I mean . . . you know, just friends.

DAVID: A Christmas party?

DIANNE: Why not . . . We're both alone, right?

DAVID: Don't remind me.

DIANNE: I could bring the Christmas tree from the party—it's just a small one. And I could make a turkey—

DAVID: *(An outburst, angry)* And cranberry sauce and sweet potatoes and dressing and dumplings and then you could trot out the crutches and I could be Bob Cratchit and carry you around on my back like Tiny Tim!

DIANNE: Okay.

DAVID: And we could go all over the building and have plum pudding with the neighbors!

DIANNE: *(Near tears)* Okay. Direct hit. *(She turns away. Short pause)*

DAVID: Look . . . it's a touchy area for me.

DIANNE: So take your touchy area across the hall and forget I brought it up.

DAVID: I don't want to forget it. It was a nice idea. *(She doesn't respond. He starts out, hesitates, turns back to her)* Let me think about it, okay?

DIANNE: You do that.

DAVID: I'm really . . . grateful . . . that you asked me.

DIANNE: I said forget it. *(She rises, moves back to the kitchen)* My mother warned me about strange men.

DAVID: *(Opens door)* Yes, but did she warn you about *very* strange men? *(Waits for a moment)* I'm sorry . . . I really will think about it. *(Short pause)* Okay?

DIANNE: Just go.

(He watches her for a beat, then exits. She stands for a long moment, then crosses near telephone, sits. After a moment she lifts receiver, starts to dial, then hesitates as lights fade slowly)

Scene Two:

Time: A half hour later.

As the lights rise, Dianne is sitting near the window in a rocking chair. She is wrapped in a shawl, knees tucked under, rocking slowly. On the stove, a boiling teakettle whistles cheerfully. After a moment, there is a knock at the door. She rises, hurriedly turns off the teakettle, then opens door. David steps inside. During the following his behavior is mercurial, nearly manic, but controlled.

DAVID: Hi there! I'm Three-F!

DIANNE: Congratulations.

DAVID: Merry Christmas!

DIANNE: Don't play with me.

DAVID: Heaven forfend! May I come in? *(She steps aside. He moves into room, adopts stuffy English accent, trilling the R's and broadening the A's, etc.)* Miss Pizzarusso, I believe? Ah! Of course you ah! The description matches—you are Italian? How Mahvelous! Now then . . . *(He pauses briefly for effect)* It gives me great pleasure on behalf of the Anglo-Italian Good Neighbor Association to present to you owah annual Tiny Tim Award for the propagation of the true holiday spirit in the face of incredible odds! The envelope please! *(Takes envelope from pocket; extracts object wrapped in toilet paper; presents it to her with a flourish)* Congratulations, Miss . . . Pizza . . .?

DIANNE: Pizzarusso. *(Takes object)* What is it?

DAVID: It's an authentic replica of the tip of Tiny Tim's crutch—a talisman of good cheer no less!

DIANNE: What is it really?

DAVID: *(Drops accent)* It's the thing off the leg of the ironing board. A poor but heartfelt token of apology and symbol of my acceptance of your invitation.

DIANNE: Are you serious?

DAVID: You bet your sweet mistletoe!

DIANNE: Okay, but first sit down. *(Leads him to couch)* You'll drive yourself crazy with all that energy.

DAVID: It's too late, nurse. I already did.

DIANNE: What?

DAVID: Drive myself crazy.

DIANNE: *(Nurse-like)* Poor thing. *(Sits him down, pats his head)* You'll just have to be patient and have faith, Lieutenant Meyer. These things happen to the strongest of men.

DAVID: And not only that—the other men are stealing all my chocolates from home.

DIANNE: Now, now, you're imagining things.

DAVID: Is there any other way?

DIANNE: *(Laughs)* You're feeling better.

DAVID: Not really. I'm persevering.

DIANNE: Well, you *seem* better.

DAVID: *(Rises)* Seems? Nay, madam—is! I know not seems!

DIANNE: *(Fixing plate of cheese, etc.)* What's that—poetry?

DAVID: Camouflage. *(She regards him curiously, then offers him plate)* No, thank you.

DIANNE: If you don't want it, don't eat. *(She sits across from him)* I need to ask you a question.

DAVID: Ah ah, not so fast. The burning question has become . . . *(Rises, imitates a Prima Donna attorney, stressing N's)* Did she interrupt the interim with an enormously interesting, interpersonal, intermarriage phone call—in short, I ask you, did she or did she not call her husband!

DIANNE: No.

DAVID: *(Shouts)* Get thee behind me, Satan!

DIANNE: Okay . . . Now . . . would you mind sitting down? I need an honest answer . . . please. *(He sits. She waits until he is settled)* Why did you change your mind?

(Short pause)

DAVID: An honest answer.

DIANNE: Yes.

(A long moment)

DAVID: I figured . . . what did I have to lose?

DIANNE: *(After a beat)* Okay. That's a good way to start. And there's something else. *(She hesitates)* I . . . wasn't sure if you'd come back, but I've been thinking about us being together.

DAVID: *(Leering, the low comedian)* So have I.

DIANNE: I'm serious. And it might not be good this way.

DAVID: What way?

DIANNE: We don't really know each other. And on Christmas Eve you should be with somebody you really know. I mean . . . intimately.

DAVID: Tell me more.

DIANNE: I don't mean that.

DAVID: I take it back. I lost my head.

DIANNE: Now, it would take us about six months to really get to know each other, right?

DAVID: About that, give or take a trauma.

DIANNE: So why don't we skip the six months?

DAVID: What?

DIANNE: *(Growing more enthused)* Just wait 'til I finish. We could think of it as . . . a shortcut. I got the idea from this guy I met. We were having coffee on our first date and he proposed to me. He wanted to move in with me right then.

DAVID: That's what I call a real shortcut.

DIANNE: Yeah, I found out he just got a divorce and couldn't adjust to being single. He wanted sort of an instant wife.

DAVID: So how did it work out?

DIANNE: It didn't. I only said I got the *idea* from him. So what do you think about that?

DAVID: How do you propose to go about this . . . intimacy?

DIANNE: By just being honest with each other. The way you told me why you came over. You know, really say what we're thinking—what's really going on and skip the in-betweens.

DAVID: You're serious.

DIANNE: Yes.

DAVID: *(After a moment)* I don't think you can skip the in-betweens. It's dangerous.

DIANNE: *(She rises, moves)* I know, but God, I don't think I can live through another day of games with anybody. I'd rather just be alone. I could always put on the kettle.

DAVID: The kettle?

DIANNE: When I'm lonely I heat up the kettle until it whistles. It's from when I was a little girl. *(Laughs)* See? I just told you something honest and you didn't make fun of me. I guess I trust you or something. Okay . . . your turn.

DAVID: I didn't say yes.

DIANNE: What's wrong? After all, like you said, what do you have to lose?

DAVID: Did I say that?

DIANNE: You can take it back.

(Pause)

DAVID: *(Rises)* Okay. Just remember I warned you. *(He moves, then finally sits across from her. There is a long moment as they become aware of each other in a new way. During the following, an exhilaration develops for them both)* I had this terrible thing for my grandmother. *(Attempts to laugh)*

DIANNE: Strike one . . . Wait, I know! *(Leads him to bed)* We'll relax first. I'll show you. I learned it in my Yoga class.

DAVID: *(À la James Cagney)* Wait a minute, wait a minute, you're not one of them Commie chinks, are ya?

DIANNE: I'm Italian, remember?

DAVID: What a relief—okay, lead on.

DIANNE: *(She sits on floor, assumes Lotus position)* Put your legs like this and your arms like this with the palms up.

DAVID: How the hell do you get like that?

DIANNE: Come on, you can do it.

DAVID: *(Struggling)* I don't know, coach. The legs are the first to go, you know.

DIANNE: That's right. Now, just relax. Close your eyes and breathe deeply—only don't raise your shoulders when you breathe. *(He tries gamely)* Okay, now just say whatever's on your mind.

(A long moment)

DAVID: My leg hurts.

DIANNE: Then you're not relaxed. Just let all the muscles sag.

DAVID: That's easy.

DIANNE: *(She watches him for a beat)* That's better. Now you can say whatever you're really thinking or you can tell something about yourself. *(She waits for a moment)* Okay, you just keep relaxing and I'll tell you one, okay?

DAVID: Don't mind me, I'm, communing with Buddha.

DIANNE: If you're not going to be serious we might as well stop.

DAVID: *(Affected by her tone)* All right . . . I'm serious.

DIANNE: Okay . . . This is a feeling I had . . . I told you a lot about myself and you never told me anything about you, right? *(He starts to protest)* No, that's okay. But every time I do and you don't I feel like I've . . . lost something.

DAVID: I'm sorry.

DIANNE: Oh no, see that's not why I told you. I just wanted you to know how I felt, that's all. I wasn't being critical.

DAVID: I understand.

DIANNE: Do you really? It's really important.

DAVID: Yes.

DIANNE: Okay, your turn. Go ahead.

DAVID: Look . . . Just let me get out of this tangle. I feel like a Kamikaze pilot.

DIANNE: You've got the wrong country.

DAVID: *(Cagney again)* What's the difference? All those slant-eyed little bastards are alike—right, Dragon Lady?

DIANNE: You know what you're doing now? Can I tell you?

DAVID: Tell me.

DIANNE: You're resisting.

DAVID: You're goddam right I'm resisting. I think I broke my pelvic area.

DIANNE: Don't you trust me?

DAVID: No! *(He laughs)* No, I really do . . . sort of.

DIANNE: Okay, now it's easy. Just like swimming in the ocean—you just have to plunge in. So keep plunging. *(Sits next to him, takes his hand)*

DAVID: *(Pulls away)* Don't do that.

DIANNE: What did I do?

DAVID: It's like you're patronizing me.

DIANNE: I'm sorry . . . So, I won't do it. See? How would I know if you didn't tell me? That's what I mean! Don't you feel better?

DAVID: Yeah, out of the frying pan into the fire. *(Dianne laughs, then impulsively kisses him on the cheek. After a beat, she returns to her chair, sits)*

DIANNE: What are you thinking?

DAVID: I was thinking that was . . . very nice. *(Short pause)* Whose turn is it?

DIANNE: You decide.

DAVID: Why me?

DIANNE: You're the man.

DAVID: Bless my soul, an old-fashioned girl.

DIANNE: You're damn right!

DAVID: I'm glad we got that straight. Okay—your turn.

DIANNE: That's not fair.

DAVID: It's the price you pay.

DIANNE: What does that mean?

DAVID: As they used to say in my neighborhood, if you can't stand the heat, get out of the kitchen.

DIANNE: I really hate it when you do that.

DAVID: Do what?

DIANNE: Say something like that. I mean this isn't easy for me either.

DAVID: You're right—I apologize.

DIANNE: I know you don't mean anything by it . . . wait, damn it, yes you do—It's like you're pushing me away.

DAVID: *(Rises)* Game's over.

DIANNE: What—?

DAVID: There's nothing worse than dime-store psychiatry.

DIANNE: Oh no, please. I didn't mean it that way. Don't be angry. I just can't say things right—explain myself. All I'm saying is don't hold me away.

(A beat)

DAVID: You're right . . . There isn't time for that.

DIANNE: What do you mean?

DAVID: Forget it. Let's go back to the kissing part.

DIANNE: It's too late. Come on, your turn.

DAVID: *(After a moment)* Okay . . . I think you're afraid of your own intelligence. You're afraid to admit you see what you see. Like about me. You were absolutely right and then you backed off.

DIANNE: Now who's analyzing?

DAVID: I owed you one.

DIANNE: Right. So why do you cover up like that—what are you afraid of?

DAVID: Let's change the subject.

DIANNE: Are you afraid of me?

DAVID: *(Rises)* I don't know.

DIANNE: That's it, isn't it?

DAVID: No, that isn't it.

DIANNE: Then what?

DAVID: *(Sarcastic)* I'm depressed, Doctor.

DIANNE: Why?

DAVID: *(Turns to her)* Why? Jesus Christ! It's Christmas, I'm alone—and I just lost my wife, remember?

DIANNE: You mean she died? I thought you said you got a divorce?

DAVID: *(Angry)* You know what the hell I'm talking about! It's like a death—with the shock, the grief, the loss and the pain. And it doesn't matter who was the victim—who left who or which one stayed to mourn—the death goes both ways—and you know that, don't you!

DIANNE: *(Starting to cry)* Yes.

DAVID: You're goddam right you know it! So don't pretend it's all another world to you! *(Dianne rises, crosses to window. He starts toward her, stops, watches her for a long moment)* I'm sorry . . . I said it was dangerous.

DIANNE: No, it's alright. I don't know where that came from.

DAVID: We both know where that came from. *(A beat)* Look, maybe I better go.

DIANNE: No, oh no. Please. It's been so long since I've been honest with anyone. And what you said is true. *(She sits)* I'm sorry to make such a mess. I've never really cried all this time. Sometimes my eyes get all swollen from the inside from holding it back . . . Please stay.

DAVID: Alright. But we change the subject.

DIANNE: Okay. You can choose—No, wait. *(Both laugh)*

DAVID: I give up. You go ahead.

DIANNE: I just wanted to ask you . . . Before, when I wanted to know about your work, you avoided it.

DAVID: And you thought I was too old to be a student, right?

DIANNE: Oh no, I have this uncle who goes to night school.

DAVID: That's different.

DIANNE: So tell me.

DAVID: *(Hesitates)* . . . I've never really tried to talk about it with anyone.

DIANNE: Why?

DAVID: There isn't anyone.

(He laughs)

DIANNE: It's really amazing. When you smile like that your whole face changes—almost like you're another person.

DAVID: Maybe I am.

DIANNE: There you go again, avoiding.

DAVID: Right . . . Okay . . . I don't know if I can really talk about it . . . Especially now when so much has been happening. *(He stops, fights back an emotion)*

DIANNE: Please try . . . please.

DAVID: First you promise you won't laugh and two, you won't interrupt.

DIANNE: I promise.

DAVID: *(He moves; during the following he covers the intensity with something of a huckster manner)* Take today . . . First, I held my breath for two minutes. Then I did my color.

DIANNE: Your what?

DAVID: Be patient. Today the color was Prussian Blue. I filled eight sheets of paper with every possible shade and hue and density of Prussian Blue. Then I decided the only thing I had ever seen that was truly, truly Prussian Blue was the Pacific Ocean off Northern California on a stormy afternoon.

DIANNE: Was it beautiful?

DAVID: Astounding . . . Then I drew a picture of my hand.

DIANNE: What for?

DAVID: The Indians believed the first man was made from corn and earth and ocean surf and the sun, and then warm winds came to give him life. The proof of that, they say, is to look carefully at your fingertips. You can see where the wind made circles and turned around.

DIANNE: *(Looks at her fingertips)* That's beautiful. But why did you draw your hand?

DAVID: I had never really looked at it before.

DIANNE: I'm lost.

DAVID: *(Intense, with great energy)* The Indians really discovered something. They believed the universe was composed of circles. The moon, the sun, the stars, the earth—they're all circles that make other circles. Are you with me?

DIANNE: Sort of.

DAVID: And they believed everything in nature was either a circle or trying to become a circle—the wind, the four seasons, a rainbow, a bird's nest, even a growing tree tries to fill a circle. Do you see?

DIANNE: I think so.

DAVID: And they thought that a man's life is like that, too—a circle that begins and ends with childhood. And once you discovered your own circle you could always touch it by reaching in any direction. But the discovery takes a very long time.

DIANNE: And that's what you're doing?

DAVID: Right.

DIANNE: How do you have time for all that?

DAVID: There isn't time for anything else.

DIANNE: How do you eat?

DAVID: Haven't you heard of Kleenex soup?

DIANNE: So where is it all going?

DAVID: Sometimes I seem to be on to something . . . But . . . *(He stops; an emotion threatens)*

DIANNE: What's wrong?

DAVID: I don't know.

DIANNE: Yes, you do.

DAVID: *(The strange, fearful agitation returns)* . . . This morning, after I made the drawing, I was staring at myself in the mirror—I do that for a half hour . . . And I had been standing there for a

long time when, all at once, there was a flash of crimson on the fire
escape outside the window. *(With wonder)* It was a cardinal. Of all
things . . . a cardinal. I hadn't seen one since I was a boy . . .
And I could watch it by just barely turning my head. I saw it was
watching me as well. We had become aware of each other at exactly
the same instant. And . . . there was no barrier between us. It
was . . . as if I was watching myself . . . *(A beat)* Then suddenly it
flew off and as it curved between the buildings everything seemed
to shift to slow motion and I saw its wing feathers—each separate
one of them—like wide, flat fingers, scooping the wind. I closed my
eyes and I could still see those wings making circles and taking the
air like water. And . . . there was no sound. *(His voice drops; there is
a fearful awe in what he is reliving)* And then I felt . . . the motion of
the earth . . . I felt myself, the building—all the goddam buildings and the bridges and the trees hurtling toward the curve of the
horizon. *(Turns to her suddenly)* Have you ever been on a roller
coaster?

DIANNE: Yes.

DAVID: Just before you start down you feel yourself going over
the edge—and you take a deep, panic breath—*(Intakes a rush of air)*
Like that—and then you're falling? That's what it was—and I felt a
rush of blood to my head and lungs and I felt tons of pressure
holding me in place, my arms were heavy—my feet like magnets
—I couldn't move . . . and . . . then . . . I felt myself pulling
free from the force of gravity—I was pulling free from the earth
. . . and I was falling . . . falling. *(Pause)* . . . It lasted only a moment, all of it. Then somebody slammed a door across the hall and
it was over.

DIANNE: *(Trying to make a joke)* Does this sort of thing happen
often, Mr. Meyer?

DAVID: Goddamit! I'm trying to tell you something!

DIANNE: I'm sorry. It made me . . . afraid.

(Short pause)

DAVID: *(Sits)* You know what I just told you? . . . It isn't true.

DIANNE: Really?

DAVID: Just the part about looking in the mirror. The rest I
made up.

DIANNE: Why would you do that?

DAVID: I was testing you.

DIANNE: That's not true. You're just afraid I'd think it was
strange.

DAVID: Have it your way. *(A beat)* Did you think it was strange?

DIANNE: No. Sometimes when I'm really happy I feel like I'm
doing somersaults backwards.

DAVID: Then you don't think there's anything wrong with me?

DIANNE: Oh, no—why do you say that?

DAVID: Because something else happened . . . *(Moves closer to her)* Yesterday I was on the Morton Street pier, watching the sunset. I was sitting on the edge with my legs dangling over. There was a tug churning along. The sun had already moved behind a bank of dark clouds stretching along the horizon. High up, there were gulls, wheeling and drifting. As they rose, the sun's rays would touch them for just an instant. Then they would drop into shadows again. *(He watches her intently before he continues)* I was sitting there . . . I could hear the slap of water on the pilings . . . and then . . . *(He stops, moved, afraid)*

DIANNE: What? . . . Please.

DAVID: Then . . . Something happened. All the sounds around me seemed to fade . . . it was like a vacuum. I looked up—I swear to God—I saw this . . . dark mass moving slowly, but everywhere at once. It was being drawn towards the sun and it made this incredible sound—like a murmur, or a moan—all around I could hear that sound as the darkness moved down the sky . . . And . . . I was . . . terrified. I said, "Wake up, wake up, wake up—Oh God, please wake me up!" And then I knew someone was behind me and I whirled around, but the pier was empty. *(He moves away; sits; pause)* Well, that was my day yesterday. What did you do?

DIANNE: *(She is affected, moved by him)* Thank you for telling me that.

DAVID: Don't mention it. *(Rises)* Well, I'll just be toddling along. After all, we made a little progress, Nurse.

DIANNE: *(Watching him carefully)* You're not avoiding me now, are you?

DAVID: Why would I do that?

DIANNE: You tell me.

DAVID: *(Mimes looking at watch)* I'm sorry, but we'll have to stop for today. Besides—I thought you were going to a party.

DIANNE: Oh, my God—I almost forgot! I have to go.

DAVID: So I'll come back. How late does this hospital stay open?

DIANNE: We never close.

DAVID: What time?

DIANNE: On such short notice I should say I'm busy.

DAVID: But you're not.

DIANNE: No . . . I'll give you a knock when I get back.

DAVID: *(Moves to door)* Fair enough. *(Sings, mimics Ezio Pinza)* GETTING TO KNOW YOU . . . GETTING TO KNOW ALL ABOUT YOU!

DIANNE: I'm glad you changed your mind.

DAVID: Yes . . . It was good. *(Quotes)* "The time and my intents are savage wild,"

DIANNE: Poetry?

DAVID: Ah, yes—a poem a day keeps the doctor away. Well . . . I'm off!

DIANNE: *(Sings softly)* WISH ME WELL, LET'S PRETEND IT'S THE FIRST TIME I FELL.

DAVID: My, my. She sings, does she?

DIANNE: *(Shyly)* A little . . . that's how I met my husband. He was a musician.

DAVID: A small world, young lady.

DIANNE: In what way?

DAVID: I used to be a musician.

DIANNE: Really?

DAVID: I used to be everything . . . Check that. I used to be. Period.

DIANNE: Aren't you exaggerating?

DAVID: Maybe. Sing the first part of that again. *(Sings badly)* SO I'M OFF . . . How does it go?

DIANNE: *(Sings)* WISH ME WELL . . .

DAVID: LET'S PRETEND IT'S THE FIRST TIME I FELL. Terrific! Now—I'm Fred Astaire and you're Juliet Prowse or somebody. *(She laughs. He grasps her waist. The rest is done to a crazy, antic waltz tempo)* WHO CAN KNOW . . .

DIANNE: WHO CAN TELL . . .

(They dance madly about apartment)

DAVID: *(Trilling the R)* ROMANCE .

DIANNE: IS SUCH A CRAZY—

DAVID: YENNNN! . . . ONE, TWO, THREE.

DIANNE: AND HERE—

DAVID: *(The mad conductor)* Orchestra! Build! Build! *(To her)* Sing, you fool!

DIANNE: I AM . . .

BOTH: IN LOVE . . . AHHHH . . . GAIN . . .!!! *(He bows. She applauds)*

DAVID: *(Exits)* See you later.

DIANNE: Goodbye, you idiot.

Blackout

Scene Three:

Time: A few hours later.
   As the lights come up, David and Dianne can be heard approaching. He is carrying a small evergreen tree. She carries a large box and a small rectangular aquarium converted to an animal cage with mesh top. They are both laughing as they enter. David is wearing a battered cap.

DIANNE: You can put the tree here on the desk. I made a place for it.
   DAVID: Whatever you say, lady. *(He places tree)*
   DIANNE: Oh, that's perfect. Isn't it pretty?
   DAVID: A thing of beauty.
   DIANNE: I didn't interrupt anything when I buzzed, did I?
   DAVID: I wish I could say yes.
   DIANNE: *(Opening the box)* Thanks for the help.
   DAVID: Anything for a neighbor.
   DIANNE: Look, I saved all these decorations from the party.
   DAVID: Forget it. You can put them away.
   DIANNE: But why?
   DAVID: I've got it all planned. It's a surprise for later.
   DIANNE: What kind of surprise?
   DAVID: We, young lady, are going to have an organic tree—none of that cheap tinsel and plastic for us!
   DIANNE: *(Laughs)* You win. I've got a surprise, too. Look. *(She motions him close to the small animal cage)* Meet Gerda and Gordon. *(To cage)* This is David, everybody.
   DAVID: What the hell are they?
   DIANNE: Gerbils—the kids love them. *(She lifts top of cage, removes one of the tiny, furred animals, kisses it, replaces it, sets cage by plants)* We're closed tomorrow so they came to visit the plants. *(She turns, looks at him curiously, smiles)* Do you always wear a hat in the house, young man?
   DAVID: Almost always. It gives me a false sense of security. I've got about ten hats for different traumatic states. I guess this one is part of my Christmas Syndrome—It's the "trying to recapture the ecstatic innocence of youth" hat.
   DIANNE: Good luck. *(She moves into kitchen area, takes bowls from refrigerator)*
   DAVID: What are you doing?
   DIANNE: Making cookies—it's part of *my* Christmas Syndrome. You can help. *(Gives him bowl)* Stir the icing.

DAVID: Yes, ma'am. *(He obeys. She pours two glasses of wine, hands him one)* No, thanks. I don't drink.

DIANNE: So excuse me if I do. *Bona Fortuna. (Takes a sip)*

DAVID: *Eh Gumba. (She laughs)* That's the only Italian I know. *(They both work. There is an easy familiarity between them now. A long moment follows, punctuated by the sounds of their activities. After a beat, David puts down bowl, removes hat, inspects it fondly)* You know, it's funny about this hat. It's a copy of a fuzzy, battered one I'd kept since I was a boy. My . . . ex-wife threw away the original.

DIANNE: Really? *(Crosses to sink)*

DAVID: Yessiree . . . You know, that was very strange. She never admitted it. But I always knew she hated it . . . Why do you think she did that?

DIANNE: Maybe she thought it was childish or something. You know, like the Bible says . . . "Put away childish things."

DAVID: Do you think it's childish?

DIANNE: No, I'm saying maybe *she* did.

DAVID: It was just a goddam devious way to get back at me.

DIANNE: For what?

DAVID: . . . You know.

DIANNE: No, I don't know.

DAVID: *(Stops work, moves away)* . . .It's strange what you remember . . . She told me once all she wanted was to be able to make a mistake . . . And once in a while, when she was tired, to be held like a little girl.

DIANNE: You think about her a lot, don't you?

DAVID: *(Half-kidding)* So now you're criticizing me. Be really honest and right away somebody judges you—Ahah! A weak spot—break out the harpoons!

DIANNE: *(Stung)* You're really something, you know that? You're incredible!

DAVID: *(Trying to banter)* Yeah, and here's something else you can use against me some time.

DIANNE: Oh, wait, wait—I'm writing it all down!

DAVID: *(Moving)* We had a small place and I used the kitchen table for a desk. I was sitting there this one time and she was at the sink, washing dishes or something. And she was . . . humming. Not anything special. Just . . . inventing sounds to please herself, like a child. *(He stops)* I wanted to go to her and hold her then.

DIANNE: Did you?

DAVID: No. I knew I was going to leave her. I mean, I knew at that moment . . . Isn't that backwards? *(He sits. Pause. She has stopped working, watches him)* When . . . we were breaking up she locked herself in the bedroom. I could hear her crying and moaning . . . They were . . . animal sounds. *(Short pause)* After a while she opened the door and walked slowly over to where I was sitting and started hitting me in the face—again and again, and again. I didn't move. Then she sat on the floor, exhausted . . . crying. She said she wanted to hurt me the way I had hurt her. And we both knew she couldn't. *(He moves; almost to himself)* An instant on the wind.

DIANNE: What's that?

DAVID: Nothing. It doesn't matter.

DIANNE: That's not fair.

DAVID: It's just a poem. *(Quotes mockingly)* "And so it was I came into the broken world to trace the visionary company of love, it's voice an instant on the wind, I know not whither hurled!"

DIANNE: Why do you do that? Like you're embarrassed to say something beautiful?

DAVID: What? A goddam poem? Words, words, words, fucking words!

DIANNE: You change so fast I can't keep up with you.

DAVID: That's the idea.

DIANNE: *(Angry)* Okay, you win. I give up.

DAVID: What did I do now?

DIANNE: The camouflage. It works too well and I just turn off.

DAVID: *(Goes to her)* Don't. Don't turn off. I'm sorry—really.

DIANNE: Can I tell you something then?

DAVID: Fire away! Damn the torpedoes!

DIANNE: Just sit here. And relax, please.

(He sits. Short pause) It's like you offer yourself with your left hand and then hit with your right.

DAVID: *(Rises)* Ah yes, the manly art of self-defense.

DIANNE: So stop defending. It's exhausting.

DAVID: *(Collapses on bed)* You must be right. I'm exhausted.

DIANNE: *(Moves closer)* That's better. *(Sits next to him; after a moment)* Can I ask you something . . . about her?

DAVID: I was wondering when you'd get around to that.

DIANNE: Don't, please.

DAVID: Sorry.

DIANNE: What was her name?

DAVID: Catherine. *(A beat)* It means consecrated to God. I looked it up once during one of my periods of insanity.

DIANNE: What was she like?

DAVID: Come on—Jesus Christ!

DIANNE: Okay, sorry. What I really wanted to ask you was . . . I'm afraid to.

DAVID: You can't stop now.

DIANNE: *(Hesitates, then decides)* How was it with her . . . I mean making love . . . was it . . . good?

DAVID: *(Watches her for a long moment)* Why do you want to know?

DIANNE: I'm not prying or anything—it's for me—I have to know. It's for something about myself.

(Short pause)

DAVID: Yes. It was . . . good. That never changed. I guess that means there was something positive underneath. We just never . . . discovered it.

DIANNE: That's what I meant. See . . . *(Watching him carefully)* When Tony and I first got married, we . . . You're going to think this is weird or something.

DAVID: No, I won't *(Gently)* Go ahead.

DIANNE: We . . . took turns being each other's slave. Do you think that's sick?

DAVID: *(After a moment)* No.

DIANNE: It was exciting, you know—like original sin or something. And there wasn't anything bad about it. It's just like giving yourself completely to the other person—trusting. And I read this book where it says nothing men and women do together is unnatural. It wasn't, was it?

DAVID: I don't think so.

DIANNE: It's almost the only part I remember—the sex part. Except the fights. But he could be sweet. He liked to act tough—he was from the neighborhood, you know? But his hobby was math and he was always trying to teach his friends. He could make it seem simple. He should have been a teacher.

DAVID: Was he a good musician?

DIANNE: No. *(Short pause)* I made him leave finally because I swore to God I never would. It was terrible. I started throwing things and screaming—it was unbelievable. He was so shocked—little me acting like a lunatic. He was so helpless. He just sat at the kitchen table and cried. I guess that's backwards, too. I didn't cry at all. *(He is watching her intently)* What are you thinking?

DAVID: *(Carefully)* Do you still see him?

DIANNE: I did for a while. But I couldn't keep on like that. And I couldn't stay in that place any more, so I moved out. I didn't take anything with me, not even my clothes. *(A long moment)* After that, I slept around a lot. Do you think that's terrible?

DAVID: No.

DIANNE: I just had to know what that was. *(She hesitates)* . . . The first time you think you'll die, but then you don't. And it gets easier. And then it's too easy. *(She starts to cry)* Oh, I'm sorry. I didn't want to do this.

DAVID: It's alright—Christ, don't apologize for being real.

DIANNE: *(Controls the emotion)* Thanks . . . I feel better already. *(Tries to smile)* The worst part is holding it in.

DAVID: I know. *(Rises; with urgency)* Now I need to ask *you* something. And please . . . I need to know this . . . When it was really bad, did you ever think about . . . suicide?

DIANNE: I don't want to talk about that.

DAVID: Wait—this is important! Please. Did you ever think about it?

DIANNE: *(Studying him)* I . . . remember thinking that if I were only dead then I couldn't feel anything any more.

DAVID: But did you ever think about just how you would do it . . . specifically?

DIANNE: No, not really. Hey, are you alright?

DAVID: *(He moves. There is a great fear now, a new intensity)* Put your hands over your ears.

DIANNE: What?

DAVID: Like this. *(Presses hands against ears)*

DIANNE: *(Imitates him)* So?

DAVID: Listen. *(She does so)*

DIANNE: *(After a moment)* That's scary.

DAVID: What do you hear?

DIANNE: My heartbeat . . . and . . . the sound of my breathing.

DAVID: Right! I do that sometimes when I feel out of touch with myself and today I was listening to all the sounds of my life roaring along and then . . . I suddenly realized that I could stop it all . . . my heart, my lungs, the pumping blood . . . and there was something sacred in that moment, you know? A power and a mystery. *(She starts to protest)* But I could never do that. *(He turns suddenly, comes closer to her, confronts her in a way she only vaguely senses. With an attempt at his former jauntiness)* Did you read the paper yesterday?

DIANNE: No.

DAVID: There was this article about this man who . . . killed himself. He must have been thinking about it for a long time.

DIANNE: That's enough.

DAVID: Wait, wait—this is fascinating! He had it all worked out. down to the split-second. He made a sort of oxygen tent out of those plastic dry-cleaning bags—split them open and melted them together with an iron. And he rigged up a gas mask and hose to the stove. He . . . even took sleeping pills and ripped out the phone so he couldn't change his mind.

DIANNE: *(Rises)* Don't—it's horrible to think about.

DAVID: Yes, but you have to think about it at least once or you aren't really alive!

DIANNE: *(A beat)* Do you think if I called the agency they would send a different Santa Claus?

(He laughs; she joins him)

DAVID: You're absolutely right! Now, I ask you, what kind of talk is that on Christmas Eve? Tiny Tim will be harsh with us!

DIANNE: *(Laughs; then abruptly)* Oh, I almost forgot—*(Crosses to oven, inspects cookies inside)*

DAVID: How are the goodies?

DIANNE: Coming right along. *(Turns to him)* I made the cookies in crazy shapes so we could tie them together with yarn to help decorate the tree.

DAVID: What a peachy idea! And you know how much I love therapy hour, Nurse!

DIANNE: Why, what a nice attitude. You're feeling better, aren't you, Lieutenant?

DAVID: Oh yes, Nurse. *(She crosses to sink)* And oh, Nurse?

DIANNE: Yes?

DAVID: *(A demented child)* Now that we know each other better, can I sleep with you tonight?

DIANNE: Why, Lieutenant Meyer! What a thing to ask Nursie.

DAVID: But it's Christmas and this is an emergency! I have this pain in my head—I'm so excited about all the presents I'm going to get in the morning. See, at home when I got like that, I always slept with Mommy.

DIANNE: *(Pats his head)* I'm sorry, but our Mommy Department is closed until after New Year's.

DAVID: *(Grabs her hand)* I want my Mommy! *(Bites her finger)*

DIANNE: Why, Lieutenant Meyer, you little savage!

DAVID: *(Lunges for her)* I want my Mommy!

DIANNE: *(Laughing, she tries to evade him)* You really are a lunatic, aren't you?

DAVID: How else do you get in this hospital?

(She laughs. He has her cornered by the Christmas tree. He comes closer,

then hesitates. She takes his hand. After a long moment, she kisses him firmly. He seems unsettled by it)

DIANNE: Merry Christmas.

DAVID: Merry Christmas.

DIANNE: *(Her face close to a tree branch)* Just smell that. Isn't that wonderful?

DAVID: Yes, indeed. Reminds me of the Great North Woods when I was a boy.

DIANNE: I can hardly wait until we trim it. *(Sings softly)* DECK THE HALLS WITH BOUGHS OF HOLLY *(Laughs)* That song makes me feel like a little girl.

DAVID: How so?

DIANNE: *(Absently removes scraps of tinsel from tree, arranges branches)* When my mother went to the movies on Thursday nights my father would take care of us. And *then,* well, we could actually bring our big toys into the *living room* because daddy didn't care. We'd make a house with cushions from the couch and then my sister and I would climb into daddy's chair. I'd get to sit on his lap because I was the youngest. And then, we'd sing Christmas carols.

DAVID: Why Christmas carols?

DIANNE: They were the only songs we all knew. *(She smiles)* It was a special time. Safe. I feel like that now. Were you ever happy like that?

DAVID: Happy she says.

DIANNE: You heard right. Here, help me with this. *(They move a small drop-leaf table away from the wall and open it)* So, come on. What's so terrible about being happy.

DAVID: *(The aging actor)* Ah yes, happiness. A rare thing, young lady! And you ask, do I recall an instant of delight—a moment of sunlit perfection amid hours of darkest agony!

DIANNE: In your real voice, please.

DAVID: Once upon a time . . .

DIANNE: Come on.

DAVID: *(After a moment)* I don't know if this is happiness, but it's something I keep thinking about. *(He moves to window, looks out)* When I first knew Catherine, she was always trying to get me to jump over puddles or run down the street with her or go to the ocean on a foggy day. But . . . I never did any of that. *(A beat)* Then one day, in spring, in Riverside Park, we were on the crest of a hill. I had this crazy impulse. I drew her down next to me in the grass. "Now close your eyes," I said. And before she could draw a breath we were rolling down that sunny hill, holding each other and bumping and giggling. Her laugh was like warm bells. *(Short pause. He sits. Dianne sits next to him, takes his hand. After a moment, she touches him, strokes his arm. Slowly, he reaches for her and then they hold each other for a long moment. They kiss)*

DAVID: *(Rises, moves away)* I can't stop thinking about her! *(She goes to him, embraces him. He is reluctant, but returns it)*

DIANNE: *(Touches his face gently)* Look at me . . . please. *(He does)* It's me, isn't it?

DAVID: Yes.

DIANNE: What color are my eyes . . . Look.

DAVID: Brown.

DIANNE: *(Lifts his hands to touch her hair)* It's my face, isn't it?

DAVID: Yes . . .

DIANNE: Say my name.

DAVID: Dianne. *(She kisses him. He responds, slowly)*

DIANNE: Do you want me?

DAVID: Yes. *(Kisses her roughly)*

DIANNE: Be gentle, please.

(She embraces him. He tries to respond fully but after a moment he moves away. There is a deep pain in his eyes)

DAVID: God damn it! *(Short pause)* I'm sorry.

DIANNE: No, it's me. I was pushing. It has to happen in its own time. *(She goes to him, embraces him. They stand for a long moment, almost rocking each other. Suddenly)* Do you smell something? Oh, my God— *(She rushes to oven, removes pan. He follows)* They'll be ruined.

DAVID: Can I help?

DIANNE: Beep beep! *(Passes him, sets pan on counter, inspects cookies)* No, they're still okay. *(Hurries to refrigerator, takes out icing bowl, applies some to one cookie, crosses to him)* Now for the test. Close your eyes. *(He does)* Smell. *(He obeys)* Verdict?

DAVID: The prisoner may live.

DIANNE: Open wide. *(He takes bite; they fumble with the crumbs, laugh)* Ah, ah, keep eyes closed, please. *(She kisses him soundly)* How was it?

DAVID: Delicious. *(She laughs)*

DIANNE: *(Taking charge)* Okay, now. it's getting late. And we're having a party, remember? First, dinner. I'm making a surprise. Then I could sing something . . . Okay? Then a few poems from you.

DAVID: If you won't sing, I won't recite poetry.

DIANNE: Come on, it's a party, remember? Please?

DAVID: Okay, I'll try.

DIANNE: Promise.

DAVID: *(Holds up hand)* I swear by Tiny Tim and all that's holy.

DIANNE: *(Growing more excited)* And then we'll listen to Christmas carols and sing along.

DAVID: That I can do without.

DIANNE: And when it gets close to midnight, we'll trim the tree!

DAVID: Like Santa's good little helpers.

DIANNE: *(Claps her hands)* Yes!

DAVID: Remember—I'm bringing the trimmings.

DIANNE: Right! And—oh, oh. How about eggnog? I've got three quarts. Is it okay?

DAVID: Okay, but heavy on the brandy.

DIANNE: I thought you didn't drink.

DAVID: I'm easily corrupted.

DIANNE: *(Stops)* And, I nearly forgot.

(She goes to window box, brings him the Mimosa plant. A red ribbon has been fixed to the base. She offers it to him)

DAVID: What's this, an appetizer?

DIANNE: Merry Christmas.

DAVID: No, I really don't . . .

DIANNE: I want you to have it. So you can start your own forest.

DAVID: *(After a moment)* Thanks.

DIANNE: Her name's Melissa; Melissa Mimosa.

DAVID: That's a nice name.

DIANNE: And you don't have to give me a present. That wasn't part of the deal. *(Pushes him toward door)* Now, go. I have to get ready.

DAVID: What's to get ready?

DIANNE: Girl things.

DAVID: Okay, okay. When should I come back?

DIANNE: In an hour. And don't eat anything. Save up.

DAVID: Right, Nurse.

DIANNE: Hey. And don't forget. You're performing at our Christmas Gala.

DAVID: How could I forget?

(He turns)

DIANNE: What are you thinking?

DAVID: I was thinking I like it here at this hospital.

DIANNE: We aim to please.

DAVID: *(In a manic whisper)* Just don't tell the other guys about this. They'll make fun of me in the exercise yard.

(He exits. The lights fade to blackout)

Scene Four:

Time: An hour later.

    The lights rise on David's cluttered apartment. It is sparsely furnished but crammed with books, stacks of papers, memorabilia, etc. David stands in front of a long mirror, holding aloft an open book of poetry. He is rehearsing his performance.

He wears a baggy sport coat and a long, woolen scarf with the long end flung jauntily over one shoulder. His behavior is manic.

DAVID:
(Reads with gusto) When all the world is young, lad,
And all the trees are green,
And every goose a swan, lad,
And every lass a queen,
Then hey for boot and horse, lad,
And 'round the World away;
Young blood must have its course, lad,
And every dog its day.
    (Laughs)
When all the world is old, lad
And all the trees are brown,
And all the sport is stale, lad,
And all the wheels run down,
Creep home, and take your place there,
The spent and maimed among.
God grant you find one face there
You loved when all was young.
    (After a moment)
No—dammit! Why do I always do that! Morbidia! Morbidia! Let's see, let's see . . .
    (He strides around the room; suddenly goes to closet, knocks on door; in a muffled voice) Five minutes, Mr. Meyer . . .
    (Louder)
Ah yes, yes, thank you, thank you.
    (He rummages through debris on his desk, produces a slim volume, opens it. Recites with an occasional glance at page. The following is simple, sincere and direct)
One Christmas was so much like another,
In those years around the sea-town corner now,
And out of all sound except the distant speaking
Of the voices I sometimes hear a moment before sleep,
That I can never remember whether it snowed

For six days and six nights when I was twelve
Or whether it snowed for twelve days and
twelve nights when I was six.
(A knock at his door. He approaches furtively, looks out through peephole. Mockingly, in grand manner)
Approach owah cahstle and identify thyself!
(Opens door. Dianne enters, carrying animal cage)
What have we here? Why, it's Dianne and Greta and Gregory!

DIANNE: They're coming to visit? Okay?

DAVID: Sure, they can share the closet with my boa constrictor. *(Hurries to desk, removes two crude red objects, exhibits them with a flourish)* Feast thine eyes!

DIANNE: What are they?

DAVID: Our Christmas stockings. Made with loving care from an old sweatshirt! I hope you appreciate the sacrifice. *(Hands her one)* Yours has Jingle Bells inside—stolen from a sleeping horse in Central Park. And, as you know, it is to be hung by the fire escape with care! *(She puts gerbils container on desk, turns to him. He rushes about, finds large bag, holds it up)* And look, preparations for the Midnight Ritual of the Tree! *(Rummages in sack, displays each item)* Oranges, apples, popcorn to pop and string . . . dates, figs, walnuts and pine cones, a spray of bittersweet from the Great North Woods and last but not least, from the thundering seas of Moby Dick, honest-to-God tallow candles—to be lit exactly at midnight! If we're lucky we'll burn down this decaying building as a sacrifice to the Gods of Christmas Day!

DIANNE: Can I sit down?

DAVID: Oh, sure, sure . . . sorry. *(Removes piles of magazines and papers from an ancient chair)* Here. *(She sits)* What's wrong?

DIANNE: I need a friend.

DAVID: What happened?

DIANNE: He called.

(Short pause)

DAVID: When?

DIANNE: Just a while ago.

DAVID: *(After a moment)* And?

DIANNE: I don't know.

DAVID: Don't give me that.

DIANNE: I . . . hadn't spoken to him in so long.

DAVID: How did it go?

DIANNE: He wants me to come back.

DAVID: . . . What did you say?

DIANNE: I said I'd call him back. I told him if I did come it would be only for tonight—for Christmas—and that was it. (*Starts to cry, stifles it, rises, turns to him imploringly*) It isn't over. I want it to be, oh God, how I want it to be!

DAVID: (*Waits a long moment*) Are you going?

DIANNE: Only if you say it's okay.

(*Pause*)

DAVID: I think you should go.

DIANNE: Really?

DAVID: Absolutely.

(*Short pause*)

DIANNE: He . . . needs me.

DAVID: Right.

DIANNE: Tell me again.

DAVID: (*Smiles*) Would I lie to you?

DIANNE: It'll be just 'til tomorrow and I'll be back early. (*Comes to him*) We can have our party then—it'll still be Christmas, right?

DAVID: Right.

DIANNE: (*Referring to stocking she still holds*) Can I take this now?

DAVID: Sure.

(*She crosses to him, kisses him*)

DIANNE: It's beautiful.

DAVID: Thanks. (*He watches as she moves toward door, stops*) And . . . if you don't get back until later, don't worry. In my neighborhood every day is a holiday.

DIANNE: (*Turns*) Tell me again.

DAVID: Merry Christmas.

DIANNE: Merry Christmas . . . (*They watch each other for a long moment*) I . . . have to go.

(*She exits, closes door softly. David stands for a long moment. Suddenly his body contracts violently. He grips his sides, then presses his hand against his chest. He straightens himself with great effort. As he moves away from the door a loud, almost animal sound is heard. He wanders frantically, searching, then finds his cap, puts it on and falls on the bed, curling his body against the pain in his chest and stomach. Long pause. Finally, David rises slowly and comes to where the Mimosa plant sits atop his desk. He touches it fearfully, trembling, then slowly strips the tiny leaves from the slender branches. Then, hurriedly, he takes the glass gerbil container, places it on his desk and stares at it. He lifts top of cage, reaches in violently, pulls back abruptly*)

DAVID: Ow! You bastard, you little fucking bastard! (*He goes quickly to sink, fills two large pans with water, returns to desk and stands poised*) And so it was . . . (*Empties first pan into cage*) And so it was . . . (*Empties second pan*) And so it was. (*He stands for a long moment*

watching the cage, then he goes to his bed, sits. Long pause. He rises, goes to phone, dials hurriedly) . . .
Catherine? . . . This is David . . . I know, I'm surprised, too . . . Fine, fine, terrific, as a matter of fact . . . I was . . . wondering—I know it's short notice and I know what we decided but I thought maybe we could see each other tonight or tomorrow . . . No, just meet for coffee somewhere—you can pick the place . . . Yes . . . No, you're right. I just thought . . . Right . . . When are you leaving? . . . Well, have a good Christmas and say hello to your folks for me—no, you better not.
(Laughs) . . . Same to you . . . Goodbye.
   (Hangs up. Long pause. Sings softly, absently, to himself)
Jingle Bells, Jingle Bells, Jingle all the way. Oh, what fun it is to ride in a one-horse open sleigh . . . eigh . . .
   (LIGHTS FADE TO:)

Blackout

Joseph Hart

THE DARK MOON
AND THE FULL

(A Chamber Play)

"To such a pitch of folly am I brought
Being caught between the pull
of the Dark Moon and the Full . . ."
W. B. YEATS

Joseph Hart

Joseph Hart is another dramatist who is making his debut in this tenth anniversary edition of *The Best Short Plays* series with his compelling drama about a family of Irish-Americans, *The Dark Moon and the Full.*

The author was educated at Fordham University where he took his B.A. in English Literature, and at New York University where he received his M.A. in Theatre. Equally adept as playwright, director, actor and teacher, Mr. Hart has been an Assistant and Associate Professor in the Theatre Arts Department of Douglass College, Rutgers University, since 1969. Prior to joining the faculty at Douglass, he was a Teaching Fellow at New York University, a director of drama for PAL (New York), and a founder-director of the Melting Pot Repertory Theatre and the New York University Drama Society.

In addition to *The Dark Moon and the Full,* his other produced plays include: *The Memoirs of Charlie Pops; Window and Wall; Ghost Dance;* and *Absinthe.*

The Dark Moon and the Full originally was performed Off-Off-Broadway at The Cubiculo in 1974. The present, and final version, which appears in these pages was presented in 1976 by the Irish Rebel Theatre in New York City.

A prolific writer, Mr. Hart also has contributed reviews and feature articles to dozens of newspapers and national periodicals.

As an actor he has appeared with the New York Shakespeare Festival, the Heritage Theatre, Rutgers' Professional Repertory Company, New York University's Youtheatre as well as on radio and television.

The Dark Moon and the Full appears in print for the first time in *The Best Short Plays 1977.*

Characters:

HELEN
GRANDMA
PATSY
MICHAEL
LORETTA

Scene:

The small back room of a comfortable house in a middle-class Irish Catholic section of Brooklyn. On one side of the stage a short hallway leads to the back door of the house. Another doorway at the opposite side leads into adjoining rooms. A window at center stage faces west, looking out over a small garden to the backs of several other houses on the block. Beneath the window, a combination radiator-cover and sideboard extends the width of the room. On top of the sideboard is an assortment of medicine bottles and a vase of fresh-cut flowers. The walls of the room are crowded with sacred images and photographs of family members who have passed on. Other furniture includes a television set, a radio-phonograph console, an old-fashioned standing lamp, and a large upholstered rocking chair with foot stool. This last is situated against the sideboard directly under the window.

It is a heavy, overcast April afternoon. The standing lamp is turned off and the light in the room is a soft, pale gray. The window is open and robins can be heard singing in the backyard.

Grandma is seated in the upholstered rocker, her hands folded on her lap and her chin sunk upon her chest. She seems to be asleep. Next to her chair are a pair of crutches and on one foot she wears a "high" shoe. She is nearing eighty and is hard of hearing—although occasionally her hearing improves in proportion to her interest in the subject at hand. She is the dowager empress of the family—willful, sardonic, "full of the devil" and by day, at least, an absolute monarch. An empty glass sits on the sideboard next to her, and a bottle of Irish Mist liquor stands just out of easy reach. Across her knees is a soft, luminous green shawl. Except for the flowers it is the most colorful object in the room.

Helen enters and stands behind Grandma's chair. She carries a pile of folded household linen. Helen is a heavyset, powerful, peasant-type, about forty years of age. Her simple values are reflected in her plain, open face, and cheerful though somewhat superstitious nature. She is ready to believe the most outlandish story or laugh at a slightly dirty joke. In moments of minor crisis she has the habit of repeating "Oo-oo!" several times and suffering momentary paralyses of indecision.

HELEN: *(Shaking her head)* Awful gloomy day, ain't it, Grandma? It looks like it's gonna rain, maybe. Do you want the light on? *(There is no answer)* Grandma?

(For the first time Helen notices that Grandma is asleep. Walking on tippy-toe–an awkward move for a big woman–she goes and removes the bottle, and is about to start off with it)

GRANDMA: *(Without lifting her head)* Where are you going with that?

(Helen stops, caught in the act. Grandma boosts herself up in the chair with a mischievous smile. She speaks with a marked Irish accent)

GRANDMA: I fooled ya.

HELEN: I was just straightening up before I go home, Grandma.

GRANDMA: You leave that right here. *(As Helen reaches to replace the bottle, Grandma covers her shawl with her hands)* Watch out it don't drip on my shawl.

HELEN: I thought maybe you had enough. Maybe you'd have a little sleep now.

GRANDMA: Where's Loretta? You're not going to leave me till Loretta gets home are you?

HELEN: You know I wouldn't do that, Grandma. I thought you were having a little sleep that's all.

GRANDMA: Well, I fooled you. *(Smiling again)* I like fooling Helen. *(Pointing to the glass)* Put a little more in that thing.

HELEN: Oh, I think you had enough to drink, Grandma. It'll be all gone soon. You'll want to save some for later on. Easter's coming in a couple of days.

GRANDMA: You pour some in there and be quick about it. *(Muttering as if to herself)* Easter's coming. Don't I know all about Easter? *(Helen begins to pour)* Watch out it don't drip on my shawl.

HELEN: I'm watching out.

GRANDMA: Just a finger.

HELEN: I know.

(Grandma takes the glass and sips. Helen corks the bottle and puts it down)

HELEN: *(Hinting)* You know Joseph gives up drinking hard liquor for Lent altogether.

GRANDMA: You're talking in my bum ear, Helen.

HELEN: *(Louder)* I said Joseph gives up drinking altogether for Lent. *(Grandma grunts and continues to sip)* Right from Ash Wednesday till Easter Sunday you couldn't get him to touch a drop.

GRANDMA: My poor son—he must be mad with the thirst by this time.

(Grandma takes her time finishing the drink. Helen stands in restless at-

tendance behind her chair. There is no sound but the occasional bird song from the garden)

GRANDMA: *(Suddenly)* Is that Loretta I hear, just now? *(She strains to look out the window)*

HELEN: *(Leaning over the back of Grandma's chair to look)* No. It's Mrs. Hanlon next door. She's waving to you, Grandma. *(Helen waves back)* Hello, how are you?

GRANDMA: What's she doing, that one? Hanging out her wash again?

HELEN: *(Still looking)* She's doing something in the garage.

GRANDMA: She don't hang out her wash till Sunday. I'm after forgetting that. The Protestant bitch!

HELEN: *(Scandalized)* Oo-oo! Grandma!

GRANDMA: Can't get over the indignity of living across the street from a Catholic Church. Every Sunday morning she's hanging out her clothes when the rest of the world is going to Mass. Got her orange drawers flapping in the breeze like a flag of defiance.

HELEN: Oh, Grandma, you like Mrs. Hanlon. She sent you those flowers just the other day. The first ones out of her garden— she said she wanted to be sure and give them to Mrs. McGrath.

GRANDMA: *(Ignoring her)* Well, she better not hang out her drawers on Easter Sunday, that's all I'm saying. I'll wrap the clothesline around her Protestant neck.

HELEN: Now Grandma, you be nice!

GRANDMA: Blocking my view to the West like that. I'll knock her for a ghoul, the orange bitch!

HELEN: Oo-oo Grandma! You're nobody to be talking about Mrs. Hanlon's religion! You haven't let the priest set foot in the door for years now. Not since Grandpa died. What kind of Catholic do you call yourself, I wonder?

GRANDMA: I'm my own kind of Catholic—that's what I call myself. Or maybe I'm only Aggie Reilly. I went back to being myself when my husband died!

HELEN: I bet you never let Grandpa see you like that.

GRANDMA: There's lots of things I never let Grandpa see.

HELEN: Well, I'm still a good Catholic whatever you may be. And I'm not forgetting what day this is. This is Good Friday, Grandma!

GRANDMA: And I'm not forgetting it either, you simp! *(She raises her glass)* Look at me celebrating it, won't you? I'm giving Jesus of Nazareth a good Irish wake!

HELEN: *(Moving toward the bottle decisively)* Oh, I think you've had enough to drink for one day.

(With a sudden thrust of her rocker, Grandma reaches out and snatches up the bottle)

GRANDMA: *(Trying to distract her)* Is that Loretta I hear coming?

HELEN: *(Glancing out the window)* I told you. It's Mrs. Hanlon. Loretta'll be home from school any minute.

GRANDMA: *(Guarding the bottle)* Maybe you ought to go out front and look for the car.

HELEN: It won't make her get here any faster.

GRANDMA: Go ahead and have a look. See if she's coming.

HELEN: *(Impatiently)* Now Grandma, Loretta will be home any minute. She'll get here when she gets here and that's all there is to it.

(Grandma slams down the bottle and strains to get out of the chair)

GRANDMA: Never mind! Never mind! I'll do it myself!—I'll do it myself! I'll go faster on four bum legs than you can on your two fat stumps.

HELEN: *(Genuinely frightened—trying to keep her down)* Oo-oo, Grandma—Grandma, you sit down!

GRANDMA: *(Slapping at Helen's feet with her crutch)* G'wan! G'wan! I'll knock you for a ghoul!

HELEN: You told Loretta you were gonna be good! I heard you promise her this morning you were gonna be good today!

GRANDMA: *(Mimicking)* "You told Loretta you were gonna be good! You told Loretta you were gonna be good!" *(Grandma surrenders and plops down in her chair with a sigh of disgust)* Seventy-eight years old. They're all after forgetting the seventy and remembering the eight.

(There is a pause as Helen stands anxious guard and Grandma fusses very particularly with her shawl. Again, the only sound is the occasional bird song)

GRANDMA: What's keeping Loretta? It's way past her time.

HELEN: I'll go out in the front and look for the car. *(She starts out)*

GRANDMA: *(Pointing at the empty glass)* You finish what you're doing here first.

HELEN: *(Protesting)* I just gave you some a minute ago.

GRANDMA: *(Irate again)* Never mind! Never mind! I'll do it myself—I'll do it myself. *(She makes a faltering effort to uncap the bottle)* Only trouble is I can't see so good. Don't know if it's one finger or a whole fist I'm putting in.

HELEN: Oh, give it to me. I'll do it.

(Helen pours a careful fingerful and stops)

GRANDMA: You can do better than that.

(Exasperated, Helen pours another finger, and recorks the bottle. Grandma begins to sip as Helen turns once again to go out)

GRANDMA: Where are you going?

HELEN: I told you. I'm going out front to look for the car.

GRANDMA: *(Matter of fact)* Don't leave me alone.

(There is another silence, punctuated only by the sound of the birds. Grandma sits sipping her drink and looking out the window. Helen stands restlessly behind her chair)

GRANDMA: *(Solemnly)* Awful gloomy day, ain't it, Helen? Spooky kinda day. Kinda day would make you think the whole house was haunted.

HELEN: *(The remark has made her uncomfortable)* Do you want me to turn on the light, Grandma?

GRANDMA: This here window faces the West. *(Enjoying the spookiness)* You know, when I was a young girl back on the other side, one of the "Ould Wans" had a story about Good Friday. She said if you looked out the West Room window on Good Friday you might see the ghost of some dead one walking by on his journey. And if you *did* happen to see one it meant you'd be joining him yourself before the full moon fades.

HELEN: Grandma, you're giving me the creeps. Do you want me to turn on the light?

GRANDMA: *(Still staring out the window)* No. Leave it be. I like it this way. *(There is another pause before Grandma turns away from the window)* What's the calendar say, Helen? What's today anyway?

HELEN: It's Good Friday, Grandma. You know that.

GRANDMA: *(Irritably)* Of course I know that. I mean the date. What's the date today?

HELEN: Today's the thirteenth, Grandma.

GRANDMA: *(Once again enjoying the spookiness)* Oh, God, now there's a full day for you. Friday the thirteenth—and a Good Friday at that. If there was ever a time for the ghosts to walk it's on a dark afternoon the likes of this one. *(Mock serious, teasing)* You know, Helen, maybe it wasn't Mrs. Hanlon at all who was waving at you just now. Maybe it was one of the ghosts waving you on to follow her.

HELEN: *(Seriously)* I'm gonna turn on the lights. You're giving me the creeps!

GRANDMA: *(Sternly)* You leave that light alone! I'm only fooling you. I'm sitting by this window every Good Friday for years and I ain't seen one of them pass by yet.

HELEN: *(Petulent)* Well, Good Friday's not the sort of day for drinking and telling a lot of old wives' tales. It's the most sorrowful day of the Catholic year.

GRANDMA: *(Sipping)* It's the darkest day of the Catholic year, that's certain. Just look at that sky, will you. Just the right kind of setting for the Three Hours Devotion. *(Musing)* Father Drane used to say to us, "What's the hard wood of the Church pew against your soft backsides compared to the hard rough beams of the cross, holding Jesus' arms outstretched in love?" He could speak well on occasion—I'll give him that much.

HELEN: Yeah, you told me Grandma.

GRANDMA: Ah, the poor ignorant little birds. Listen to them, will ya? *(Smiling)* They don't know they're not supposed to sing and be happy on Good Friday. Father Drane would have frowned on that. Just outside the church there was a big dogwood tree. It was always in bloom for Holy Week. I wonder now just how much of the Three Hours I spent smelling the perfume and listening to the birds.

HELEN: *(Absently)* There were trees behind St. Thomas here a few years ago. They knocked them down when they built the new wing. I don't know what kind of trees they were.

GRANDMA: Father Drane used to tell us, "The tree's got the word that Christ is coming back to life and she's opening her arms to give him a hug."

HELEN: Yeah, you told me, Grandma.

GRANDMA: Sometimes he spoke well, I have to give him that much. You remember how he used to speak, Helen.

HELEN: That was in Ireland, Grandma.

GRANDMA: *(Not hearing, lost in thought)* Oh, but he was a devil out of Hell all the same. Still, it *was* a pretty notion—whoever it came from. It kept running through my head all through the Easter Week trouble. "He'll be coming back," I kept saying to myself. "He'll be coming back sure as the life comes back to the trees."

HELEN: *(Starting to worry)* Grandma—Grandma, it's almost four o'clock now. Do you want a cup of tea? Maybe you'd like a cup of tea and something to eat.

GRANDMA: All that long week I kept saying it to myself over and over—like I was trying to shut out the sound of the women weeping and the whizzin' justice of the firing squads.

HELEN: Now, Grandma, I don't want you getting yourself all upset.

GRANDMA: *(With rising anger)* And all that week not one of the good, pious Catholics I knelt with in Church on Good Friday had the courage to lift up a finger for freedom—or to give help to the boys who was fightin' for it!

HELEN: Oh, Grandma, that was a long time ago.

GRANDMA: *(Defiantly)* Ay, ay—a long time ago. And its a long time ago that I made up my mind. If Good Friday's a sad day for the whimpering likes of them, then Aggie Reilly won't make it sadder still! That was the last Three Hours I ever did! *(Taking up her glass as in a "toast")* And now that I'm old I got a fine new way of keeping the Three Hours Devotion!

HELEN: *(Quickly)* Well, it's almost four o'clock now, Grandma— the Three Hours is up. *(Gently)* Maybe you want to close your eyes and have a little sleep. Have a little sleep till Loretta gets home.

GRANDMA: *(Mimicking)* "Have a little sleep till Loretta gets home." And then what happens, I wonder? Loretta takes over the job of changing my diapers and mashing my food into goo for me. Aah, Helen. I got all the rest of you fooled with these crutches and pills. I'm younger than all of you by sixty years! *(Dreamily, as if to herself)* "He'll be coming—he'll be coming back." And now I can't even see his face at all. Too many crowded years between us. Oh, she's a worse old bitch than I am, old Mother Time! Fooling us all with little tricks like that.

(Again there is another lull as Grandma looks out the window, rocking in her chair and sipping her drink. Helen finds a few trifling tasks to occupy her before she goes back to standing behind Grandma's chair. Once again she stares restlessly out of the window. The only sounds are the birds in the garden. After about a minute the back door opens and Patsy leans into the hallway and calls)

PATSY: *(Disguising her voice)* Howdy!

HELEN: Who's that!

PATSY: Howdy Doody! Where's everybody?

HELEN: Grandma—Loretta's home, Grandma.

GRANDMA: *(With a wave of high disdain)* Well, tell her to be quiet. I'm listening to the birds.

(Patsy comes into the room like a burst of light. She is pretty and vivacious, with long dark hair and a trim, graceful body. Her style of dress is the deliberately old-fashioned, "hip-chic" of attic chests and rummage sales. But for all her effort there is more Brooklyn Irish in Patsy than the influence of the counter-culture. She is seventeen years old and expects to stay that way)

PATSY: *(Entering)* Howdy!

HELEN: Oh—it's you!

PATSY: Why's it so dark in here?

HELEN: Look who it is, Grandma. It's Patsy.

GRANDMA: *(Happily)* Who's that—Patsy? You sounded just like Loretta.

HELEN: You sounded just like Loretta. That's how she always comes home.

PATSY: I thought I'd try and fool you, Grandma. I didn't see Aunt Loretta's car in the driveway. Hi ya, Grandma—how are you? Mm-wah! *(She kisses Grandma with a loud exhuberant smack)* I came down to see what's keeping my mother. *(To Helen)* Daddy's coming home soon, Ma. You better get the supper going.

HELEN: Loretta's late. We been waiting for her.

GRANDMA: Aah, Patsy's come down here to sit with me. That was nice, Patsy.

PATSY: *(Quickly)* Well, only just for a little while, Grandma. My father's coming home from work soon. We're gonna have supper soon. *(To Helen)* Why's it so gloomy in here? Put on a light so we can see each other at least.

HELEN: Grandma don't want the light on.

GRANDMA: Loretta'll turn on the lights when she gets home. How are you, Patsy? Come over here and give me a kiss.

PATSY: I just gave you a kiss, Grandma. Okay—you want another one? Here's another one. *(She gives her another loud smack)* And one more for good measure. *(She kisses Grandma again)* Oh, that's a real pretty shawl you got there, Grandma. I don't remember seeing that on you. *(Sitting on Grandma's foot stool)* So how are you feeling today, Grandma?

HELEN: She's full of the devil.

GRANDMA: I'm fine, Patsy. Fine and dandy.

HELEN: *(Pointing at the bottle)* High as the sky. Talking "ragtime" ever since twelve o'clock.

PATSY: *(Picking up the bottle, teasing)* Oh . . . I see. Grandma, have you been a bad girl today?

GRANDMA: *(Seriously)* You put that back where you found it!

HELEN: Every year since Grandpa died. And what a day she picks for it.

PATSY: *(Setting the bottle down, teasing)* Now you go and tell that to the priest in confession, Grandma. And on Good Friday, too. I'm surprised at you. You tell the priest what a bad girl you are, Grandma.

GRANDMA: You tell the priest to come on over here. A little drop of this and he'll be telling me *his* confession. *(Slyly)* Did it ever make you wonder, Helen, what kind of sins the priest has to tell in confession?

HELEN: Now, Grandma, don't you get started—

PATSY: Oh, I don't know about all this. Are you sure you're over eighteen, young lady? Where's your driver's license? Come on, show me some proof. Everybody always asking *me* for proof!

HELEN: *(Sternly)* Who's always asking you for proof?

PATSY: *(Caught)* Oh—well, you know. Places you go. They ask you sometimes. That's a real pretty shawl, Grandma. I love it on you. Is it Irish?

HELEN: You mean places like you went to last night, I suppose.

GRANDMA: *(Fondling the shawl)* This here is older than any of the rest of you, Patsy. Nearly sixty years old—and just look at how new it is.

HELEN: It's a good thing your father didn't smell your breath when you came in the door.

(During their little spat, Helen and Patsy talk to each other over Grandma's chair on her "bum ear" side)

GRANDMA: Here, Patsy—run your hand over it. It's just like a cloud.

HELEN: It's a good thing I was there waiting up with him. Three o'clock in the morning—and him having to get up at seven-thirty. He was *rippin'* mad.

PATSY: It's beautiful, Grandma. *(To Helen)* Well, my father couldn't have done any worse than he did, could he? Standing out in the middle of the street, blowing a gut. He musta woke up the whole neighborhood.

GRANDMA: It's only this time of the year that I take it out of hiding. Sixty years old, and it's the color of springtime.

PATSY: Yeah, I'm crazy about old clothes, Grandma.

HELEN: Couldn't get you out of bed with a bomb this morning. Nice place to spend Good Friday—in bed all day with a hangover.

PATSY: I didn't have a hangover!

HELEN: Oh—so maybe you had something worse then!

GRANDMA: *(Still dreamily fondling the shawl)* It was an Easter present to me, long, long, ago.

PATSY: If you want to know, I spent the whole day in the house hiding from the neighbors. How much beer did my father drink while he was waiting up worrying about me? Cursing at Billy a mile a minute! Calling him a Brooklyn College Communist!—And a faggot! And there's a convent full of nuns right across the street!

HELEN: Well, the nuns were up long before your father got started. Pulling up to the door in that little tin-lizzie with the radio blasting. I thought it was a jukebox rolling down the street!

GRANDMA: *(Becoming aware of the argument for the first time)* What are you saying? What's the matter with the both of you?

PATSY: It's nothing, Grandma. Never mind.

HELEN: And don't think I didn't see the steam all over the windows!

PATSY: I don't care what you saw!

HELEN: What do you have to go hanging around Brooklyn College for? Why can't you go out with the boys you used to know from the Confraternity?

PATSY: Oh, God . . . !

GRANDMA: *(Slapping the arm of her chair for emphasis)* What's the matter with the both of you? Helen, you leave Patsy alone.

PATSY: It's okay, Grandma.

GRANDMA: Patsy's my girl—aren't you, Patsy?

PATSY: I sure am, Grandma!

HELEN: Well, you're welcome to keep her anytime you say the word, Grandma. Anyway, I'm going home. *(Announcing)* Grandma, I'm going home. I have to go shopping for Joseph's supper. Patsy'll sit with you till Loretta gets home.

GRANDMA: You're not going to leave me alone, are you, Helen?

HELEN: Patsy's gonna sit with you, Grandma. Joseph's coming home from work. I haven't got a thing in the house.

GRANDMA: Terrible gloomy day. I don't want to sit here alone.

PATSY: *(To Helen)* What's keeping Aunt Loretta?

HELEN: *(Getting her things together)* Oh, she's busy doing something I suppose. She's always busy doing something.

PATSY: Maybe it's the Belt Parkway. It's a big holiday weekend.

HELEN: Or maybe its a teacher's meeting—or the Garden Club—or the Rosary Society—or some other g.d. thing!

PATSY: What are you mad at Aunt Loretta for?

HELEN: Maybe she oughta stay home from work once in a while and watch the ghosts walking West on Good Friday!

PATSY: What?

HELEN: Never mind. You just stay here till she gets home. *(With an emphatic whisper)* And keep her glued to that chair whatever you do. All we need is for her to fall down and break the other hip— then we're all in big trouble.

PATSY: How long's she gonna be? I only came down to see what was keeping you.

HELEN: You came down so you wouldn't be alone when your father came home. You just stay here, that's all. And today's Friday. You be sure and get the twenty-five dollars from her.

PATSY: Oh, Ma—you know I hate doing that!

HELEN: I don't want to hear about it. It's little enough for all the time I spend away from my own house. Five days a week—eight in the morning till four in the afternoon. And days like this I don't get paid for overtime!

PATSY: I don't know why you do it. I hate it.

HELEN: I'm a good natured slob, that's why. Now make yourself useful instead of gallivanting around with a lot of Brooklyn College hippies!

PATSY: *(Resentfully)* You know, you don't even know Billy. You have no right to talk.

HELEN: You're right—I don't know Billy. Except he keeps me up till all hours babysitting with a crazy husband. *(Relenting)* Who knows? I might even get to like Billy—if he'd take that terrible-looking thing off his face. *(Patsy laughs as Helen chucks her under the chin)*

GRANDMA: Helen—Helen!

HELEN: *(Speeding up her "getaway")* I'm going now, Grandma! Patsy's gonna sit with you.

GRANDMA: *(To Helen)* Come over here and sit with me, Helen.

PATSY: *(Urgently)* What do I do if she has to go?

HELEN: Patsy's gonna sit with you, Grandma! *(To Patsy)* Don't worry. I put her on the pan a little while ago. She'll be fine till Loretta gets home. Don't forget the twenty-five dollars.

(Helen hurries out the back door. Patsy mopes awhile in the doorway. She hooks her fingers around the edge of the molding and swings her body slowly side to side, humming to herself)

GRANDMA: Helen! Helen! *(Patsy comes back into the room)* Where's Helen, Patsy?

PATSY: She's gone to the store to get supper, Grandma.

GRANDMA: Come and sit with me, Patsy. Don't leave me alone.

PATSY: *(A little annoyed)* I'm not going to leave you alone, Grandma. *(Patsy sits on the foot stool as Grandma looks out the window. There is another pause.)* Can I get you anything, Grandma?

GRANDMA: No, no. I'm fine, Patsy. Fine and dandy.

PATSY: Looks like rain, don't it?

GRANDMA: Mmmh. The robins are letting us know. They're telling the world to get under cover. Did you ever notice that about them, Patsy?

PATSY: *(Absently)* Yeah, I guess so.

GRANDMA: Be a nice sky for Easter Sunday, I bet. *(There is another pause, then Grandma turns and smiles at Patsy a moment)* Is there a young man you're fond of Patsy?

PATSY: *(Surprised at the question)* Yeah, I guess there is, Grandma.

GRANDMA: What's his name?

PATSY: Billy.

GRANDMA: Is he a Catholic?

PATSY: Oh, I don't know what he was.

GRANDMA: Well, he's got to be something.

PATSY: *(Laughing)* I asked him one time what his religion was. He said it was political science.

GRANDMA: You're talking in my bum ear, Patsy.

PATSY: *(Louder)* I said he was fooling with me, Grandma. He said he was a poly-sci major in college. *(Grandma looks blank)* It means he's learning all about politics, Grandma.

GRANDMA: Politics? You don't need college for that. That's something you're born with.

PATSY: Well, I mean he's into all kinds of radical theories, Grandma. You know, like the redistribution of income and the overthrow of the capitalist system. That kind of stuff.

GRANDMA: What's that when it's cooked?

PATSY: Well, I guess back in your day, Grandma, you'd of called him a rebel.

GRANDMA: Oh, God help us—don't tell me that!

PATSY: What's the matter?

GRANDMA: *(Musing)* A rebel . . . another one . . .

PATSY: Grandma?

GRANDMA: Mmmh? Oh, never mind—never mind, Patsy—I was just trying to remember. *(To herself)* If I only had a picture or something.

PATSY: You know, Grandma, you look tired. Do you want to have a little sleep?

GRANDMA: *(Annoyed)* Now tell me, Patsy, am I crazy or does this damned room have an echo in it? Everybody's always telling me to go to sleep. I'll have plenty of time for sleeping when I'm tucked away under the ground. Why's everybody in such a g.d. hurry to get me there?

PATSY: *(Admonished)* I'm sorry, Grandma.

(There is another pause as a light rain begins to spatter the window. Grandma continues to look out as Patsy fidgets and hums to herself)

GRANDMA: Look—it's raining, just like the birds said it would. Terrible dark day.

PATSY: Do you want me to turn on the light, Grandma?

GRANDMA: No, no. Loretta will turn on the lights when she comes home. I like it this way.

(There is another pause as the rain continues and Patsy hums in restlessness)

GRANDMA: Patsy—put on a little music for us like a good girl.

PATSY: You want the radio, Grandma?

GRANDMA: No, no. The other thing. Put on one of the records Joseph gave me. One of the Irish records. He give them to me . . . ah, I don't know when it was. The same time he give me the bottle.

PATSY: *(At the record cabinet, reading the jackets)* "Songs of the Irish Rebellion." And—"Drinking Songs from a Public House." Which one do you want to hear, Grandma?

GRANDMA: Let me hear the rebellion. That's the proper stuff for a day like today. But keep it turned down. I don't want that Hanlon bitch thinking we're all gone Protestant.

PATSY: *(Putting the record on)* Good Friday's a Protestant day too, Grandma. Anyway, I think Mrs. Hanlon's an agnostic.

GRANDMA: *(With a wave of disdain)* Aah, Agnostic, Presbyterian . . . they're all cut from the same loaf.

PATSY: By the way, Mrs. Hanlon was asking for you when I was coming up the street just now.

(Grandma pays no attention. The music goes on and the song is "Foggy Dew," a solemn, stirring ballad of the 1916 Easter Rising in Dublin. Grandma listens for a while, looking out the window and humming softly to herself)

GRANDMA: *(After a few minutes)* That's a grand song. Don't you like that song, Patsy?

PATSY: Yeah, it's okay, I guess.

GRANDMA: *(After a pause)* Is he good to you, your young rebel fella? Does he treat you good, Patsy?

PATSY: *(A little embarrassed)* Yeah, he treats me okay, Grandma.

GRANDMA: *(Softly)* Be careful, Patsy. *(There is another pause. The song continues and Grandma hums the tune as she gazes out the window. Patsy watches her, a little puzzled)* Oh, but that's a grand song. You know, when I take a little drop the words seem that much clearer to me. . . . Will you have a little drop yourself, Patsy?

PATSY: *(Surprised)* Oh, I don't know, Grandma. There was a big party last night. I'm still a little shaky.

GRANDMA: Oh, you can have a little drop. A little drop's not gonna hurt you. Go find yourself a glass. You and me will have a little drop together. *(With a wink)* It's the most sorrowful day of the Catholic year. It'll help dilute some of the sadness for us.

PATSY: *(Enjoying the mischief)* Well . . . okay, I guess I will!

(Patsy goes out to find a glass. The music starts again with "Nell Flaherty's Drake," a snappy, satirical song of humor and defiance. Grandma's mood picks up as she hums and keeps time by tapping her hand on the arm of the chair. Patsy comes in with a freshly rinsed tumbler, more appropriate for holding milk than a cordial. She pours too much for herself)

PATSY: Just don't go telling my father if he comes down here later. After what happened last night, I think he'd try and kill me.

GRANDMA: Aah, never you mind about him. Joseph means well

in his own way. He just can't help being what he is, the simp.

PATSY: *(Shocked and delighted)* Grandma!

GRANDMA: *(Apologetically)* He can't help it, the poor fella. All the McGraths were simps. Your own grandfather—good man that he was. If there was a lump of manure in the middle of the road he'd be the first one to put his foot in it.

(Patsy laughs)

GRANDMA: Don't laugh. I seen him do it.

PATSY: I'm sorry I don't remember Grandpa better.

GRANDMA: Well, he lived just long enough to see you make your first Communion. That's the sort of thing he enjoyed. That and being the first one in the first pew of the first Mass on every first Friday of the month, and every Sunday of the year. Marching me and the little ones up the aisle in a line behind him. "A good solid foundation," he'd say. "A good solid foundation and they'll never get away from it."

PATSY: That's what Daddy's always saying!

GRANDMA: And "Good morning, Father this," and "How are you, Father that . . ."

PATSY: *(Laughing with recognition)* And taking off his hat whenever he meets one of them in the street! Even in the pouring rain with the water running off his nose!

GRANDMA: *(Tentatively)* Well, I couldn't never quite share his enthusiasm for the clergy. It always seemed to me that they had it too easy for the high and mighty things they were preaching at you. But still and all it was the only way I knew to raise a family. I mean, what else was I to do when you come right down to it? *(She pauses as if she expects Patsy to respond)* An ignorant little immigrant skirt right off the boat—what else could I do? All the Irish troubles behind me—and a big new world standing over me shouting questions in my face.

PATSY: I guess I'd be frightened to death.

GRANDMA: Sure you would! Sure you would! No friends or family to go to. *(Grandly)* No family at all but the One Holy Catholic and Apostolic Family of all of us. I met your Grandpa at a Church Caeli dance. It was held special for those of us just off the boat.

PATSY: Yeah, you told me, Grandma.

GRANDMA: Six months later I was married to him. Then the little ones started coming along. All so fast—so fast . . . But it was the only life I knew and I stuck to it. The letter of the law—year after year. What other way was there? I mean I'm asking you, Patsy. When you come right down to it—what other way did I know?

PATSY: *(Taken aback by Grandma's sudden intimacy)* Well, you were just saying how frightened you were. You didn't see no other—

GRANDMA: A frightened little immigrant skirt right off the boat. Oh, fear's a terrible thing, Patsy. It'll lead you around by the nose if you let it. It'll lead you right back to whatever makes you feel all safe and sound. Never mind the questions you got deep in your heart. So that's what I done—just like all the other ignorant little skirts before me.

PATSY: *(Sipping the drink)* Mmmh. This is really good, Grandma. Now I see why you like it so much.

GRANDMA: Isn't it good though? Now you see why I like it so much.

PATSY: *(Playfully)* What about Aunt Loretta? Is Aunt Loretta a simp?

GRANDMA: Loretta? Oh, God help us, no. Loretta's perfect. Perfect. Just don't never live with nobody perfect. *(Quietly)* Not man or woman good enough for that one there. Oh, I did a fine job of raising those two, didn't I now? Passing on the same malarkey that was passed on to me. Still, what other way did I have I'd like to know? *(With a sigh)* But your Grandfather's under the ground now where he's happy, and the other two are all grown up and out of my hands. So, now I'm back trying to be Aggie Reilly again. With what little time is left me anyway.

PATSY: Aunt Loretta's awful late getting home, isn't she? What's keeping her I wonder?

GRANDMA: Oh, whatever it is she'll have a good excuse when she gets here. Whatever it takes to get her out of the house and away from sitting with me. *(Laughing suddenly)* I bet she's in Church catching the tail end of the Good Friday show, and praying for her wicked old mother. *(Smiling and shaking her head)* Aah, but what can she do? Isn't it the way I raised her myself?

PATSY: Well, I guess it does look kind of funny. It being Good Friday and you making a party out of it.

GRANDMA: *(Severely)* It's no party, Patsy. It's a wake. And there's others beside the Son of God can use the remembering. *(The music has changed again. Now the song is "Reilly's Daughter," a strong dancing lyric. Grandma pauses to listen with pleasure)* Oh, now there's a fine piece of music for you. Just listen to that, will you? I could do a fine little step to that once upon a time.

PATSY: *(Leaping up suddenly and launching into an Irish folk dance)* Do you mean something like this, Grandma? Is this what you're talking about.

GRANDMA: *(Delighted)* Oh, now look at that, will you?

PATSY: *(As she dances)* It's easy. I learned it a long time ago—the eighth grade assembly—on St. Patrick's day. The nuns made all the girls dance in a line. The boys were too clumsy.

(Grandma watches for a moment with great pleasure. Then suddenly her expression changes and she leans forward urgently)

GRANDMA: Patsy! Patsy! Stop a minute! Stop a minute and come over here!

PATSY: *(Taken aback)* What's the matter? *(She lifts the needle arm off the record)*

GRANDMA: *(Holding her shawl out to her)* Here, take this. Put it around your shoulders. Go ahead—go ahead. Just do what I say. Do what I say.

(Patsy takes Grandma's shawl and wraps it around her shoulders. She feels self-conscious and overplays the role of "model." Grandma stares at her intently)

PATSY: *(Strutting and turning)* Well? What do I look like?

GRANDMA: You look like a ghost.

PATSY: What?

GRANDMA: Your dancing like that—it made me think I was seeing somebody else. Start the dance again, Patsy.

PATSY: Grandma, are you fooling me?

GRANDMA: Start the dance again, Patsy! I want to see it. Start it again I'm telling you!

PATSY: *(Mystified)* Well—okay, I will. If you really want me to.

GRANDMA: It was beautiful watching you dancing like that. I was struck how beautiful you looked.

(Patsy starts the song again, but before she begins the dance, she takes up her glass and drains it off)

PATSY: *(Laughing)* Maybe this is what's got me looking so beautiful to you!

(Patsy begins to dance again, as Grandma watches her, intently. When Grandma begins to speak, the scene lights fade out until Patsy is dancing in a pool of light surrounded by darkness. As Grandma continues to speak, and Patsy continues to dance, other lights slowly rise on the scene of a bare tenement room. Midway in her speech, as the scenes are changing, Grandma's voice is joined by a male voice speaking the lines in unison with her. As Grandma's voice fades and the tenement scene emerges, the character of Michael comes into focus. He stands with his hands in his pockets watching Patsy dance. The phonograph music has become the "live" music of masculine voices rising from the street below the tenement window, and Patsy is no longer Patsy, but Aggie herself as a young girl on a bright Palm Sunday in Dublin, 1916)

GRANDMA: *(As Patsy resumes dancing)* It's like a green spring breeze blowing around your shoulders. I love watching you dance Patsy . . . you've such beautiful hair . . . *(Michael's voice joins Aggie's)* I love watching the way your hair moves . . . take out the pin and let your hair go free . . . *(Patsy takes out her hair clip as the lights come up full on the tenement scene)*

MICHAEL: Your hair has a music all its own, Aggie.

(The young Aggie continues to dance to the sound of the street song. Michael watches her, enchanted. He is a slightly built young man about twenty-three years old. He wears glasses and the rough clothing of the Dublin poor. But there is nothing of the working-class in his manner or physique. He is a student and something of a poet. There is a shy, yearning recluse in him who loves Aggie for her beauty and exhuberance)

MICHAEL: *(Teasing)* If you kick up your skirts any higher you'll be showing the freckles above your knees!

AGGIE: *(Stopping suddenly and grabbing at her skirt)* Michael! Don't you be saying such things!

MICHAEL: I'm only saying what I saw.

AGGIE: You saw no such thing. Freckles above my knees. I'll have you know I have no such thing.

MICHAEL: I know you don't.

AGGIE: Oh, Michael O'Neill, you're a terrible liar. I've no right to be dancing in front of you at all.

MICHAEL: Why not?

AGGIE: Because it isn't decent, that's why. A young girl all by herself dancing a jig in a young man's flat. And here we are—still in the middle of Lent.

MICHAEL: Palm Sunday doesn't count. It's a holiday from all the fasting and breast-beating of the rest of the season. Even the weather's taking a holiday. Just look at that sky. Come over here by the window.

AGGIE: I can't do that. Somebody's liable to look up and see us. Then what would we do, I wonder?

MICHAEL: There's nobody down on the street but a bunch of the old fellas banging out their song and waiting for the pub to open its doors.

AGGIE: Well, I don't think its a proper thing to be singing on the street in the middle of Lent.

MICHAEL: But it's proper for you to dance a jig if they do.

AGGIE: Oh, aren't you the smart one? Well, I'm not to blame for my actions.

(Aggie kneels to Michael in the attitude of a mock "confession." Michael assumes the attitude of Father Drane, the pastor)

AGGIE: *(Plaintively)* It was this here magic shawl made me do it,

Father Drane. He whispered some sort of poetic incantation over it, Father. Some terrible mumbo-jumbo from the works of Swinburne and Yeats. Oh, it was awful, Father. Once he clapped it on my shoulders I couldn't stop dancing. I danced and danced till I tumbled down with shame and exhaustion. Oh, Father, you'll forgive me—won't you, Father?

MICHAEL: *(Making the sign of absolution)* Of course I will, my child. And for your penance, you can thank the young man and give him a kiss.

AGGIE: *(Moving away invitingly)* It seems to me that I thanked the young man once already.

MICHAEL: *(Pulling her to him)* Just once more. We call it a "firm purpose of amendment."

(He kisses her. At first she resists—but not too severely. Gradually she surrenders and their embrace becomes passionate. Suddenly Aggie pulls away from him)

AGGIE: Now, Michael—Michael, that's enough. I don't want anything bad to happen.

MICHAEL: *(Frustrated)* Anything good, you mean. You have your adjectives backwards, don't you Aggie?

AGGIE: Now, please Michael—please. I don't want to go on about it. *(Brightly, trying to change the subject)* It's such a lovely shawl you gave me. Just wearing it's liable to give me notions. Thank you again, Michael.

MICHAEL: *(Sourly)* You're very welcome, I'm sure.

AGGIE: Of course I'll have to bunk it when I get home. I'd have a time explaining to my father how I came by it.

MICHAEL: Tell him it's an Easter present from the four-eyed atheist. I'll surely be invited to dinner.

AGGIE: *(Quickly)* Michael, let's go outside. We'll take a stroll through the flower beds at Phoenix Park. Come on now. I came up here to rescue a poor, lonely student from the tyranny of his books. Now I'll go downstairs first. Then you wait ten minutes and join me around the corner. That way we won't run the risk of arousing suspicion.

MICHAEL: And what would anybody be suspecting *you* of, Aggie? Unless you done something bad on your way here. God knows, you done nothing bad since you came.

AGGIE: *(Defiantly)* Well, I'm sorry, Mr. O'Neill, for being what I happen to be. And I'm sorry that some of your wilder words were lost on my father's poor, dark, working-class mind.

MICHAEL: *(Angrily)* It's in support of the working people that I say the things I do!

AGGIE: Well, then you'll just have to find another and better way of expressing yourself!

MICHAEL: Yes! Yes, I will! On that score I'm in full agreement with you!

AGGIE: *(After a brief pouting silence)* Well, now—do you think we can put these things behind us and take advantage of a beautiful day? You're just after saying yourself what a glorious sky it is. Like the first Palm Sunday when they welcomed the Savior into the city like a conquering hero.

MICHAEL: *(Brooding)* And a week later the same city hanged him for a traitor and drove his people into hiding.

AGGIE: *(Stamping her foot with impatience)* Oooh . . .!

MICHAEL: *(At the window, looking down on the singers),* Oh, why don't they stop their croaking, the damned old fools!

AGGIE: You liked it well enough when I was dancing to it and lifting my skirts. Oh, Michael—Michael, what's the matter with you today?

MICHAEL: Come look at them down there and you'll see for yourself.

AGGIE: I can't come to the window!

MICHAEL: *(Still at the window)* Old dead faces, wrinkled with thirst, waiting for the pub to open its doors. There's our National Gallery for you! Four dead men leaning against a padlocked door, singing songs of rebellion a hundred years old. God, is it any wonder the young people are fleeing this land by the thousands before the blood in their veins turns to Guinness? It's something I've often thought of myself.

AGGIE: *(Startled)* That's the first I heard you speak of it.

MICHAEL: I've thought of it. Believe me I have.

AGGIE: *(Bravely)* Well, go then if you feel you must. There's nothing that's tying you down here—that's for certain. It's a cheap enough steerage on the steamer to Liverpool.

MICHAEL: Liverpool? What are you saying, girl?

AGGIE: Well, then there's always America. The way the letters come back from some of them you'd think the Irish were running the country!

MICHAEL: But the Irish can't run their own country, can they? America . . . I met one of them the other night when I was walking back from the college. He comes busting out from the smoky light of a pub house door. "Hey you! Hey you!" he calls to me. "Where are the Leprechauns?"he says, "Where are the Leprechauns? You're an Irishman, ain't you? Well, let's you and me go catch a leprechaun to take back on the boat to the States." Well, I jerked up my knee and slammed it right into his pills. "Is it the Little People you're looking for?" I shouted while he was rolling on the cobblestones holding himself. "Are you looking for the 'Ould Wans' you bastard? Well, there's one just down the street there! An old grandmother sitting on top of her few sticks of furniture, pounding her hair and calling out to Jesus Christ to find out what plans he's made for looking after the poor he created!"

AGGIE: Oh, that was terrible, Michael!

MICHAEL: What was terrible, Aggie? What I did to that bastard? Or what was being done to that old woman by the powers that be?

AGGIE: Both! Both those things. And the way you talk, Michael.

MICHAEL: I've no other way to say what I'm feeling! If it's dirty talk, then it's a dirty world!

AGGIE: No! It's Palm Sunday—and it's a beautiful sky outside! And there's music coming from the streets below. These are the only things I want to know about, Michael. I hate hearing you talk so wild.

MICHAEL: The facts are the facts and that's all they are. There's nothing *wild* about the *facts,* Aggie!

AGGIE: I don't want to talk about it today, Michael!

MICHAEL: *(In a fury)* And the fella in the flat just two doors down—back from France for Christmas with the half of his face shot off and the light in his mind blown out forever! Fighting the Great War he was for the freedom of all the little nations of the world! All the little nations except his own! *(At the window)* Now look—look! C'mon to the window—you can see his old mother, wheeling him around the block like he was a baby again. And the drool running out of his mouth like twenty-five years of life never happened at all!

AGGIE: *(Wailing and covering her ears)* Oh, Michael, Michael! Why do you tell me these terrible things?

MICHAEL: *(Shaking her roughly)* To make you see them, Aggie! To make you understand who I've become now—and *why!*

AGGIE: *(Struggling in his grip)* You're spitting out the words so fast I can't even hear what you're saying!

MICHAEL: *(Slowly and carefully, his face close to hers)* Then can you hear this much, Aggie? I'm a Socialist now. I've gone with the Republican Brotherhood.

AGGIE: *(In a shocked whisper)* The Republican Brotherhood?

MICHAEL: *(Letting her go)* I'm with them the better part of two months now. I'm calling it quits with the college.

AGGIE: You've gone with The Brotherhood? Why it's a brotherhood of crazy men you're joined with! Standing on soap boxes spouting crazy speeches in the park!

MICHAEL: And when all the rest of you are through talking, they're the only ones who are telling the truth!

AGGIE: Calling for rifles and dynamite—for fighting house to house in the street—for women and children, anybody who can pull the trigger of a gun—!

MICHAEL: *(Grandly)* They've forced us at gunpoint to take up guns ourselves!

AGGIE: Those aren't your words, Michael.

MICHAEL: They're my words now!

AGGIE: And it's for crazy business the likes of this you want to throw away your hope of the future?

MICHAEL: Oh, for God's sake, girl!—Was there ever a rebel who stopped in his tracks to take a bachelor's degree?

AGGIE: Oh, this isn't you, Michael. This isn't you I'm listening to!

MICHAEL: *(Furiously)* It is! It is I tell you! I'm changed! I'm not the same fella I used to be!

AGGIE: It's not a gun but a book that belongs in your hand, Michael!

MICHAEL: I'll be the best judge of that!

AGGIE: *(Going to him)* Michael, you're a scholar—you're a poet. If it's fighting you want, do your fighting with words.

MICHAEL: *(Breaking away from her)* I'm sick of words! I'm sick of reading about the pain all around me! I'm sick of *writing* about it! I'm sick of words! I'm sick of the sound of my own *voice!*

AGGIE: But you're not a soldier, Michael!

MICHAEL: *(Hysterically)* I am! I am I tell you! I have to be!

(Michael breaks down, sinking to the floor on his knees. He clutches himself tightly about the chest, looking away from her and trying to stifle his sobs. Aggie stands over him helplessly. Then she kneels beside him and wraps her arms around his shoulders)

AGGIE: *(Softly)* Michael, it was only this morning at Mass that Father Drane said members of groups like the Republican Brotherhood were committing a mortal sin.

MICHAEL: *(With a sudden sad laugh)* Oh God, did he now? Well, good for Father Drane and all the rest of his kind. If I only had the fare handy I'd buy them all a one-way steerage to hell.

AGGIE: Michael, don't say such things! You're talking against God.

MICHAEL: Aggie, you're so afraid. You're so afraid of just wanting things. And I know. I know you are. I know it because I'm afraid myself. I'm afraid of looking in the mirror twenty years from now and being ashamed of what I see!

AGGIE: Oh, Michael, I wish I could understand. I do. But all your talk about guns and history. I'm afraid of that. Maybe its got to do with my being a woman and all—but I can't see no glory in the drool spilling over that young fella's lip!

MICHAEL: *(Gently turning her face towards him)* Aggie—just answer me this much then. Do you love me?

(The question comes as a shock to her. Instinctively she tries to pull away from him. He holds her tightly)

MICHAEL: No—no, for God's sake don't start blushing and being coy. Not now, Aggie. Not now. There's no time for that now. We're not at a Caeli dance or a parish picnic. We're hanging onto the earth by our fingernails and its spinning faster than you or me know. Just say it to me—simple and straight. Do you love me?

AGGIE: *(Softly)* Yes. I love you, Michael. You know that I do.

MICHAEL: *(Taking her face in his hands)* Then there's something I have to tell you. *(Quickly)* And I can't tell you no more or I would, Aggie. I swear to you I would. *(Slowly, looking for the words)* We maybe have only a little time left to be together. We maybe have only a little time left not to be afraid. Maybe only as little time as Jesus himself had when they cheered him into the city, waving their palm fronds and calling for miracles.

(Slowly, almost reverently, their lips come together in a kiss. Then, as kiss follows kiss, their passion grows and Aggie abandons herself to the freedom of her love. Michael slips the green shawl from her shoulders and spreads it open on the floor. Aggie lies back upon it. Then, with a sudden cry of joy, she welcomes her lover into her arms. The lights and the street music fade out as the figure of Grandma re-emerges in a pool of light surrounded by the darkness of the rest of the stage. She is rocking gently in her chair and smiling softly at her memories)

GRANDMA: And for all the rest of that week I was as happy and as guilty as any girl alive had ever been before me. I visited Michael's flat twice more—wearing my beautiful green shawl and walking down the street as bold as you please. And the National Gallery was right there with their mouths wide open, enjoying the scandal of it all. Their whispers were burning the hair on the back of my head when I lifted my skirts and trotted up the tenement steps. And they were watching and whispering still when I came down a few minutes later. That whole week Michael was never at home. His chums had an idea he was off in the hills playing toy soldier with the Citizen Army. It was a lot of damned nonsense they laughed. He'd be back at his books so fast the Republicans wouldn't catch him for dust. But all that week I didn't see him. And there wasn't a word from him waiting for me anywhere. Come Good Friday, I took a deep breath and sneaked behind the purple curtain of the confessional—all the while practicing what I was gonna say when the little wooden window slid open. I surrounded my terrible sin with a lot of little made-up ones that didn't amount to a hill of beans. A few before it and a few after it—like I was making some kind of sandwich for the priest. But he fooled me—he stopped me short when I got to the main event. "What is it you said you did?" he bellowed. "And what's the name of the man you did it with?" He was puffing so hard his big bald head near glowed in the dark. "An atheist," he says, "A heathen!" One of Satan's own lawyers, with a library full of lies to turn the head of an ignorant little skirt the likes of me! And I kept saying "Yes, Father" every time he stopped for breath. I wore him out just agreeing with him. Then he tossed his absolution at me, and I walked out of there, holding up my head, and trying not to think what was meant by "a firm purpose of amendment." I spent all the Three Hours Devotion working off the sentence he gave me. But every so often I'd look up from my beads, hoping I'd see Michael standing in the vestibule looking to find me there. But no—Good Friday went by, and Jesus was taken down from the cross and sealed in the tomb. Then all day Saturday the family was talking in whispers, walking on tip-toe, like we was mourning the great Loss—and trying not to wake the Savior up before His Time on Easter morning. Come Sunday my father made a big effort at shining his boots, and off we all went to hear the High Mass and stand inspection in front of the Parish. I wanted so bad to wear my beautiful shawl for Easter—but I just didn't dare. Afterwards I looked for Michael in the crowd on the steps. I found every familiar face but his own. Then I walked home alone, fighting the tears, and wondering what could have happened to the world in the space of a little week.

(As Grandma's monologue of Holy Week ends, the spotlight fades, and the lights and phonograph music rise again in the West Room of the Brooklyn house. Patsy stands near Grandma's chair holding her head and breathing heavily as if she has just finished her dance. She seems a little shaky and has lost the exuberance of the earlier scene)

PATSY: Oo-oh. I shouldn't have been jumping around like that. I feel dizzy or something. I better sit down.

GRANDMA: *(She is speaking to herself, not even aware of Patsy)* Next day was Easter Monday—as bright and blue as Palm Sunday the week before. I put on my new shawl and took another walk down Michael's street.

PATSY: *(Still preoccupied)* I don't know what's the matter with me. I think it must be that stuff you gave me to drink. On top of last night it's done something to me.

GRANDMA: I wasn't so bold now. I pretended to be window shopping along the way.

PATSY: This shawl, too. *(She takes it off)* It's so muggy in here—it's got me dizzy.

GRANDMA: I'd only squint up real quick at Michael's window, looking for signs of life.

PATSY: Did Aunt Loretta say she'd be late getting home?

GRANDMA: Michael was never home.

PATSY: *(At last focusing on Grandma)* What did you say, Grandma?

GRANDMA: *(Still giving no sign of noticing Patsy)* I went to the park and sat on the grass. I watched a little girl with a big bunch of balloons. She was laughing out loud, and letting them go one by one, making freckles of color in the clear blue sky.

PATSY: Grandma, did you hear what I said to you?

GRANDMA: Then I heard the guns. Pop—pop—pop. I thought it was the balloons breaking. Pop—pop—pop. Way off—in the heart of the city.

PATSY: *(Growing concerned)* Grandma . . .?

GRANDMA: *(With rising excitement)* Then a flood of rumors came filling the streets from every direction. They're out! They're out—and the tri-colors flying! It's the Republic! The Republic—and the Tommies are running away from our boys! The Germans are landing and there's U-boats in the Liffey! Seven hundred years and its all chucked over in the space of a morning. It's the Republic!

PATSY: Grandma—Grandma, who are you talking to? Here, try and sleep—sleep a little bit. You're talking wild, Grandma.

(As Patsy spreads the shawl on her lap, Grandma seems to notice her for the first time. She seizes Patsy's wrist and holds it in a ferocious grip)

GRANDMA: Well, that's all that it was, wasn't it? Wild talk! Nothing but wild talk!

PATSY: Grandma, what are you talking about?

GRANDMA: Wild talk! A little cluster of men trapped and fighting their hearts out. And Michael trapped in the midst of it all—trapped and waiting for the end to come!

PATSY: Grandma, you're pinching my arm! *(Pulling free)* Here, don't talk about that anymore, Grandma. Let me get you a cup of tea—do you want a cup of tea, Grandma?

GRANDMA: And the end come all right. It come. Quick, and neat, and efficient it come. Rolling street by street, and flat by flat, crushing any man with the courage to lift up his face off the floor.

And the navy's big guns from the river, smashing down tenement walls and setting off fires—roasting the rebels who refused to come out! Then the tri-color flag came fluttering down. And all over the city the broken windows were blossoming with the colors of the Union Jack. And every Protestant Union-boy stuck a smile on his face and an orange ribbon in the band of his hat!

PATSY: Grandma—

GRANDMA: It was a long, long time before I heard about Michael. It was months of waiting before any word came. Then one of the boys just out of prison told me. It was an accident, he said. Easter Monday—the first day of the Rising. A couple of the boys were fixing a bomb to use if the Tommies had tanks. Michael was standing over the thing, with his hands in his pockets, looking on and trying to learn. The fella said it was an accident the thing went off.

(Grandma pauses, her lips working silently as if she is praying or dwelling over the memory. The story has begun to affect Patsy)

PATSY: Please, Grandma. I don't want you to talk about it any more.

GRANDMA: *(Still speaking as if to herself)* I made visits to Church every day. Every minute I had—till my knees were sore with the kneeling. And when I went walking it was only to look at the flowers in Phoenix Park or hear the birds singing over and over that things were still alive in the world. Then one day, when I was leaving the church, Father Drane was coming up the steps. He grabbed me by the arm and looked at me hard before he said a word. "You were the lucky one, weren't you?" he said. "Here you're walking around alive and absolved—and there's the other poor fool lying tortured in hell the very minute we're standing here." For a second I couldn't say nothing at all. It was like my own face a bomb went off in. "You liar!" I shouted at him. "You liar! You liar! I'll take no absolution from the likes of you! I'll take no forgiveness for what we done! I'm proud of what my man done—and I'm proud of the love I gave to help him do it! May God forgive me for ever asking forgiveness at all! Do you hear me, you liar! Do you? Do you hear me, you liar, you!" Over and over, screaming it and screaming it into his face. Holding onto the iron railing like a drunken woman—till he hitched up his skirts and went running into his church for safety.

PATSY: Grandma, Grandma, please. You'll make yourself sick, Grandma. I don't want you to talk about it any more.

(There is a sound at the back door and Loretta enters, her arms full of books and term-paper envelopes. Loretta is in her mid-forties, neatly but

not smartly dressed. She still has her figure and must have been an attractive girl when she was Patsy's age. But her face is pinched with seriousness and the business of life. Her movements are quick, efficient, and full of authority. She is the sort of person who prides herself on her ability to act with dispatch in times of emergency. As she enters, her call of greeting has a cheerfulness more Pavlovian than genuine)

LORETTA: *(At the back door)* Howdy! Howdy Doody!

(Grandma sits transfixed in her chair her lips moving in silence and her eyes wide-open, staring at her memories. Patsy gives her an urgent shake on the wrist. It has no effect)

PATSY: Here's Aunt Loretta now, Grandma!

LORETTA: *(Setting down her books and entering)* Ma! Helen! It's me!

PATSY: Don't let Aunt Loretta see you like this.

(Loretta steps into the room. Immediately she senses that something is wrong. Grandma gives her no sign of recognition)

LORETTA: What's going on? Patsy, what are you doing here? Why's it so dark?

GRANDMA: *(Still speaking to her memories)* I remember holding a rifle in my hands one time.

LORETTA: What's the matter with Grandma? *(Going to her)* Ma?

GRANDMA: It was so heavy I could hardly lift it at all.

LORETTA: What's the matter with her? Ma, look at me.

PATSY: She's been like this a little while now, Aunt Loretta.

GRANDMA: A long, cold, hard thing it was. Hard, and cold, and ugly as sin.

LORETTA: *(Angrily, to Patsy)* What happened to your mother? How did she let her get like this?

PATSY: My mother waited. She had to go shopping.

GRANDMA: *(With growing intensity)* Not an inch or an ounce of beauty in the whole ugly thing! Oh, what is it men find to *love* in such things?

LORETTA: I stopped off in Church for a few minutes on my way home—your mother couldn't have waited a little while longer? *(Putting her face close to Grandma's and shaking her)* Ma—Ma—

PATSY: *(Timidly)* She waited as long as she could.

GRANDMA: *(With a sudden wail of anguish)* Oh, Michael— Michael—was the touch of it better than my own willing body lying naked in your arms?

LORETTA: *(Pulling back from her)* Oh, my God! Oh, my God! My God, we're at it again. *(Shaking her)* Ma! Ma! I want you to look at me!

PATSY: I never seen her like this before.

LORETTA: *(Almost savagely)* Well, *I* have! I've seen it! And I've heard it, too—year in and year out! Who do you think's alone here with her night after night! *(Roughly)* Ma! Ma!

GRANDMA: *(Softly)* Michael . . . Michael . . .

(Loretta uncaps a small bottle from among Grandma's array of medicines and passes it under her nose)

LORETTA: Loretta, Ma. It's Loretta. Look at me, won't you? It's Loretta. Patsy, make yourself useful and turn that damned thing off!

(Patsy lifts the arm off the phonograph and silence returns to the room)

LORETTA: What's the matter with your mother, letting her get in a state like this?

PATSY: She was all right till just a little while ago. I don't know what happened to her.

LORETTA: *(Pointing at the liquor bottle)* That's what happened to her! Right there! Oh, I could kill that Joseph for giving it to her. And I warned your mother only this morning! What's the matter with her anyway?

PATSY: *(Sullenly)* There's nothing the matter with my mother.

(As Loretta continues to apply the smelling salts, Grandma slowly comes around. She blinks as if just awakening from a trance or a sleep. Slowly her eyes focus on Loretta)

GRANDMA: Who's that—Loretta?

LORETTA: It's me, Ma. You were having a dream.

GRANDMA: Is that Helen?

PATSY: It's Patsy, Grandma. How are you feeling?

GRANDMA: Where's Helen?

LORETTA: Helen's gone home, Ma. I'm here with you now. Everything's gonna be all right.

GRANDMA: Is that Patsy over there?

PATSY: It's Patsy, Grandma.

GRANDMA: What happened to me just now?

LORETTA: You were dreaming, Ma.

GRANDMA: *(Trying to remember)* No. No, you're wrong. That wasn't no dream. I seen something just now. What was it I was saying to you, Patsy?

LORETTA: *(To Patsy)* For God's sake don't get her started all over again!

GRANDMA: I know I was saying something just now.

LORETTA: *(Quickly)* It was nothing, Ma. Patsy, maybe you oughta go on home now. It's getting late.

PATSY: *(Hesitantly)* Aunt Loretta—my mother said you could give me the money. I'd bring it down to her.

LORETTA: Oh—yes. I was forgetting. This is Friday, isn't it? *(At her pocket book)* Well, I'll have to give you a check. I'll be short on cash the rest of the weekend. *(She begins to write out the check)*

GRANDMA: It's like knowing you had a dream and not being able to remember it. But this *wasn't* no dream! Patsy—what was I saying just now?

PATSY: *(Uncomfortable)* Oh, you were just talking about Ireland, Grandma.

LORETTA: *(Quickly)* You were talking "ragtime," Ma. You weren't making any sense at all. *(To Patsy)* Don't even answer her. I'll be stuck with it all the rest of the night. And by the way, tell Joseph I need him down here by eight o'clock. There's a Parish Club meeting. Tonight of all nights I can't miss out on it.

GRANDMA: *(Struggling)* I feel like there was something I was trying to get at. Patsy—what was it I was saying?

LORETTA: *(Giving Patsy the check)* What are you standing around here for? Go on home now.

GRANDMA: *(Urgently)* Why don't you let the girl speak? Patsy—I was trying to say something. I was just coming to it. Don't leave me alone not knowing what it was.

PATSY: *(Hesitantly)* You were talking about Michael, Grandma.

LORETTA: Oh, damn you! What did I just finish telling you?

GRANDMA: *(Softly)* Michael . . . Oh, yes. Yes, I remember it now.

LORETTA: *(To Patsy)* Are you happy now? Are you happy? We'll have the same old story over and over the rest of the night. Oh, you damned little fool, you!

GRANDMA: Loretta! Don't you be taking out after Patsy so! You leave Patsy alone. Patsy's my girl.

LORETTA: *(Bitterly)* Patsy's your girl. And you're my mother—God help me. Though I'd be ashamed to admit it, seeing the way you're carrying on the day Christ died.

GRANDMA: *(With a grand disdain)* Never you mind how I'm carrying on. *(Raising her glass)* I been giving Jesus of Nazareth a good Irish wake! *(Leaning forward in her chair and speaking in a hard whisper)* And that's not what's eating at you, Loretta. I know what your trouble is well enough.

LORETTA: Sitting here in the dark, drunk as a lord. Making yourself sick with the same old sob story.

GRANDMA: And don't you worry none either, Loretta. There'll be no more need to tell the same old sob story ever again. Because today I seen the whole thing happen! I seen him right here with me!

LORETTA: *(Plaintively)* What are you talking about, Ma? Do you even know what you're talking about?

GRANDMA: All this time there's one fella I been looking to see. And today I seen him. I seen his face clearer than I'm seeing your own! That's what I was trying to get at, Patsy! That 'Ould Wan' was right after all!

LORETTA: *(Gently, stroking her wrist)* Aah, Ma, Ma, you're talking "ragtime."

GRANDMA: *(Pulling her hand away)* The 'Ould Wan' was right! And here I was thinking all along it was only a crazy old notion she had. Well, today I seen the ghost myself. I seen the bare wood boards of the tenement floor! And I seen the way it was when we said goodbye! I seen the pride and joy and the beauty we had! I seen him right here—today! *(Passionately)* And it means it's not done with *yet*—or I wouldn't be seeing him still!

LORETTA: *(Stroking her wrist, soothing)* Now Ma—Ma, go easy. Go easy now.

GRANDMA: Life don't quit once it gets started! That's what that 'Ould Wan' meant all along! It only walks West and waits for you to catch up! *(With a sudden joyous laugh)* No—this is a good day, Good Friday. I can look West out the window and see clear to the other side. So you pour me another two fingers, Patsy.

LORETTA: *(Quietly, to Patsy)* You leave that right there, Patsy.

GRANDMA: That's right. That's right. You listen to Loretta, Patsy. Listen to her good. It seems I always get the faintest quiver of fear in her voice. Her and Joseph both. You listen to them long enough you'll be sounding the same way yourself.

LORETTA: *(Breaking contact)* All right—now I've had just about enough!

GRANDMA: *(Quietly, with a deep sense of anguish)* Oh, Loretta, I'm sorry what I done to you.

LORETTA: *(No longer listening)* Go ahead, Patsy. And tell your father to be down here quarter of eight. I'm not going to be locked up in prison all night.

GRANDMA: It's just that I didn't know no other way. *(Patsy starts out)* No, Patsy, wait—give me two fingers before you go. Like my own good girl.

(Patsy hesitates, then moves towards the bottle. Loretta snatches it up and stands between her and Grandma's chair)

LORETTA: Don't you dare!

GRANDMA: Well, then you better come kiss me goodbye, Patsy.

LORETTA: *(Holding her ground between the two)* Never mind—

never mind. Your supper must be getting cold. *(Patsy hesitates)* Do what I tell you now!

(Suddenly Patsy breaks past Loretta and rushes to Grandma. Taking her face in her hands she kisses her once and then once again. For a moment she studies her Grandmother's face as if it is a fine work of art and she is seeing it for the first time)

PATSY: *(Softly)* Goodbye, Grandma.

GRANDMA: Goodbye Patsy. *(Patsy rushes past Loretta and exits out the back door)* Loretta's right. It's getting late in the day. *(Looking out the window)* Oh, look at that, will you now? It's stopped raining and the sky is beginning to break. We'll have a fine full moon tonight, that's certain. Well, I'm ready for it—I'm ready for it now. And listen to the robins, will you? They tell you when it's gonna rain and they tell you when it's gonna stop. *(Looking up at Loretta)* And every afternoon at four o'clock Loretta comes home and turns on the lights. *(There is a note of sadness in her soft laugh)* Oh, Loretta, if you could only have seen . . . *(She moves her hands as if she is searching for the words. But there are none. She shakes her head wistfully)* I'm younger than all of you by sixty years.

(Loretta moves to the standing lamp and places her hand on the switch)

LORETTA: Watch your eyes, Ma.

Blackout

Jonathan Reynolds

RUBBERS

and

YANKS 3 DETROIT 0 TOP OF THE SEVENTH

Jonathan Reynolds

Since Jonathan Reynolds' double bill of *Rubbers* and *Yanks 3 Detroit 0 Top of the Seventh* was an outstanding success of the 1975 Off-Broadway season, this editor has chosen to include both plays in this volume. When it opened at the prestigious American Place Theatre in New York, it was acclaimed both by reviewers and audiences and for the very first time in its long and prodigious history, the American Place suspended its subscription-only policy and swung open its box office for the sale of tickets to the public on a regular basis.

Even the generally caustic John Simon recounted in his *New York Magazine* coverage how he almost parted company with his theatre seat because of his continued and unabashed hilarity: "*Rubbers* and *Yanks 3 Detroit 0 Top of the Seventh* is the funniest double- (or single-) header of the season, bar none. Certainly, the first item, *Rubbers,* made me laugh more than anything all year. I had to abandon my usual dignified inner laughter and primly seated posture for fallings out of my seat accompanied by unseemly hollers and howls."

His fellow journalistic aisle-sitters concurred. Jack Kroll of *Newsweek* declared: "The American Place Theatre has come up with something really important—a very, very funny new playwright. Jonathan Reynolds' double bill is by far the funniest event of the season. During *Rubbers,* which takes place in the Assembly Chamber of the New York State Legislature, I didn't stop laughing from start to finish.

"Reynolds has the healthiest irreverence I've seen on a stage in years. *Rubbers* concerns a typical day of lawmaking among his inanely insane solons. The pivotal event is a Marx Brothers donnybrook over a bill to allow the public display of contraceptives in drugstores . . . This lunatic debate rises to an unhinged climax of sexo-political dementia."

Marilyn Stasio reported in *Cue* magazine: "Is any laughter more satisfying than the tart laughter of satire? Come and get it now, from a terrifically talented new writer named Jonathan Reynolds. His two one-act satirical comedies are full of spicy laughter and rich with the social comment that makes such laughter meaningful. *Rubbers* is a devastating comic rip-up of the New York State Legislative Assembly. Actress Laura Esterman suffers gorgeously as a Brooklyn Assemblyperson fighting for a mildly liberal bill regulating the display of contraceptives. Against her is pitted a hilarious sideshow of dumb, self-serving, incompetent, prejudiced, provincial colleagues.

"*Yanks 3 Detroit 0* employs the same style to satirize the big-business nature of major-league ball, and the small-business character of a Yankee pitcher who has an anxiety attack on the mound . . . It is full of sidesplitting moments, as the paranoid pitcher, played to perfection by Tony Lo Bianco, sees his big-time ambitions ("the razor-blade league") slipping away beneath his spikes.

"Under Alan Arkin's direction an excellent cast romps through playing field and Assembly Chamber as if to the idiocy born. Jonathan Reynolds and the APT have hit a Grand Slammer."

The author studied at Denison University, the Eagles Mere Playhouse in Pennsylvania, and at the London Academy of Dramatic Art. And according to the production's program notes: "He has been an actor, a director, a farmer, a travel writer for the *Times,* a dishwasher, and a gummer for the *Associated Press*."

In addition to his work for the theatre, Mr. Reynolds has written several screenplays, one of which is entitled *A Moderately Amusing Scandinavian.*

RUBBERS

Characters:

MRS. MARJORIE BRIMMINS, *38 years old, Democrat from Brooklyn. She wears horn-rimmed glasses, a suit, and her hair pulled back.*

MR. WILLIE CLEGG, *45-50, fat, and sloppy with thinning hair. He is Irish, the Republican Majority Leader from Queens.*

MR. VIC DAMIANO, *35-40, very slick dresser, but nothing matches except his white patent leather belt and shoes. His hair is oily, he is heavily on the take from everybody. He has a hoarse, show-biz laugh, and wears rings. Republican.*

MR . LARRY PARD, *The oldest man in the world. A Democrat who was an aide to FDR, or so he says.*

MR. DICK BAPP, *35-40, short, stocky, with a crew cut. He wears shortsleeved shirts, a tie pin and always has lots of pencils in his pocket. An upstate Republican.*

MR. PAULIE VLITSIAK, *About 50 with handsomely greying hair. Very dull, but not slow. A Republican from the western part of the state.*

MR. AUGIE TOMATO, *35-40. A Republican.*

MR. VALERIE TOWNSEND, *About 40, a handsome black man who wears a three-piece, pin-striped suit, a watch chain, and a carnation. A Democrat.*

DICK BLEAK, *65-70, crusty-looking, dressed in a green uniform, possibly wears a hat.*

ACTING SPEAKER, *45-55, a Republican who is moderate, dull-witted, and obeys orders.*

SPEAKER, *50-60, a beautiful voice, large hands, a stunning shock of silver or white hair. He looks like Warren Burger and wears flowing black judicial robes.*

CLERK, *No specific age or type. Same for PAGES. Both may be women.*

Scene:

The lights come up on a scrim on which is depicted the New York State Capitol Building in Albany. All is quiet for a moment. Then the lights bleed through, revealing the Assembly Chamber, a handsome neo-Gothic room.

The Acting Speaker of the Assembly sits behind an elevated, wooden desk up center, surrounded by Officers and a Clerk on a lower level.

The other desks fan out below him on the floor level, Republicans to his left, Democrats to his right. Mrs. Brimmins sits downstage just right of center; Clegg is across from her just left of center; Mr. Damiano, Mr. Vlitsiak, Mr. Bapp, and Mr. Tomato all sit up left of Mr. Stimola. Mr. Pard sits up center of Mrs. Brimmins; Mr. Townsend sits up right of her. Other chairs are filled with very lifelike dummies.

Above and around the Chamber—but never seen—is the Visitors Gallery.

The floor itself is filled with constant motion —Legislators popping up and down to speak, visiting with each other, coming and going; the Pages, too, exit and enter frequently. The background is never quiet.

Each Legislator stands whenever he talks and speaks through a microphone attached to a box in his desk by a coiled wire long enough to allow two or three steps movement in each direction. The volume of the mikes is the same as the volume of each speaker's normal voice — the mikes are not used for loudness but for vocal quality.

As the lights come up, there is a loud grumbling from everyone.

MR. DAMIANO: On the bill, Mr. Speaker.

ACTING SPEAKER: On the bill, Mr. Damiano.

MR. DAMIANO: . . . Ladies and gentlemen, in conjunction with my wildlife legislation, I would like to illustrate the desperate need my constituents up in beautiful Schroon River feel for a bounty on the rattlesnakes that are biting them so recklessly by introducing Mr. Dick Bleak, the reptile executive of the Nosewater Game Preserve, who has something scary named Bridget the Rattler to show you—

(Dick Bleak enters carrying a reptile case marked with a skull and crossbones)

MR. CLEGG: Wait a minute, Vic, you got a snake in there? You can't do that, this is the New York State Assembly, we're not in Georgia, ya know.

MR. DAMIANO: C'mon, Willie, I brought this snake all the way down here, I put her up in a hotel for two days, I had to buy her a mouse to eat — it's for my bill.

MR. CLEGG: All right, but make it snappy!

MR. VLITSIAK: Has he got a snake in there?

MR. DAMIANO: Presenting: Bridget the Rattler!

(Dick Bleak produces the snake. Everyone reacts unhappily)

How'd you like that to bite through your boots, Mrs. Brimmins! How'd you like little children and babies torn to pieces by that oily creeper!

MR. BAPP: Look at those fangs! They'd cut through bone!

MR. TOWNSEND: Look at those fangs? Look at that face!

MR. TOMATO: Atlantic Ocean!

MRS. BRIMMINS: Mr. Speaker! Mr. Speaker!

ACTING SPEAKER: *(Banging gavel)* Just a moment, Mrs. Brimmins, everybody'll get a chance. This is your state government in action. Let's settle down now, settle on down.

(The noise gradually subsides)

MR. TOWNSEND: Mr. Speaker!

ACTING SPEAKER: Mr. Townsend!

MR. TOWNSEND: How on God's green earth does Mr. Damiano think he has the right to bring a deadly poisonous, furiously writhing timber rattler from the Schroon River area into this hallowed chamber, its body held and fumbled by a gamekeeper clearly inept at snake handling!

MR. DAMIANO: Dick Bleak is head of the snake pit at Nosewater! The finest gamekeeping snake handler in or out of my district, and I apologize to no man for his presence!

MR. TOWNSEND: Some of us have children at home, homes themselves, outside concerns that depend on us for guidance! How could you! And how do we know now that your so-called snake handling gamekeeper will be able to control Bridget the Rattler? What about the visiting school-children in the halls! They're wearing shorts!

MR. BAPP: What on God's green earth was the purpose of bringing Bridget the Rattler in here in the first place, Mr. Damiano!

MR. DAMIANO: Audio-visual, audio-visual! Children up in beautiful Essex County are being snakebitten by Bridget the Rattler and her friends, and there's gotta be a bounty on them!

MR. TOWNSEND: Couldn't you have gotten that across without terrifying all the people in this room?

MRS. BRIMMINS: Never mind terrifying the people—what about the snake!

MR. CLEGG: Oh, please.

MRS. BRIMMINS: It was the height of inhumanity to bring Bridget the Rattler in here, Damiano! I cannot bear to see a frightened, defenseless creature, particularly a female, tortured and plied thusly for purely political reasons!

MR. CLEGG: Hey, whatta ya talkin' about, whatta ya talkin' about—it's a snake! He'll bite ya and kill ya! I know according to *The New York Times* compassion is supposed to be your middle name, Mrs. Brimmins —

MRS. BRIMMINS: For whom do I have insufficient compassion in your view, Mr. Clegg?

MR. CLEGG: Victims of violent crimes insteada their perpetrators, that's who for one thing.

MRS. BRIMMINS: Can I believe I once went to bed with this man for five months?

ACTING SPEAKER: Mr. Clegg, Mrs. Brimmins . . .

MRS. BRIMMINS: Children starving in India, 8 to 10% unemployment . . .!

MR. CLEGG: Not now, Marge.

MR. PARD: Snakes frightened Melissa once.

(There is a pause. Everyone freezes and listens to this old sage)

MR. CLEGG: Who's Melissa?

MR. PARD: One of my hundreds and hundreds of grandchildren. Little girl blondie wears taffeta sometimes . . . Looks so cute when she eats a burger. Well sir, some kind of a snake or a duck come over and just frightened her all up. So I say kill the buggerer!

ACTING SPEAKER: Thank you, Mr. Pard, as always.

MRS. BRIMMINS: What I'm looking forward to is 6843-D—*my* bill.

MR. DAMIANO: Mr. Speaker, I have a great and sincere caring for all of God's living things—

MRS. BRIMMINS: Who are you fronting for, Damiano, who's slipping you the greenbacks on this one! You don't care about Essex County snakebite! Who it is, Damiano!

MR. DAMIANO: Listen to this, listen to this! I don't have to pay attention to bilge and garbage from a toxic Brooklyn shrew! You're here on charity, little lady, and don't you forget it. Victory by plurality is charity, Mrs. Brimmins, if that really is your name!

MRS. BRIMMINS: He's hiding something, Mr. Speaker, putting up the old Nixonian offense as the world's most transparent defense—trying to distract our attention from Nam, as it were, with the trip to China!

ACTING SPEAKER: Mrs. Brimmins, you are out of order.

MR. DAMIANO: Pluralities are for sissies, lady, and dried-up brown bags!

ACTING SPEAKER: Mr. Townsend.

MR. TOWNSEND: Mr. Speaker, either this body should institute a limited bounty on timber rattlers, or it should not. We have much work to get to in the morning of this long winter light and I suggest we call for a vote and move onward.

MRS. BRIMMINS: At last, the voice of reason.

MR. CLEGG: *(Disparagingly)* Reason, reason.

ACTING SPEAKER: Mr. Vlitsiak.

MR. VLITSIAK: Mr. Speaker, I would like to call your attention to the arrival of Joe Paella and his little league football team, the

Paella Marvels who have just entered the gallery above. The Paella
Marvels have compiled an admirable 8-and-1 record last year behind the standout quarterbacking of Pieter Carvalho, the 13-year-
old Dutch whiz. Would you kindly extend the usual greetings?

ACTING SPEAKER: On behalf of the Speaker of this Assembly
who is otherwise engaged, I, the Acting Speaker, cordially extend
a warm state welcome to Mr. Paella, the Paella Marvels, and
Dutchman Pete Carvalho, whom we have all heard so much about.
We hope they enjoy the deliberations.
(The Assembly applauds)
MR. DAMIANO: I now move the bill.
MRS. BRIMMINS: I demand a slow roll call.
ACTING SPEAKER: Willie?
MR. CLEGG: No.
ACTING SPEAKER: Request for a slow roll call is denied.
MRS. BRIMMINS: It's always turned down. But I can't let up;
someone has to keep these moral surrealists clipped and shorn.
MR. DAMIANO: I could really use this bill, Willie.
MR. CLEGG: It ain't gonna come back to embarrass me, is it, Vic?
MR. DAMIANO: Oh, no! On my mother's fingers, Willie—it's for a
friend of mine in the cement business. It's legit.
(Willie nods, waves his finger almost unnoticeably)
ACTING SPEAKER: Mr. Clegg.
MR. CLEGG: Mr. Speaker, after a thoughtful perusal of Mr.
Damiano's bill, it is my firm conviction that this legislation would
enormously benefit the people of this great state as well as the good
people of Schroon River, and I am proud to endorse its passage. As
is customary, of course, each member is free to vote his own convic-
tions.
MRS. BRIMMINS: Free to vote his own convictions; in the first
place, no one in this room is free, and second, no one in this room
has any convictions.
ACTING SPEAKER: Read the last section.
CLERK: This act shall take effect immediately.
ACTING SPEAKER: The clerk will call the roll.
CLERK: Aabey, Gwathmey, Dallenbach, Zyzzeroso.
ACTING SPEAKER: The bill is passed.
MR. DAMIANO: *(Giving him a wrapped present of some hot jewelry)*
Thank you, Willie. From the bottom of my heart.
MR. CLEGG: Anytime, Vic, but dispense with the soipents, from
now on, huh?
ACTING SPEAKER: Calendar of the day. The clerk will read.
MR. CLEGG: Joey . . . get me a container of cottage cheese and
some prunes, will you? I don't know what's going on here.

CLERK: Assembly Number 10501, Mr. Tomato. An act to amend the alcoholic beverage law allowing beer wholesalers to also merchandise syrup-based soda pop.

MRS. BRIMMINS: Syrup-based soda pop. I came up here to argue in the Socratic-Platonic tradition, to ease suffering in cold water flats, and syrup-based soda pop is my just desserts. I demand a slow roll call.

ACTING SPEAKER: Willie?

MR. CLEGG: Nope.

ACTING SPEAKER: Request denied.

MRS. BRIMMINS: Every day, questions of syrup-based soda pop. Oh, I cared about the Bridget the Rattler bill—I'm a humanitarian after all. In fact, if I had to be categorized, I'm sure everyone here would concede with opens arms that I'm a professional, militant liberal—with discerning, unflinching stances on all issues of the day. I was, of course, against the war, that goes without saying; I brought local opposition to its uncaring knees during the lettuce strike; I was one of the first to call blacks blacks, even when most of them were still insulted by it.

MR. TOMATO: *(Approaching Mr. Clegg)* I hate to ask you, Willie . . .

MR. CLEGG: Don't be shy, Augie, I'm very accessible. Who's it for?

MR. TOMATO: My step-nephew. He's in the brewery business and he's very unhappy with his lot. It'd mean so much to the family.

(Willie waves his finger again)

ACTING SPEAKER: Mr. Clegg.

MR. CLEGG: Mr. Speaker, after a thoughtful perusal of Mr. Tomato's bill, it is my firm conviction that this legislation would enormously benefit the people of this great state as well as the good people of Mr. Tomato's constituency, and I am proud to endorse its passage. As is customary, of course, each member is free to vote his own convictions.

ACTING SPEAKER: Read the last section.

CLERK: This act shall take effect immediately.

ACTING SPEAKER: The clerk will call the roll.

CLERK: Aabey, Gwathmey, Dallenbach, Zyzzeroso.

ACTING SPEAKER: The bill is passed.

MRS. BRIMMINS: All he has to do is wave that index finger, and the bill is passed; I can't even get the floor.

MR. TOMATO: God love you and yours, Willie.

MR. CLEGG: How's Joleen?

MR. TOMATO: Fine, Willie, fine. She asks after you every day.

MR. CLEGG: Give her my hellos.

MR. TOMATO: Oh, I sure will, Willie.

MRS. BRIMMINS: That fat, balding Republican over there with the stranglehold on all who enter is the one who I earlier intimated lay with me for five months two years ago. He confuses me lately. I think he hates me, but I can't be sure. In a way I hope he does—it can be kind of exciting when someone hates you. I thought he would tie me to the four corners of the room and lasciviate me like a 220-pound flesh jockey, my truckdriver fantasy. But he never did. He's an ex-cop, and he can be so mean and thrilling in here—he broke one Assemblyman's knuckles over the milk dispute last year—but at home he just never came alive. Shame is what drives most men away, and he was out the door from the very first.

MR. BAPP: Willie, could I ask a favor? I know you don't like me particularly, but—

MR. CLEGG: In a minute, Dick, when your bill comes up. And cut out this "don't like me" stuff. You're one of my all time greats.

(He squeezes Mr. Bapp's neck hard in a friendly gesture)

ACTING SPEAKER: Calendar of the day. The clerk will read.

CLERK: Bill 6843-D, Calendar number 660, Mrs. Brimmins.

MRS. BRIMMINS: At last! My bill. The fearful slumber hath an end. The giant awakes.

CLERK: An act to amend the education law in relation to the display of—yicchh—contraceptives in pharmacies.

MR. CLEGG: Oh, no, not this again.

(There is general angry consternation)

MR. DAMIANO: On the bill, Mr. Speaker

ACTING SPEAKER: On the bill, Mr. Damiano.

MR. DAMIANO: Mr. Speaker, this bill has been introduced four times in the last three weeks! Surely we don't have to suffer another one of these schoolteaching, moralistic explanations — particularly from a woman who's up here only on a plurality. I have an extremely important license plate bill to get to, Mr. Speaker . . .

MRS. BRIMMINS: This is the purpose of my bill. The law currently states that a pharmacist must keep all prescription and non-prescription contraceptive items hidden behind his counter and that customers must ask often-embarrassing and inhibiting questions just to see them, let alone buy them. My bill changes that to allow non-prescription contraceptives and their advertising literature to be displayed *openly*—so customers may examine their prices and ingredients comparatively, just as they do now with toothpaste and shampoo. This is all the bill intends — nothing subversive. As for the number of times this bill has been brought to the floor—

MR. DAMIANO: Uh-oh, here comes the moral—I can see the glint from here—

MRS. BRIMMINS: Such continual amendment wouldn't be necessary, Mr. Damiano, if it weren't for the repressive, Nineteenth Century blindness of my tightly corseted opponents, most of whom, I might add, voted for restoration of the death penalty with glazed eyes bordering on the sexual . . .

MR. CLEGG: All right, all right . . .

MR. PARD: No advertising in the window this time, is there?

MRS. BRIMMINS: No advertising in the window, Mr. Pard.

MR. PARD: You know what this legislature thinks of making sport of natural bodily functions, don't you?

MRS. BRIMMINS: I was made painfully aware of that last week, Mr. Pard.

MR. PARD: *(Furiously)* Good. Stool is not funny, lady.

MRS. BRIMMINS: Mr. Speaker, this is an important, humanitarian bill. It may help prevent a few unwanted pregnancies, stop even a fraction of venereal disease. Not like Damiano's self-serving, back-scratching Bridget the Rattler bill.

MR. DAMIANO: Watch it, lady, I'm a lawyer.

MRS. BRIMMINS: A lawyer!

MR. DAMIANO: I am!

MRS. BRIMMINS: If it wasn't for no-fault you'd still be chasing ambulances, you sleaze.

MR. DAMIANO: Listen to this! Listen to this!

MRS. BRIMMINS: You couldn't stop no-fault, no matter who you bribed, could you? Marrying the Speaker's daughter didn't help you on that one, did it? So now he's Mr. Medical Malpractice Suit, driving all our doctors into Pennsylvania. Ho, I'd never even *listen* to a bribe from you!

MR. DAMIANO: Who'd ever offer you one? Pluralities don't get offered bribes, lady, pluralities just fill up a chair.

MR. CLEGG: All right, all right, Mrs. Brimmins, Mr. Damiano, let's just try to stick to the contraceptive bill, okay? *The New York Times*'ll be keenly disappointed if you keep wandering around like that.

MRS. BRIMMINS: This plurality business will drive me screaming into the cold. Is it my fault I come from the most conservative district in Brooklyn and possibly the world? My fault two Viet vets split the vote and I sailed through the middle—not once but twice?

MR. DAMIANO: What about my license plates bill, Willie! Tell her to hurry up.

MRS. BRIMMINS: Your license plates bill—You know what that is? His daughter's name is Gussie Ogilvie Damiano, her initials boil down to G-O-D, God, and G-O-D, God, isn't allowed on license plates in New York State, so he wants to pass a law—A LAW!—allowing the initials G-O-D, God, on license plates in New York State. Over my livid body!

MR. VLITSIAK: Oh, come on, it's for his daughter—we're allowed to do that up here. I think it's kind of sweet.

MR. CLEGG: Will you get back to the contraceptive bill, Marge!

MRS. BRIMMINS: Open display of contraceptives and their advertising literature. Period.

MR. PARD: You mean according to this bill little children can sell these things?

MRS. BRIMMINS: No, Mr. Pard, little children can't sell these things—no one who isn't at least sixteen and who doesn't have working papers can be employed in a pharmacy in the first place.

MR. PARD: Haw, kids can get around *that*.

MRS. BRIMMINS: Mr. Pard, I doubt seriously boys and girls under sixteen are going to lie about their ages and forge working papers just to be in close proximity to boxes of contraceptives.

MR. PARD: Then you don't know kids—which you don't, by the way. Cross—eyed Sephardic!

MRS. BRIMMINS: Mr. Speaker . . .

MR. PARD: She don't know kids. *I* know kids. I'm the oldest man in the world! Goodtime Larry Pard! Chairman of Ways and Means, a hammerlock on the Rules Committee, for years before that a harsh and unbending judge! The very best friend Franklin Eleanor Roosevelt ever had!

MRS. BRIMMINS: On the bill, Mr. Speaker.

MR. VLITSIAK: Mr. Speaker.

MR. DAMIANO: C'mon, Willie, I got my license plates to get to!

ACTING SPEAKER: Mr. Vlitsiak.

MR. VLITSIAK: Mr. Speaker, I would like to introduce several of my constituents who have just arrived here to watch these proceedings—the Nina Rohan Five, a singing group of elderly widows from Conewango Valley over in beautiful Cattaraugus County, and the Douzy Saints Gang, a rehabilitated street mob gradually integrating into the wonderful community of Skaneateles in the great county of Onondaga. They are here with their faculty adviser, Monseigneur Honest Nick O'Cake.

ACTING SPEAKER: On behalf of the Speaker of this Assembly who is otherwise engaged, I as Acting Speaker welcome The Nina Rohan Five, The Douzy Saints Gang and Monseigneur Honest Nick O'Cake to this hallowed chamber and hope you will all enjoy the deliberations, so help me God.

MRS. BRIMMINS: My childhood wasn't easy. Only Jewess of a middle-class Central Park West family, I was forced into a life of competitive and aggressive art early on—mastering the flute, failing terribly with the cello, a puberty jam-crammed with the Brontës and Virginia Woolf. Music and Art, Radcliffe, nominee for a Woodrow Wilson, honors at Harvard Law. Politics I learned in the hot and salty crucible of '68 — '68, when protest was an art form!

MR. PARD: I hate her!

MR. CLEGG: Easy, Mr. Pard.

MRS. BRIMMINS: Children starving in India! Rising cost of the defense budget!

MR. CLEGG: Mr. Speaker, will Mrs. Brimmins yield for a question?

ACTING SPEAKER: Will you yield for a question, Mrs. Brimmins?

MRS. BRIMMINS: Yes! If it's relevant to my contraceptive bill, Mr. Speaker.

MR. CLEGG: If it's relevant to your contraceptive bill, eh? Always the little barb, always the little eye gouge. Well, you're gonna see some blood flow like wine in a minute. Here's the question, Mrs. Brimmins, and it's relevant all right: You finished?

MRS. BRIMMINS: Yes.

MR. CLEGG: Good. I'm sick of this bill. Let's get this debate movin', Terry. *Him* first.

ACTING SPEAKER: Right. Mr. Tomato.

MR. TOMATO: Thank you, Mr. Speaker. I have mail from all over the state on this bill, Mr. Speaker. The people are aroused, and I don't mean maybe. I have letters from Schaghticoke, Schenevus, and Schodack Landing; Sagaponack, Oriskany Falls, and Kenoza Lake. I have mail from Sodus and Shandaken, even some from Scipio Center in the great county of Cayuga. Everyone—concerned mothers in Felts Mills, common laborers in East Pharsalia, two shut-ins from Cropseyville; good Lord, even the people of Claverack just down in Columbia County sent mail—and Claverack doesn't really write as a rule. Pifford; Nedrow; Hoosick Falls six letters. I have a small *drawerful* from Beemus Point! I don't think you're all aware how much commotion this woman's bill has stirred up. Ho, they're dancin' mad over in Arkport, furious in Bible School Park, drained of all hope in Blodget Mills. That ain't all, Mr. Speaker—oh, no, you bet your socks. It just doesn't stop—I got mail from the likes of Sparrow Bush, Tupper Lake, Waccabuc, Wappingers Falls, and West Coxsackie. Even Chenango Forks in the usually happy county of Broome.

And you know something? Every piece of mail except one from a family named Wormser in Ballston Spa urged me to vote against this wretched bill. Some even threatened my family with physical violence if I didn't. The people in this state are stirred up by this bill, Mr. Speaker, up to the throat. I tell you, once you get outta your big cities—particularly that one Big City down there which I don't need to mention by name, everybody knows what I'm talkin' about—once you get outta there, I'm proud to say this state's filled with decent, God-striving families who decry hookers on every corner and one-on-one skin flicks where they're always showin' penetration. Down to a man—'cept for this one Wormser family in Ballston Spa—everybody I've heard from believes open display of rubbers—for that's all they are, rubbers! rubbers!—and their advertising'll lead to more and more porn and more porn and more and more porn more. No sir, I'd never vote for this bill, hand on the Bible! I thank you.

(He sits to applause. The Page delivers Mr. Clegg's lunch)

MR. CLEGG: Thanks, Joey. That was quick.

MRS. BRIMMINS: I can answer that, and with celerity.

ACTING SPEAKER: Mr. Vlitsiak.

MR. VLITSIAK: What about little children, Mrs. Brimmins—what if these things become popular with little children, Mrs. Brimmins? Start catchin' on in stores, establishin' themselves in kiddie buying habbits, becomin' fads like Pez machines and Silly Putty, Mrs. Brimmins? What if kids start tradin' 'em like ball cards, flashin' 'em around near urinals, wearin' 'em in their lapels—

MR. PARD: Blowin' 'em up in public places!

MR. VLITSIAK: Blowin' 'em up in public places, Mrs. Brimmins, thank you, Mr. Pard. Ladies and gentlemen, this mass of brazen wants to destroy our children with this bill, to make public jokes of their private parts, to force aimless, wandering permissiveness on them though they clearly long for heavy and corrective spanking. You boys know what I've always said: if the Lord above had wanted a permissive society, he would have given Moses ten suggestions, not ten commandments. I ask you. And what of those poor little kids who will choose *not* to play with rubbers, Mrs. Brimmins? Do you know how venomous and rat-like little children can be, Mrs. Brimmins? "Aram doesn't want to play with rubbers! Dooley's afray-ayd! Let's make everyone hate them!" Lord, this is a disgusting, dirty bill. For remember: every freedom of is a freedom from. I wouldn't vote for this bill if you attached an anti-abortion amendment and reneged on open housing. Not now, not later, not never!

(He sits down to thunderous applause)

MR. BAPP: Vote it down!

MR. TOMATO: Clear the floor!

MR. DAMIANO: Go home and polish the silver!

MRS. BRIMMINS: Willie, I want to talk.

MR. CLEGG: Sure. Hold it, Terry.

(They huddle downstage center. A pool table wheels on. Mr. Clegg plays)

MR. CLEGG: Shoot.

MRS. BRIMMINS: Is this sort of argument going to continue for the life of the debate, Willie?

MR. CLEGG: I don't know what's on their minds, Marge.

MRS. BRIMMINS: Oh, yes, you do. Mr. Majority Leader, you put them up to all this. Whose knuckles did you have to break this time?

MR. CLEGG: Ball in the pocket with my own brand of English.

MRS. BRIMMINS: But why not, Willie? It's a good bill, a decent bill. Even the pharmacists are in favor of it. You know how much work I've put into it, Willie—three months of research, hundreds of interviews, endless midnight committee meetings with the likes of Goodtime Larry Pard—

MR. CLEGG: Yeah, but in all that time you never changed one provision of that bill, Marge, not one provision, not one paragraph.

MRS. BRIMMINS: Of course I haven't! This bill shouldn't be changed one comma!

MR. CLEGG: Know what your problem is, Marge? You got no political savvy. On every issue you always get all your As, Bs, and Cs in the right order, all your ones, twos and threes, but you know something? In the three years you been up here you ain't once changed one person's mind about anything. You gotta bend up here, Marge, you gotta flex. You shoulda learned that with all your *summa cum laude* Phi Beta Kappa.

MRS. BRIMMINS: I am not up here for bending and flexing! I'm up here because I believe in things!

MR. CLEGG: That's it, bring out the sanctimony. That ball in that pocket with my own brand of English. Look, Marge, your bill ain't a bad bill. In fact it's a pretty good bill—I'd probly vote for it myself if I was my own man. But you know who runs things in here—the Speaker. And the Speaker says bury it. So I'm buryin' it. Period. End of caucus.

MRS. BRIMMINS: Oh, yes, the silver-haired, golden-tongued Speaker we never see, the Byzantine, celestial Speaker who's always off in the halls somewhere making deals! Why is he never here?

MR. CLEGG: The Speaker is a very busy man, Marge. He comes when he's needed. You shouldn't get so emotionally involved with these things.

MRS. BRIMMINS: I get emotionally involved with everything I do,

Willie Clegg. You know that! Have you forgotten 1900 and 68 so soon?

MR. CLEGG: Yeah, yeah, everybody knows about you and 1900 and 68, Marge, but those traitors you played around with in '68 ain't been seen too much lately.

MRS. BRIMMINS: Do you know what the happiest day of my life was, Willie?

MR. CLEGG: Of course I do, Marge. When you and that dike named Heather exposed the capitalist system for the sham it really is by dropping those hundred one-dollar bills on the floor of the New York Stock Exchange and causing all the brokers to panic for twenty entire seconds. You only told me that twice a day for five months.

MRS. BRIMMINS: Heather was not a dike, Willie! She was a saint! She had a stridency that was the envy of us all, ideals that cut through fog like a laser.

MR. CLEGG: Lest we forget, Marge, ya mind tellin' me once more what it was became of Miss Heather with the ideals that cut through fog like a laser?

MRS. BRIMMINS: Oh, she moved out west . . .

MR. CLEGG: And what does she do for a living, this wonderful woman who dropped the hundred one-dollar bills on the floor of the New York Stock Exchange?

MRS. BRIMMINS: You know what she does, Willie! She works for a Hollywood game show.

MR. CLEGG: She works for a Hollywood game show. So much for 1900 and 68. *I* know what the happiest day of *your* life was, Marge, now let me ask you somethin': what was the happiest day of *my* life? *(A pause)* You don't know, do you? That was what our relationship was all about.

MRS. BRIMMINS: Who cares about the happiest day of your life, Willie! The people need this bill—!

MR. CLEGG: Want me to be frank with you, Marge?

(He feels her rear end)

MRS. BRIMMINS: You get your dampened hands off me, Willie Clegg—I'm not one of your fifteen-dollar Hoboken tootsies!

MR. CLEGG: You got a real bad mouth on you, ya know that, Marge? I can get angry at you just sittin' around watchin' television. Everybody up here feels that way—you make us furious just sittin' around! Just like the first day you came up here, somebody whistled at you—

MRS. BRIMMINS: Damiano!

MR. CLEGG: —and you turned on him with your eyes all crazy and hollered "I will not be whistled at! I am an Assemblyperson!"

MRS. BRIMMINS: I will not be whistled at! I *am* an Assemblyperson! What's the matter with that?

MR. CLEGG: Bad legislative style, Marge. Ball over there, this time with Swedish.

MRS. BRIMMINS: Bad legislative style!—I suppose yours is good legislative style? Pouring dark beer over your head on New Year's, sleeping with a gun under your pillow, and cowering in front of a mysterious Speaker who's never here—that's good legislative style? You're just his patsy, Willie Clegg, his spineless, quivering patsy!

MR. CLEGG: I am the Speaker's man! I have more raw power than any man in this Chamber! I control every man on my side of the aisle like a martinet and damn near everybody on yours! And those I can't handle with my jaws, I treat like pool cues! *(He smashes the pool cue into bits, possibly over his head)* If you was a man, which you may well be despite my experience, I'd make *you* into a pool cue! Now, you wanna know the real reason you ain't gonna get your bill through?

MRS. BRIMMINS: *(Thrilled at his display)* How come you were never like that at home.

MR. CLEGG: *(Furious; in one breath)* I ain't gonna vote for your bill 'cause the Speaker, wherever he is, wants it killed once and for all and even though I'd probly vote for it if I was my own man 'cause it ain't such a bad bill, ya know why I couldn't use my considerable influence and occasional violence to get anyone else to vote for your bill? *(Another breath)* 'CAUSE EVERYBODY HATES YOU, THAT'S WHY!

MRS. BRIMMINS: *(After a pause)*
Oh, they don't hate me, Willie. They don't understand me, true —I'm not the usual politician. I'm consistently right on the issues. I'm supported by *The New York Times,* which infuriates everyone. I'm an idealist, a pragmatic realist—

MR. CLEGG: You know what ya ain't, though, Mrs. Brimmins? You ain't married.

MRS. BRIMMINS: Who needs to be married!

MR. CLEGG: Ya wanna be a political success up here, Marge, ya gotta be married. Nobody wants to vote for somebody nobody wants. Look at Bella, look at Shirley the Chiz, look at Mary Ann Krupsack—they're all married. I don't know to what, but they're all married.

MRS. BRIMMINS: Married! I don't need to be married! No man can hold me down—you saw that! I made your life a living hell, and don't you forget it! I turned you into a waffle!

MR. CLEGG: *(Furious)*

Ya know, if you were funny, I'd start laughin', but you ain't funny, anymore, Marge!

MRS. BRIMMINS: I am too funny! I am very funny! In fact, one of my strongest electoral traits is my sense of humor.

MR. CLEGG: Oh, yeah, many's the time you'd break me up with one of your snappy one liners from the *New York Review of Books*. Whadda ya gonna do—get this bill through with jokes?

MRS. BRIMMINS: I do have some jokes, yes, now that you mention it, Willie.

MR. CLEGG: Oh yeah? This is gonna be good. Get this table outta here! Let's hear one.

(The table exits)

MRS. BRIMMINS: What, now? I'm not really prepared.

MR. CLEGG: C'mon, ya gotta try 'em out sometime.

MRS. BRIMMINS: Uh . . . well, once upon a time there was this . . .

MR. CLEGG: No, no, not to me, I'm no audience. Tell it to them. C'mon, c'mon. Mr. Speaker, the sensual version of Ralph Nader here has something to say on the bill.

ACTING SPEAKER: On the bill, Mrs. Brimmins.

MRS. BRIMMINS: Thank you, Mr. Speaker. Oh, hiya fellas, what's new? What'cha up to? Jets won Sunday, didja see that? Hey, whadda ya say! By the way, got a good joke for you, you know, just to loosen up the air a little. You know me! Well, once upon a time there was this kindly old white-haired couple who lived together in a big white house. One day they decided to adopt a pet to take the place of the children they never had. But they wanted something really special, and after weeks of looking at dogs and cats and boring tropical fish they finally found the perfect thing: a baby octopus. They took him home, gave him his own room, and, because he was such a smart baby octopus, even sent him off to school, because they loved the baby octopus and he loved them. A year passed, and it became time for the baby octopus's birthday. Naturally, the old couple wanted to get him something wonderful. And after weeks of looking they found it: a beautiful grand piano. So on the night before his birthday, when the baby octopus was asleep, they snuck the grand piano home, wrapped it up with beautiful ribbons and tags and went to bed too excited to sleep. The next morning they brought the baby octopus sleepily downstairs. He tore off the ribbons and tags gleefully, stepped back, and suddenly a large tear slowly formed in one eye. "Baby octopus, baby octopus, what's the matter?" said the woman, "Don't you like your grand piano?" "Yes," said the baby octopus, "but I thought you were going to get me something I could fuck." *(The Assemblymen are stunned. They make no reaction)* Think I'm daunted by this? I'm not daunted by this! Can't stand subtlety, can they? Makes them squirm. This room is where elephants go to die! And I don't mean just Republicans. You knew they wouldn't laugh, Willie Clegg, you little sneak, you humpy little gargoyle!

MR. CLEGG: That's all you ever do—talk, talk, talk, shake that index finger and talk!

MRS. BRIMMINS: You second-rate boss! Third-rate hack!

MR. CLEGG: I ain't no boss! I ain't no hack!

MRS. BRIMMINS: Boss boss boss! Hack hack hack!

MR. CLEGG: The bill's a dead duck and so's anything you ever touch up here again—ever, ever, ever!

MRS. BRIMMINS: No, you don't, smoke-filled boss! Oh, I know, you think you've got all the numbers, don't you—Vlitsiak and the West, Damiano the sleaze, Goodtime Larry Pard—but I'll show you! All of you! Nobody's ever seen me with my righteous indignation all a-pump!

MR. CLEGG: That's the only way anybody's ever seen you—with your righteous indignation all a-pump! You and that wagging index finger!

MRS. BRIMMINS: I'm going to the mat with this one, Willie! I'm going to mash your face in it, you skunky little weasel! See this smile? This smile can melt hearts of the purest gold!

MR. CLEGG: I won't even have to lift a finger!!!

(They return to their desks, both smoking with fury. The floor action continues as if uninterrupted)

MR. PARD: Mr. Chairman, Mr. Chairman!

ACTING SPEAKER: I'm not the Chairman, Mr. Pard, I'm the Speaker. The Acting Speaker.

MR. PARD: Oh, that's right. Forgive me, Terry, I was lost back there in the Army-McCarthy hearings. Oh, those were grand days, weren't they? Such substance. I want to go back there so much, see those guys again. And Franklin! He ran this state with a glove of iron! Better than the sanctified Herbert Lehman or the Beloved Rocky, stronger than grand old Averell, who's gone deaf now and let his eyebrows grow. *(He speaks in tongues for a moment)* Ah. Now. Hey! Hey, you, will you yield for a question?

MRS. BRIMMINS: You talking to me, Mr. Pard?

MR. PARD: Who you think I'm talking to—Harold Ickes? Lord, how I hate you woman. If you only knew. Answer me this question. Does this bill of yours mean that little children can buy these things?

MRS. BRIMMINS: No, unfortunately.

MR. PARD: Oh, you'd like little children to be able to fool with these things, wouldn't you, Madame Porno! Little children not even old enough yet to shave!

MRS. BRIMMINS: I'd like everyone to be able to buy contraceptives if they need to, Mr. Pard.

MR. PARD: Lord! Little children just buy 'em and blow 'em up anywhere they like?

MRS. BRIMMINS: Or not, Mr. Pard.

MR. PARD: Oh, the hate that's in the air! This is all such a disgrace, like not being able to control your bladder.

MRS. BRIMMINS: On the bill, Mr. Speaker.

ACTING SPEAKER: It's not your turn, Mrs. Brimmins. Mr. Bapp.

MR. BAPP: Mrs. Brimmins, do you have any idea what you're letting loose when you allow advertising free license in a pharmacy? Do you have any idea of the average ad man's mentality?

MRS. BRIMMINS: Well . . .

MR. BAPP: Well, I do, Mrs. Brimmins, because I'm in advertising myself. Oh, not one of your big Park Avenue firms down in the Big City—I had my chance with those bozos years ago, turned 'em down flat. Oh, they may have all those thousand-dollar-a-day copywriters, all those picture-windows overlooking St. Patrick's, but I've got something far more valuable than that, Mrs. Brimmins! I've got my freedom!

MRS. BRIMMINS: Mr. Bapp . . .

MR. BAPP: I'm not tied down to big corporations who won't even let you look at the Volkswagen *proofs!* They made me come back six days running, waiting in their reception rooms with a frizzy blonde temp who didn't even know where the men's john was! And me with my portfolio between my legs like a beaten dog! A *dog!* Those people, that city . . . just let them try to get their mass transit through up here, by God! I'll show them "Hold, please, he's in a meeting, can we get back to you!"

MR. PARD: The last man to say "You're welcome" in New York City died in 1925!

MRS. BRIMMINS: On the bill, Mr. Speaker.

MR. BAPP: That woman is out of order, Mr. Speaker! No long French lunches for me, no bombed in the middle of the day and having to think up golf jokes or keep up with the fashions all the time, growing moustaches one year, shavin' 'em off the next. No sir, I'm my own boss, I can wear plaid to work if I want; and whenever I want, I can just take the week off in the camper with Dodi and little Dick Junior, free, free as the breeze. Got my own company up in Au Sable Forks, oh, not a biggie, not a lotta clients, no pretentious initials either, just direct and straight: DICK BAPP ADS. That's all.

MRS. BRIMMINS: Mr. Speaker, please . . .!

MR. BAPP: You open the door to public advertising, you open the door to public smut! Before you know it, fourteen by thirty-six wallposters, three-dimensional fold-out displays, two-for-one specials on Four Exx lamb membranes, penny sales at Christmas on Trojans and contoured reservoir ends in all the colors of the TV networks. Worst of all—and I know my field—French ticklers with tiny rubber protrusions that can drive a woman or a little child hysterical with pleasure, screaming and banging on the walls . . . I know all this stuff, Willie. That woman knows it, too. She comes from the Big City.

MRS. BRIMMINS: Well, Brooklyn.

MR. BAPP: Don't you try to get applause on me! Not while I have the floor! Miss Big City where everything happens first! These Big City admen know all the tricks. Which rubbers make you look younger, which one'll get you into the country club? I mean a little innocent girl like Mr. Pard's Melissa! Entrapped in a drugstore ablaze with neon—her nightmares'd never end! I'm voting my absolute convictions on this one! I'll never change to the end!

MRS. BRIMMINS: Mr. Speaker, will the gentleman yield?

MR. BAPP: No, I will not yield.

MR. PARD: Atta boy!

MR. BAPP: But I have finished.

MRS. BRIMMINS: I'm going under, I'm suffocating.

MR. DAMIANO: That woman is out of order, Mr. Speaker!

ACTING SPEAKER: I'm afraid you're out of order, Mrs. Brimmins. Mr. Damiano.

MR. DAMIANO: Thank you, thank you, Mr. Speaker. You're very kind. It's great to be here, just great. And that's why I always say . . .*(Singing)* When . . . the . . . moon hits your eye
Like a bigga pizza pie, that's amore!
When your eyes start to shine
Like you've had too much wine, that's amore! *(He breaks himself up and laughs horribly)* Thank you . . . thank you . . . you're beautiful.

MRS. BRIMMINS: This isn't happening.

MR. DAMIANO: Ha ha ha! Ladies and gentlemen, it was so cold today—how cold was it, Vic? It was so cold today, Ed, that the drunks on the Bowery were actually lighting their Sterno instead of drinking it! Now that's cold! Ha ha ha! May the clangbird of paradise put camel chips in your fruit loops!

MR. CLEGG: Let's get goin', Damiano.

ACTING SPEAKER: On the bill, Mr. Damiano.

MR. DAMIANO: Right, ha, ha, right! The tears came to my eyes. Whew. Uh, as you know, I've given this legislation a great deal of thought, and I think we're wasting valuable time with all this palaver. The good little people who are my constituents don't really need any more info about contraceiving in their pharmacies. They won't read it if it's there, they won't like it if they do read it, and on the off-chance they do read it and they do like it, they won't listen. Look to me now, I know—reading about rubbers just gets people mad. And that's why I always say . . .
(Singing) Lady of Spain, I adore you
Right from the night I first saw you;
My heart has been yearning for you;
Lady of Spain, I love you!
Ha ha ha. You're too kind. But let's get down to the real reasons for this bill, shall we? Mrs. Brimmins, was not this legislation introduced solely to boost sales of contraceptives in this state? Be honest now!

MRS. BRIMMINS: Of course not.

MR. DAMIANO: I submit it is entirely possible that this woman—yes, this woman!—is a bag-person for the entire prophylactic scumbag lobby in this great and revered state! Passage of this bill would increase sales of these awful things by the millions. This great land would be inundated with rubbers and their facsimiles within minutes. This woman!

MRS. BRIMMINS: Sit down, Damiano! No one listens to you, no one trusts you, you're a fraud, a gamecock!

MR. DAMIANO: What do you mean no one trusts me! I'm a lawyer!

MR. TOWNSEND: Mr. Speaker, I cannot believe what I have seen and heard this morning. The discussion presented here today makes an absolute mockery of the legislative procedure and the concept of democratic representation.

MR. PARD: You're the only person here wearing a suit!

MR. TOWNSEND: I cannot for the life of me see the logic of any of the arguments against this tiny bill. Furthermore, parenthetically, I lament the absence of wit in this Chamber. You should read the Gladstone-Disraeli debates—now there was wit! Why, on one occasion, my fellow colleagues, Gladstone—six-foot-three, who used to split logs to relieve tension, addressed Disraeli on the Commons floor: "Sir, you will die, I pray, either on the gallows or by a terrible disease." To which Disraeli replied, "That depends entirely on whether I embrace your politics or your mistress." That was wit, my friends, and spontaneity!

MR. CLEGG: Wit? That wasn't funny. First reason, now wit.

MR. TOWNSEND: As to the treatment this fine lady has thus far received—

MR. CLEGG: Hey Townsend, c'mere.

MR. TOWNSEND: *(Crossing to Mr. Clegg)*
This august body claims it realizes there is an epidemic of venereal disease, a critical birth rate, and yet when presented with two viable methods which might relieve these problems—abortion and contraception—most of you are aghast at the former and hysterical at the latter. Yes? *(Mr. Clegg suddenly bops Townsend on the head with his blackjack, then bops him again on his way down. Townsend recovers slowly)* You really hate this bill, don't you?

MR. CLEGG: Yeah, what about you?

MR. TOWNSEND: Oh, I don't care so much about it one way or the other.

MR. CLEGG: Good. Let me help you up.

MRS. BRIMMINS: My brains are fogged with the heat. Platitudes usually on the tip of my tongue have dried up, my paradigms've vanished. I can't talk. I can't think. The only argument that comes to mind is the one about children starving in India, and I'm not sure that's relevant here. I hate to admit it, but I need a gimmick desperately.

MR. VLITSIAK: Why is it no one's brought up house and home yet? What about parents? I'm a parent. We all know how embarrassing little kids can be in public, always askin' stupid questions in real loud voices. I mean suppose these things *are* lyin' all around and advertised everywhere like he says, and my wife and me and my kid go in, and my kid says to me, real loud, "Hey Dad, hey, Mom, what are those funny lookin' things over there? I think I'll put one on my head"? See how embarrassing that could be? You should think about the plight of the parent for a second. Go ahead. Let's just have thirty seconds of silence while we think about the parents for a minute.

MRS. BRIMMINS: Mr. Speaker . . .

MR. VLITSIAK: Sshhh!

MRS. BRIMMINS: Mr. Speaker, will Mr. Vlitsiak yield?

MR. VLITSIAK: Shhh! No!

ACTING SPEAKER: No, he won't. And you're a prune, by the way, woman. I've been meaning to tell you that. Only thirty-eight and already a prune!

CLERK: Y'oughtta gussy yourself up, buy a corsage or something, get a new perm—then maybe somebody'd listen to you in here.

MRS. BRIMMINS: But you two are supposed to be neutral.

ACTING SPEAKER: Not when it's a matter of taste.

(Mr. Damiano whistles at her, but she doesn't see him)

MRS. BRIMMINS: Who did that! Huh? I will not be whistled at! I am an Assemblyperson!

MR. VLITSIAK: You're just making it longer, Mrs. Brimmins! I have the floor! It's thirty seconds from the last word that's spoken. Now.

MRS. BRIMMINS: I'm rabid! I want to eat my desk!

MR. VLITSIAK: Ah ah! Begin again. *(There is silence for thirty seconds)* Okay.

MRS. BRIMMINS: Mr. Speaker, I demand to be heard!

ACTING SPEAKER: All right.

MRS. BRIMMINS: *(Surprised)* What?

ACTING SPEAKER: You've been asking for the floor, lady, now you got it.

MRS. BRIMMINS: Children starving in India! 8 to 10% unemployment!

MR. CLEGG: Oh, please!

MRS. BRIMMINS: I hardly know where to begin. But I doubt that anything in history can rival the vapidity of this morning's floor debate. . .

MR. PARD: Don't you quote history to me. I *am* history! I've been a legislator in this Chamber nigh on to seventy years. Some say more. Chairman of Ways and Means, a hammerlock on Rules, and for years before that a harsh and unbending judge. And don't forget—FDR's very best friend.

MRS. BRIMMINS: On the bill, Mr. Speaker.

ACTING SPEAKER: You're out of order, Mrs. Brimmins.

MRS. BRIMMINS: But I just got started!

ACTING SPEAKER: That's not my fault, Mrs. Brimmins. Mr. Damiano.

MR. DAMIANO: Mr. Speaker. I hardy think this woman's in a position to legislate anything regarding children. She's never had any of her own, never adopted any, to the best of my knowledge she's never even had a miscarriage! And no one knows *what* the story on this *Mr.* Brimmins is — nobody's ever seen him, nobody's even ever heard of him. It's only your word, lady, there's no records anywhere.

MRS. BRIMMINS: If the hair I'm wearing was a wig, I'd tear it off and throw it on the table, that's how mad I am! This bill isn't for children, it's for adults!

MR. PARD: What about my little Melissa?

MRS. BRIMMINS: It's to avoid bringing morons like your little Melissa into the world in the first place. This is a bill to help prevent venereal disease and unwanted pregnancies among adults! And it isn't just about contraceptives for men. It isn't even *mainly* about contraceptives for men!

MR. DAMIANO: Oh yeah? What's it about then?

MRS. BRIMMINS: Contraceptives for women!

(There is a pause)

MR. DAMIANO: Contraceptives for women? Such as what?

MRS. BRIMMINS: Such as what? You can't be serious.

MR. DAMIANO: Never mind heaping on the scorn, just such as what.

MRS. BRIMMINS: *(Slowly, with passion)*
Foams . . . jellies . . . pills . . . suppositories . . diaphragms . . .

MR. PARD: Suppositories?

MRS. BRIMMINS: Uterine devices . . . even voluntary sterilization . . .

MR. PARD: Suppositories . . .

MRS. BRIMMINS: You all think it's about penises! What's complicated about a penis! Nothing! They're either hard or soft, some bend a little to the left, they shrivel up after swimming! That's it! *We* . . . have tubes, valleys, nooks and crannies, hairpin turns . . .

MR. DAMIANO: Mr. Speaker! Stop this!

MRS. BRIMMINS: *(Her eyes closed, oblivious to everything)*
Grand adventure, high dark places . . .

MR. PARD: Suppositories?

MRS. BRIMMINS: Roadways, channels, sacks, fluids . . .

MR. VLITSIAK: Mr. Speaker! Where is this woman's sense of propriety!

MRS. BRIMMINS: Delicious secretions . .

MR. PARD: Go on, lady, go on!

MRS. BRIMMINS: *(Still enraptured)*
Cushy softnesses you wouldn't understand . . . dreams, desires, flights of fancy . . .

MR. BAPP: There is such a thing as legislative good taste!

MRS. BRIMMINS: Pockets for our secrets . . a pinwheel of lights . . .

MR. TOWNSEND: Never heard such in all my born days!

MR. PARD: Shut up, you nick-nack!

MRS. BRIMMINS: Canals, poetry, street festivals, grassy knolls Pudendum, pudendi . . . a good brioche . . .

MR. PARD: Mr. Speaker

ACTING SPEAKER: Mr. Pard.

MR. PARD: *(Salaciously, his voice low in his throat)* Can I ask you a question without interruptin' your rhythm?

MRS. BRIMMINS: Mmmmmmmmmm.

MR. PARD: Are these things . . . you . . . put right inside you?

MRS. BRIMMINS: Yes, Mr. Pard.

MR. PARD: Do they give you pleasure?

MRS. BRIMMINS: What?

MR. PARD: Do they feel good? Y'know, d'you get off on them?

MRS. BRIMMINS: No, they don't feel good! They're boring! Sometimes they hurt!

MR. PARD: *(Chuckling to himself)* They hurt? Oh, Franklin! Where . . . could I see this?

MR. CLEGG: No you don't, don't fall for it! She's always like that! Brings you to the peak of sexual frenzy and then cuts you short! For five months she tantalized me with sexual imagery and the moment I caved in, she'd start lecturing!

MRS. BRIMMINS: What!

MR. CLEGG: All that finger-shaking, all that moralizing—you don't know what's in store for you! And all those organ meats! A woman like you's supposed to be a vegetarian, everybody knows that! But not you! All that liver and kidneys, sweetbreads, all those brains, Marge!

MRS. BRIMMINS: Brains aren't organs!

MR. CLEGG: They are when they're on a plate!

MRS. BRIMMINS: This is absurd! I'd never even go out with a man like him! He's too fat for me!

MR. CLEGG: Always making me exercise for my heart! My heart's strong as an ox! You just couldn't stand to be seen with a fat man! Well, I'll tell you something—Damiano was right! This woman never had a husband!

MRS. BRIMMINS: What!

MR. CLEGG: She's never been married or anywhere near it!

MRS. BRIMMINS: MR. SPEAKER! MR. SPEAKER! POINT OF HIGH PERSONAL PRIVILEGE! I DEMAND THAT MAN'S MICROPHONE BE TURNED OFF! *(She runs to Mr. Clegg, kicking him and hitting him with her purse)* How dare you say that, Willie! This is the floor of the New York State Assembly—you're not at home taking a crap with a cigar in your mouth! Take that back, Willie, and on the floor of this Chamber or I'll tell them you were impotent for one hundred fifty days running! And then I'll kill you!

MR. CLEGG: But it's true, Marge—you never were married, you did make me exercise though my heart's strong as an ox, and you did lecture all the time!

MRS. BRIMMINS: I don't care if it's true or not, Willie, we had a deal! I'm going to find the Speaker wherever he is and tell him you're impotent! Impotent, Willie! Think you'll be Majority Leader after that, Little Willie Clegg?

MR. CLEGG: You got a point.

MRS. BRIMMINS: I want this bill, Willie!

MR. CLEGG: Your bill's dead, Marge—ya need a gimmick and you haven't got one! You won't bend, ya won't flex!

MRS. BRIMMINS: I do not need a gimmick and I wouldn't resort to one if I did. Now take back this not married stuff, Willie, or I'll shake the rafters and rattle your eyes! Mr. Acting Speaker! Him!

MR. CLEGG: *(Meekly)*
I was only kidding. She was married.

MR. DAMIANO: *(Holding up a jar)*
Who cares! No one was listening! See this? This is the fetus of an unborn child—a murdered unborn child! Mutilated, chopped up, death by anguish! That's what passage of her contraceptive bill'll do!

MRS. BRIMMINS: Put that away, Damiano, you used that in the abortion debate. It's not the same thing. Mr. Speaker, I should like to quote Statute 34, Section 8 from *McKinney's Statutes* . . .

MR. PARD: Don't you quote things at me, little sister! I knew the greatest quotemaker ever to stalk this fearful and abundant land! Ladies and gentlemen, our great Governor, Hyde Park's own, I give you Franklin Eleanor Roosevelt! I was with him in Warm Springs, Georgia—oh, how those waters loved his legs—his cigarette a-cock, irrepressible grin slapped a-jaunt on his face when he said to me, "Larry, my grand old and probably best friend, the buck stops here. If you don't like the heat stay out of the kitchen." I was with him when—

MRS. BRIMMINS: Just a minute, Mr. Pard, Franklin Roosevelt didn't say those things—Harry Truman did!

MR. PARD: Harry Truman! Harry Truman was a breadstick. I suppose Franklin didn't say "I shall go to Korea" either! Oh, he was the greatest of men—but not without his enemies. People thought he was stupid. When he first arrived in Washington, know what they said about him? "That man's so dumb he can't wheel and chew gum at the same time." But he showed 'em. "54-40 or fight," "Win With Willkie," "I love a parade"—FDR said 'em all. A dynamo in a rolling box, a razzle-dazzle stand-up comic with an eye to the international, re-elected nine or ten times and still going strong. So don't you ballyhoo me, you little whiner, fine-looking and sizeable-breasted as you may be, hot and juicy as I got when you said "suppository" to me. I'd give half-a-hundred in meaningful money for a quick look at you naked, lambie. I'd suck on you 'til my bugle playing days're numbered. Fine as your secretions may be —

MRS. BRIMMINS: Is that really what you think of me, Mr. Pard?

MR. PARD: Suck, suck. *(She crosses to him, looks down on him)* What're you doin' here?

MRS. BRIMMINS: I've come for your vote, Mr. Pard.

MR. PARD: Come for my vote? You're sure daffy, even for a woman. *(She rips her blouse open, popping the buttons all over the floor. Everyone gasps and freezes)* Oh my, oh my!

(For a moment, he is paralyzed; then he touches one breast with one hand, then the other breast with the other hand, slowly, and, finally, all the fight gone out of him, lays his head on her breasts)

MRS. BRIMMINS: May I have your vote, Mr. Pard?

MR. PARD: Yes, my dear . . . if I live to cast it.

MRS. BRIMMINS: Mr. Damiano? For a touch and a fondle?

MR. DAMIANO: I can get this for free, you know!

MRS. BRIMMINS: I'm sure you can. But not from me. And not now.

MR. DAMIANO: Okay.

MRS. BRIMMINS: I've got your word? In front of everybody?

MR. DAMIANO: Uh-huh.

MRS. BRIMMINS: Upstate and Onondaga?

MR. DAMIANO: This better be good.

MRS. BRIMMINS: The best.

(He goes to her, touches her breast, and groans)

MR. CLEGG: Jesus, Marjorie!

MRS. BRIMMINS: Mr. Vlitsiak?

MR. VLITSIAK: Yes, yes, and the West, too, just for the asking.

MRS. BRIMMINS: Here you go. *(They bury their faces in her breasts)* Boys? *(Everyone onstage except Mr. Clegg runs to her and fondles her)* You're the only one left, Willie.

(Willie starts to rise, but he is interrupted by an amazing burst of lightning and thunder. The Speaker appears and mounts the rostrum)

MR. VLITSIAK: Oh, my God, it's Mr. Fermrlnr—the Speaker!

MR. CLEGG: It's the Speaker!

A PAGE: Good Lord, the Speaker!

MRS. BRIMMINS: Is that what he looks like?

SPEAKER: *(Calmly)*
What's going on, Willie? I trusted you to look after things.

MR. CLEGG: *(Nervously)*
Oh, it's nothing I can't handle, Mr. Speaker. Just the boys having a little go-round. Okay, fellas, Vic, Dickie, knock it off, we got some legislatin' to do.

MR. BAPP: But this is such good stuff, Willie!

MR. DAMIANO: Y'oughta see what's under here, Willie!

MR. CLEGG: C'mon, fellas, knock it off—you're makin' everything look outta hand.

MR. DAMIANO: Get outta here!

MR. BAPP: Go soak your face!

MR. TOWNSEND: Leave us alone!

SPEAKER: I'm very disappointed in you, son. Leave you by yourself a few minutes and the sky rains chaos. Where's the old legislative loyalty?

MR. CLEGG: Just a minute, Mr. Speaker, I can do it! Remember me and the milk dispute?

SPEAKER: It's too late, Willie.

MRS. BRIMMINS: You're dealing with the wrong man, Mr. Speaker. I hold sway over this caucus. See?

SPEAKER: Don't be silly. Which do you want, boys — that with her shirt open there, or . . . THIS!
(He points his fingers at Willie and sparks fly out)

MR.   CLEGG: AAAARRRRRGGGGGGGGHHHHHHH!!   My shoulder!

MR. VLITSIAK: Mr. Speaker, Mr. Speaker, what'd you do?

SPEAKER: I gave him arthritis.

MR. VLITSIAK: Now that's what I call clout.

MR. BAPP: Talk about your political muscle.

SPEAKER: And THIS!
(He points his fingers at Willie again, and an explosion occurs)

MR. VLITSIAK: What'd you do this time?

SPEAKER: I took away his newspaper support, indicted his chief fund-raiser for fraud, and re-districted him right out of the ballpark. His next election will be won by a Democrat.

MR. CLEGG: No, Mr. Speaker!

SPEAKER: Not only that — I also know the secret of fire! *(He either lights a Zippo or strikes a match. A moderate flame shoots up. All the Assemblymen cower and mutter "Ooooo")* Well, boys, the choice is simple—me or that raven-haired vixen over there.
(There is a pause. Mr. Damiano suddenly breaks for his desk)

MR. DAMIANO: I didn't have nothin' to do with this, Mr. Speaker! I was lured over there by Mr. Clegg and his honeyed bimbo here under the misapprehension we were going to dole out a little patronage!

MR. BAPP: *(Crossing to his desk)*
I was on my way to the library for some religious research! My hands are clean!

MR. TOWNSEND: *(Returning to his seat)*
I was just looking for paper clips!

MRS. BRIMMINS: What about your promises to me?

MR. VLITSIAK: *(Moving away from her)*
Mr. Speaker, Mr. Speaker!

SPEAKER: Mr. Vlitsiak.

MR. VLITSIAK: Mr. Speaker, Rabbi Wonderling from West Chazy in beautiful Clinton County has just arrived in the gallery above with remnants of his beatific congregation. Would you be so kind as to extend your customary salutation?

SPEAKER: On behalf of the people of this great state, I welcome Rabbi Wonderling and the remnants of his beatific congregation to this hallowed chamber and hope they enjoy the deliberations. *(Applause)* See how nice I can be? *(Everyone returns to his desk except Mrs. Brimmins and Mr. Clegg)* And now the contraceptive vote. The Clerk will call the roll.

CLERK: Aabey, Gwathmey, Dallenbach, Zysseroso.

SPEAKER: The contraceptive bill is defeated.

MRS. BRIMMINS: *(Collapsing at her desk)*
No-o-o-o-o-o-o-o-o!

(Mr. Clegg sits at his desk)

SPEAKER: Ah-ah. That's not your seat anymore, Willie. Mr. Damiano.

MR. DAMIANO: *(Moving right in with his supplies and his fetus and his gifts, sweeping Mr. Clegg's onto the floor)*
Oh, Mr. Speaker, I don't know how to begin my thank-yous.

SPEAKER: It's all right, son. You'll find a way. I've got work to do now, boys, and I'd like to vanish as quick as I came.

MRS. BRIMMINS: Just a minute, Mr. Speaker! What about me? I've done everything I've been told to, I've even learned how to bend up here, how to flex! And the answer is, I just don't get it! What am I doing wrong?

SPEAKER: Why nothing, dear. In fact, I think you're doing rather well, considering. It's just that it's not that kind of club. Right, boys?

(They applaud and laugh. He exits accompanied by mammoth lightning and thunder)

ACTING SPEAKER: *(Crossing back to his desk)*
The calendar of the day. The Clerk will read.

CLERK: Bill 7883, Calendar Number 584, Mr. Damiano. An act to legalize the letters G-O-D, God, for imprint on state motor vehicle license plates.

(March music begins quietly here)

MR. DAMIANO: On the bill, Mr. Speaker.

ACTING SPEAKER: On the bill, Mr. Damiano.

(Curtain .   . and loud march music)

NOTE: On April 18, 1974, Bill Number 6843-D, Calendar Number 660, an act to amend the education law in relation to the display of contraceptives was unanimously defeated in the Assembly of the State of New York.

YANKS 3 DETROIT 0
TOP OF THE SEVENTH

Characters:

EMIL "DUKE" BRONKOWSKI
LAWRENCE "BEANIE" MALIGMA
OLD SALT
LUCKY JOHNSON
DONNA LUNA DONNA
LINCOLN LEWIS III
GUIDO MANCINI
BRICK BROCK
BASEBALL PLAYERS

Scene:

Emil "Duke" Bronkowski, dressed in the uniform of the New York Yankees, is in the middle of his windup in the pitcher's mound at Yankee Stadium, right of stage center. He is thirty-six years old and husky.

His teammates are all offstage.

An electronic score board would be helpful to keep the audience informed of balls and strikes, but it isn't essential.

The bases are located either in the audience or on a platform suspended above the stage, or on the stage itself. The noise of the crowd is constant (silent only once during the play), reacting wildly when the Yankees do well and silently or unfavorably when they do poorly.

The ball is real. So are the bases. So is the rubber. Duke pitches to his catcher, offstage left.

UMPIRE: *(Offstage)* STEE-RYE!
(The crowd approves enthusiastically. The ball comes back to Duke and he rubs it up, digs into the mound, and otherwise makes himself at home. He steps on the rubber, winds up and pitches again.)
STEE-RYE!
(The crowd approves and the ball comes back to him once more)
DUKE: Well, it's going' pretty good now.
(He winds up and fires another pitch and the crowd applauds wildly again)
UMPIRE: *(Hoarsely)* STEE-RYE!
(The ball comes back from first base side)

DUKE: One down. Slider's workin' good. Lookin' good. Always could get 'em by Carvalho. Who's this?

P.A. SYSTEM: Number twenty-three, the third baseman, Butch Dietrich.

DUKE: Oh, yeah, Dietrich. Bounced to short in the first, popped up to Bubba in the fourth. Inside and high fast one or he'll go for a good curve, or go ahead and scroojie him. If I had a scroojie.

(Looking offstage at his catcher, Duke shakes off two signs, then winds up and throws)

UMPIRE: STEE-RYE!

(The crowd approves)

DUKE: I tell ya, when the slider's goin' good, when it's got the rotation, I can't be beat! *(The ball comes back to him. He feels great)* Once more, Beanie. Atta baby.

(He pitches)

UMPIRE: STEE-RYE!

DUKE: God, am I on! I can't wait. *(Ball comes back. He fiddles with the rubber, the resin bag, and so on. He shakes off a sign, then steps off the rubber)* That's the one thing Beanie's never learned—how to call 'em for me. He can call 'em for everybody else on the staff but he can't call 'em for me. When m'slider's hot, it can't be hit. He should know that after all these years we been together, but he don't. Aaron couldn't hit my slider when it's hot. Carew couldn't hit my slider when it's hot. But Beanie don't know that yet. *(Duke shakes off two more signs)* C'mon, Beanie, c'mon, the slider, the slider. I don't care if he is looking for it, no one's gonna hit this Polack's slider today, particularly no German. Atta boy.

(Duke pitches. The crowd doesn't react. The ball comes back)

DUKE: Well, it's okay, it's okay, it's only one and two, one and two, I'm way ahead of him. Just missed with it. He was goin' for it, he was gonna bite, checked it just in time. It's goin' okay now. Don't wanna talk about the whole season, of course, but right now it's goin' okay. Somehow I knew it, too. This morning I got up and told Jeannie, "My arm feels like a cannon today, hon, it's my day in the slot, and I'm gonna do it." and here I am, top of the seventh, a perfect game under m'belt, a real return to m'form of '65-'66, a complete reversal of what was destined to be m'swan song to the big time. I'm so happy I can hardly keep myself together. Just two innings to go after this one—eight lousy outs—and I can write my own ticket. One or two games like this one, I can write my own ticket.

And so far, no pangs of fear. Usually 'bout this time little terrors confront me, little doubts gnaw at my neck. But not today. Couple pangs of hunger, maybe, but no pangs of fear. And I'm okay at home, too. As the late, great Ed Sullivan used to say, "Are you all right at home? Then you're all right." I got a wonderful wife named Jeannie watching me on the tube, two fine boys named Mitch, seven, and Eric, six, one good with puzzles, the other of a more artistic bent, strong and loyal friends, a rambling, two-story white Victorian house in Roslyn that's almost paid for, I got a year-old Buick Luxus Cononnade, m'66 Lincoln, a Black and Decker Self-Starting Roto 380, two good trees planted outside, plenty of electrical appliances, ham radio band W2-LEO, barbecue aprons with funny slogans on 'em, lotsa hobbies, and just today, everything's startin' to look up like a bandit. Triumph's in m'blood.

I'm financially secure (it looks like), I'm puttin' in my sixth year doin' P.R. in the off-season for Connecticut Federal and my fast food burger franchise's doin' swell. Some people might even consider me a pillar of society—Roslyn society, whatever that means, Yessir, startin' today, after five years in the sewer, life's lookin' grand. I'm comin' back—all the way back.

Back to business, now, back to business. Can't wander around like that, no goin' back to bad habits. Let's see: Beanie's gonna ask me for the curve; Dietrich's gonna expect the curve; he knows Beanie won't ask for the fastball so that means the change-up's out. Sinker's murder, and I haven't got a scroojie, so I say, guess what, the slider. Won't be ready for it four times in a row. The curve; I haven't had a grip on the curve since Norm Cash on this very same Detroit Tiger baseball team six years ago. *Then* I had a grip on the curve. But that was some year all around. Awright, awright, concentrate, concentrate. *(He looks offstage at the catcher)* The curve. *(He shakes it off, looks again)* Not again! *(He shakes it off again)* C'mon, c'mon, Beanie. *(He nods, winds up and pitches. The crowd makes no reaction)* Okay, okay, okay, boy, okay, okay, okay, okay, it's all right, all right, waste a few, waste a few, all right. Wind wasn't right on it. Remember: top of the seventh, nobody's even reached base yet, you're pitchin' better than *any time* this year, better'n *any pitcher* on *any team* this whole year! The fire's comin' back, too, the perfect eye, the control, the confidence; knock this one off, you'll be right back in the Razor Blade League — $50,000 buy-out from Schaefer or Gillette's New Foamy. Just don't lose your grip and you're in. *(The ball comes back)* Know what I like about baseball? Part of it's that it's calm, it's dependable, it isn't scary. It's got good, simple, faithful structure, a structure you can count on. But most of all I like it 'cause it's a game of individuals. One against one. Hitter against pitcher; fielder against ball; runner against time.

Oh, you can have teamwork in baseball, but you don't have to depend so much on blocks and tackles from guys who don't care; in baseball you always know just who's at fault. Like now . . . it's just me against this one guy, a former Nazi, Butch Dietrich. I love baseball.

Okay, okay, now just concentrate on this boy. High and inside with the slider, or try the scroojie, which I don't have, Goddamnit. He's a little nothing, doesn't know his bat from a bratwurst, battin' .207, something like that, a little lampshade-making Kraut. It's all he can do to pick up the occasional grounder at third. He couldn't hit me today if I was throwin' tomatoes. ZA CHANCELLOR OF 86TH STREET! YOU ARE NUSSING! He's nothin'. Okay, Beanie, breeze me in there, boy, make his little Deutsch balls sing in the wind at my smoke. I'll do whatever you want, Beanie boy, whatever you want. You call it, I'll throw it. Whatever you want. *(He gets the signal)* Jesus Christ, the curve! Can't you have a little faith in my slider, for Chrissake? I don't know who's more against me, you know that, Beanie—you or the Nazi! The slider, Beanie, call for the slider, just this once more, he'll never know it's comin'. Atta boy. *(He winds up and pitches. The crowd murmurs)* Goddamn son of a fuckin' bitch, what the hell's happenin' to my slider? *(The ball comes back to him. He throws his resin bag down)* Jesus, Jesus, Jesus! Can't lose m'slider. There goes my comeback, there goes m'no-hitter. All I've got's m'slider. If I lose that . . . I don't get Donna Luna Donna if my slider goes. Rizzuto's up there, jackin' up enthusiasm, puttin' me down like a bandit. "Ho-ly cow, Duke Bronkowski's got himself in a little Polack jam here, folks! He's pitched five straight sliders and it looks like he's just lost his toehold! The string's run out!" Lost his toehold. The string's run out. Baseball talk'll turn your brain to meat loaf. I mean "bunt" —what the hell does "bunt" mean? How d'ya like this, Des Moines? *(Duke blatantly scratches his testicles)* TV executives go crazy when balls are scratched on the tube. They don't acknowledge them. For all they know. I got a mixed floral arrangement down here. Once more, Des Moines. Or Queens, I guess, I know this ain't goin' any farther'n Queens. Jesus, I don't know. It's happened so often like this before. Goes real good for awhile, then my slider goes, and I lose it. All right, all right, come on, easy . . . you're a seasoned ballplayer, fourteen years' experience under your belt, you're a *veteran*. Just breathe in . . . slowly. Quit talkin' to yourself. That's it. Hooo. That was a little glimpse of the fear I mentioned earlier. I get frightened pretty easy these days.

(He steps in the rubber, shakes off a sign, then steps off the rubber and rubs up the ball. Beanie, the catcher, enters)

BEANIE: Hey, whadda ya doin'? Why ya keep shakin' me off?
DUKE: Beanie, you gotta ask for my slider.
BEANIE: Oh, yeah? Why?
DUKE: *(Quickly)* 'Cause I wanna set a record for the most sliders ever pitched at 4:05 on a sunny afternoon to a Nazi Third Baseman from Detroit! I don't know, I wanna pitch it 'cause it's goin' good!
BEANIE: You missed wit' it three times, Duke.
DUKE: Look, Beanie, I got problems.
BEANIE: I thought you looked sorta fragged. What's ya problems? C'mon, c'mon, that's what ol' Beanie's here for. What're ya problems?
DUKE: Secretly I don't think I can make it today, Beanie.
BEANIE: Look, Duke, we all got problems. Listen to this. My twelve-year-old wants a Snowmobile—a Snowmobile! He's tired of his Honda, now he announces he wants a Snowmobile.
DUKE: Your boy's got a Honda? He's only twelve!
BEANIE: Sure, all the kids got 'em. That's only openers. Try this. Ya know that baton twirler from Toledo I been ballin'? Bobbi? Suddenly she wants a car to keep it outta the papers. An' yesterday, Rowena tells me she wants custody of the kids, the house, and the legal right to tell me when I can quit playin' ball. To tell me when I can quit playin' ball!
DUKE: You gettin' a divorce?
BEANIE: No.
DUKE: Then why'd she say all that?
BEANIE: Just feelin' her oats.
DUKE: But *you're* supposed to be takin' care of *me*, Beanie, you're supposed to be listenin' to *my* problems.
BEANIE: Whatever they are, you'd better get over 'em, fella, or Old Salt'll be out here like the Fordham Flash.
DUKE: Old Salt.
BEANIE: Yup. An' quit shakin' me off, or Old Salt'll be out here for that, too.
DUKE: Can I throw m'slider?
BEANIE: Think I care? Sure. Throw it all afternoon. I don't care. *(Beanie trots off. Duke steps back on the rubber, shakes off two signs. Beanie runs out again)* What's goin' on? Quit shakin' me off! You're makin' me look bad!
DUKE: How can I quit shakin' you off unless you ask for my slider? We had a deal.
BEANIE: All right, all right, I'll ask for your goddamn slider.
DUKE: How come you didn't ask for it just now?
BEANIE: I wasn't sure you meant it. *(Beanie starts to trot off)*
DUKE: Hey, Beanie.

BEANIE: Yeah?

DUKE: I always wanted to know—how come you call yourself Beanie?

BEANIE: Oh, well, a ballplayer's gotta have a nickname, you know that. Just like yours, Duke-o. Otherwise you don't fit in, people forget you. You know, something like Boog or Yogi or The Babe, something that's fun to say over and over again. Or, 'course, a good way is to be born with a good name—like Mickey or Johnny. Johnny's a great name for a jock—people think of you as a kid all the time, a son. Y'know, Johnny, Hey, Johnny, Hey, Johnny, Johnny.

DUKE: Yeah, Johnny is a great name for a jock. Jimmy and Bobby are okay, too.

BEANIE: That's right, Jimmy's real good. Even Jim ain't bad. Chico's real good if you're a spic. There are just some names that can really increase your earning potential.

DUKE: But why'd you choose Beanie?

BEANIE: Why not?

DUKE: Beanie's so . . . coy.

BEANIE: Beanie ain't coy.

DUKE: Sure it is. You could just as easily have called yourself Pretty Boy or Cutie Pie or . . . Candice. Really, what's the matter with Cutie Pie? Cutie Pie Maligma. Gets the same idea across.

BEANIE: All right, look: I won't ask for nothin' but your god-damn slider! Just don't shake me off, got it?

DUKE: Right.

(Beanie trots off, fuming)

DUKE: Cutie Pie Maligma. If anything, he should change his last name. Okay, let's see. Dietrich the Nazi. Slider high and inside or the nonexistent scroojie.

(Duke winds up and pitches. The ball is hit a few feet upstage of him. He dives after it acrobatically, retrieves it and fires it offstage right. The crowd goes wild, indicating the runner is out. Duke picks himself up and heads back to the mound. In an instant, two players, a Trainer, Beanie and Old Salt run out to him, all yelling and carrying on)

VARIOUS AD LIBS: Hey, hey, hey ya, Duke. Hey ya, hey ya, how ya doin? Great play, Duke-o!

(The Trainer rubs Duke's shoulders avidly, then dusts off his uniform, offers him a drink, and combs his hair. Finally, he splashes talcum on his face. Old Salt and Duke walk around the mound as the Trainer massages Duke)

OLD SALT: A great play, son. How's the shoulder?

DUKE: Fine, fine. But I got problems, Old Salt.

OLD SALT: Walk it off, boy, walk it off.

DUKE: They're problems inside m'head, sir, I can't walk 'em off.

OLD SALT: Do as I tell ya, boy, I know what I'm talkin' about. Walk 'em off, boy, walk 'em off.

DUKE: I don't know if I can.

OLD SALT: You goddamn college kids! Can't get anything straight! Can't just get on with it! You never shoulda gone there. College is the source of all your troubles.

DUKE: I know, I know. But I soon saw the error of m'ways; I left after two years.

OLD SALT: Makes no difference. Two months is enough to catch the taint. What good d'it do ya? *(Quickly)* Can you tell me for sure that it was the decline of the Baltic herring industry at the end of the Fifteenth Century that led to the dissolution of the Hanseatic League? No. D'ya know the chemical formula for common table salt or the subtrahend in the remainder is factorial three and the minuend factorial seventeen? No. Can you explain fully the symbolism of the bar of soap in Bloom's pocket in *Ulysses*? *(Pause)* Well, can ya?

DUKE: No.

OLD SALT: There y'are—what good d'it do ya? Ya didn't learn nothin', you don't remember nothin'—all it did was make it impossible for you to come to any conclusions, am I right? There's nothin' worse than an indecisive jock.

DUKE: I know, I know, but I've always been like this, even before college. I was like this in high school.

OLD SALT: High school! That's another thing!

DUKE: I know I did wrong, I know I did, but that's all in the past. I got big troubles right now, sir.

OLD SALT: Well, you're right, my boy. Remember: only fools and chickens scratch at yesterday's feed. But from now on, Goddamnit, you remember: too much bookin', not much cookin'.

DUKE: Yes, sir. But what about the trouble I'm in?

OLD SALT: You're not in trouble, son. You got two down, top of the seventh, you're seven outs away from a perfect game! That's not trouble! Beanie's in trouble! Don't look a gift horse in the mouth, boy. Remember: he who plants sproutlings before breakfast will reap mung beans by noon. Your slider's in there tight, your form's good, what more could you ask?

DUKE: I don't know where I'm headed, Old Salt. I had two good years for you '64 and '65, and in '66 I led the majors with an E.R.A. of 1.41 and won twenty-four games. I got married in '66, confident of my future, ready to raise a family and settle down. '67 was okay but not great—a big disappointment according to the Associated Press. Then I started to crumble. My fastball lost its zip, I couldn't get the rotation on my curve, I never learned a scroojie—and it's too late to start now. All I've got left is my slider and maybe a knuckleball somewhere by the fireplace in my future.

OLD SALT: See how I'm listenin' to ya? Watch. Can ya see it?

DUKE: Yeah.

OLD SALT: Remember: the best talker is a good listener.

DUKE: Yeah. But ya see—

OLD SALT: Cross at the green, not in-between. Now what's botherin' you, boy? See me listenin'?

DUKE: I don't think I can do it, Old Salt.

OLD SALT: You'll see—the eagle that flies lowest flies longest.

DUKE: I never had any luck. I never had the charisma like Namath or the press like Mantle, or even the arrest record like Lance Rentzel. That can mean an awful lot to a fella. I never made the big money in my prime and now I'm past my prime and I can't seem to get back on the track. I know I woulda been shipped back to the minors if this team wasn't so rotten.

OLD SALT: It's that goddamn college shit! All this crap's in your head, boy!

DUKE: I know it is! That's the problem!

OLD SALT: Pshaw, boy, pish-shaw, pis-haw, washpi. You got a perfect game goin', son, a no-hitter, a shutout. What else could you want?

DUKE: I just feel it inside—my game's goin' into the toilet. I don't get it—I'm almost thirty-seven years old and the person I admire most is still Holden Caulfield.

OLD SALT: Don't be crazy. Just pitch good. Now let me pat you on the ass and let's get on with it. I'm sick of this.

DUKE: Can't you tell me anything? I'm so confused.

OLD SALT: Why, sure, son, I wouldn't let you down. I been waitin' for this the whole game! Ready? Ready. I HAVE CONFIDENCE IN YOU, SON. I'M THE MANAGER OF THE NEW YORK YANKEES, AND I HAVE CONFIDENCE IN YOU! That's all you need, boy. Repeat after me: CONFIDENCE. I HAVE OLD SALT'S CONFIDENCE, AND THAT MEANS THE WORLD TO ME.

DUKE: (Depressed) Confidence, right. Thank you, sir.

OLD SALT: Come on boy, let's hear the old pep—I HAVE OLD SALT'S CONFIDENCE! HEY HEY!

DUKE: (Embarrassed) Okay, I have Old Salt's confidence. Whadda ya think, I'll stick to the slider . . .

OLD SALT: Louder! More gusto! HEY HEY! I HAVE OLD
SALT'S CONFIDENCE!
DUKE: I HAVE OLD SALT'S CONFIDENCE.
OLD SALT: AGAIN! AGAIN! I HAVE OLD SALT'S CONFI-
DENCE! HEY HEY!
DUKE: I HAVE OLD SALT'S CONFIDENCE!
OLD SALT: ATTABABY POOCHIE! LET'S HEAR IT JES'
ONE MORE TIME FOR THOSE COMMIES IN HAVANA! I
HAVE OLD SALT'S CONFIDENCE!
DUKE: I HAVE OLD SALT'S CONFIDENCE!
OLD SALT: All right, then, Now lemme pat you on the ass and
let's get on with it. *(They all leave, patting Duke on the behind and mak-
ing additional cheer-leading noises)*
DUKE: I don't believe it. Old Salt? Old Saltine. That man lives
for one thing: his obituary. Just keeps pumpin' out those quotes.
Sooner or later he's bound to hit the right one—and then there'll
be nobody around to take it down. Boy, was he furious when Vince
Lombardi died first. Now he's just staying alive to put some
distance between the two legends. If he was smart, he'd kick off this
afternoon before anyone finds out what a goon he is. YANKEE
MANAGER DIES AT 65 OF EXCESS WISDOM. NATION
MOURNS LOSS. PRESIDENT EXTOLS VIRTUES: "TO THE
BEST OF MY KNOWLEDGE, OLD SALT NEVER URINATED
IN HIS ENTIRE LIFE—AN EXAMPLE, ONE OF MANY GOOD
ONES, FOR THE YOUTH OF AMERICA." *(He yells to the umpire
offstage)* Hey! Can I throw a couple? *(He quickly throws two pitches,
each time limbering up his bruised shoulder. The ball doesn't return after
the second pitch)* I know this sounds silly, but whenever he does that
"I have confidence" routine, I actually feel a lot better. Some of the
brambles get cleared away. But it doesn't last.
   Lookit this team. I never felt so insecure in my life. If it hadn't
been for those back-to-back homers by Popeye and Bruno in the
second, I'd be in the toilet already. They came through. Not like
my coconut buddy at third. Lookit him. All he does is flash his
gums and say, "I'ng no Paneech, I'ng Coob'n." Lookit him? Lookit
me—I just dove after that Nazi's grounder like a fag was after my
boy Mitch. I could've dislocated my shoulder! Oh, this is a dopey
game. *(The ball comes back)* There's no strategy in baseball. You
know what the strategy is in baseball? When you got a right-handed
pitcher, you put up a left-handed batter, when you got a left-
handed pitcher, you put up a right-handed batter. That's it. That's
all the strategy there is.
   I used to be so excited with all this, but I'm not anymore. I'm ex-

cited . . . but I'm also bored. I'm bored with the excitement. When I first came up, whew, when I was doin' good, this game meant everything to me. I could lick anyone. Now it's just bases . . . changin' clothes . . . fake dirt . . . 20,000 paid and furious fans dyin' for me to fail. I just don't have the confidence to know what to do next.

Look: suppose your career's over—what're ya gonna do? *(Pause)* I don't know. Breathe. I'm gonna lose Donna Luna Donna, that's for sure. She's outside in m'66 Lincoln right now, listenin' to the game on the radio and protectin' my hubcaps from the Cuban's cousins. She's my Texas groupie, and I think about her all the time. What I like best about her is her body. What she likes best about me is that I'm famous. C'mon, c'mon, back to business, back to business. Let's see, who's this?

P.A. SYSTEM: Number forty-one, the second baseman, Lucky Johnson.

DUKE: How d'ya like that—a WASP. What can you say bad about a WASP—they-re all perfect. They have so many advantages. They own all the banks; they don't have to take life seriously; they can be dull and nobody cares. They're so much better than other folks—leaner; tighter; sharper round the edges. I'm not a WASP. I'm a Polack. Not a Pole; not Polish—Polack. I get very suspicious of people who call me "Polish." Y'know inside they're all thinking "starched bowling shirt, six to turn the ladder, count the basement windows and multiply by six . . . "

The main advantage they got is that they're so many of 'em. All those southern sheriffs! All those midwestern governors! *(Suddenly dejected)* I can't fight that. I'm fed up with this. I wanna take a shower. I'm gonna let him hit. I'm gonna give up my perfect game and my no-hitter and just get the hell outta here. It's all outta my hands anyway. I'm gonna give up my razor blade commercials and my whole economic future and I'm just gonna let Lucky Johnson hit this next one as far as he can make it go. WASPs are the chosen people and they should be allowed certain graces in times of stress. Let's see . . . Lucky baby: switch-hitter, popped to Bruno in the first bounced to Popeye whenever it was the last time he was up. Can't hit it low and away 'cause he steps into the bucket, so we'll put it right across his letters where he can't miss it, and we'll make it a medium fast one—which is the only kind of fast one I can throw anyway. *(He shakes off a sigh)*

He'll never ask for the right one. Gimme another sign, Cutie Pie. The hell with it. Here comes Sunday, Lucky Boy. *(He winds up and throws. The crowd cheers. Duke is amazed)* He missed! That was the fattest pitch I ever threw anyone! Right down the alley! Helen Keller coulda hit that one with a fishing rod! An' he missed it! Boy, Old Salt is a goddamn genius. If I can get by with that sort of stuff, I got it knocked. I could put a wing on the house, I could keep a little apartment in the Village for the snatch, I could even give Jeannie a bauble of some kind. Let's go, baby. He's no better'n me. That's all the charity you get, you pasty-faced bigot. Hoo, I'm hot today. C'MON, CUTIE PIE, THROW THE BALL BACK. *(The ball comes back)* Old Lucky Boy, the golden WASP must've been droolin' for my slider. Well, this time he's gonna get it. All right, here we go, Lucky Johnson, outside and low. *(He pitches. The ball is hit to third. Duke follows the ball along the ground, then the throw to first, narrating the play all the time)* 'At's it, little bingle along the ground, scoop it up, baby, fire it right on target, a perfect strike, easy out . . . SAFE?! *(The crowd boos loudly. To Camacho:)* You stupid Camacho, you pulled him off the bag! You blew my perfect game! I don't believe it! I just don't believe it!

Goddamit, you come over here, you make us advertise our beer in Spanish, you paint all your walls green, you get us all addicted to plantains—and now you and your neon gums ruin my perfect game! I'll get you for this, Gummo! *(The ball comes back to him from the first base side)* All right, all right, who cares, who cares? It's my old buddy the self-fulfilling prophecy . . . although if I'm gonna be self-destructive, you stupid banana, lemme do it on my own! Who cares, still a no-hitter, still a shutout, still a big, big victory. This ain't even a jam. Who's this?

P.A. SYSTEM: Number twenty-two, the left fielder, Lincoln Lewis.

DUKE: Thanks. Ah, one of our dusky brethren, da highly mobile Lincoln Lewis Da Third. He get mah singin', dancin', watermelon pitch, right down da alley.

Don't be bitter, don't be hostile. It's just self-defense. Concentrate, concentrate. Still got a no-hitter, still got a shutout, still a big win for ya.

Lincoln Lewis . . . popped to Felez in the second, hey! He's one of my strikeouts! That's right! Don't pitch him low and outside, don't pitch him low and inside, don't pitch him high and outside . . . don't pitch him high and inside. Where the hell did I pitch this guy? On the hands? Across the letters? With my eyes closed? I forget. A slider, I guess. Or a scroojie, which I don't have. Ask for my slider, Cutie Pie, ask for my slider. *(He shakes off two pitches)* ASK FOR MY SLIDER, CUTIE PIE!

(Beanie marches out)

BEANIE: All right, that's it, knock it off, cut out this Cutie Pie shit! My name's Lawrence or Larry. My friends call me Beanie. You can call me Mr. Maligma. Mr. Maligma.

DUKE: Gee, I'm sorry. I didn't know it meant so much to you.

BEANIE: All right, then. From now on, Mr. Maligma.

DUKE: But I can't do that. Who ever heard of a pitcher calling his catcher "Mister"? I can't go around calling you "Mr. Maligma."

(Beanie takes the ball)

BEANIE: If you don't, the next time I throw this back, there's gonna be a grenade in it. And don't think I ain't man enough to do it.

DUKE: Gee. Okay.

(Beanie leaves. Duke realizes he doesn't have the ball)

DUKE: Uh . . . Mr. Maligma? Could I have the ball please? *(The ball comes back to him)* I wonder if the President has to put up with stuff like this. Command is sure lonely. Okay, one more for Des Moines, and we're off.

(Duke scratches his testicles, winds up and goes into the stretch. Lucky Johnson is on first base)

LUCKY JOHNSON: You haven't got it anymore! You're finished! Finished!

DUKE: Whew, I forgot how rattled I get with someone on base. Concentrate now.

LUCKY: Your only good pitch is the slider and anyone can see that coming from left field! You're not famous, never were! You're nothing! You never had a piece on you by Jimmy Cannon or Arthur Daley, and now they're dead, and you'll never get one! Never anything by Red Smith, either! Or anyone! Your scrapbook's full of pressed leaves!

DUKE: Jesus, Red Smith.

LUCKY: You're a failure as a man, a failure as a husband, a lousy father, and you can't mambo!

DUKE: My whole life's been like this. Just as I start goin' up the corporate ladder, wham, the pressure gets me. Rizzuto starts watchin' me up there, I can feel his eyes on the front of my face. I can feel that camera cutting to my right cheek, then my left cheek, then a close-up of the sweat on my forehead. I can't get away from it — that damn camera sees everything: my arm, my lack of concentration, I'm always on the spot. I freeze at the pinnacle. I'm afraid of success, that's it.

LUCKY: Mambo! Mambo!

DUKE: *(Dreamily)* '67 was sure a good year. The curve had rotation, the fastball had zip . . . I got the loan for the fast food franchise, Jeannie's breasts didn't sag. Everyone knew my name, even at away games. I could've been dating Mamie van Doren in '67. All right, all right, concentrate, concentrate.

LUCKY: Mambo! Mambo!

(Duke winds up and throws a wild pitch. The crowd groans and Lucky Johnson trots down to second base)

DUKE: Oh, no! A wild pitch. Nothin' looks as bad as a wild pitch. Jesus! Okay, okay, no problem. You're a *veteran*, a fourteen-year veteran, you've been through situations like this dozens of times. Dozens. Yeah, but what did I do to get out of them? My memory's gone, wiped out like the crease in my grey double knit. What do I care? This is the New York Yankees! This is the Big Apple! As the Yanks go, so goes New York, and as goes New York, so goes the world! Everybody knows that. Wait a minute . . . is that still right? Breathe. Figure it out. Two down, WASP on second, old chocolate face at the plate.

LUCKY: You're through! You're too old, Bronkowski! Can't even find the box! You're undisciplined, scatterbrained, inarticulate!

DUKE: Jesus, what's he sayin'? YOU GOT ON BASE ON A GIFT, YOU KNOW! That son-of-a-bitch don't bother me. To think I almost gave him a hit. Sure wish I could think of something mean to say to a WASP. All you can do is insult their taste and hope for the best. THE KINGSTON TRIO'S NEVER GETTING BACK TOGETHER AGAIN! THANKSGIVING IS BO-RING! JEWS ARE SMARTER! Oooo, that'll get 'em, Jews'll get 'em. JEWS ARE SMARTER! MORE CREATIVE! They don't like *that.*

LUCKY: Don't try to get out of it! You just can't throw anymore! You can't even pay for the furniture! What about that couch, huh? Poor Jeannie was in tears! You're a washout, a wet rag, a failure!

DUKE: Gee, these insults are awfully personal. Whatever happened to, "Hey, pitch, hey, pitcher"? Ah, forget it. Two down, you still got your no-hitter. You got the best infield money can buy backing you up. Except for that El Exigente reject at third who just ruined my life forever. Okay, okay, Lincoln Lewis Da Third. Old handkerchief head. One and oh. Time for the Old slider. *(He shakes off two signs)* I SAID THE SLIDER!

(He goes into the stretch, looks at second)

LUCKY: Failure! Fraud!

(He steps off the rubber)

DUKE: In '67 I made two Rapid Shave commercials and a public service spot against TB. I barely lost out on an Oldsmobile radio spot to Sandy Koufax which grossed him thousands. I had an agent and a lawyer and broads with thighs of honey all year long, whenever I wanted, way before groupies. I started to hang out with Mantle, did a spot on the Carson Show, almost got invited to the White House. I should've known it wouldn't last.

C'mon, c'mon, concentrate, concentrate, no more talkin'. You're behind on him two and oh. I'll throw whatever you want, Mr. Maligma. Boy, the first six innings were fantastic, weren't they? Got 'em down 1-2-3 in the first, 1-2-3 in the second, 1-2-3 in the third, and so on. Christ, I not only live in the past, I live in the past few minutes.

(He goes into the stretch. Johnson dances off second. Duke pitches and the crowd groans again. Beanie comes trotting out)

BEANIE: What's happenin' to you?

DUKE: I threw what you wanted, didn't I? You asked for the curve and I threw it, didn't I?

BEANIE: You asked for a curve and I threw it, didn't I, what?

DUKE: What? What what?

BEANIE: You asked for a curve and I threw it, didn't I, Mr. Maligma?

DUKE: Oh, Christ.

BEANIE: You asked for a curve and I threw it, didn't I, Mr. Maligma? Say it.

DUKE: You asked for a curve and I threw it, didn't I, Mr. Maligma . . . this is stupid! I feel stupid.

BEANIE: Well, you should. It's your own fault, you know.

DUKE: Look, Beanie, Mr. Maligma, I'm sorry, I didn't mean to make fun of your name — but I got problems.

BEANIE: Everybody's got problems. You'll just have to walk 'em off, just like Old Salt says. Did I ever tell you about my boy? He's twelve and he wants a Snowmobile.

DUKE: Yeah, you told me.

BEANIE: And Rowena wants custody of the house, our children, and my career.

DUKE: I know, I know.

BEANIE: And Bobbi, the baton twirler, wants a car to keep it outta the papers.

DUKE: I know all this!

BEANIE: Well, those are problems! Those are real problems!

DUKE: But they're the only ones you got! Anybody can solve those problems!

BEANIE: Oh, yeah, Mr. Dear Abby? How?

DUKE: Don't buy your son a Snowmobile, you're bigger than he is and you can beat him up if he gives you any trouble; don't worry about Rowena, you're not gonna get a divorce; and buy dopey

Bobbi a Honda like your boy's — they're cheaper and more chic than a car. Okay?

BEANIE: Not bad.

DUKE: Now your problems are solved.

BEANIE: Not so fast — what about my slump?

DUKE: Keep your eye on the ball.

BEANIE: Okay. Now what's the matter with you?

DUKE: I'm suffering from malaise, I feel downtrodden. I have problems of the spirit. Ya see, what's weird—I know what the problems are . . . I even know what's causin' 'em. I just don't know what to do about them.

BEANIE: Aww, it's all in your head.

DUKE: I know that! That's the problem!

BEANIE: Well, you better do somethin' about 'em or Old Salt'll be out here faster'n the Fordham Flash.

(Beanie pats Duke on the behind and starts to leave)

DUKE: Hey, Mr. Maligma!

BEANIE: You can call me Beanie—you've learned your lesson.

DUKE: Whadda we do about Lincoln Lewis Da Third?

BEANIE: Wanna try your slider?

DUKE: Okay. Good idea. *(Beanie leaves)* I had a cheerleader once, out of Detroit, too, in '68, my first bad year. I would've left home for her. She was the beginning of the end for me. I fell in love with the insides of her thighs, too, but she got tired of me when I didn't pan out professionally. I knew it was all over the last road trip of the season; I kissed her at the ballpark and her lips turned to ashes, her mouth wouldn't open. I never felt so undesirable. *(He goes into the stretch)*

LUCKY: You don't finish with a better won-lost record or E.R.A. than last year, you ain't gonna be back! Connecticut Federal ain't interested in a P.R. man with no P.R.!

(Duke pitches and the crowd groans again. The ball comes back)

DUKE: Jesus—another ball. Well, the rest is history. It's out of my control completely. I can't keep anything on my mind for longer than a single second—except Donna Luna Donna, and I can't keep her *off* my mind. I think of her and her honey thighs constantly. They're overpowering; they make me lose my balance. And she's always so *bronzed*. I can't stand it. She loves to lie in the sun — it's the only thing she cares about. I met her six months ago in Texas, and . . . and, why, here she is now, just as you like her . . .

(Donna Luna Donna enters, singing quietly, dressed briefly and very sexily)

Hi, Donna Luna Donna. Your tan sure looks great.

DONNA: If I could spend my whole life lying on sand in the sun, I would. I mean it, sugar. I love it, I love it. I used to love other things—fleshy things in my mouth, whispering sex words in your ear, but now I only love the sun.

DUKE: I understand. I used to love big breasts — breasts you could wrestle with, thrash around in and manhandle, twist into pretzels, Christmas decorations and interesting antique bottles. When I married Jeannie, her breasts were firm, but not any more. Big breasts used to be very popular — but the times have changed and I've changed with them. See the breasted Donna Luna Donna. Small. Compact. Barely noticeable. Just a hint of mammary.

(He moves behind her, pressing against her and rotating her breasts with his palms. They both moan quietly)

Mmmmm, these are so good. I love your honey thighs, how they come together like this. And I love your navel. There isn't a navel in the land that isn't sexy—even Kate Smith's navel is sexy. If only'd she get rid of all the clutter in there — copies of the Constitution, the Declaration of Independence, the lyrics to the *Ella Sings Irving Berlin* album, other assorted documents relating to our national history. Clear it out! Too much stuff, Kate!

DONNA LUNA DONNA: Duke first came to my attention a year ago. He looks like my father, and there's the essence of failure about him which is very attractive to me. Besides, there's hardly any competition for baseball players anymore, and none at all for unsuccessful ones, so I've got nothing to lose.

All my friends were after guitar players or else just busy with their boyfriends in parked cars—that still happens, you know, very few parents actually allow their kids to fuck right in the house, despite all the talk. Duke always provides a good, clean HoJo's. Also, there's some nice peer notoriety in going with a middle-aged ballplayer. And I wasn't otherwise engaged at the time, having just recovered in seclusion from some serious skin grafts necessitated by Duane the automobile mechanic's fondness for putting out his cigarettes on me. So one night at the ballpark about six months ago, when Duke'd been taken out of the game in the bottom of the third — when I see him failin' like that, I just get hot as hell, even now — I approached him outside the locker room and put my hand right inside his pants.

He's warmed to me ever since. He never says an unkind, restless word to me; he never treats me with anything but the kindest consideration. He's a true sweetie.

I reckon I'll have to dump him if he can't stay on the team—I do have a failure threshold. San Antonio Normal is a very demanding institution in that regard. But right now, I still lather for him right off.

DUKE: No hair gluts these armpits!

DONNA: I know it's just a phase, but for what it is, it's a good relationship. I have to go now.

DUKE: Okay. Still want me?

DONNA: You know I do, shoog.

DUKE: How's m'Lincoln?

DONNA.   Apple red and clearwater shiny.

DUKE: I'm doin' okay out here, ya know?

DONNA: I sure do, and I'm real proud and pouty. I better let you get on with it. Soon I believe I'd like to go to California where they say there's sun all the day long, and a person can truly get her brains baked. 'Bye now.

(She leaves. Duke is ferocious with passion)

DUKE: Where's the ball, where's the ball? *(He finds it in his glove. He yells to Beanie)* HEY, LINCOLN LEWIS—IT'S GONNA BE A FASTBALL!

(He winds up furiously and pitches. The crowd cheers)

UMPIRE: *(Hoarsely)* STEE-RYE! *(The ball comes back)*

DUKE: I knew it! FASTBALL SMOKIN' IN! *(Again he pitches)*

UMPIRE: *(Hoarsely)* STEE-RYE! *(The crowd cheers. The ball comes back)*

DUKE: Okay, mama — I knew she'd get it back for me. She always does. I sure don't wanna lose her. Hey! What's the count?

LUCKY: Six outs! Three balls! Trouble comin' back!

(Duke waves to Beanie, who runs out)

DUKE: What's the count?

BEANIE: Three and two. Christ, were those fastballs beauts! I haven't seen you pitch like that in years!

DUKE: Two down?

BEANIE: Yup. Smoke on more of 'em in, this boy'll be back in the minors by breakfast.

DUKE: Gotta do it with m'slider.

BEANIE: What?

DUKE: The fastballs were quirks of fate. I know my own arm. I gotta do the slider. I'd rather lose with my slider than win with my fastball.

BEANIE: Jesus, you're stupid.

DUKE: You're a real consolation, you know that? Mr. Maligma?

BEANIE: Beanie's okay.

DUKE: Oh no, not after all that. I like Mr. Maligma.

BEANIE: Just get on with it.

(Beanie trots off)

DUKE: Three and two. The payoff pitch. Gotta do it with the slider. Low and outside, make him hit it on the ground, and let's end this goddamn inning.

(Duke goes into the stretch)

LUCKY: Male chauvinist pig! Base Hungarian wight! Brazen hussy!

(Duke pitches and the crowd groans. The ball comes back and Lincoln Lewis trots down to first base)

DUKE: Jesus, I walked him. Now it really starts to be my fault. Can't blame it on the Cuban anymore. *(To Lincoln Lewis)* Welcome to first base, colonel. That Donna Luna Donna inspiration stuff never lasts very long. I could be slipping. Hey, what's that?

(In an aisle of the theatre, a right-handed relief pitcher named O'Donnell warms up with a Catcher. Their throws rhythmically emphasize Duke's action)

For Chrissake! One walk and they bring out the fire truck! "I got confidence in you, son," says that fart Old Salt and then he starts warming up O'Donnell after one walk and an error that wasn't even my fault. He looks pretty sinister, don't he? All right, all right, who we got here?

P.A. SYSTEM: Number twelve, the third baseman, Guido Mancini.

DUKE: Ah, the clothing magnate. In '71 this sleaze-o batted .321 and then went out and started up a whole line of clothing. Now he sells his outfits everywhere — every time he gets up to bat, it's a network commercial. Let's see, bounced to the Cisco Kid in the second, lined one to Popeye in the fifth. Let's try the curve. *(He goes into the stretch)*

LUCKY: What about your poor Jeannie? You haven't snookered her in three months! Think she's not playin' around? She wears a mattress to work every morning! That's the trouble with you guys that cheat — so much guilt it never occurs to you she may be taking remedial pelvic action of her own! With a guy built like a swimmer!

DUKE: Jesus!

LINCOLN LEWIS: Unctuous suburbanite! Ivory tower thinker!

DUKE: Christ, there's two of them now.

LINCOLN LEWIS: I'ze frightenin'! I'ze frightenin!!

DUKE: Jesus, do I hate bein' yelled at by a brown brethren. You can never call 'em what ya want to call 'em without bringing down the bleachers on you. They got a copyright on the word N, and they're mighty stingy with the rights. Only they can call each other Ns. *(In imitation:)* Hey, you N. See that N? Who's that N think he is? *(Yelling at LINCOLN LEWIS)* N,N,N,N,N! There. God, is this bad.

LINCOLN LEWIS: Boo-shee! Movin' in! Movin' in! What I'm gonna do to you! What I haven't done already!

DUKE: Don't answer him. Don't dignify with a reply. Oh, yeah?

LINCOLN LEWIS: Maximize your terror! Play upon your fears! Plunge headfirst into little Mitchie's nightmares! Oooo, you should see me when I wear a hat!

DUKE: I'm starting to shiver. I feel acrophobic all the time. I can't remember what I was gonna pitch. *(He pitches and the ball is hit to deep left. Duke follows it foul)* Aaaaaaggghh. Foul. Jesus, was that long. No more curves for lilla ginny-ginny-wop-wop-wop. I'VE SEEN YOUR CLOTHES, YOU KNOW! You should see some of his stuff. Hang a Mancini sportjacket in the bedroom, you don't need a nightlight. Hang one in the bathroom, you don't need a mirror. This is it. The beginning of the end. I'm crumbling fast. I'm no fatalist, but this is it. *(He looks at O'Donnell warming up)* He looks happy. IT WAS FOUL, YA KNOW! But hoo, was it long.

LUCKY: Hey, man, whadda you think of this guy?

LINCOLN LEWIS: You kidding? He extinct!

DUKE: Quit talking about me like I wasn't here! I can hear it all! All! *(He pitches. The crowd groans)* Ball one. *(As the ball comes back to Duke, O'Donnell throws one at him that narrowly misses)* Hey! Hey, what the hell is that? You threw a baseball at me! I'm havin' a hard enough time up here — knock it off!

LUCKY: Freemason! Homesteader!

LINCOLN LEWIS: Opponent ɔf the Patrolman's Benevolent Association!

DUKE: Jesus, I never heard such insults. The curve or the slider — I'll throw anything you want. Just tell me what to do. *(Goes into the stretch as Doc Matthews, a left-handed relief pitcher, warms up in another aisle)* Hey, what's this? Another reliever? Doc Matthews, too? All my fairweather friends.

LINCOLN LEWIS: Fantasy monger! Prince of Daydreams! This is what you get for breaking all those windows at thirteen! *(Duke pitches, the crowd groans. The ball comes back)*

DUKE: Two and one. There are times when a fella really needs a resin bag. *(As he plays with a resin bag, O'Donnell and Matthews throw baseballs at him, and one of them hits him)* Hey! Knock it off — what's goin' on here? I don't need this! This is aggravation! Since when do relief pitchers throw baseballs at the guy in a jam? Jesus! It's getting awfully lonely out here.

Here's the part of the game where inevitability asserts itself. I don't like this part, but I'm sure familiar with it. Hope m'Lincoln's okay. Sure is ugly, but it's such a nice reminder. Two and one. Ask for the slider, Beanie boy. *(He shakes off a sign)* You can always count on Lawrence Larry Beanie Maligma to be in your corner the night of the big fight.

LINCOLN LEWIS: Neighbors hate you—even friends! Mainly friends! Now you know why Brademas wouldn't lend you that mower! Not 'cause it didn't work! *(Duke goes into the stretch, pitches, and the crowd groans. The ball comes back)*

LUCKY: I told ya! I told ya!

DUKE: Christ, I feel like I'm falling off the side of the earth. Let's approach this logically. Suppose my career in the majors is over, A; B, suppose the burger franchise has one more bad year like last year when McDonald's moved in two blocks away; C, suppose the Golden Wasp there is right, suppose Connecticut Federal doesn't want a public relations man with no public relations. *(Pause)* I've got no answers! Grab the ball! Tighter! Whew. That was close. I was fucking scared! *(O'Donnell and Matthews unleash balls at once)* Hey! Cut it out! Jesus! How come you guys are throwin' baseballs at me! Huh? Now where the hell's the ball? I'm being bruised black and blue by these two so-called friendly teammates of mine, and now I can't even find the ball. *(He motions to Beanie to throw the ball back. Nothing happens)* THROW ME THE BALL! *(A basketball bounces out from stage left)* This is a basketball. Hey, c'mere! GET YOUR ASS OUT HERE! *(Beanie jogs in)* What's the wise idea?

BEANIE: Whadda ya mean?

DUKE: What's the idea of throwin' out this basketball?

BEANIE: Just pitch the ball. I'm tired of your problems.

DUKE: This is a *basketball*. This is the *wrong ball* for this game.

BEANIE: C'mon, c'mon, you gonna let a little ball get the better of you? I'll ask for the slider if that'll make you happy. *(Beanie trots off)*

DUKE: I don't believe it. Not only do I have to put up with these clowns out here—not to mention a third baseman wearing mittens — now this. What if I make it to the next inning? I have to pitch with a hockey puck? *(Duke goes into the stretch, pitches the basketball. Mancini singles to shallow left, but it's too short to drive in a run. The bases are loaded)* Jesus, a single. There goes my no-hitter. There goes everything. The razor blades, Donna Luna Donna, everything, forever. I can't take it. Oh, no!

(Old Salt enters)

OLD SALT: I mean business. Listen to me, son, and listen hard.

The worst pig gets the best pear.

DUKE: What?

OLD SALT: *(Singing)* The best minute of the day; the best minute of the da-aa—ay.

DUKE: But wait a minute—

OLD SALT: Listen to me, son: a vision for the ages. I love you like you were my own boy—that goes for all of you! Listen. Remember: women, priests, and poultry, are never satisfied.

DUKE: What?

OLD SALT: You've gotta do some of the work yourself, Dumbo Doody, Jesus! Remember: life is too short to waste time on truffles. He ain't heavy, father, he's m'brother; never trouble trouble til' trouble troubles you. We won't stop tryin' til' we get your WEO; it's a blind goose that comes to the fox's sermon. Huh? Huh? Here's Johnny. Peaches with honor. No house without a mouse, no throne without a thorn. Get it?

DUKE: No . . . I . . .

OLD SALT: Jesus! Mail early in the day, it's the better way. Here's the kicker. Listen: morals are the core of culture, and therefore letters without virtue are like pearls in a dunghill. Right, Beanie?

BEANIE: Damn right!

OLD SALT: Does that help you, son?

DUKE: They made me pitch with a basketball!

OLD SALT: DOES THAT HELP YOU, SON?

DUKE: Oh, yeah, yeah. There's much wisdom in what you say, much wisdom. But they made me pitch with a basketball!

OLD SALT: I know, son, I know. The swine! I'll see that it doesn't happen again.

DUKE: Then Mancini's hit doesn't count?

OLD SALT: Of course it counts! And I'm saying that for your own good.

DUKE: Even though I had to pitch with a basketball?

OLD SALT: Why you so upset about that?

DUKE: Because a basketball's harder to pitch than a baseball!

OLD SALT: True, but it's also harder to hit. Think of that for a moment. You have to learn respect for your opponents when they do well, son, even if you don't like them personally. Remember: when the going gets tough, the fuffle gets sluddy. Now if there's anything else I can do for you, son, don't hesitate to let me know. I can't come out again in this inning, you know, except to replace you, but you can phone me. Now let me pat you on the ass and let's get going.

DUKE: Sure. Thanks. *(Old Salt runs off to wild crowd approval)* At least I got a baseball back. I'm gonna have to do this all on my own. Two down, bases loaded, bottom of the ninth. No, it's the top of the seventh; it just seems like the bottom of the ninth.

P.A. SYSTEM: Number three, the center fielder, Brick Brock.

DUKE: Oh, Jesus, not brick Brock. Bases loaded and I get Brick Brock, the home run king of America. He hit m'slider so hard in the second, Digiatelli damn near broke his hip diving into the stands to catch it. I whiffed him in the fifth, but only by not looking where I was throwing. Jesus! Brick Brock. *(He takes a full windup and pitches as he finishes the last line of dialogue. The crowd groans. The ball comes back)* Ball one. I know what's gonna happen. It's inevitable. First my perfect game, then my no-hitter, in a minute my shutout, then victory. Either this guy hits a home run, winning the game and ending my career, or I do something humiliating like hit him in the face with m'slider. Gotta be. Rizzuto must be goin' crazy up there in the booth. I wonder if the cameras are pickin' up my panic — Jeannie'll be able to see that, if she's watching. Get those cameras off me, Rizzuto!

GUIDO: You're doomed!

DUKE: Jesus, not another one. I can't take it!

GUIDO: Can't you see the handwriting on the wall? What'll you do when you're through here? Nobody'll want you, you won't be traded. Back to the minors!

DUKE: Oh, God, no, I couldn't stand that. Jeannie couldn't stand that. My boys'd start lookin' in my underwear. Donna Luna Donna'd be gone for sure.

LUCKY: You're gonna lose her anyway, you know that. Your last chance to be young! Blow this and you'll be thirty-six goin' on seventy! *(Duke fires a strike)*

UMPIRE: STEE-RYE! *(And the crowd cheers. The ball comes back)*

DUKE: Jesus, I made it! A goddamn strike! *(To Lincoln)* Did you see that? I'm gonna make it. Did you see that, honkey?

LINCOLN LEWIS: One strike, one strike, that's all, you got two to go, you'll never get it by him! You could, but you'll talk yourself out of it!

DUKE: Jesus, you guys won't budge, will you? ALL RIGHT, FROM NOW ON, I'M NOT LISTENIN' TO YOU ANYMORE! YOUR WORDS MEAN NOTHING! THESE CANALS ARE CLOSED TO INSULTS!

GUIDO: *(Seductively)* Oh, Dukey . .

DUKE: . . . Yeah?

GUIDO: *(Harsh again)* The trick ain't to keep us out. It's to keep us in!

DUKE: *(Winding up and pitching)* Christ, Christ, throw the ball, throw the ball! *(He pitches. It's a ball)*

LINCOLN LEWIS: What'd I say? What'd I say?

LUCKY: Ball Two! Ball Two! Soon ball four or outta the park! *(The ball comes back to Duke)*

GUIDO: Your future's blank! Lasts five minutes! No horizons, Bronkowski, no safe places!

DUKE: *(Whispering intensely)* I got a future! It's a secret! It's a knuckler! I ain't ever pitched one before, but I know I can do it right now. I can feel the shaft. Tips of the fingers, right, Whitey? Tips of the fingers, right, Old Salt? Tips of the fingers. Let's see a little forecast of what's comin' up.

LUCKY: *(As Duke pitches)* This is a knuckler? This is your future! *(Duke pitches a wobbly knuckle ball and makes a terrible face)*

DUKE: God! A crazy pitch. I hate to say it, but thank God for Mr. Maligma.

(Beanie trots out, just barely onstage, and throws the ball back angrily. Then he disappears)

BEANIE: You almost killed me!

DUKE: SERVES YOU RIGHT! What's that bad knuckler s'posed to mean — I got no future?

LINCOLN LEWIS: *(Almost in falsetto)* Breee! Breee! Breee!

LUCKY: *(Pointing to Brick Brock)* He's got fourteen girls! You got one!

GUIDO: *(Overlapping)* Breee! Breee! Breee!

DUKE: They're whistling like cranes! The loons are closing in. I'm no closer to an answer. CUT IT OUT! SETTLE DOWN! *(The yelling dies down)* I know what the solution is! God, why didn't I think of this before? I've been pitching all these years — it's so simple, Jesus—with the *wrong arm*! I'm a natural left-hander, momma knew that!

GUIDO: What about the kids? What if they find you wanting? They laugh at your jokes now, but what about their adolescence? They'll see right through you! You've no flesh, no spunk, no saving grace!

DUKE: God! It's gonna be left-handed. It's my last hope.

(He winds up. The insults come as he pitches)

LUCKY: Still can't dance! Still no savvy!

LINCOLN LEWIS: Slapdash tramp! Got no flash! Got no verve!

(Duke pitches. The crowd cheers. He is amazed)

DUKE: Jesus, a strike! How ya like that? All well and good, but what do I do now? Pitch again left-handed? Is that the answer? Arbitrarily change my way of life in midstream?

LINCOLN LEWIS: Left-handed's just a trick, just a gimmick!

LUCKY: Don't be stupid! You can't do it!

DUKE: Jesus!

P.A. SYSTEM: He's a better man than you are, plain and simple.

DUKE: Hey!

LINCOLN LEWIS: He's a better man than you are, plain and simple.

ALL THREE: Plain and simple, plain and simple!

GUIDO: You're through! Your life is over and you're only thirty-six! What're you gonna do? What *can* you do?

DUKE: Don't be stupid—I could always be a football coach, football coaches are very respected. Look at Woody Hayes, look at Bear Bryant . . .

LINCOLN LEWIS: Woody Hayes! Bear Bryant!

DUKE: Look at Bud Wilkinson! He's in the President's cabinet, for Chrissake! Or he was, anyway. I could manage a movie theatre or a bowling alley, be a dental assistant . . . I've got a nice sense of irony, I could be a newscaster. I could be a chauffeur to someone famous, or a counselor . . . a bootblack . . . think up new names for automobiles or cigarettes . . . There're lots of things I could do! I'm not helpless, you know!

ALL THREE: Woody Hayes, Bear Bryant! Woody Hayes, Bear Bryant!

(Duke goes into the stretch)

DUKE: Three and two, the big one due. This is it — I got no place to hide. This is the final pitch, this is the end of my life. Okay. I'm ready. I'm prepared. Bases loaded, two down, the count's unavoidable—three and two. Gotta be the slider. And in the slider, he's gettin' my best. This is it. Here it comes.

LINCOLN LEWIS: This is it! Here it comes!

ALL THREE: This is it! Here it comes! This is it! Here it comes!

(The Baserunners chant like maniacs until Duke releases the ball, at which point everything–including the crowd–becomes silent for an exaggerated moment. Then the sound of bat hitting ball lifts the roof off the theatre. It's a home run. The Runners clear the bases)

LUCKY: Thanks, Duke.

LINCOLN LEWIS: Thanks, Duke.

GUIDO: Thanks, Duke. Nothing personal.

BRICK BROCK: Thanks, guy. You're okay in my book.

(Duke walks off the mound into the audience. Beanie and Old Salt enter stage left)

DUKE: Well, that's it, folks. Maybe Old Salt's right—maybe it was those two years of college.

OLD SALT: Just where d'ya think you're going?

DUKE: Me? To the showers.

OLD SALT: Come back here.

DUKE: Why?

OLD SALT: Come back here!

DUKE: My life's fallin' down around me! My future's an empty barrel. My slider won't break, my fastball isn't fast, my catcher hates me, my teammates are throwin' things at me, three guys on the other team somehow found out all about my life and are torturing me with it, my house is infested with termites and was burgled early this morning. My wife's in bed with a swimmer's body, my two boys have become fags, my darling Donna Luna Donna's taken her thighs out of circulation, my ham radio's been dismantled and broken for good, the vote's been given to eighteen-year-olds, I'm thirty-six going on seventy, and I don't know what to do! Why should I come back?

OLD SALT: For the good of the game, son.

DUKE: For the good of the game.

OLD SALT: That's right, son, for the good of the game.

(Duke walks back to the mound)

DUKE: I don't believe this. Why'm I goin' back? You mean I'm not out of the game?

OLD SALT: Oh, you're out of the game. Whoo, are you out of the game!

DUKE: Then why'd you make me come back?

OLD SALT: So I could tell you that. My power must be absolute.

DUKE: Oh, no.

OLD SALT: You don't play the piano when the house is afire, boy. And thou hadst better eat salt with the philosophers of Greece than sugar with the courtiers of Italy. I'm a father figure to all of you, goddamnit, how come you never got that?

DUKE: You mean I have to walk back across the field in front of all the fans again?

OLD SALT: Of course.

DUKE: Why?

OLD SALT: Why? Why? Why? Why? 'Cause that's the way it's done. This is ball! This is organized ball!

DUKE: Oh. Yeah.

OLD SALT: With your head down, boy. You know. Or at least you should by now.

DUKE: Don't I get a pat on the ass this time?

OLD SALT: No, sir, bob-o-linky. You been a bad boy. No son o' mine.

(Duke walks into the audience)

DUKE: Well, that wasn't so bad. At least the uncertainty's over.

BEANIE: *(To Old Salt)* You wanna go with the right-hander or the southpaw?

(Old Salt flips a coin, gestures with his left hand)

OLD SALT: The southpaw.

Blackout

Marc Alan Zagoren

KNIGHT OF THE
TWELFTH SAUCER

Marc Alan Zagoren

With *Knight of the Twelfth Saucer,* a tender and poignant play about people attempting to fulfill themselves, Marc Alan Zagoren makes his debut in *The Best Short Plays* series.

The author was born in Perth Amboy, New Jersey, in 1940, and received his academic degrees from the University of Michigan and the Yale School of Drama. While at Michigan, he studied playwriting with Kenneth Thorpe Rowe and twice was the recipient of the Jule and Avery Hopwood Award administered by the university.

In addition to *Knight of the Twelfth Saucer* (published here for the first time), Mr. Zagoren has written several full-length plays: *The Signorina; Henry's Day;* and *Dalliance.* Readings and productions of his plays have been presented across the country from the Manhattan Theatre Club to the Shubert Theatre in Los Angeles.

He is also the author of two screenplays, *Chasing Rainbows* and *Sydna Areson,* as well as the television drama, *For the Price of Three Roses.*

In collaboration with David S. Meranze, Mr. Zagoren wrote the play, *Curtains,* which is currently under option for Broadway production, and the screenplays: *Second Fiddle; Dutch Treat;* and *Gilbert.*

As an adjunct to his writing, he teaches theatre and film at Fairleigh Dickinson University, and lives in nearby Montclair, New Jersey, with his wife, Stephanie.

Characters:

TILLIE
ROSE
SHANAKIND (EDNA)
ARNOLD

The play takes place in the late nineteen fifties.

Scene One:

Spot on a table at an automat in Manhattan.

Rose Wittman, a very large middle-aged woman, who despite her mammoth size manages to retain about herself a remarkable delicate quality, has spread herself out and is seriously considering which delicacy in front of her she should sample first. Unable to decide among the tuna fish platter, the ice cream sundae and the chocolate layer cake, Rose employs a child's ritualistic method for selection. The ice cream sundae is thus designated. But Rose, somehow not completely satisfied with this choice, gives a shrug of the shoulders, and with a somewhat explanatory "Eh" cuts for herself instead a very large piece of the chocolate layer cake. As she does this a tired and frail woman is making her way to Rose's table. On Tillie's tray is a cup of black coffee only. Tillie speaks first.

TILLIE: Is there anybody sittin' here?
ROSE: No. Nobody.
TILLIE: Well, there ain't no more empty tables left. You mind if I park myself a minute?
ROSE: No. No, of course not. Go right ahead. Sit down.
(Tillie sits as Rose begins to busy herself with the sundae and the chocolate layer cake. Tillie lights a cigarette and is staring vacantly into space when:)
ROSE: Oh, no. Now I spilled myself. *(To Tillie)* Excuse me a second, but have you got a hankie or a Kleenex? I used my last tissue in the bakemaster.
TILLIE: Wait a minute. I'll take a look.
ROSE: Really, I'm sorry to bother you this way.
TILLIE: No bother. *(She begins to rummage through her handbag now)* Someday I gotta give this pocketbook one good cleaning out. Here. I got a hankie, only it's a little soiled.
ROSE: Not a napkin anywheres on this table. *(Turning to Tillie)* You're sure you haven't got yourself a Kleenex or something?
TILLIE: Here's a fresh tissue.

ROSE: Thank you. Thank you very much. *(Gesturing towards Tillie's water)* May I?

TILLIE: Sure, sure. Be my guest.

ROSE: I think I made myself a good stain here. Just took this dress out of the cleaners yesterday, today I think I'm going to have to return it.

TILLIE: Look, instead of taking it to the cleaners, before you go home today, why don't you take yourself a walk over to the Food Fair and pick up a bottle of stain remover? Four months ago I bought a bottle of stain remover. Now you should see. I never have to send anything to the cleaners no more.

ROSE: *(Beginning to swirl her dress a bit to get it dry)* Such a nice dress. Such a shame I had to spill anything on it. I'm sorry I ordered the chocolate sundae . . . Here, why don't you have my little tuna? I didn't even taste it. Lost my whole appetite.

TILLIE: *(Anxiously eyeing the platter)* I can't.

ROSE: Listen, they make a very good tuna salad here. I really wish you'd take it.

TILLIE: Oh no, no. It's your tuna.

ROSE: Nonsense. Go on and take it. Besides if you don't eat it, it's only going to go to waste . . . *(Extending her plate generously)* Here. Go on. Have it and enjoy it.

TILLIE: *(Taking the plate)* Not hungry really. I mean if I were hungry—Just that I don't want it to go to waste . . . Thank you. Thank you very much. *(She starts to eat and then:)* You're right. Certainly is very good . . . Very nice dress you're wearing, lady. I'm sure the stain'll come out easily.

ROSE: You like the dress?

TILLIE: Very good material. I can tell.

ROSE: Last summer I bought this dress. My husband, for our anniversary, he took the day off and helped me pick it out. He liked the way the dress looked on me. That's why I bought it. Maybe why I'm so extra specially fond of it even today. Everybody in the family always said, Rose's Louie, he's got the taste of a prince . . . Oh Louie, when Louie was alive we certainly were a happy family the three of us. One child we got—a daughter. Even today she misses her daddy so much. Such a good girl she is, look what she just gave me for my fiftieth birthday.

(Rose points to the wrist watch on her hand)

TILLIE: Very nice. Very, very nice.

ROSE: Of a heart attack Louie died. They told him beforehand. Louie, you gotta stop all your between meal eating. You heart's not that strong anymore. Who should know that better than a heart doctor like you? But Louie and me, well, we both come from a family of big eaters, if you know what I mean. And Louie—I think he loved my cooking almost as much as he loved me. *(Swallowing hard)* Lost him in less than a minute. Twenty six years. Not a moment to say goodbye . . . You see the stain yet?

TILLIE: Just the outline a drop.

ROSE: I think maybe I should let it dry a few seconds more.

TILLIE: Your husband—I'm not a question asker—he went to school in the city?

ROSE: Columbia. That's where I first met Louie. Eight years Louis spent at Columbia.

TILLIE: That Columbia's got a good medical school I'm very much aware of. I'm sure if it weren't for the interview my son Arnold would've been accepted also. Just whenever Arnold gets a little nervous, he begins his scratching. Was the scratching that made him end up at NYU. And you shouldn't shrug your shoulders neither. NYU's got a very fine reputation.

ROSE: I wasn't shrugging my shoulders. Why Louie himself thought NYU was a very fine medical school. Anyways you certainly ought to be very proud of your son for going out for medicine. It's a very difficult course of study but a rewarding and noble profession.

TILLIE: Of my Arnold I'm proud. Proud to have even got him this far. My Arnold's going to finish NYU if it's the last thing I do. He's not going to end up like his father Philip did. Not if I have anything to do with it . . . Philip, I mean who was Philip? With my sister's husband it was different. Highly educated. He was an important man. Family respected him. Community respected him. When he died they all showed the respect. But Philip, Philip was just some poor little cocker shoemaker. Worked himself to the bone. Little bit Philip made from a heel here, sole there, we three had just about enough to eat. Used to get up every morning of the week, seven a.m., Sundays included, to open the store. Said he was happy. Happy just to have a little place of his own to work in. Always would tell me, we're not rich people, Tillie, at least we got the world of friends. We're rich with all the friends we've got. *(Biting her lip now, each word an effort to get out)* Friends! Some friends! To the funeral . . . three people. My sister . . . Arnold . . . me.

ROSE: I don't understand. Your husband, if he had such good friends, a man's funeral—

TILLIE: The doctor gets a big funeral. The lawyer gets a big funeral. The shoemaker only gets a lick and a smell. Well, with my Arnold it's going to be different. Very different, and that I'm going to see to. My Arnold's going to be somebody. A very important man. If I have to keep working night and day to do it, my Arnold's going to finish NYU, and that you can be rest assured.

ROSE: I admire you very much. Really I do. No, I don't know if I would be strong enough to do the things you're doing.

TILLIE: Anything I can do for my Arnold, my Arnold deserves, and it's only my privilege and pleasure to do so. Arnold's a good boy. Always minds and is well liked at school. One year. Thank god, that's all Arnold's got left yet. Just one more year.

ROSE: Just one more year. You should be thankful the worst part is over.

TILLIE: Come here. I'm going to tell you something on the q.t. Strictly confidential . . . I haven't been feeling up to par as of late, so two weeks ago I take myself a little walk over to see my doctor. Bladder troubles I got. The doctor says I got a stone the size of a mush melon growing on top of one of my kidneys. An operation he says I need. Big shot I tell him. Who can afford an operation?

ROSE: Kidneys. You always got to look after the kidneys.

TILLIE: Listen, I'll tell you right here and now no mush melon growing on top of one of my kidneys is going to stop my Arnold now.

ROSE: I had a friend once who didn't look after her kidneys. Here one day, gone the next. Kidneys are nothing to fool around with.

TILLIE: Still, still I ask you just where do you think I'm going to be able to get the money for an operation and still have enough money for Arnold's schooling besides. Where! Where!

(For a moment there is silence. Then Rose, slowly looking down at her wrist watch pauses several seconds before she starts to speak)

ROSE: Uh, tell me, your Arnold. Listen, you wouldn't happen to have a picture of your Arnold now by any chance?

TILLIE: Sure. Sure. *(She begins rummaging through her pocketbook)* What kind of mother wouldn't carry around the picture of her only son? *(Proudly pushing the photograph forward)* Look!

ROSE: *(Very carefully scrutinizing the photograph)* This is your son? Your Arnold?

TILLIE: *(Enormously proud)* Yeah. Handsome, ain't he!

ROSE: *(Making certain).* This is the Arnold that's going to become the doctor?

TILLIE: *(Almost in awe)* This is the Arnold that's going to become the doctor.

ROSE: The picture here, it's very nice. Only your Arnold, he looks so skinny. Got a nice smile though. Very gentle. Very easy to see that.

(Tillie looks at her son's photograph again)

TILLIE: Arnold's got a nice face, eh? Even here where Arnold's just finishing up with exams and his skin is all broken out. Even here he's got a nice face. Besides, what's a pimple here and there mean anyways? A pimple is certainly no measure of a man's character. And that's what my son Arnold's got. He's got character.

ROSE: Tell me, your Arnold, he's a healthy boy, huh? I mean no sickness.

TILLIE: Strong like an ox Arnold is. Hasn't had a cold since he had his tonsils removed. Athletic also, if you ask me. Every night thirty-five push-ups he does, one sitting, before he goes to bed. I'm telling you, Arnold, he's like a regular bulldozer.

ROSE: Thirty-five push-ups. Very interesting.

TILLIE: A skyscraper. Everybody says Arnold's the skyscraper of the family. My Arnold's like a tree he is, no shorty like my husband or myself. *(Most proudly of all)* Why my Arnold is practically five-foot-eight!

ROSE: Five-foot-eight. My, my, five-foot-eight! *(As lightly as possible)* Why five-foot-eight would be just the perfect height for my sweet little daughter Edna. Oh, not that I'm suggesting anything, but Edna, she's twenty-four years old, five-foot-five, such a lovely, lovely child butter wouldn't melt in her mouth. Oh, sure I don't want you to think I'm imposing in the least but from the little I know about your Arnold, well I wouldn't be too surprised if your Arnold wouldn't just enjoy meeting my darling Edna.

TILLIE: *(There is a long moment. And then a bit too quickly)* Oh, Arnold, Arnold's first got another year of medical school yet, two years of interning, even two years with the army. Well, Arnold, he's just not going to be ready for any one girl for quite some time yet . . . You say you call your daughter Edna?

ROSE: Her real name's Edna, but ever since I don't know when we've been calling her Shanakind.

TILLIE: You actually named your daughter Edna?

ROSE: Edna—such a pretty name, isn't it? Sweet like a blossom. She even looks like an Edna. Everybody's always telling her that. I'd show you a picture of her only a picture'd never begin to do her justice.

TILLIE: Tell me something I don't understand. You got a daughter twenty-four years old and she ain't married yet? So what's wrong? Girl from Brooklyn not married by the time she's twenty-four, that's certainly very strange.

ROSE: Just my daughter's very fussy, that's all. I'm quite certain if Edna wanted to, well, she could've been married a dozen times over already. She's studying . . . medical technology at the

Brooklyn Institute. Since I don't remember when Edna's only been
going out with the very finest of medical students. In fact, to be
perfectly truthful, only a medical student would my Edna even
consider to date. Certainly a very lucky girl she can afford to be so
selective.

TILLIE: Puh, puh. Only a medical student. Sounds like you got
yourself some fancy thing on your hands.

ROSE: I said, Edna, you really ought to get down on your hands
and knees, and be thankful for all the wonderful things you've got.
For your sweet-like disposition, for the very fine clothes you're able
to wear, for all the very very nice things your teachers have always
had to say about you in school and . . . and also for that nice little
bit of money your father left you as a dowry so maybe you could
help your husband finish medical school, get himself a little established as well.

TILLIE: Finish medical school? Get established did you say?

ROSE: I said, Edna, to be such a lucky, lucky girl you really have
to be just so grateful. *(In the most distinct tones of all)* After all, twenty
thousand shares of AT&T is certainly nothing to sneeze at.

TILLIE: *(Aghast)* Twenty thousand shares of AT&T?

ROSE: Oh, my goodness, my goodness. You will excuse me.
Somehow for the moment I must've gotten a bit carried away and
completely forgot myself. I mean talking about money, dropping
such figures to strangers.

TILLIE: Please, please. We're not such strangers.

ROSE: Where was my head?

TILLIE: Think nothing of it at all.

ROSE: Oh, well, I guess I better gather myself together. Won't
be more than an hour before I'll have to be putting up supper.

TILLIE: *(She is on the verge of being frantic now)* Look, about what
you said before. I mean about your Edna and my Arnold.

ROSE: Well, someday perhaps. Anyway it certainly was pleasant
meeting you.

TILLIE: Listen, well I just know your Edna would enjoy meeting
my Arnold. After all an almost doctor and a, a—

ROSE: Medical technologist.

TILLIE: Yes, yes, medical technologist. Well, certainly they've
got a lot in common just to begin with . . . But look, look if you'd
rather just forget about it maybe—

ROSE: Whatever you want. I mean whatever you want to do
would suit me perfectly.

TILLIE: Well, to me it really doesn't make any difference. I
mean Arnold, well, he goes out just the same with girls one way or

another. I mean, well, I just thought the idea of getting the kids together purely for professional reasons—Look, if you'd like to make a specific date—

ROSE: Well, what about Monday? I'm gonna put a couple of pullets into the oven for us. There's certainly no reason I can think of why I possibly couldn't put an extra one in for your Arnold. Would Monday be all right?

TILLIE: *(Just a little too quickly)* Monday? Why Monday would be just fine!

(Blackout)

Scene Two:

Rose's living room in a two-family Brooklyn brownstone apartment house. It is late afternoon the following Monday.

The living room which opens on to a comfortably airy sun porch is pleasantly decorated and distinguished only by a curious set of end tables which really act to serve as tiny twin refrigerators. Inside one end table are all sorts of ice cream confections while the other is crammed full of chicken legs and cold meats. Open boxes of candy are generously strewn about the room. The dining room table is set for company.

Shanakind (Edna) enters the living room from the sun porch. As bountiful as Rose, she is unfortunately neither delicate nor beautiful. Shanakind spends the bulk of her time alternating excessive eating with perspiring and powdering herself. Shanakind crosses to the end table with the chicken legs inside it and picks for herself a choice bone to nibble on. She then sprawls herself on the couch, fan in one hand, chicken leg in the other and a magazine on her lap. Although it is five-thirty and the company is expected shortly, Shanakind is still not dressed for dinner. She is busy nibbling on the chicken leg as Rose enters.

ROSE: Shanakind, what am I going to do with you? I spend ten minutes puffing the whole sofa up, and you come in here just like Madam Fifi and spread yourself all over the place. Now come on and get dressed.

SHANAKIND: *(Totally lacking any expression in her voice)* You invited him to dinner, Mama. Anything that may possibly go wrong tonight, you got no one to blame for but yourself.

ROSE: Nothing is going to go wrong tonight, Shanakind. You hear what I'm saying?

SHANAKIND: Mama, it's bad enough you got to invite a boy over for dinner without first asking me. But you got to invite him for Monday night no less. You know Monday's the only night I go to the movies. You know Monday's the only night they give the dishes away.

ROSE: Shanakind, be quiet.

SHANAKIND: For eleven weeks I've been collecting saucers. For eleven weeks I've been looking forward to this night more than anything else. Looking forward to completing my saucer service. For my trousseau. So how do you think it's going to look if I've got twelve cups and only eleven saucers? Next week they start on spoons already.

ROSE: Shanakind, for God's sakes be still!

SHANAKIND: You know what the manager of our neighborhood Orpheum said about my taste in dishes just last Monday, Mama? He said my Fragrant Flower pattern suited me to a "T".

ROSE: Spoons and dishes and dishes and spoons! That's all that ever comes out of your mouth. For once I want to hear a little something else.

SHANAKIND: The manager himself told me he thought the pattern of my dishes was very strange and very oriental.

ROSE: Shanakind, get dressed. Get dressed before I completely lose my patience! Five-thirty already. He's going to be here in less than an hour and there's absolutely no reason in the whole world why you're going to keep him waiting even five seconds. Now come on. Get dressed and let me puff up the couch.

SHANAKIND: I think I should go and take myself a little dip in the tub. I feel kind o' sticky.

ROSE: Not half an hour ago I just got done cleaning the whole bathtub out.

SHANAKIND: I feel sticky, Mama. And you shouldn't get so upset about it either.

ROSE: With you I certainly didn't get any bargain. What's the matter? Madam Fifi couldn't't've marched herself into the bathtub maybe an hour earlier? Well, just listen to me. There's no time left for bathing now. Tonight if you want to freshen up, you'll just have to take some talc from the bathroom and dust under the arms.

SHANAKIND: Mama, I am very hot and very dirty. I already checked myself very carefully under the arms. Powdering won't do.

ROSE: Get dressed!

SHANAKIND: *(She now takes an enormous bite off the chicken bone)* You could wring me out, Mama. Positively wring me out. I was very uncomfortable all afternoon in the laboratory.

(She then emits a belch. There is a stunned silence)

ROSE: *(Absolutely furious now)* Shanakind, for God's sakes, put down that bone this minute!

SHANAKIND: I'm sorry. Just that I got a little piece of chicken leg stuck in the back of my throat.

ROSE: God, God, just tell me what kind of animal am I bringing up in my house anyways? Always a little piece of food stuck in your mouth. Always a little chicken leg lying around for you to nibble on. Just once I'd like to see you with your mouth empty. You know what you are, Shanakind? I'll tell you what you are. You're a pig. A pig! A pig! A pig!

SHANAKIND: *(Slowly and devastatingly)* Go on, Mama. Go on and insult me more. Only now I got a nice little surprise cooked up for you. *(There is an altogether dreadful pause)* I don't think I'll be coming to your dinner party tonight. I—I just remembered I've got a—a conflicting engagement someplace else.

ROSE: Shanakind, don't push me too far.

SHANAKIND: For shouting at me and for calling me a pig, I sincerely thank you. I'll tell the truth. I was looking for an excuse to get out of coming to dinner anyways. You invited him to dinner, Mama. Well, then you have dinner with him alone.

ROSE: Shanakind!

SHANAKIND: As for me I think I'll take myself a little walk over to the neighborhood Orpheum and finish off my saucer service.

ROSE: You are not going to leave this house tonight! You hear me? You are not going to throw away your one opportunity to meet a nice unmarried boy. I'm not going to let you.

SHANAKIND: Mama, you wouldn't want me to make one of my scenes tonight, would you? Remember how embarrassed you were when I had that little trauma when you took me to Uncle Harold's up in the mountains? You wouldn't want me to make a scene in front of this boy, Mama?

ROSE: Shanakind, listen to me. For once open your ears and try to hear what mama's saying. Oh Shanakind, Shanakind, who do you think I arranged this dinner party for anyways, huh? You think I made it to entertain myself? Shanakind, look at me. It's just I want you to meet a nice boy. Twenty-four, Shanakind. You were twenty-four last March. A girl your age should be seriously considering marriage.

SHANAKIND: Please don't start up with the marriage again, Mama. I don't think I'm up to talking about marriage again tonight . . . Mama, Mama, why is it I have to worry about meeting anybody anyways? I'm happy, believe me, here with you. Everything I could ever want anywhere, I've got it all here. Even if I want to nibble. For my last birthday Granny Esther gave me my own little refrige in my bedroom.

ROSE: It isn't right you should want to nibble so much. And it isn't right you shouldn't want to go out to meet a nice boy. Shanakind, so worried am I about you. Can't you understand that, sweetheart? I'm not always going to be here. Someday you're going to have to get used to that idea. And when that someday comes you should have somebody to turn to. You should have a husband and you should have a family.

SHANAKIND: Mama, I don't understand you since papa died. What is it! All of a sudden you have to get rid of me. All of a sudden you have to marry me off. Tell me, Mama, am I so much in the way since papa died you got to get rid of me?

ROSE: Shanakind, sweetheart, of course that's not it.

SHANAKIND: Then I don't understand. I don't understand at all.

ROSE: Just look around you. Only the people who were in your graduating class, alone, Shanakind. Last week I'm standing in the butcher's and Mrs. Miller comes up to me. Sweetheart, so, so excited she was because her Lois is going to have her first baby in November. And in the bakemaster Mrs. Greene tells me her daughter's working on her third already. And even, even Monroe Brown—Monroe Brown who used to come to all the sweet sixteens, was so wild everybody said he'd never settle down, he used to steal all the centerpieces—today I hear that even he's going to be a papa soon. And they ask about you, Shanakind. Just this morning they were asking about you.

SHANAKIND: Mama, Mama, you act as if this boy that's coming, you act as if this boy's going to be my one and only. There'll be others, Mama. Plenty of others. *(A pause in which she is not so certain now)* There will be others, won't there, Mama?

ROSE: Sure, sure, sweetheart. It's just from the little picture his mother showed me of this Arnold, and from all the wonderful, wonderful things she had to say about him, well, who knows? Why this Arnold might just walk in here and what might happen, sweetheart, might be like what happens with knights and ladies in fairy tales.

SHANAKIND: That's not going to happen, Mama. I got eyes and I can see. I'm fat and I'm ugly.

ROSE: Shanakind, don't speak that way! You hear me?

SHANAKIND: I'm fat and ugly, and I know it, Mama! *(Urgently)* Please, not tonight.

ROSE: Tonight.

SHANAKIND: Mama, I—I just . . . can't.

ROSE: It's too long since you've been out with a boy.

SHANAKIND: *(She begins to cry now)* Oh, Mama, if you make me stay here tonight and entertain this boy, Mama, I can tell you right now from the way I feel, that when he rings the doorbell I'm going to be so nervous. I'm going to have a trauma right there and then. Oh, Mama, I'm so scared!

ROSE: There's nothing to be frightened of, you hear me, sweetheart?

SHANAKIND: Mama, I know everything's going to go wrong tonight. I got a premonition. I'll perspire and I'll belch, and I'll have a trauma.

ROSE: Shanakind!

SHANAKIND: Perspiring and belching all over the house.

ROSE: *(She takes Shanakind in her arms and begins coddling and lulling her)* Everything is going to be all right, sweetheart, all right. Oh, I remember when you were a baby and I used to hold you just like this in my arms and would sing to you when you cried. Want mama to sing to you now, huh, sweetheart? Mama'll sing. *(Rose begins to chant a soft melody)*

Shanakind
Klanakind
Smile for Mama
Smile for Papa
Auntie's standing near
Uncle's making shame, shame, Shaney
Granny loves you, darling.

Shanakind
Smile for me
When you're smiling
Little lady
Mama's heart soars high.
Cling to me, I'll sing to you
Sweet Shanakind's lullabye.

(Shanakind's crying has somewhat subsided now)

ROSE: Now everything is going to be all right, sweetheart. This boy will come. You'll be nice and polite to him. You'll both have a very pleasant evening. Oh come, come, mustn't cry now, Shanakind. Tonight, tonight more than any other night I want my sweetheart happy, carefree. Here Shanakind. You want to blow your nose? *(Shanakind gives Rose the chicken bone to hold while she takes the handkerchief to blow her nose)* Come on, sweetheart. Come on and get dressed. This Arnold's going to be here any minute now. Wash away your tears, baby. You want to make a good first impression, huh? *(Beginning to shoo Shanakind out now)* First impressions, they're very important. Now stand tall and walk straight. Always you don't have to waddle. For one night in your life walk straight. For me. Huh? Shanakind?

(Blackout)

Scene Three:

A corner of Tillie's shabby apartment in Brooklyn. It is immediately thereafter.
Spot on Arnold. He is dressed in a tie and suit and sitting in a chair.

TILLIE: *(From off)* Arnold, you ready yet? Arnold, it's getting late. *(Coming into the room)* Here, let me take a good look at my boy, see if he looks all right, eh?

ARNOLD: *(Slowly and deliberately)* I am not going through with this, Mama. You hear me? I am not going through with this.

TILLIE: There's no sense starting up now, Arnold.

ARNOLD: I don't want to go. Just what have I got to do to make you understand that?

TILLIE: Arnold, I'm not that strong a woman. You know what the doctor said. *(Arnold turns away. Tillie tries a new approach)* Oh, Arnold, Arnold, it's just I want so much for you to be happy. Believe me nothing in the whole world matters as long as you're happy and healthy. It's just I want you to have all the things your father and I could never have. You can only get them with an education. An education and profession people can look up to you for.

ARNOLD: Leave me alone, Mama. Just leave me alone.

TILLIE: *(Mimicking him)* Leave me alone, Mama. Just leave me alone. Oh, Arnold, all my good years. I gave every one of them up for you.

ARNOLD: Keep your voice down, Mama. Must all the neighbors always hear us when we fight?

TILLIE: *(Bitterly mimicking now)* Keep your voice down, Mama. Keep your voice down. Must all the neighbors always hear us when we fight . . . Oh, Arnold, I too could've been a lady, lady of leisure like your Aunt Blanche, department-storing every afternoon, mah-jonging all over Brooklyn every night. I didn't have to get up mornings when it wasn't even light yet, run three blocks down the street all out of breath to catch the BMT to Manhattan so you could abuse me like this?

ARNOLD: Enough, Mama? Enough?

TILLIE: You work, you scrimp, you save, you do without. And you go to bed late and you wake up early. And always you're so tired.

ARNOLD: Pushing, pushing, pushing. Mama, don't you ever get tired of the pushing?

TILLIE: My pushing?

ARNOLD: Yes, Mama. Your pushing. Always pushing and nagging after me.

TILLIE: You just listen to me, Arnold. You ought to thank the Lord above you got a mother who knows how to push. Tell me, you just tell me where you think you'd be today if you didn't have a mother always pushing after you, eh?

ARNOLD: I might've done what I wanted.

TILLIE: Meaning what?

ARNOLD: I might've become a florist.

TILLIE: Always the florist you throw in my face.

ARNOLD: You know how much I wanted to become a florist, Mama?

TILLIE: A florist. Don't make me laugh. Please . . . Tell me, what kind of profession you think it is to be a florist, eh? Just tell me, why do you think I wanted you to become a doctor for anyways? Because a doctor makes money, and that's what it takes to be somebody in this world. What kind of living do you think you'd make from selling roses and gardenias? I'll tell you where the real money is. It's in gallstones. Gallstones and kidneys.

ARNOLD: Never get tired of the pushing, do you, Mama? All the way back from the beginning. Make Arnold a doctor no matter what in the world Arnold might ever want to be. Such drive you got, Mama. Such push. Such a pity how you waste it.

TILLIE: *(Gesturing out to an imaginary audience)* The "thank you, Mama" you get when you try to give your children all the things you never had for yourself.

ARNOLD: Please don't start up with the gratitude now. Gratitude's not what you want. You know it. I know it.

TILLIE: Oh, I deserve everything I'm getting tonight for wasting my whole life on a good-for-nothing nippish like you.

ARNOLD: Know what you wanted? Let me tell you what you wanted. You wanted everybody to say how she gave her life to make her Arnold a doctor. Only it wasn't your life you gave. It was mine.

TILLIE: So quit. Quit. Nobody's stopping you. Go on. Throw all your education out the windows. Forget the books. Forget about ever being somebody. Go on and be a nothing. Be like your father. See if I care. See if I try to raise a finger to stop you.

ARNOLD: I can see right through you like you were a pane of glass or something.

TILLIE: These hands—you just remember these hands, not the books—they're what made you what you are. You just remember without these hands you'd still be another cocker nobody. You wouldn't be talking down so high falutin' like you are.

ARNOLD: You—you wanted so much for people to think you were a martyr. A—A Saint Tillie of Ocean Parkway.

TILLIE: Go on. Go on. Make fun. You can afford to. You've been highly educated.

ARNOLD: Well, just listen to me. You're not Saint Tillie one—one-tenth so much as you're—you're Yenta Tillie!

TILLIE: All right, so I'm Yenta Tillie.

ARNOLD: You don't have to yell it so loud, Mama. I mean everybody knows.

TILLIE: And you want to know why I'm Yenta Tillie, Arnold? You want to know why? I'm Yenta Tillie because I want you to meet a nice girl, a girl who'll bear your children, and maybe one whose father left her comfortably fixed enough to help you set up a nice little practice besides. I'm Yenta Tillie because I want you to be happy and settle down. And because I want you to have all the things your father and I could never afford. *(Softer now)* I'm Yenta Tillie because I got a stone the size of a mush melon growing on top of one of my kidneys. And the doctor said I gotta have an operation. And I'm Yenta Tillie because I gotta sit up nights sewing to send you through medical school. And I don't have enough money for the operation besides. *(With compassion)* I'm Yenta Tillie because I want to live to see my only son become a doctor. Because I want to live to see people finally looking up to you. To Tillie's son. To you. *(After a very long pause)* Now you gonna go, Arnold? You gonna go and be nice to this Edna. Eh?

(Arnold lowers his head and nods)

(Blackout)

Scene Four:

Rose's living room. It is half an hour later.
Rose is lighting the candles on the dining room table.

ROSE: Shanakind, any second now he's going to be here. How long does it take for Madam Fifi to put on her little party dress and dust up under the arms?

SHANAKIND: *(She calls from off)* Mama, I can't find my little fan.

ROSE: Forget the fan. You hear me? For once in your life is it please possible you could hurry and be on time? *(The doorbell rings)* Well, I certainly hope you're satisfied now. He's here. He's here already, and you're not through powdering yourself.

SHANAKIND: The fan. The fan. I'm lost without my little fan.

ROSE: You coming yet? Madam Fifi, you coming?

SHANAKIND: Without my little fan I don't know what I'm going to do with the hands. You better get the door yourself, Mama, before he goes away.

ROSE: *(She begins muttering to herself)* Oh, Shanakind, for you I haven't got the patience no more!

(Rose touches her hair for a moment to see if it is in place before she opens the door to admit Arnold. Arnold stands in the entrance carrying a small carton)

ARNOLD: *(After a moment)* Edna Wittman lives here?

ROSE: You must be Arnold, right? Well, I'm Edna's mother, Mrs. Wittman . . . Well, my goodness. Come in, come in. Please don't just stand there.

(Arnold makes a somewhat helpless gesture as Rose almost pushes him into the living room)

ROSE: Here, here. Let me take your package and make you feel really comfortable.

ARNOLD: If you don't mind, I'd just as soon hold on to it.

ROSE: I'll just put it right up in the closet here.

ARNOLD: Just a little something I thought maybe, well, Edna would like.

ROSE: *(She is at once surprised and touched)* A present for Edna?

ARNOLD: I mean really it's nothing. Honestly.

ROSE: *(Very warmly now, not knowing what is good enough for Arnold to enjoy)* Here, here. Until she comes out, why don't you just sit yourself down in this nice comfortable chair.

ARNOLD: Oh, no.

ROSE: Most comfortable chair in the whole house. Dr. Wittman, when he would come home from a long day at the office, used to love to sit here.

ARNOLD: Please, really. It's not necessary.

ROSE: Just spread yourself out and make yourself feel really at home.

ARNOLD: *(Picking what seems to be the straightest back chair of all)* This—this'll be just fine, thank you.

ROSE: Edna, I'm sure'll be right out in a minute. *(Extending to him a box of chocolates)* Here, Arnold. Help yourself, huh?

ARNOLD: No, thank you.

ROSE: Brown paper with the two stars, they're really very tasty. They're the chocolate creams.

ARNOLD: I got an allergy to chocolate.

ROSE: Chocolate creams are just out of this world. Sure you won't try one now? . . . Maybe later, huh? . . . Look, Arnold, you'll excuse me if I call Edna a minute. I wouldn't be too, too surprised if she doesn't even know you're here yet. *(She begins to call)* Edna, Edna sweetheart, there's somebody here to see you.

(There is a moment of silence and then:)

ARNOLD: Maybe she doesn't hear you.

ROSE: Oh, she hears. She hears . . . Oh, I'm sure you know just how fussy girls can be about the way they look. Got to be just so-so. *(Calling Shankakind again)* Edna, your company is here. We don't want to keep our company waiting now, do we? *(There is still no answer. Then Rose calls out in a very firm voice)* Edna, you hear me? Edna!

SHANAKIND: *(Shrilly)* Oh, for God's sakes, Mama, can't you hold your horses a minute!

ARNOLD: *(Not really believing what he has just heard)* That was Edna?

ROSE: Edna, please come out here!

SHANAKIND: I can't find my fan.

ROSE: Edna, come out here this minute!

SHANAKIND: Explicitly, I told you not to take the tassles off. The tassles always made it easier to find.

ROSE: *(Furious now)* Edna, you can look for that fan later. Come out here this minute. *(To Arnold, as lightly as possible)* Oh, I tell you it's not bad enough she always has to carry that little fan of hers around, but the tassles, you should've only seen the tassles.

SHANAKIND: *(She makes an unfortunately clumsy entrance)* You don't have to get so excited, Mama. I'm not deaf.

(Seeing Arnold for the first time Edna stands there more or less mute, her mouth wide open)

ROSE: Edna. *(Gently coaxing her)* Close your mouth, sweetheart. We're not catching flies.

SHANAKIND: Mama, you wouldn't want me to make one of my scenes now would you, Mama? I ask you not to tempt me.

ROSE: *(To Arnold)* Edna's always a little shy at first until she really gets going. *(And now momentarily embracing the two of them)* Well, I guess this is certainly as good a time as any to make the little introductions. Arnold, I want you to meet my daughter Edna. And Edna, sweetheart, I want you to meet Arnold Rothstein. *(Arnold and Edna nod vaguely at each other)* You know, Arnold, Edna's just finished studying medical technology at the Brooklyn Institute.

ARNOLD: *(Dutifully)* That's very nice. Very nice.

(There is another awkward pause and then:)

ROSE: Edna, come over here and let me see how your little hem came out. Edna's wearing a nice dress tonight, isn't she, Arnold?

ARNOLD: Very nice dress, Edna.

SHANAKIND: Thank you.

ROSE: *(To Arnold)* Pink has always been Edna's shade. Edna always looks her best in a little something pink.

(There is another pause and then Arnold looks around)

ARNOLD: I wonder what that was.

ROSE: You hear something? Funny, I didn't hear anything.

SHANAKIND: Probably just my stomach growling.

ROSE: That will do, Edna!

SHANAKIND: Mama, when do you think our pullets will be ready for a polishing off?

ARNOLD: Polishing off?

ROSE: That will do, sweetheart. I'm sure you're not so hungry you can't maybe wait a little while longer. *(To Arnold now)* I bet you must have a king size appetite by about now, am I right, Arnold? I know Dr. Wittman used to be just famished whenever he finished up after a day at the hospital.

ARNOLD: Don't worry about my being hungry tonight, Mrs. Wittman. I never eat much anyways.

ROSE: *(Almost coyly)* Well, then tonight, I absolutely insist you make an exception for me.

SHANAKIND: Mama, I hate to interrupt, but I ate a very early lunch at the Moderne. If dinner isn't going to be ready for a little while yet—*(She begins to rise now)*—maybe I ought to go and get myself a little snick-snack from the refrige.

ROSE: No snick-snack so soon before dinner. You'll only ruin your little appetite. *(Shanakind gives Rose one devastating stare)* The face, sweetheart. The face. *(A few seconds pass before Shanakind begins sniffing obviously around the room)* Edna, please. The sniffing. It's really not necessary.

SHANAKIND: You smell something burning? I think I smell something burning.

ROSE: Now I know dinner can't be ready yet, sweetheart. It must be just your imagination.

SHANAKIND: It's not my imagination. I really think I ought to go in the kitchen and take a little peek. I mean, maybe the whole house is burning down.

ROSE: Edna, sit down. A young lady has certain definite responsibilities when a gentleman comes to call. Honestly, I'm very surprised the way you're acting tonight. *(To Arnold)* Arnold, you'll excuse me if I go inside a minute and begin to get dinner ready, all right? *(To Shanakind)* Never can let anybody sit still in peace two minutes can you. *(Rose crosses to the kitchen. After Rose leaves Shanakind takes one last peek to be absolutely certain Rose is gone. Then Shanakind crosses to the table with the cold meats inside, opens the top, takes out a chicken leg and begins to munch. Arnold is stunned)*

ARNOLD: *(Incredulously)* My God, my God, what is that? That's a refrigerator.

SHANAKIND: What's wrong? Doesn't the wood match the other furniture in the room?

ARNOLD: Edna, what's a refrigerator doing in here? I never heard of a refrigerator in a living room before.

SHANAKIND: Oh, we just bought it so we wouldn't have to run all the way out to the kitchen if we wanted to nibble a little. We got a unit in practically every room of the house. Say, maybe you want a little something to suck on also before dinner.

ARNOLD: No, no. I'll wait for dinner, thank you.

SHANAKIND: How about a Popsicle, OK? We got all the flavors. Dairyman was just here today.

(Arnold shakes his head)

SHANAKIND: Well, all right. Suit yourself then. *(For the first time Shanakind notices the box next to Arnold)* Hey, what's that, huh?

ARNOLD: Oh, I almost forgot. I—I brought you a present.

SHANAKIND: *(Excited beyond words)* A present for me? A present for me in there?

ARNOLD: Nothing. I mean, really nothing. Just something I figured, well, if I was coming anyways—*(He hands her the carton)* You might as well go on, open it up.

SHANAKIND: *(Seizing the package, she begins to tear it open)* Oh, I get so excited when it comes to opening a present!

ARNOLD: Easy now. It's gentle.

SHANAKIND: *(Finally getting the package open, she screams with abandoned joy at the contents)* Oh! OH! OHHH!!! . . . Oh, excuse me for screaming like that. Just that they looked so beautiful there for the moment.

ROSE: *(She calls from off)* Everything all right in there?

ARNOLD: Everything's all right. *(To Shanakind)* You like them, Edna?

SHANAKIND: They're beautiful. Beautiful, beautiful, BEAUTI-FUL! *(Calling)* Mama, guess what Arnold brought me, Mama? Flowers!

ROSE: *(She calls from off)* Roses, darling?

SHANAKIND: Narcissus, Mama. *(To Arnold)* Oh, I'm just so ex-cited.

ARNOLD: Bought the bulbs and grew them myself in my bedroom. Kind of funny looking plants, aren't they, 'til they start to bloom. Here, give them to me. I'll put them on the table right over here. *(Arnold puts the narcissus on the other end table as Shanakind begins to sprawl herself out on the sofa with the chicken leg. Rose comes in backwards, carrying two bottles of wine on her tray. For the moment, Shanakind does not see her)*

ROSE: Tell me, Arnold, are you going to want raspberry or blackberry wine tonight?

(In an effort to get rid of the chicken leg before Rose sees it, Shanakind starts to open the table refrigerator on which the narcissus are standing. Arnold, in a move to save Shanakind from dropping his prized narcissus, accidentally pushes the plant over himself, and it smashes, spreading soil all over the carpet)

ROSE: *(She is absolutely furious with Shanakind now)* Edna!

SHANAKIND: I didn't mean to do anything wrong. It's just I got a little hungry.

ARNOLD: *(Helplessly)* I'm—I'm sorry.

ROSE: *(Softly to Shanakind)* Well, I certainly hope you're satisfied now—satisfied with what you've done.

ARNOLD: *(Bending over to begin cleaning up the soil from the carpet)* Here, let me clean it up for you.

ROSE: Now Arnold, I positively won't hear of such a thing. Why, you just stay right where you are. This little mess will take me just a jiffy to clean up.

ARNOLD: Feel so bad I spilled anything on the carpet.

ROSE: *(A little too nervously)* It's nothing. Nothing.

ARNOLD: In a fine house like this I know you must have a very fine carpet.

SHANAKIND: Mama, I'm scared. Mama, I'm so scared I'm afraid I'm going to have a trauma!

ARNOLD: *(He begins nervously edging towards the door)* Look, maybe, maybe it would be better for everybody if—if I just left.

ROSE: Now everything's going to be all right. No harm's been done.

SHANAKIND: Mama!

ROSE: Arnold, I got raspberry and blackberry wine. And I made a whole big dinner just for you.

ARNOLD: I—I caused you enough trouble.

ROSE: And Edna—how much she looked forward all week to your coming over. So serious she's been to talk to you, spend a little time with you, right, Edna?

(Shanakind is dazed by all that has happened and does not respond. A moment passes where Arnold looks squarely at Shanakind. Rose sees this and makes prime use of the moment)

Arnold, please. Please sit down to dinner now. You'll have a nice time this evening. You'll see. I promise you. Stay now. Won't you, Arnold? *(Pushing the dining room table out to beckon him)* Please?

Blackout

Scene Five:

It is about half an hour later.
Rose, Shanakind and Arnold are finishing their dinner.

ROSE: Arnold, I've got some good pie for dessert. How about a delicous little baked apple, Okay?

ARNOLD: Please, no. I can't eat anymore.

ROSE: Dr. Wittman—why, he would consider the little chopped liver, vegetable soup, and chicken you ate tonight a mere trifle.

ARNOLD: Trifle?

ROSE: At least let me give you a little piece of watermelon.

ARNOLD: I can't.

ROSE: For watermelon you don't have to be hungry. *(Then realizing perhaps he really cannot eat anymore)* All right, so I'm not going to feel insulted if you don't have dessert now. But before you go home tonight I absolutely insist you taste the fluffy little apple pie I baked just for you this morning. With a smidgen of ice cream on top, I tell you your tonsils will go absolutely wild.

SHANAKIND: Mama, if it's all right with you, I would like my piece of apple pie and ice cream right now.

ROSE: Later, sweetheart.

SHANAKIND: Mama, I don't think you heard what I just said. I said, I would like my piece of apple pie and ice cream right now.

ROSE: Sweetheart, I'm quite certain you can't be that hungry not to be able to wait half an hour more.

SHANAKIND: Mama, I am not full.

ARNOLD: *(Astonished)* Not full?

ROSE: My, my, such a sense of humor we have tonight, don't we, sweetheart. Only sometimes our friends don't know when we're playacting and when we're not. *(Rising)* Come, Edna, come. While I'm cleaning up a little in the kitchen, why don't you take Arnold out and show him our nice little sun porch.

SHANAKIND: *(Speaking under her breath to Rose so Arnold can't hear what's being said)* Mama, please. Not alone, Mama.

ROSE: *(Playfully poking Shanakind in the ribs)* Up, up, sweetheart.

SHANAKIND: *(Warningly)* Mama!

ROSE: Come, come.

SHANAKIND: *(More ominously)* Mama!

ROSE: *(Softly)* Sweetheart, please. The teeth. Really, it's not necessary to show me the teeth.

SHANAKIND: *(Erupting almost ferociously)* MAMA!

ROSE: Such a little comic show-off we are, aren't we? I really can't imagine what our company must think of us. *(Then beginning to beckon Arnold)* Come, Arnold, come. While Edna is finishing up, I want you to see the little view from our sun porch before the sun goes down. Dr. Wittman would try to see it whenever he was able.

ARNOLD: *(Clumsily to Shanakind)* Ex—Excuse me.

ROSE: Edna will be right out. I'm quite sure of that. *(Rose leads Arnold out to the sun porch)* Nice and quiet out here on the porch after dinner, isn't it? Here, I'll turn on a little lamp, make it really nice and cozy.

ARNOLD: *(Uncomfortably)* Thank you.

ROSE: Dr. Wittman always used to tell everybody just how much pleasure it would give him to sit here after supper, light his cigar, and read his newspaper. *(Gesturing persuasively towards a highly cushioned chair)* Here. Sit over here. Okay, Arnold?

ARNOLD: *(He again chooses what seems to be the least comfortable chair in the room)*
Thank you very much, but this—this is just as good.

ROSE: Arnold, I feel very uncomfortable when people come to my house and don't make themselves feel at home. *(She coyly gets Arnold to move from one seat to the other)* Oh, come, come. When a man finishes a hard day's work at the office, he should always relax in a nice easy chair. There we go now. Better?

ARNOLD: *(Just a little lost with all the cushioning)* Thank you.

ROSE: While I finishing cleaning up a bit, why don't you get nice and comfortable with the evening paper here . . . Everything all right now, huh?

ARNOLD: Sure, sure.

ROSE: I'll be right back before you even know I'm gone.   *(Rose crosses to the living room. A moment after Rose is out of view Arnold, very uncomfortable in the overly cushioned chair, moves back to the first one he sat in. Rose crosses to her daughter in the dining room. Shanakind is scraping mashed potatoes off her plate with a fork)*

ROSE: Edna, I want you to go outside now this minute. You hear me?

SHANAKIND: Mama, I would like my dessert now.

ROSE: Edna, there is not going to be any dessert this evening unless you get up and go out on the sun porch and entertain your company.

SHANAKIND: Mama, if it doesn't inconvenience you, I would like my ball of chocolate ice cream right now.

ROSE: Edna, I've had just about enough tumult from you for one evening. Get up from the table this minute.

SHANAKIND: If I get up from this table without the dessert I have thought about having all morning and all afternoon long, it will only be to go to our neighborhood Orpheum to finish off my saucer service.

ROSE: *(Totally losing her patience now)* Get up! Get up!

SHANAKIND: There's no need for you to get red as a beet over a little ball of chocolate ice cream.

ROSE: *(Violently thrusting Shanakind's chair out, wildly forcing her to her feet)* You can push somebody just so far, just so far. Edna, you hear me!

SHANAKIND: *(Frightened now)* Mama!

ROSE: *(Beginning to push her in the direction of the sun porch)* Edna, you're going to go out on the sun porch in five seconds. You hear me? If I have to push you out there myself.

SHANAKIND: Mama! Mama, please!

ROSE: Your father, if he ever saw the way you've been carrying on—

SHANAKIND: Mama, I'm scared.

ROSE: For once, Shanakind, you're going to try and act like the grown lady you're supposed to be.

SHANAKIND: Mama, I'm afraid I'm going to . . . Mama, my whole supper up.

ROSE: *(They are on the threshold of the sun porch)* Shanakind, Shanakind, stand tall and walk straight. Edna, Edna, for God's sakes, he's such a nice boy. (Imploringly) Edna. Please, Edna?

SHANAKIND: *(Feebly)* Mama? *(Shanakind is on the sun porch now. Rose motions for her to go to Arnold. There is a terribly awkward and painful moment. Clumsily and jarringly, Shanakind then crosses to the end table on which Arnold's arm is resting. She stops, then starts backing away. A moment passes. Again she crosses clumsily to the end table. This time she gestures for Arnold to move his arm away)* I—I want a cracker with a little raw meat and egg on it.

ARNOLD: *(Moving his arm, realizing this must be another refrigerator)* Sure, sure.

SHANAKIND: Look, if—if you want—

ARNOLD: No, no, thank you.

(As Shanakind is opening the top)

Very . . . nice piece of mahogany. I—I bet it's not so easy to find a piece of wood like this. I mean refrigerated, you know.

(Shanakind takes out a couple of crackers with raw chopped meat neatly wrapped in cellophane covers)

They come like that from the market?

SHANAKIND: No, no. These snick-snacks I make by myself. *(Beginning to eat now)* Mama thinks it's terrible to guzzle down raw chopped meat, so I have the butcher deliver the chopped meat to the laboratory where I work. Then I slip the meat in my little purse without mama knowing anything.

ROSE: *(She calls from off)* Listen, I hope you young people don't mind my putting on a little soft music while I finish my little cleaning up.

(The scene is set now. A perfectly romantic scene with the little park across the way, the star-filled night, and even the gentle background music. Shanakind sits with her hands in her lap not at all certain what she should do with them. Arnold is obviously equally uncomfortable. Neither seems to know what to say. And then during an especially ambitious violin section:)

SHANAKIND: *(She calls so loudly for the moment, she startles Arnold)* Oh, for God's sakes, Mama, turn that music off this minute! Honest to God, I can't even hear myself think with all that racket going on. *(The music fades immediately. Shanakind now realizes her scream has startled Arnold)* Oh, I'm—I'm sorry.

ARNOLD: *(Trying to brush the incident off as quickly as possible)* Nothing.

SHANAKIND: I mean, I didn't mean to scare you that way.

ARNOLD: Not important really.

SHANAKIND: You're all right?

ARNOLD: Sure, sure. Just sometimes before an exam I get a little high-strung that's all.

SHANAKIND: Just—just that I—well, I got a pair of lungs. If you know what I mean.

ARNOLD: Nothing worth getting upset over.

SHANAKIND: Mama—she always wanted me to learn how to play the piano. But my music teacher—well, he said that with a pair of lungs like mine, I should definitely learn how to play the tuba.

ARNOLD: Uh, very nice the way your mother set everything up tonight. Flowers, candlelight. Very, very nice.

SHANAKIND: Oh, yes. Candlelight's very nice. Only you gotta watch when you blow the soup you don't blow the candles out also.

ARNOLD: Medical technology. Very nice, Edna. Very impressive field for a girl.

SHANAKIND: Thank you. Mama is also very impressed with your field.

ARNOLD: *(Looking around)* Nice-sized porch here. It's really very nice out here, you know it?

SHANAKIND: Yes, yes. It's a good place to cool your parts off a little, especially after such a hot stinking day like today.

ARNOLD: Beautiful view you've got across the way in this direction. Little park over there, small lake running through it. Trees. Flowers. Everything all nice and green. Really very nice.

SHANAKIND: Not such a bad view from the other side also. I mean, if you look really closely all the way down the street you can just about make out our neighborhood Orpheum from here. Ya see, huh? . . . Besides from this side of the porch you can also get a nice view of the people going by in the street. You ever sit back and watch the people go by?

ARNOLD: No.

SHANAKIND: I'll tell you, it's very nice to watch. Really very nice. Saturday nights—that's when I like to look. Everybody goes out for the evening.

ARNOLD: Saturday nights—sometimes I watch television. Sometimes I just go to sleep.

SHANAKIND: You . . . don't go out on Saturday nights?

ARNOLD: Oh, sometimes I'll call up a friend. I don't know, sometimes Davy and me, we'll take in a movie. Maybe go out afterwards a little while bowling.

SHANAKIND: You—you mean you don't go out with—well, with people of—of the opposite gender, so to speak, on Saturday nights?

ARNOLD: I—I guess I don't go out that much.

SHANAKIND: Mama always told me that I was the only one who never went out on Saturday nights.

ARNOLD: Me, I—I don't go out that much either.

SHANAKIND: Very interesting. I mean, it's always nice to find out somebody else is peculiar like yourself also . . . Sometimes mama and me—we fight because I haven't been going out—socially you might say. You might say since I was sixteen . . . Uh, quite a long time now.

ARNOLD: I really just can't get over how beautiful that little park is over there, you know it? Must be really something to see in the springtime when everything is first coming into bloom.

SHANAKIND: Oh, yes. The very first warm Sunday of spring, when my daddy was alive, we always used to make a little picnic on the grass. Me, best part of the picnic always was when I could take my shoes off, my socks off, just squish my feet on the grass.

ARNOLD: *(Shanakind has accidentally struck upon a responsive chord)* Dig your feet into the ground, huh?

SHANAKIND: Yes, yes. Especially if it rained the night before and everything was really muddy.

ARNOLD: Really feel the earth below you.

SHANAKIND: Mama would holler at me from the moment we came 'til the moment we would go because I used to get my feet all dirty during the day, and then at night track the mud into the house over the good broadloom. *(Secretively)* I used to leave prints.

ARNOLD: Tell me something. You ever squiggle your toes in the early morning dew?

SHANAKIND: Oh, no, no. I never did it in the dew.

ARNOLD: Oh, some morning, some morning you'll really have to get up early, Edna. Really have to squiggle your feet in the dew . . . I—I remember when I was a kid, I had an Aunt Sophie that lived up in the country. Every summer I used to go there for a week or so, and every morning I'd wake myself up six, six-thirty just to run barefoot all over Aunt Sophie's grass . . . Aunt Sophie was my father's sister.   *(Arnold begins to laugh lightly)*

SHANAKIND: *(Very upset)* What'sa matter?

ARNOLD: *(Laughing a bit more now)* Nothing.

SHANAKIND: I say something wrong?

ARNOLD: No, no.

SHANAKIND: Look, I hope you're not laughing at me. I mean about things like that I'm very sensitive.

ARNOLD: Oh, no, no. Not laughing about you. I—well, I was just thinking of the first time mama took me up to Aunt Sophie's. Aunt Sophie—she used to grow Bermuda buttercups all over the place. Bermuda buttercups on the front lawn. Bermuda buttercups on the back porch. Bermuda buttercups on all the window sills. First time mama saw all the Bermuda buttercups growing all over the place . . . *(He begins to laugh)* Well, she thought Aunt Sophie was really wacked up and she didn't want me to stay . . . Oh, I would have myself some good times every summer the week I used to go up to Aunt Sophie's. Last summer I was up there, I decided right there and then what I really wanted to do when I finished school. I mean I never really wanted to become a doctor. You know what I always wanted to be?

SHANAKIND: *(Bluntly)* No.

ARNOLD: Come on.

SHANAKIND: *(Uncomfortable now, actually getting a bit hostile)* I don't know.

ARNOLD: Go on and take a guess.

SHANAKIND: I'm no good at guessing games. *(And then finally)* A poet.

ARNOLD: A florist. Ever since the last time I came back from Aunt Sophie's up in the country, I wanted to become a florist. When I told my mother what I wanted to be, she threw every plant out of the window. That's how much she wanted me to become a doctor. Even the rhododendron that was sitting on the window sill she threw out.

SHANAKIND: I don't think I ever knew anybody who wanted to become a florist before. I once knew somebody who wanted to become an undertaker, but I never knew anybody who wanted to be a florist.

ARNOLD: Oh, you should only hear my mother when she gets going on my wanting to become a florist. *(Having a good time, mimicking his mother's manner of speech)* "What kind of money you think you'd make from selling roses and gardenias, Arnold? Real money's in gallstones! Gallstones and kidneys!" *(Then returning to his own voice)* Well, I ask you, what does she think I want so much with other people's gallstones and kidneys for anyways?

SHANAKIND: Your mother's a harpist also?

ARNOLD: My mother's an accomplished harpist . . . For God's sakes, what does she think I want so much anyways? Just a little store to sell plants and pots and seedlings. A place for people to come every now and then, maybe ask a couple of questions about propagation here and there, that's all. Tell anybody you want to be a florist and they look at you as if you're cockeyed or something. I said to my Aunt Blanche from Brooklyn, "Aunt Blanche, I want to be a florist." She laughed for half an hour. I said to my Uncle Charley from Jersey, "Uncle Charley, I want to be a florist." He said, "That's nice boy, now go and play a little more. One morning I want to sit down and read my New York Times in peace."

SHANAKIND: Why do they laugh at you if you say you wanna become a florist? I mean, well look, well, if you've got the thumb, I don't see what they should care what you want to do with it.

ARNOLD: It's not that. I mean, not that I can't see a little to their point also. Well, a boy like me, well, to become a florist . . . well, you do have to admit it does sound a little, I don't know, well, wacky! . . . Well, what does it sound like to you?

SHANAKIND: Florist sounds like florist to me. I mean, well, what's it supposed to sound like? *(There is a very long moment. And then Arnold looks around questioningly)* But listen, if I were you, I wouldn't put too much stock in what I say anyways. *(Confidentially)* Everybody thinks I'm very strange.

ARNOLD: *(More comfortable with her now, he is able to be more spontaneous)* You—when you were a kid, you must have had pipe dreams also.

SHANAKIND: Sure.

ARNOLD: Come on.

SHANAKIND: Oh, no.

ARNOLD: Look, I told you mine.

SHANAKIND: *(Almost ashamed)* . . . It's screwball.

ARNOLD: Look, what could be more screwball than me saying I want to become a florist.

SHANAKIND: You'll laugh. You will.

ARNOLD: No, I won't. Honest.

SHANAKIND: Now you promise you won't laugh if I tell you now? *(Arnold nods)* Oh, you will.

ARNOLD: *(A bit impatiently)* Come on now.

SHANAKIND: *(There is a very long silence in which she looks about the room not quite certain yet whether she should divulge this confidence. And then all of a sudden blurting it out)* An actress! I always wanted to become an actress.

ARNOLD: An actress?

SHANAKIND: There I told you, you'd make a face when I'd tell.

ARNOLD: I wasn't making a face.

SHANAKIND: Listen, you're not the only one that made a face when I told them I wanted to become an actress. You should've seen them all when I made the big announcement at my cousin's wedding in the Brooklyn Community Center. "I want to become an actress" I shouted into the microphone just before the bride started to cut the cake. My mother fainted right there and then—took quite a lot of doing just to get her back up on her feet again. They said, "Edna, be a teacher. Edna, be a nurse. Edna, be an office girl. For God's sakes, Edna, be something reasonable." Well, being an actress is reasonable—if you know what I mean. I mean an actress can be anything she wants . . . Besides, I always wanted to be in one of those great big technicolored affairs where everybody sings, dances, everything comes out happily. I mean, once, too, I wanted

to go to the beautiful parties with the beautiful ladies in the beautiful gowns. I mean, it would hurt somebody if just once a handsome
gentlemen came up to *me*, asked *me* if I would give them the
pleasure of the dance—that would hurt somebody?—'stead of just
sittin' around in a little corner somewhere watching the clock,
waitin' 'til ten past twelve to sneak out, meet my daddy around the
corner where nobody was looking. I mean, it would really bother
somebody if once, too, I sang the little duet on one of those
staircases, pianos and candelabras on both sides . . . Hey, what're
you makin' me talk like this for anyways? I know all this movie
stuff's impossible. I know what I look like. Sometimes the mirror
catches me unawares. I feel what people are thinkin' when they
pass me by on the streets starin' after me.

ARNOLD: *(A long pause and then very clumsily)* Uh, look, well.
Look, you're not that bad-looking.

SHANAKIND: Listen, about the way I look I don't want you hand-
ing me any malarkey.

ARNOLD: I mean, well, if I said you looked pretty, I wouldn't be
telling the truth . . . Listen, I'm not what you might call good-
looking either.

SHANAKIND: About looks I don't like no kidding.

ARNOLD: Your face—uh-in the twilight just now, I don't know,
well, I—I kind of thought it maybe had a—a softness.

SHANAKIND: Softness?

ARNOLD: Yeah, softness. Well, I don't know. Maybe twilight becomes you or something. Maybe you look your best in a little twilight.

SHANAKIND: Never thought of myself as having a softness
before. Fat, yes. Ugly, yes. Softness, no. You sure you got 20-20?

ARNOLD: Yeah.

SHANAKIND: . . . Uh, thank you . . . I—I guess I'm just not
used to such talk from strangers . . . Uh, come here. Come here a
minute. I—I want—I want to show you something, Okay? I mean,
what with you always wanting to become a florist—well, I—I want
to show you my dishes. Dishes I get from the movies. *(Beginning to
open the cupboard)* For my trousseau. *(Putting several dishes forward)*
How do you like my pattern, huh?

ARNOLD: Very nice.

SHANAKIND: 'S called Fragrant Flower. A different flower on
every dish.

ARNOLD: Very good drawing of an ipomoea here.

SHANAKIND: Pretty, aren't they?

ARNOLD: This one over here looks like a species of African
Violet.

SHANAKIND: That was the first plate. I remember a romantic comedy was playing that night.

ARNOLD: Cattleya orchidaceae, anthurium—

SHANAKIND: You don't say?

ARNOLD: Good sketch of a monstera deliciosa here.

SHANAKIND: A what?

ARNOLD: Monstera deliciosa.

SHANAKIND: Oh. *(Condescendingly)* Well, when they gave this one out, a lot of the ladies were very disappointed with this particular piece.

ARNOLD: I don't know why. I mean, in the right room the monstera can make a very fine ornamental plant.

SHANAKIND: Oh, I wouldn't want you to think that I was disappointed with this particular selection. I mean, I myself of course wouldn't make a fuss, but Mrs. Gimpleman—I remember she made quite a commotion.

ARNOLD: *(Smiling)* Even a Bermuda buttercup.

SHANAKIND: Oh, let me see.

ARNOLD: Oxalis cernua. Know how you can always tell one of these babies? By the color. I mean no other flower in the world has such a bright yellow sunshine color like this one.

SHANAKIND: Very nice.

ARNOLD: Yeah, very nice.

SHANAKIND: Sure know your flowers, don't you?

ARNOLD: Little, I suppose.

SHANAKIND: You—you like my Fragrant Flower pattern? I—I mean it meets with your approval, huh?

ARNOLD: Very nice drawings, Edna. Very scientific. I'm—I'm sure it'll be very nice to someday eat off these.

SHANAKIND: *(A long moment)* Look, I'm going to say something, something I know it's not my business to say, but saying something that's not my business never really stopped me from saying anything anyways . . . Uh, tonight you—look, I—I—I . . . I don't know . . . *(Groping, stammering)* Well, look, look, if you want to be a florist—*(Until finally)* Well, sometimes it's just not possible to do what everybody wants you to do, and if you start listening to what everybody says you can go right out of your mind. Uh, well take me for an example. Every morning my mama says, "Edna, stop eating, Edna, get married. Edna, stop eating! Edna, get married! EDNA, STOP EATING! EDNA, GET MARRIED!" Every morning she asks me the same two impossible things. Well, if I listened to her— well, I would go a little looney—if you know what I mean. *(There is a long pause and then:)*

ARNOLD: . . . Look, uh—you want to take a walk?

SHANAKIND: Walk?

ARNOLD: *(Gesturing across the way)* I thought maybe we could talk down there a little . . . look, look, you'd rather not, you got someplace else to go—

SHANAKIND: No, no, please. Whatever you want to do. Me, I mean I really haven't got anything planned for tonight.

ARNOLD: . . . I—I'd like to take the walk.

ROSE: *(There is a long moment. And then calling from off:)* Edna, Arnold, come children. Your pie à la mode's waiting on the dining room table.

SHANAKIND: *(Shrilly)* Oh, for God's sakes, Mama, can't you hold your horses a minute? *(To Arnold)* Her with the food. Always the food!

Curtain

Israel Horovitz

STAGE DIRECTIONS

.

Israel Horovitz

A prolific and outstandingly successful modern playwright, Israel Horovitz makes his fourth appearance in *The Best Short Plays* series with his inventive drama, *Stage Directions*.

Mr. Horovitz first came to international prominence in 1968 with *The Indian Wants the Bronx*, a powerful and terrifying study of violence on a New York street. A striking Off-Broadway success, it also scored heavily in other major American cities, at the 1968 Spoleto Festival (Italy), the World Theatre Festival in England (1969), as well as in numerous other foreign countries. The play (which was published in *The Best Short Plays 1969*) won a 1968 Drama Desk-Vernon Rice Award and three "Obies," as well as a commendation from *Newsweek* magazine citing the author as one of the three most original dramatists of the year.

Israel Horovitz was born on March 31, 1939, in Wakefield, Massachusetts. After completing his domestic studies, he journeyed to London to continue his education at the Royal Academy of Dramatic Art and in 1965 became the first American to be chosen as playwright-in-residence with Britain's celebrated Royal Shakespeare Company.

His first play, *The Comeback*, was written when he was seventeen; it was produced in Boston in 1960. In the decade that followed, Mr. Horovitz's plays tenanted many stages of the world. Among them: *It's Called the Sugar Plum* (paired with *The Indian Wants the Bronx* on the New York stage); *The Death of Bernard the Believer; Rats; Morning* (originally titled *Chiaroscuro*, it was initially performed at the Spoleto Festival and later on a triple bill, *Morning, Noon and Night*, Henry Miller's Theatre, New York, 1968); *Trees; Acrobats* (introduced in *The Best Short Plays 1970); Line* (included in this editor's anthology, *Best Short Plays of the World Theatre: 1968–1973*); *The Honest-to-God Schnozzola* (for which he won a 1969 Off-Broadway "Obie" award); and *Spared* (which appeared in *The Best Short Plays 1975*).

His other works for the stage include: *Shooting Gallery; Dr. Hero* (presented at Amherst and various other colleges as well as Off-Broadway by The Shade Company, 1973); *Turnstile; The Primary English Class* (a 1976 Off-Broadway success); and *The Reason We Eat*, which held its world premiere at the Hartman Theatre, Stamford, Connecticut, in November, 1976, with Academy Award-winning actress Estelle Parsons in one of the principal roles.

Mr. Horovitz's most ambitious project to-date is his trilogy, *The Wakefield Plays*. Set in Wakefield, Massachusetts, where he grew up, the three plays are *Alfred the Great, Our Father's Failing* and *Alfred*

Dies, and they are scheduled for a major Broadway production next season.

A collection of his plays, *First Season,* was published in 1968, and his first novel, *Cappella,* was issued in 1973.

Twice the recipient of a Rockefeller Foundation Playwriting Fellowship, he also won a similar fellowship from the Creative Artists Program Service, funded by the New York State Council on the Arts. In 1972, he received an Award in Literature from the American Academy of Arts and Letters, and in 1973 he was honored with a National Endowment for the Arts Award.

The author, who lives in New York City, also has written several major screenplays, notably *The Strawberry Statement,* which won the *Prix de Jury,* Cannes Film Festival, 1970.

Author's Note

There are four related short plays, of which STAGE DIRECTIONS *and* SPARED *(The Best Short Plays 1975) are two, that may be performed in a series under the umbrella-title* THE QUANNAPOWITT QUARTET. *The title refers, of course, to Lake Quannapowitt, the setting of all of the plays of the series.*

The other two plays that complete the quartet are HOPSCOTCH *and* THE 75th. *which should be performed on an evening, or bill, of their own, in that order.* STAGE DIRECTIONS *should precede* SPARED *when they are coupled together on the alternate evening or bill.*

A company of just three performers may be sufficient to play the entire quartet.

Scenic elements designed for the four plays should be minimal, with maximum attention instead given over to the design of lighting and sound effects.

Characters:

RICHARD, *a thin, hawk-like man, forties.*
RUTH, *a thin, hawk-like woman, thirties.*
RUBY, *a small, wren-like woman, twenties.*

NOTE: *The people of the play will speak only words that describe their activities and, on occasion, emotions. No other words or sounds are permitted. By definition, then, all activity and conveyed emotion must be born of spoken stage directions.*

Scene:

Time: Late afternoon, fall. Place: Living room, New England home, overlooking Lake Quannapowitt, Wakefield, Massachusetts.

Lights fade up. Sofa slightly right of room's center. Bar wagon and liquor, upstage right. Overstuffed chairs, right and left of sofa, slightly downstage. Large framed mirror, 24" x 36", draped in black fabric, upstage left wall. Equal sized framed photograph, draped in black fabric as well, opposite wall, upstage of center of sofa. China cabinet filled with bric-a-brac, wall beside upstage chair. (Optional.) Single door to room, upstage right wall. Copious bookshelves and books, wherever space permits. General feeling wanted that room belongs to bookish person. Small desk downstage right. Writing stand, memo pad, stationery, on same. Wastebasket at upstage front foot. Oriental carpet, subdued tones, under all of above.

RICHARD: *(Enters)* Richard enters, quietly. Looks about room to see if he is alone. Certain he is, closes door. Pauses, inhales, turns and leans his back against door, exhales, sobs once. He wipes his eyes on his cuffs, notices black armband, which he removes and into which he blows his nose. He then stuffs armband into pocket of his overcoat which he then removes and folds somewhat fastidiously over back of sofa. He pauses, looking about room, taking a private moment: possibly adjusting his underwear and then discovering and dealing with a day-old insect bite in the pit behind his knee. A fly buzzes past his nose, breaking into his thoughts. He swats at fly carelessly, but somehow manages to capture same in hand, which he brings down and then up close to his eye. He opens hand ever so slightly, watching fly awhile. Although it appears certain that he will open hand allowing fly her freedom, he suddenly smashes hands together, finishing fly and causing clap to sound in room. He walks to desk and using slip of memo paper from pad, he scrapes fly from palm and into wastebasket at foot of desk. He inspects stain on palm, lowers hand to side, pauses, returns to chair, sobs once, sits, bows head, notices shoe, removes same, places single shoe in his lap, sobs again, searches for and finds lightly plaided handkerchief into which be blows nose enthusiastically, unclogging same and producing substantial honking sound in room. He settles back in chair, stares vacantly up at ceiling.

RUTH: *(Enters)* Ruth enters, quietly, closing door with her heel. She looks cautiously about room to see if she is alone, sees Richard sitting in chair.

RICHARD: Richard quickly bows his head and assumes somewhat grave look on his face, rather a studied vacant stare at his black-stockinged foot.

RUTH: Ruth smiles, as though she has been acknowledged.

RICHARD: Richard flashes a quick look at Ruth, to be certain it is she who has entered.

RUTH: Ruth catches Richard's glance and smiles again.

RICHARD: Richard is forced to return her smile and does. He then returns to former position in chair, head-bowed, eyes vacant, staring down toward black-stockinged foot.

RUTH: Ruth leans her back against door, exhales.

RICHARD: Richard adjusts his underwear, discreetly.

RUTH: Ruth sighs.

RICHARD: Richard wipes the palm of his hand behind the knee of his trouser-leg, accomplishing both a wipe and a rub of the day-old insect bite.

RUTH: Ruth touches her black armband to be certain it has not been lost, sighs again.

RICHARD: Richard glances at his hand to be certain now that fly stain has been completely removed. Satisfied, nonetheless, he wipes his hand on his trouser-leg again.

RUTH: Ruth pretends to be removing her overcoat while never removing her stare from the back of Richard's head. She slips her hand inside her coat and discreetly adjusts her brassière . . .

RICHARD: . . . Just as Richard turns to her . . .

RUTH: She recoils quickly, pulling her hand from her coat.

RICHARD: Seeing that he has startled her, he turns away, reviving his former position, head bowed, vacantly staring at his black-stockinged foot.

RUTH: Ruth pauses a moment and then moves directly to bar and surveys liquor supply atop same.

RICHARD: Richard senses her presence at the bar and turns to look disapprovingly at her.

RUTH: Ruth, sensing his disapproval, quickly pours an inch of bourbon, which she downs in a gulp.

RICHARD: He continues his disapproving stare, while unconsciously touching his nose.

RUTH: She raises her glass toward him, nods: blatantly hostile. She smiles, unconsciously touching her nose as well.

RICHARD: She is smiling, deliberately handling her nose . . .

RUTH: He turns away, pompously . . . She clears her throat, attempting to regain his attention, but he remains unmoved, disapproving . . . She pulls open her coat and adjusts her brassière . . .

RICHARD: Raising his hip and thigh, slightly and quickly, he adjusts his briefs, scratches his day-old insect bite and then spits directly on to his palm and fly-stain, wipes his hand on his trouser knee, smiles . . . He turns now and faces her directly, but she is pretending not to notice, not to be paying attention to him. She searches for and finds a rather gaudy orange nylon handkerchief, into which she indelicately honks her hooked nose . . .

RUTH: He removes his sock and pulls at toes, playing with same . . .

RICHARD: She flings her coat sloppily over back of sofa . . . His other shoe off now and . . .

RUTH: (N.B. Words and actions overlap competitively) Ruth removes her gloves . . . and hat . . .

RICHARD: (Overlapping) . . . placing it precisely beside his first shoe . . .

RUTH: (Overlapping) . . . tossing them in a heap on the sofa . . .

RICHARD: (Overlapping) . . . He then peels off his other sock . . .

RUTH: (Overlapping) . . . She then hoists her skirt and unhitches her stocking-top from the front and back garters on her garter-belt . . .

RICHARD: (Overlapping) Richard averts his eyes!

RUTH: Ruth stares at the back of Richard's head, directly. The affect should be one of deep hostility. She is, however, surprised to notice that she is weeping.

RICHARD: . . . as is Richard.

RUTH: There is a moment of absolute silence. (Five count)

RICHARD: Sock clenched in fist, Richard will pound the arm of his chair, three times. He stares straight ahead, eyes unblinking. Three . . . dull . . . thuds . . . And then silence. *(Five count)*

RUTH: Ruth approaches Ruby's chair, stands behind it a moment, pauses.

RICHARD: Richard turns to her and their eyes quietly meet.

RUTH: Ruth is the first to turn away.

RICHARD: Richard bows his head.

RUTH: Ruth walks quickly to the bar wagon and liquor supply, pours two inches of bourbon this time, tosses bottle cap on to floor and then returns to Ruby's chair.

RICHARD: Richard does not look up. He picks at a loose thread on his trouser-knee.

RUTH: Ruth sits, crosses legs, removes shoes, floors them.

RICHARD: Richard turns his body away from her, staring off vacantly.

RUTH: Ruth notices now she wears one stocking pulled taut, the other dangling loose by her knee. She removes first stocking and allows it to stay on floor near her foot. She reaches under her skirt and unhitches other stocking from her garter-belt.

RICHARD: Richard glances at her, discreetly touching his nose.

RUTH: She senses his glance, but neither looks up nor acknowledges same. She instead removes stocking which she crunches and holds in same hand with glass of bourbon.

RICHARD: Richard suddenly stands, floors shoes, crosses room to bar.

RUTH: Ruth watches him, unconsciously touching her nose.

RICHARD: Richard searches for and finds small clear bottle of club soda, which he neatly uncaps, pouring liquid into small clear glass. He recaps bottle, replacing same precisely where it was found. Taking glass in hand, returns to chair, sits, sips.

RUTH: Ruth sips her bourbon and notices stocking crunched in hand. She reaches down and finds other stocking, joining both in loose knot, which she flings on to sofa seat.

RICHARD: Richard stares at her disapprovingly.

RUTH: Ruth remembers armband on coat. She stands, goes to it.

RICHARD: Richard stares after her.

RUTH: Ruth begins to remove armband, but thinks better of it, returns to chair, begins to sit, thinks better of it, drains glass of its bourbon, returns to bar, pours three inches of fresh bourbon into same glass.

RICHARD: Richard turns away from her.

RUTH: Ruth glances at back of Richard's head.

RICHARD: Richard rubs his knee.

RUTH: Ruth tosses bottle, now empty, into wastebasket.

RICHARD: The sound startles Richard, who turns suddenly . . .

RUTH: . . . startling Ruth, who recoils, spilling her drink . . . on the rug.

RICHARD: Richard stares at stain . . . on the rug.

RUTH: Ruth rubs stain with her toe.

RICHARD: Richard turns away.

RUTH: Ruth turns, cupping her forehead in the palm of her right hand. She then moves her hand down over her nose and mouth and sobs.

RICHARD: There is a moment of silence, which Richard breaks first by dropping his glass on to floor.

RUTH: Ruth looks quickly in direction of sound.

RICHARD: Richard is amazed. He grabs his nose.

RUTH: Ruth smiles.

RICHARD: Richard leans forward and picks up glass.

RUTH: Ruth drains her glass of its remaining bourbon, one gulp.

RICHARD: Richard wipes his stain on rug with his socks, never leaving his chair, but instead leaning forward to his stain.

RUTH: Ruth, for the first time, notices his body, now stretched forward. Her smile is gone.

RICHARD: Richard seems perplexed. He pulls at his earlobe.

RUTH: Ruth places glass atop bar. She searches for and finds dish towel, which she aims and pitches on to floor near Richard's stain.

RICHARD: Richard looks first at dish towel, then at Ruth, disapprovingly. He then picks up dish towel and covers his stain with same.

RUTH: Ruth crosses to Ruby's chair, sits. She is weeping.

RICHARD: Richard, too, is weeping.

RUBY: (Enters) Ruby enters somewhat noisily, clumsily.

RUTH: Ruth turns to her from chair, smiles.

RUBY: Ruby returns the smile.

RUTH: Ruth looks away.

RUBY: Ruby looks about the room until her eyes meet Richard's.

RICHARD: His expression is cold, the muscles of his face taut, his mouth thin-lipped, angry.

RUBY: Ruby nods to Richard.

RICHARD: Richard turns away, fists clenched on knees.

RUBY: Ruby closes door, bracing back against same.

RUTH: She has Richard's enormous Tel Avivian nose . . .

RICHARD: . . . Ruth's hawklike eyes, her hopelessly flat chest . . .

RUTH: . . . Richard's studied pomposity: his gravity . . .

RICHARD: . . . Ruth's unfathomable lack of courage . . .

RUTH: . . . Richard's incomprehensible lack of feeling . . .

RICHARD: . . . Ruth's self-consciously-correct posture . . .

RUBY: Rich girl's shoulders.

RICHARD: Richard loathes Ruby.

RUTH: As does Ruth.

RICHARD: Evident now in his stern glance.

RUTH: As in Ruth's sudden snap from warmth to disapproval: from passion to ice.

RUBY: Ruby moves four steps to center of room and then stops, suddenly, somewhat squashed by their staring.

Note: The following speeches are to be spoken as though interruptions, often overlapping, as often blending. No considerable movement wanted during this section

RICHARD: N.B. Richard was first to hear news of father's death . . .

RUTH: N.B. Ruth heard news of plane crash and mother's death from Richard . . .

RUBY: N.B. Ruby was last to hear news of plane crash and mother's death . . .

RICHARD: . . . Mother's call put through by Betsy—the secretary—Mrs. Betsy Day, the secretary—Conference room, cigar smoke thick, business trouble, no time, distractions impossible. . . .

RUTH: . . . Richard's phone call, Asian Studies Office, University of Vermont, town of Manchester, employed as nobody, researching nothing, touching no one . . .

RUBY: . . . Read news in Chicago *Sun-Times.* Heard same on FM station, midst of news, interrupting Bach's *Concerto in D Minor for 3,* harpsicords and orchestra, *Alla Siciliana,* my name, them famous, now dead, now famous death . . .

RICHARD: . . . Father's body must be gotten. Died in Hot Springs, Arkansas, getting cured . . .

RUTH: . . . Ruth had not known her father had died . . .

RUBY: . . . Flew from O'Hare International to Logan International, United Air Lines, 707, morning flight, a clot of doubleknit polyester leisure-suited businessmen, whispering loudly. Her second flight only, entire lifetime . . .

RICHARD: . . . Arranged for mother to fly to Hot Springs, Arkansas, to collect father's body, fly it home . . .

RUTH: . . . Ruth had not even known her father had been ill . . .

RUBY: . . . Her first flight was three years prior, visited father, first news of illness . . .

RICHARD: . . . Had reserved and paid for American Airlines First Class ticket. Had ticket hand-delivered to mother, two days prior . . .

RUTH: . . . Had years ago conquered fear of air travel. Had flown to and from all continents of the earth . . .

RUBY: . . . Met with doctors, disease incurable, all hope lost . . .

RICHARD: . . . Had summoned surviving siblings to family home, New England September, all chill . . .

RUTH: . . . Had preferred Asia to all others. Had preferred living in countries possessing languages she could neither read nor speak . . .

RUBY: Brother Robert, gone as well, same disease, spared no pain, three years prior, family . . . curse . . .

RICHARD: . . . Had not spoken even one word to Ruth in four years' time, since her third divorce . . .

RUTH: . . . Had preferred most of all living with Cantonese dialect, Northern China, most difficult, words impossible to separate, blend together, words as din . . .

RUBY: . . . Missed brother Robert's funeral, fear of airplanes, trains too slow, Jewish custom, grave by sundown, arrived during night . . .

RICHARD: . . . Had not spoken even one word to Ruby in four year's time since her first divorce . . .

RUTH: . . . Had stayed in room once, one full month, three years prior, Northern China, never straying, never speaking, not one word, not aloud, voice postponed . . .

RUBY: . . . Jewish Law, beat the sundown. Only mirrors, covered, missed her absence . . . All else saw . . .

RICHARD: . . . Had not spoken even one word to father in five year's time, since news of father's irreversible disease . . .

RUTH: . . . Ruth had loved her brother, Robert, deeply . . .

RUBY: . . . Family shocked by Ruby's absence, never forgiven, never heard . . .

RICHARD: . . . Richard was first to hear news of plane crash, second half of ticket, both together, Ozark Mountains, hillbillies found them, picked their clothing clean of money, pried their teeth clean of gold . . .

RUTH: . . . Mourned brother Robert's death, deeply, endlessly, silently . . .

RUBY: . . . Ruby, youngest, most degrees, PhD, Modern British, Joyce and Woolf her favored pair . . .

RICHARD: . . . Pried their teeth clean of gold . . .

RUTH: . . . Never forgiven parents' not reaching her in time. Never said "Goodbye" to Robert . . .

Note: Overlapping ends here

RUBY: . . . One brief marriage, to a surgeon .

RICHARD: . . . Mother's death . . .

RUTH: . . . Never reached her . . .

RUBY: . . . Engendered nothing, born barren, ovaries broken at birth . . .

RICHARD: . . . Richard feels responsible . . .

RUTH: . . . Ruth feels angry . . .

RUBY: . . . Ruby left husband; her, first to door, first to street, first to forget . . .

RICHARD: . . . Richard feels responsible . . .

RUTH: . . . Ruth feels angry . . .

RUBY: . . . Lived with friends, always male .

RICHARD: . . . Richard feels responsible . . .

RUTH: . . . Ruth feels angry . . .

RUBY: . . . Loved her brother, Robert, deeply. Mourned his death, not forgotten. Parents and siblings never forgiven, they never forgave . . .

RICHARD: . . . Richard feels responsible for his parents' death . . .

RUTH: . . . Ruth feels angry at her parents' death . . .

RUBY: . . . Jet from Chicago, late as usual, missed their funeral, struck again. Ruby still stunned, unable to weep . . .

RICHARD: . . . Richard feels responsible for the death of his parents . . .

RUTH: . . . Ruth feels angry at the death of her parents . . .

RUBY: . . . Ruby is unable to weep at the death of her parents . . .

RICHARD: N.B. All of above.

RUTH: N.B. All of above.

RUBY: N.B. All of above.

RICHARD: Richard glances at Ruby.

RUTH: Richard smiles, seeing Ruby's pain . . .

RICHARD: As does Ruth.

RUBY: Ruby regains her strength. She moves to the sofa where she flings her black coat, after tossing small Vuitton weekend case to the floor beside sofa.

RICHARD: Richard is contemptuous of her gesture . . .

RUTH: As is Ruth, who is, however, somewhat amused at the same time and is surprised to find herself smiling. She adjusts her skirt.

RUBY: Ruby adjusts her skirt, re-tucks her blouse into skirt by reaching under skirt, pulls down blouse-ends from bottom, straightening blouse perfectly into skirt and, at the same time, pulling blouse tightly over her breasts.

RICHARD: Richard studies her breasts, certain there is no brassière supporting them.

RUTH: Ruth studies her breasts, certain there is no brassière supporting them.

RUBY: Ruby adjusts her brassière.

RUTH: Ruth adjusts her brassière.

RICHARD: Richard scratches his chest and coughs.

RUBY: Ruby moves to bar and pours glass full with ginger ale. She lifts brandy decanter from shelf, holds and studies same, somewhat lovingly.

RICHARD: Richard glances at dish towel . . . on his stain . . . on rug . . . near his foot.

RUTH: Ruth looks cautiously at her own stain.

RUBY: Ruby drops decanter . . . accidently. It crashes down on bar top, causing loud noise to sound sharply in room.

RICHARD: Richard turns quickly to see what Ruby has done.

RUTH: As does Ruth.

RUBY: Ruby is amazed by what she has done. She takes the bar-towel and feverishly wipes the spilled liquid.

RICHARD: Richard bows his head. He removes wallet from pocket, studies photograph of daughters and ex-wife, replaces wallet in pocket.

RUTH: Ruth bows her head. She pauses. She quietly slips from her chair and removes black veil from mirror. She studies her own image.

RUBY: Ruby moves discreetly behind Ruth, so that she is now able to see her own image in mirror as well.

RUTH: Ruth sees Ruby seeing herself and moves away from mirror, turning directly to face Ruby . . .

RUBY: . . . who is unable to meet the stare and turns her face downward, to the floor.

RUTH: Ruth smiles, crosses to sofa; sits.

RICHARD: Richard stands and walks directly to the mirror. He avoids looking at his reflected image, but instead recovers mirror with black fabric veil, moves to Ruby's chair; sits.

RUTH: Ruth crosses to Richard's chair and sits.

RUBY: Ruby clenches eyes closed, three count.

RICHARD: Richard adjusts his underwear.

RUTH: Ruth adjusts her underwear.

RUBY: Ruby crosses to what appears to be second veiled mirror and removes black fabric from it.

RICHARD: Richard averts his eyes from image . . .

RUTH: As does Ruth.

RUBY: Ruby exposes 24-by-36-inch tinted photograph of their parents, posed, taken on occasion of their 40th wedding anniversary. Ruby stares at photograph.

RICHARD: Richard is weeping. He silently mouths the word "Mama."

RUTH: As does Ruth.

RUBY: Ruby continues to stare at photograph a moment before taking two odd steps backwards, stiffly. She stops. She silently mouths the word "Papa."

RICHARD & RUTH: *(Silently)* Mama.

RUBY: *(Silently)* Papa.

RUTH: Ruth glances at photograph and then at Ruby. She faces Richard, three count. She is openly contemptuous of her sister and brother.

RUBY: Ruby looks first at Richard and then at Ruth. She replaces veil over photograph. She moves to bar . . .

RICHARD: Richard follows her with his eyes, openly staring . . .

RUBY: . . . Ruby leans against bar, somewhat slumped, anguished . . .

RICHARD: Richard coughs, turns away . . .

RUBY: . . . Ruby covers her eyes with palm of left hand. Right hand slides discreetly across stomach to waistband of skirt. She is adjusting and turning same.

RUTH: . . . Ruth remains silent, staring at stain on rug, lost in a memory . . .

RICHARD: . . . Richard strokes a tear from his cheek.

RUTH: Ruth stands, moves toward Ruby, tentatively: painfully slow, frightened. She plans to embrace her sister, but will not have the courage to do so.

RUBY: Ruby senses Ruth approaching, turns, faces her, smiles.

RUTH: Ruth is suddenly stopped.

RUBY: Ruby spies bottle-cap on floor, scoops it up, bending quickly, tosses same easily into wastebasket, leg of desk. Ruby turns, suddenly facing Richard . . .

RICHARD: . . . who has been discreetly admiring Ruby's upper thigh, made quite visible during her rapid bend and scoop . . .

RUBY: . . . Ruby giggles . . .

RICHARD: Richard turns quickly away from her, outraged.

RUBY: Ruby contrives a serious stare in his direction, but giggles again.

RUTH: Ruth is now holding her hand to her mouth, attempting unsuccessfully to contain a chortle.

RUBY: Ruby chortles openly.

RUTH: Ruth looks across stage to Ruby . . .

RUBY: . . . who looks across to Ruth.

RUTH: Ruth takes a step again in Ruby's direction.

RICHARD: Richard produces a wailing sound, suddenly, burying his face in his lap.

RUTH: Ruth turns to him and watches him awhile . . .

RICHARD: Richard is sobbing.

RUBY: Ruby walks to the back of Richard's chair, stops, reaches forward and allows her hand to rest a moment atop Richard's bowed head.

RUTH: Ruth watches, quietly, disapprovingly.

RICHARD: Richard seems unable to move. He neither turns toward Ruby nor away from her: he is instead frozen. His sobbing is now controlled: stopped, quenched.

RUBY: Ruby is embarrassed, sorry she negotiated the touching of Richard's head. She steps back now, three odd steps, stiffly; stops.

RUTH: Ruth stands staring at Ruby.

RUBY: Ruby looks directly at Ruth now. The sisters' eyes meet and hold an absolutely fixed stare.

RUTH: Ruth neither looks away, nor does she smile.

RUBY: Nor Ruby.

RICHARD: Richard stands and moves directly to veiled photograph . . .

RUBY: . . . Ruby does not break her stare at Ruth . . .

RICHARD: . . . He pauses a moment, touching black fabric with the back of his hand . . .

RUBY: . . . Nor does Ruth break her stare at Ruby . . .

RICHARD: . . . Richard carefully, silently, removes black fabric veil from photograph, allowing fabric to fall to floor beside his feet.

RUTH: Ruth is the first to break the stare between the sisters. She turns now to watch Richard.

RUBY: As does Ruby.

RICHARD: Richard stares intently at the photograph, reaching his left hand up and forward, touching the cheek of the man in the photograph. He rubs his finger gently across the face of the man, through the void between the man and the woman, finally allowing his finger to stop directly on the chin on the image of the woman in the photograph.

RUTH: Ruth stands, head bowed, silently mouths the word "Papa"

RUBY: Ruby stands, head bowed, silently mouths the word "Papa."

RICHARD: Richard turns, stares first at Ruth and then at Ruby. He points at the photograph, but then causes his pointing finger to fold back into his hand, which he clenches now into a fist, beating same, three times . . . against . . . his . . . hip. He relaxes. He silently mouths the word "Mama."

RUBY: Ruby moves to Richard's chair, sits, allowing her skirt to remain pleated open, high on her leg.

RICHARD: Richard notices her naked thigh.

RUTH: Ruth notices Richard noticing Ruby's naked thigh.

RICHARD: Richard notices that Ruth has noticed him.

RUBY: Ruby tugs her skirt down to her knee. With her left hand, she wipes a tear from her left cheek.

RICHARD: Richard moves to the bar. He studies the bottle of Scotch whiskey a while before filling five inches of the liquid into a fresh glass. He turns and faces Ruth, lifts his glass to her, then to his lips, drains it of its contents, drinking same.

RUTH: Ruth stares, silently amazed.

RUBY: Ruby bows her head and sobs.

RICHARD: Richard walks quietly to his shoes and socks and collects them. He sits on the sofa, center, and re-dresses his feet, sitting carelessly atop his sisters' outer garments.

RUTH: Ruth watches, standing straight now.

RUBY: Ruby notices the towel on the floor next to the chair in which she is sitting, rubs and moves same with her toe.

RICHARD: Richard looks up from tying his shoe to watch Ruby nudging his stain with her toe. He stares disapprovingly.

RUBY: Ruby senses Richard's disapproval and stops nudging at the stain. She instead leans forward and rubs the stain with her fingers, returning same to mouth licking them with her tongue.

RUTH: Ruth gags.

RICHARD: Richard is disgusted, completes tying his shoes hurriedly. He stands and tosses on his overcoat.

RUTH: Ruth takes three odd steps backwards, stiffly, stops.

RUBY: Ruby turns in her chair and stares openly at Richard.

RICHARD: Richard walks to bar, finds Scotch whiskey bottle which he raises to his lips and drains, unflinchingly. Richard moves directly to position beneath photograph and stares at same, lifting bottle to image of mother and father.

RUBY: Ruby continues her stare at Richard, amazed.

RICHARD: Richard allows bottle to fall to floor near his feet. He touches photograph, precisely as he did before: man first, then woman. He then bows head, sobs.

RUTH: Ruth bows head, weeps, covering her eyes with palm of right hand.

RICHARD: Richard closes his coat fully now, lifting collar to back of his head. He discovers armband in pocket, removes it, clenching same in fist. He stares at Ruth, arm outstretched in her direction, fist pointing accusingly.

RUTH: Ruth glances up and then, suddenly, down, averting eyes from Richard's, but then looking up quickly, she stares directly into Richard's eyes.

RICHARD: He waits a moment, watching to see if she will have the strength to cross the room to him.

RUTH: Ruth moves one step toward Richard, not breaking their joined stare. But then she does. She stops. She lowers her eyes.

RUBY: Ruby stands, looks at Richard, but remains, unmoving, at the foot of her chair.

RICHARD: Richard watches Ruth a moment and then shifts his stare to Ruby.

RUBY: Ruby smiles.

RICHARD: Richard moves to door, opens same, pauses a moment, turns again into room, unclenches fist, allowing armband to drop to rug, pauses a moment, exits, never closing door.

RUBY: Ruby moves to door and closes same, leaning her back against it. She stares a moment at armband on rug.

RUTH: As does Ruth.

RUBY: Ruby moves to photograph and stares at same.

RUTH: Ruth finds shoes, slips quickly into same, moves to sofa, rapidly collecting her outer clothing.

RUBY: Ruby, suddenly realizing she might be left alone in room, moves quickly away from photograph, sees Ruth; stops, frozen.

RUTH: Ruth races to re-dress herself in her coat, jamming hat on to head, stockings in coat pocket.

RUBY: Ruby has her outer clothing now in her hands but realizes she is too late.

RUTH: Ruth has moved quickly and successfully, assuming an exit position at the door, coat buttoned closed.

RUBY: Ruby is stunned and allows her outer clothing to drop back down on to the sofa.

RUTH: Ruth smiles, touches doorknob.

RUBY: Ruby leans over sofa, her back to Ruth.

RUTH: Ruth stares at Ruby's youthful body, her thighs, her straight back, her rich girl's shoulders.

RUBY: Ruby lifts her face, but cannot turn to Ruth.

RUTH: Ruth glances at photograph, but cannot sustain look at same. She straightens her back, inhales, quietly opens door, exhales. She glances a final glance at Ruby. Exits.

RUBY: Ruby hears the door . . .

RUTH: *(Off)* click . . .

RUBY: . . . finally closed. She turns quickly. Certain now that Ruth has exited, Ruby stands frozen, sad-eyed, staring at the still closed door. She moves to bar and finds glass decanter on it, which she holds a moment before suddenly smashing same on bar. After shock of glass breaking, there is silence in the room. Ruby moves again to photograph, carrying jagged neck of glass decanter with her; considers destroying photograph, but instead softly caresses same with palm of right hand, touching first the image of the man, then the image of the woman and then again the image of the man. She moves to sofa, still carrying jagged remains of decanter with her. She thinks to sit but does not, instead turns, faces photograph, fully. Leaning forward over sofa, Ruby allows the weight of her body against the final point of the glass, causing the remains of the decanter to enter her body just below the breast, not suicide, but, instead, something more severe. She turns away from photograph, faces front, allows her body to relax on to sofa. Her hand unclenches. The jagged remains of the decanter fall. Blood drops from hand, staining rug. Ruby faces front, pauses a moment. She opens her mouth, screams, but there is no sound.

(The lights fade to black)

Curtain

Rochelle Owens

THE WIDOW AND THE COLONEL

Rochelle Owens

Rochelle Owens is the award-winning author of many controversial and innovative plays, including several "Obies" (the *Village Voice* Drama Awards), the Drama Desk Award, and honors from the New York Drama Critics' Circle. Her plays have been produced throughout the world and presented at festivals in Edinburgh, Berlin, Paris and Rome. In addition to writing for the theatre, she has published five books of poetry, three collections of plays and has given many readings throughout the country and in Europe. A recipient of Guggenheim, Yale School of Drama, Creative Artists Program Service, Rockefeller, and The National Endowment for the Arts Fellowships, she is a founding member of The New York Theatre Strategy and a sponsor of The Women's InterArt Center, Inc.

Miss Owens stepped into the international theatrical limelight with her first play. *Futz,* which excited considerable critical and audience interest. Described by Edith Oliver of *The New Yorker* as "a witty, harsh, farcical, and touching dramatic poem," it was presented at Café La Mama in 1967, subsequently toured England and Europe and was performed at the Edinburgh Festival. In 1968, the drama returned to Off-Broadway, this time at the Theatre De Lys where it ran for 233 performances and garnered an "Obie" award for distinguished playwriting. *Futz* and his companions, however, would not stay ballasted to Greenwich Village, and soon they were to be seen in theatres of Sweden, Germany, Canada and other countries, as well as on the screen in a movie version released in 1969.

Miss Owens' plays have engendered much journalistic space, both approbatory and disparaging, but whether one is pro or con, it must be conceded that she has an exceptionally gifted hand for stirring the cauldron of theatrical excitement. Harold Clurman, one of her many distinguished votaries, has written, "Her work is not realism; it is real. It is the product of a complex imagination in which deep layers of the author's subconscious emerge in wild gusts of stage imagery . . . I know of no contemporary playwright like Rochelle Owens."

At the time of publication of *The Karl Marx Play* in *The Best Short Plays 1971,* Miss Owens supplied the following biographical information: "I was born in Brooklyn, New York, on April 2, 1936. Having completed my public school education, I moved to Manhattan where I studied at the New School for Social Research and with Herbert Berghof at the HB Studio. At that time, neither an academic degree nor a career as an actress appealed to me, so I worked at numerous jobs, read a great deal, and wrote poetry. In

1959, my poetry began to appear in several of the most prominent 'little magazines,' and since then I have published three books of poems and have contributed to many literary journals and anthologies.

"In 1962, I married George Economou, poet and college professor, then editor of *Trobar* poetry magazine. Shortly before meeting my husband, I wrote my first play, *Futz*. Since then I have written many full-length and short plays, among them: *The Queen of Greece; Istanboul; He Wants Shih!; Beclch; Homo;* and *Kontraption*.

"Although I wrote *The String Game* after *Futz*, it was the first of my plays to be staged, in 1965, at the Judson Poets' Theatre. Subsequently, my plays have been performed Off-Broadway, Off-Off Broadway, in regional and college theatres, on television, and abroad."

The author's published works include: *Not Be Essence That Cannot Be; Salt and Core; Futz and What Came After; I Am the Babe of Joseph Stalin's Daughter; Poems from Joe's Garage; The Karl Marx Play and Others; The Joe 82 Creation Poems;* and *Spontaneous Combustion*.

Under a grant from The National Endowment for the Arts, Rochelle Owens was commissioned by Borrowed Time Productions to write a radio drama in honor of the American Bicentennial and sponsored by Voice of America. The initial broadcast was directed by Shepard Traube in March, 1976. The play, *The Widow and the Colonel*, has been adapted for the stage by Miss Owens, and it appears in print for the first time in *The Best Short Plays 1977*.

Author's Note

There are as many ways to approach this play as there are combinations of people who might involve themselves in it. The script is designed to accommodate various concepts which can prove to be fascinating and rewarding. The play can be directed literally or as a fantasy or dream. The director should choose his approach. Although this play is based on certain historical facts, it is fictional and not intended as literal biography. The action takes place in Williamsburg, Virginia, in the years 1758 and '59. Costumes should be historically appropriate.

Characters:

NARRATOR: MRS. CHAMBERLAYNE
MARTHA CUSTIS
COLONEL WASHINGTON
SALLY FAIRFAX
MAJOR CHAMBERLAYNE
DANCING COUPLES: MEN AND WOMEN

Scene One:

A ballroom brightly lighted and with an animated group of dancing couples. At the front of the stage Narrator: Mrs. Chamberlayne and her younger friend, Martha Custis, are engaged in conversation.

NARRATOR—MRS. CHAMBERLAYNE: And so, Martha Custis, you want to know about Sally Fairfax? Well, I'm not surprised.

MARTHA CUSTIS: Yes, I am curious, a little curious about her. She is incredibly vivacious and lovely!

MRS. CHAMBERLAYNE: She goes like wine to the head of Colonel Washington and all he can do is blush like a young Virginia farmer when she graces him with a dance.

MARTHA CUSTIS: Who is she?

MRS. CHAMBERLAYNE: She is Mrs. George William Fairfax conspicuously devoted to her older, her much older easy-going husband—but having a liaison with a younger man.

MARTHA CUSTIS: Mrs. Chamberlayne, you are a little judgmental, I think. And she is the most fascinating woman that I've ever seen in Williamsburg. Colonel Washington is a man emerging into civilization after months in the wilderness. I am sure he thinks she is the most beautiful and certainly the most fashionable woman—shh! They are passing us now.

(Colonel Washington and Sally Fairfax dancing the minuet)

COLONEL WASHINGTON: The life of a soldier provides little opportunity for courtship, Sally.

SALLY FAIRFAX: So that is why you are a bachelor at an age when many men have a growing family. *(Ironically)* Because you are a soldier.

COLONEL WASHINGTON: Don't torment me, Sally.

SALLY FAIRFAX: *(Mimicking)* "Don't torment me, Sally." A little melodramatic for Colonel George Washington.

COLONEL WASHINGTON: You are beginning to attract attention and you are not dancing well. Shhh, my dearest, Mrs. Chamberlayne is staring at us.

SALLY FAIRFAX: Yes, she is and so is the little plump bird, Martha Custis. Poor little Martha, a widow with two babes. And only twenty-five herself. Martha Custis . . . small and soft—

COLONEL WASHINGTON: And my Sally Fairfax, tall and taut and distracting—and excitable! *(They laugh)*

MARTHA CUSTIS: The colonel and Sally are talking about me! I heard them say my name.

MRS. CHAMBERLAYNE: *(Dropping a glass of wine)* How terrible! O, I splashed a little wine on the hem of my dress! I had a . . . a . . . feeling . . . an omen about Colonel Washington! I know who he will marry. *(To audience)* Martha Custis stared at me—so surprised she was—that she bit the inside of her cheek when I told her the name of the woman who would be Colonel Washington's bride. There was no disputing the fact that the tall, masterful soldier had enchanted Martha. How did I know then that they would marry? Intuition! But I'll continue the story. Colonel George Washington had enchanted Martha not just because of the blue and scarlet regimentals that made his eyes glint like ice or blue hazy fire, and certainly not his wealth nor dazzling prospects, only a small house on the Potomac and some land. George Washington was a silent man and not socially extroverted, perhaps that is why he was so struck by Sally Fairfax. So it was not his telling long and amusing anecdotes that made Martha's pink cheeks warm and caused her to laugh lightly and nervously. At receptions I had observed how Colonel Washington would watch the person carefully as they told overdrawn stories about themselves. And he would smile as they rambled on. He never told anything about his colorful military career in company. But there was his reputation, his achievements at twenty-six, his overwhelming, thrilling presence, his way with a horse—how that would delight Martha's little children. O, I believe it shocked Martha to discover that people expected her to promptly marry again after her husband Daniel, who was twenty years older than she, had died, leaving her a rich widow with so much responsibility of the estate and the future of the children, little Jack and Patsy. Her husband Daniel had been so kind, capable and comfortable. They had had a good life together. As a matter of fact I remember now that it was her husband who had first pointed out to Martha in the street—towering above his companions, the grave, soft pink-skinned face of George Washington, with his erect straight-stepping carriage, like an Iroquois Indian. Williamsburg society had always been aware of the rebelliousness of George's nature. The relationship with the wife of his old friend, though it was disciplined, was fervent and constant. The signs of fatigued sadness were in the man's eyes. I, who have always loved Greek mythology, decided to give Cupid a hand and so the very day that Martha arrived on horseback from her home to our estate . . .

Scene Two:

Martha, on horseback, at the estate of Major and Mrs. Chamberlayne.

MARTHA CUSTIS: It is the year 1758, I am a widow of six months and three days. I have two children, Jacky, four, and Patsy, two. Soon I will be talking with the tall frontier colonel again, wearing uniform and riding boots and sword, his hair unpowdered, so thin and sick after weeks of dysentery. I am so nervous! I want us to be cordial and at ease together. This evening we will be sitting side by side during dinner at the Chamberlayne's. Yes, Martha Custis, you are here at the home of Major and Mrs. Chamberlayne, wonderful and dear friends. There is no reason to be nervous when you meet Colonel George Washington tonight. I almost wish he were not coming here; odd, but I think I would have preferred reading Voltaire or John Locke this evening or just thinking. I feel this odd pressure of other people's expectations. And George is so tall, I wonder if I look ridiculous by his side—if I were only a little taller and *(Horse whinnies)*—I'm even upsetting this horse. *(Laughs)* I wonder if the Colonel is interested in Greek mythology. Perhaps we can discuss Voltaire—some of the military men are so indifferent to culture. Of course, they have not the tranquility or leisure to read much. But he dances well, that I have seen, but perhaps only with that lovely adulteress Sally Fairfax. What a paradoxical individual, George Washington! He looks so severe and moral most of the time and all the time he's obsessed with Mr. Fairfax's wife. How ironic! He has a reckless side that is almost self-sabotage. Will he be good with the children? Do we really have anything in common? I wonder what we want from each other? *(Horse whinnies)* Easy, Duncan, easy! Be gentle with Martha Custis and take us back to the Chamberlayne's. Now, ride, Duncan, ride! *(Crack of whip and galloping)*

MRS. CHAMBERLAYNE: I believe it was at that first dinner party that events began to take shape. My husband, Major Chamberlayne, was speaking.

Scene Three:

The dinner party. Soft music.

MAJOR CHAMBERLAYNE: We are in the process of solving serious and original political problems. England regards the American scene as a secondary theatre of war. George, what do you think will happen?

COLONEL WASHINGTON: The principal object for England should be the conquest of Canada and the American West!

MRS. CHAMBERLAYNE: Under young and energetic generals! How wonderful the way Colonel Washington's militia held the Shenandoah Valley against the Indians!

COLONEL WASHINGTON: Unfortunately, I might have contracted consumption. Let us hope it is only a simple case of dysentery.

MARTHA CUSTIS: Colonel Washington, you ought to drink a little wine with the food.

COLONEL WASHINGTON: Perhaps I should. Mrs. Custis, you are right—wine causes the energies to flow in happier directions!

MAJOR CHAMBERLAYNE: Colonel Washington is skilled in conversation with the women folk! *(Laugh)* I enjoyed that remark about the wine causing the energies to flow.

MRS. CHAMBERLAYNE: The Major is relaxing! I can tell, by what he considers to be amusing—his own interpretation of dinner conversation. Why not ask our dear Martha to sing a refrain or two of a song she likes?

MARTHA CUSTIS: I don't think I want to sing a song now, this minute. . . . I really would like to know whether we will always be a Colony of the mother country?

MAJOR CHAMBERLAYNE: Only a woman could think such an idea. If we in this brave new world were not always a part of the body of England—if ever I had such a conviction I would divorce Mrs. Chamberlayne and marry a squaw!

(Laughter. Music)

COLONEL WASHINGTON: I'm inclined to agree. There will never be a break between England and the Colonies.

MARTHA CUSTIS: Can you be so sure? It is such a natural thing— the inevitability of separation. All things divide or even—break.

COLONEL WASHINGTON: You are a philosophical woman, Martha Custis.

MRS. CHAMBERLAYNE: Martha embroiders beautifully and she is a wonderful mother to the children.

COLONEL WASHINGTON: And would you sing one of your songs,
Martha Custis?

MAJOR CHAMBERLAYNE: Yes, yes, Martha, a little sweetness and
light the Colonel can take back with him—a memory of a song! A
woman's singing voice!

MARTHA CUSTIS: *(Sings)*
"Come, cheer up, my friends
In this lamb-white year
The battles of England
Bring triumph and fear
Come, cheer up, my friends
For an infinitely better time
When the land brings forth
A heraldic time, a heraldic,
A heraldic, a heraldic time!"

MRS. CHAMBERLAYNE: How lovely, Martha! Martha Custis, you
must perform at a musical event after the services at the church.
The mood is often terribly grim here in Virginia. So many men
returning from the frontier in broken health.—O, I'm terribly
sorry, Colonel Washington—

COLONEL WASHINGTON: I am sure that I will be perfectly healthy
soon. Especially after having the good fortune to have heard the
lovely voice of Mrs. Custis.

MARTHA CUSTIS: My children enjoy the songs. But then
children are so devoid of adult judgments. And little Jacky is delighted with songs about horses! You know how children are.

COLONEL WASHINGTON: I am interested in what you stated
before, Martha—about the possibiltiy of a break between the
Colonies and England! Though the idea unnerves me.

MARTHA CUSTIS: Why, why, because it is so unconventional?

MRS. CHAMBERLAYNE: I think the Major and I will leave you two
while you discuss this serious matter and intriguing idea.

MAJOR CHAMBERLAYNE: I intend to stay and participate with my
ideas. I've thought about this revolutionary possibility—and I—

MRS. CHAMBERLAYNE: You will accompany me, Major. Colonel
Washington and Martha want to discuss the idea of American independence without an old bird like you hanging around—*(Laughter,
as they depart. The sounds of a fire being fed. Music)*

COLONEL WASHINGTON: I'm glad they are gone. As good-
hearted as she is her voice began to grate on my nerves.

MARTHA CUSTIS: It's because of your illness.

COLONEL WASHINGTON: Perhaps. Why are you looking at me
like that?

MARTHA CUSTIS: Like what?

COLONEL WASHINGTON: As if you know what's in—what's in my thoughts.

MARTHA CUSTIS: I was just thinking that never have I seen a man with such a fine complexion as yours—so many poor people have had the pox. But you—your skin is so perfect.

COLONEL WASHINGTON: Yes, I've wondered why I have not been marked by the pox. So many of my men have had it. The beastly pox! You also have been spared.

MARTHA CUSTIS: My husband Daniel was unlucky. Poor man, he suffered with the disease when he was a small child. Thank the Lord, that my children have never had it—but still, perhaps—it might overtake them, too.

COLONEL WASHINGTON: I'm sorry about the passing of your husband. He was a good man. He was a fortunate man to have had a woman like you, Martha Custis.

MARTHA CUSTIS: The Lord did not want me to be his wife for the rest of my life. For whatever *His* reasons were.

COLONEL WASHINGTON: There is a saying that only the good die young. These hellish wars with the French and Indians kill off many young men.

MARTHA CUSTIS: True. And Daniel was not a young man. No, he was not so very young . . . like you. I am twenty-five years old, Colonel—I wonder what I want to do with the rest of my life? There are no available solutions.

COLONEL WASHINGTON: You could do anything you really desired, Martha. Martha, what exactly do you wish to do?

MARTHA CUSTIS: I see you looking at my hands. Why?

COLONEL WASHINGTON: They are soft and a little full. Like a painting I once saw of a French milkmaid.

MARTHA CUSTIS: What was she doing, milking a cow? *(Laughs)*

COLONEL WASHINGTON: As a matter of fact the title of the painting was called "The Milkmaid."

MARTHA CUSTIS: So, you are a man who secretly longs for a comfortable, perhaps a maternal woman—unlike your Sally Fairfax!

COLONEL WASHINGTON: What shall I say to that, Martha?

MARTHA CUSTIS: I am a maternal woman—*(Laughs)* I even have two children. Unlike the forever youthful vivacious Sally Fairfax. Why do you keep that liaison continuing, why let it burn you up and make your eyes so tired and sad?

COLONEL WASHINGTON: Perhaps I don't know what is right for a military man. Perhaps I should even resign from the army. Perhaps, I should go to the south of France and recuperate from the consumption that I might not even have. Let's understand one another, Martha Custis. Life often gives us more than we bargain for.

MARTHA CUSTIS: Sally Fairfax is just another facet of a knotty problem in Colonel Washington's life.

COLONEL WASHINGTON: If you want to understand something about me, know then that I'm very tired and afraid sometimes.

MARTHA CUSTIS: We will only make conversation that will keep us both at ease.

COLONEL WASHINGTON: I will not tolerate any insincerity between us, Martha Custis.

MARTHA CUSTIS: I forget that we are almost strangers.

COLONEL WASHINGTON: True. We have met as acquaintances with mutual friends and recollections. I saw how you noticed that I ate very little. Did you think that I was in pain? Then you suggested that I drink a little wine with the food. Martha, your eyes had a look of amusement in them. Did you think that I needed looking after?

MARTHA CUSTIS: Men cannot bear being ill. And they need a woman to be interested in them.

COLONEL WASHINGTON: And I have no woman in my home. No wife. You seem to know the right questions and answers to things.

(Footsteps approach, door opens and shuts)

MARTHA CUSTIS: Mrs. Chamberlayne has just looked in at the door.

COLONEL WASHINGTON: She is very kind.

MARTHA CUSTIS: She knows that—that you are a lonely man.

COLONEL WASHINGTON: And what should a lonely soldier have to ease his . . . yearning? I am worn down and exhausted, too many frustrations and humiliations in my military duties, the incompetence of subordinates! And the absurd pride of my superiors.

MARTHA CUSTIS: Why don't you resign?

COLONEL WASHINGTON: I almost was at the point of quitting, almost at the point to prepare for death like my brother Lawrence who served as a captain on the Spanish Main. And Sally Fairfax, the wife of my friend . . . that relationship is very painful.

(The fire crackles)

MARTHA CUSTIS: You are like a harassed boy—so proud and so humble. But, Colonel, I have problems, too, and such terrible responsibilities beyond a woman's scope and judgment. You are a landowner, you can understand. . . . The fire is reflecting on your shoe buckles. You look like a French Marquis, in your snowy white wig. Would you really like to retire in Southern France?

COLONEL WASHINGTON: No, I don't think I ever really could. You know, Martha, it is easy and agreeable to talk to you beside this fire.

MARTHA CUSTIS: You needn't wonder how much of your military affairs I could comprehend—

COLONEL WASHINGTON: Or find of interest.

MARTHA CUSTIS: If you want to talk of your military concerns— *(Laughs)* I am certain that I can listen.

COLONEL WASHINGTON: Why did you laugh, Martha?

MARTHA CUSTIS: Mrs. Chamberlayne was eavesdropping. I saw her holding a candle with her nightcap under her chin. *(Both laugh)*

COLONEL WASHINGTON: Your comment about me looking like a Marquis—*(Joking and laughing)* Perhaps, Mrs. Chamberlayne thinks that I'm an Indian scout posing as a French Marquis—

MARTHA CUSTIS: Posing as Colonel George Washington!

COLONEL WASHINGTON: You know there are complicated questions concerning the Indian problem.

MARTHA CUSTIS: I believe their hunting grounds must be reserved for them in the interests of humanity.

COLONEL WASHINGTON: French and Spanish ambition, with the Indian danger is very real. I fear that the Colonies will not even cooperate for their own defense against the Indians.

MARTHA CUSTIS: There is no doubt that stronger imperial control is needed.

COLONEL WASHINGTON: How perceptive of you, Mrs. Custis. Our time is not only revolutionary and destructive, but creative and constructive.

MARTHA CUSTIS: These times are bewildering for all of us.

COLONEL WASHINGTON: You are a very different type of woman, Martha Custis.

MARTHA CUSTIS: Different from whom?

COLONEL WASHINGTON: Sally Fairfax.

MARTHA CUSTIS: It must be disconcerting to be so enamored of a woman.

COLONEL WASHINGTON: A man in military life must appear formal and remote. And suppose he is not only that—suppose—

(Distant thunder)

MARTHA CUSTIS: Suppose he is like you, Colonel Washington, a frontier hero who is not always shy with women. I once said that to someone about you, behind your back—

COLONEL WASHINGTON: You gossiped about Colonel George Washington! *(Ironic, amused)* I ought to imprison you, somewhere, dark and terrible.

MARTHA CUSTIS: No, I don't believe that you are always shy with women.

(Rain storm with some thunder)

MAJOR CHAMBERLAYNE: *(Entering)* We don't allow our guests to leave after sunset. Particularly during a very nasty storm. I've already sent the horses to the stable with their attendant, Colonel Washington. And the drawing room candles are lighted.

(He leaves)

MARTHA CUSTIS: *(Rising)* I must say good-night to the children. Little Jacky loves to tell how well he can ride his pony . . .

NARRATOR—MRS. CHAMBERLAYNE: *(Appearing)* I will never forget how little Jacky clutched the forefinger of Colonel George Washington as he lead him to watch the joyful event of riding the pony. I think that Martha's children were already half in love with the Colonel when he lifted them both onto his fine saddle horse. That first wonderful evening together was a reflection of the joy that would come to all. At noon Colonel Washington rode away, in a different, yes, a far different mood than when he had arrived. Martha's face was shining. *(To Martha)* There was a sort of magic about last evening in the parlor, Martha. You and the colonel.

MARTHA CUSTIS: Colonel Washington accepted my rather impulsive invitation to pause at my home when his business in Williamsburg is finished, and see Jacky ride his pony!

MRS. CHAMBERLAYNE: The nature of his errand in town is grim.

MARTHA CUSTIS: He expects to hear a fatal diagnosis.

MRS. CHAMBERLAYNE: That he has consumption?

MARTHA CUSTIS: Yes.

MRS. CHAMBERLAYNE: No. He does not have consumption! And believe me, Martha, because of you he is not willing to die yet!

MARTHA CUSTIS: Mrs. Chamberlayne, I hope that your prophetic gifts are true! How I hope so.

MRS. CHAMBERLAYNE: Never fear, Martha. You will marry George Washington.

(Martha Custis leaves. Music)

I had been right for the dreaded interview with the doctor had proved reassuring. There was no consumption. He went away for several months to complete some unfinished business including a meeting with Sally Fairfax.

(She goes, as Sally Fairfax appears)

SALLY FAIRFAX: Like the vases filled with flowers in spring bloom! George, your face is full with improved health. I am amused that the doctor's nasty prescriptions hastened you to full recovery. Amused at the irony, the rather comic irony of your interest in Martha Custis. Another remedy for the failing health of a lonely military man.

COLONEL WASHINGTON: I am prepared to be susceptible to . . . a little sympathy from a woman. Martha Custis gives me that.

SALLY FAIRFAX: You feel deadlocked in your army ambitions! Defeated.

COLONEL WASHINGTON: I will be twenty-seven soon. I feel I have too little—

SALLY FAIRFAX: Too little! Your name is known throughout Virginia as the foremost young officer America has produced so far!

COLONEL WASHINGTON: Rank and reputation are very little good to me so long as the King's commission outweighs a colonial one. And my hard-bought experience and opinions could be dismissed by any commander sent out from England! And if I left the army, and won an election, and settled down at Mount Vernon to become an influential planter and member of the Assembly, like your husband, for instance—

SALLY FAIRFAX: Then the devotion, useless devotion to me would not give you peace or comfort or provide you with heirs for the estate you cherish, nor make a gracious hostess for the guests you would entertain. You require a wife not a mistress.

COLONEL WASHINGTON: Mount Vernon requires a wife. My leisure hours indoors would be happier—

SALLY FAIRFAX: And if you married who would be easier to be with—to love—than the practical little widow, Martha Custis, who lacks a manager for her own estate. Together you both could build an establishment, the best in Virginia!

COLONEL WASHINGTON: You yourself advised me to marry. You said it a few times. I'm at a crossroads. I've drifted too long. Mount Vernon is my home and the secondhand family life I found with you is not enough.

SALLY FAIRFAX: Yes. I have no legitimate place in your life . . . And you will not forget me for we will always be neighbors. . . Even our relationship need not change.

COLONEL WASHINGTON: Distracting and unpredictable and challenging Sally!

SALLY FAIRFAX: And is she better read than you?

COLONEL WASHINGTON: No, better read than I. Voltaire, John Locke! *(Laughs)*

SALLY FAIRFAX: George and Martha, Martha and George. How

substantial the names sound. How constant! Like bread and butter! Like salt and soup! A permanent union!

COLONEL WASHINGTON: We will share plans and difficulties together. Like any married man and woman.

SALLY FAIRFAX: You have such a grave look on your face, George.

COLONEL WASHINGTON: I am tired.

SALLY FAIRFAX: When she is your wife—when Martha Dandridge Custis becomes Martha Washington she will want a portrait of you looking serene and dignified with your snowy wig. Something for your children's children. I know a wonderful portrait artist from France. I will tell your Martha his name one day at the right time.

COLONEL WASHINGTON: You are a true gold coin, Sally Fairfax.

SALLY FAIRFAX: You always fail to notice that I come out short on wifely virtues.

COLONEL WASHINGTON: I will be fond of you as long as I shall live.

SALLY FAIRFAX: And since it can never be me in the chair across the hearth from you at Mount Vernon—

COLONEL WASHINGTON: It will be she. Martha Custis.

(Music)

SALLY FAIRFAX: You have finally taken my advice and bespoken a wife. Congratulations! *(Laughs)*

COLONEL WASHINGTON: I never supposed that you would show any sorrow for the loss of my exclusive affections.

SALLY FAIRFAX: You are as discreet as I. I never wanted our relationship unduly noticed and commented upon that you believed yourself to be in love with me.

COLONEL WASHINGTON: So be it. A conventional end to our . . . feelings for each other.

SALLY FAIRFAX: I promise to receive your bride cordially into the Fairfax circle, and help her to feel at home there.

COLONEL WASHINGTON: Everyone has met during the Assembly times at Williamsburg. But Martha has never visited among the Potomac households—

SALLY FAIRFAX: And you believe that she might feel uprooted at first. Some adjustment will naturally take place. And you, George, must make sure that she is never homesick.

COLONEL WASHINGTON: I will remind myself of that often.

SALLY FAIRFAX: You are a restless person and a dedicated soldier—but often rather preoccupied. Do not disappoint her.

COLONEL WASHINGTON: Perhaps I should never marry.

SALLY FAIRFAX: Don't lie, Colonel Washington. You are tickled pink that Martha will be your wife. *(Both laugh)*
COLONEL WASHINGTON: Yes, it's true. Martha is so uncomplaining, so good. But I am a soldier and so many times my mind is probing the odds there, devising arguments, preparing defenses, laying down stratagems. There are old scores that must be resolved!
SALLY FAIRFAX: Martha Custis is a tactful little person—let us hope! You have much to learn about living with a woman. Adieu, Colonel, Adieu.

Scene Four:

Music. Martha is having tea with her friend, Mrs. Chamberlayne, on the portico.

MRS. CHAMBERLAYNE: You went to Colonel Washington's heart and I think he fears that he might lose you.
MARTHA CUSTIS: I don't know if I ought to marry again. If I want to marry anyone at all.
MRS. CHAMBERLAYNE: Colonel George Washington is not merely anyone. I have a premonition that he will be immensely important in a high position one day! Perhaps he will be *General* Washington!
MARTHA CUSTIS: Or King of England! *(Both laugh)* Let us go into the music room.
MRS. CHAMBERLAYNE: O, Martha, you will be the General's lady!
MARTHA CUSTIS: Is that another prophesy of yours, Mrs. Chamberlayne?
MRS. CHAMBERLAYNE: Colonel Washington has exactly the right blend of authority and courtesy. Yes, and to your question about you becoming the General's lady—
MARTHA CUSTIS: I did not ask that, Mrs. Chamberlayne. You said it. I shall not ever forget the image of little Patsy toddling forward to offer him a limp bouquet and how he went on one knee to accept it. Wearing his blue and scarlet regimentals, and how little Jacky loved to exclaim that when he grew up he, too, would wear a snowy wig and shiny buckles like George Washington.
MRS. CHAMBERLAYNE: Your children love him. It seems right that they are with him, I mean that when they are with him—it is right. And it seems right for him to oversee your property, dining at your table and sharing life together.

MARTHA CUSTIS: We have visited together a few times and now you have Colonel Washington and I sharing life together, as you sentimentally put it.

MRS. CHAMBERLAYNE: Sentiment is a human virtue, Martha.

MARTHA CUSTIS: Women are secondary to a dedicated soldier.

(Harpsichord) (Sings)
"Come, cheer up, my friends
In this lamb-white year
The battles of England
Bring triumph and fear
Come, cheer up, my friends
For an infinitely better time
When the land brings forth
A heraldic time, a heraldic,
A heraldic, a heraldic time!"

MRS. CHAMBERLAYNE: Martha, when you first sang that song— why, his face was radiant as he looked at you!

MARTHA CUSTIS: I'm not a very good singer. One day soon I shall pack up the children and go to Italy. How I love the opera!

MRS. CHAMBERLAYNE: Have you promised to be Colonel Washington's wife?

(Harpsichord comes to an abrupt, dramatic halt)

MARTHA CUSTIS: Colonel George Washington! Must we always talk about him—and whether I will be his bride or not! Well, I shall tell you, Mrs. Chamberlayne, and forgive me for being so agitated! I am so very fond of you and the Major—I'd like a breath of air! Let's sit awhile on the portico.

MRS. CHAMBERLAYNE: O, you needn't apologize.

MARTHA CUSTIS: Well, I shall tell you what I believe about him. He thinks that to begin a life with me is a fair new beginning!

MRS. CHAMBERLAYNE: Like a new leaf turned.

MARTHA CUSTIS: Yes. That's what he wants! When he spoke his words—his honest offer of marriage—the words came clumsily.

MRS. CHAMBERLAYNE: Sometimes a big man has a lack of assurance!

MARTHA CUSTIS: He is not a conceited man at all.

MRS. CHAMBERLAYNE: You ought not to doubt him. A man like that.

MARTHA CUSTIS: When he left he was on his way to a war.

MRS. CHAMBERLAYNE: Martha, look at the sky—there's an eagle flying across the horizon!

MARTHA CUSTIS: Yes, how magnificent! They make their nests

on the top of icy mountains! Their young break forth from the eggs on the peaks of mountains. A magical moment of new life!

MRS. CHAMBERLAYNE: I have never seen one flying with others!

MARTHA CUSTIS: The image is most beautiful! A single great bird across the sky! Splendid and heroic! Back to earth again. Anyway, when Colonel Washington left he was on his way to a war and I fear for him—the inevitable camp ailments, dysentery and fever.

MRS. CHAMBERLAYNE: It's been about six months since your last meeting, hasn't it?

MARTHA CUSTIS: Yes, and I wonder how to begin again—the mood of our last time together.

MRS. CHAMBERLAYNE: When will you see the Colonel again?

MARTHA CUSTIS: During the Christmas season.

MRS. CHAMBERLAYNE: How perfect! The rooms will be decked with Christmas greens and glowing with log fires.

MARTHA CUSTIS: Yes, and the voices of my children, the toys and pretty dresses and garments ordered from England.

MRS. CHAMBERLAYNE: You ought to make certain that you have a gift ready for him to give to the children! He has probably never spent a Christmas season in a household where there are children.

MARTHA CUSTIS: I can see him putting his hand to his pocket for coins! *(Laughs)* Coins are meaningless to my children, only what they can fetch. I have an idea—a toy horse and a velvet cap trimmed with lace. They will be given to Jack and Patsy in his name.

MRS. CHAMBERLAYNE: You are a tactful woman.

MARTHA CUSTIS: I really *do* want to marry him!

MRS. CHAMBERLAYNE: You are going to be the bride of a man everyone in Williamsburg is delighted to honor! That is indeed something to look forward to!

MARTHA CUSTIS: My dress will be yellow brocade, the skirt open down the front over a white and silver petticoat; my slippers perhaps will be lilac silk embroidered in gold and silver, with high heels, because he is so tall. There will be pearls looped through my powdered hair.

MRS. CHAMBERLAYNE: George and Martha. George and Martha Washington! How right the names sound! *(Music)*

Curtain

Lou Rivers

THIS PIECE OF LAND

Lou Rivers

This Piece of Land, in its final manifestation, was presented by The American Theatre Company, New York City, on December 19, 1975, and is published for the first time anywhere in this anthology.

In reply to a request for biographical information, author Lou Rivers wrote to this editor: "I was born in Savannah, Georgia, on September 18, 1922. I attended the Savannah public schools, and in 1946 graduated from Savannah State College with a Bachelor's Degree in English. My college years had followed my honorable discharge from the U.S. Army in 1943. During both my high school and college years, I was duly recognized as a student with "great literary promise." I wrote poetry, plays, short stories and essays. It was also during these years that I was most active as a youth leader in the N.A.A.C.P. I was also a leader and a founder of the Youth Association for Community Betterment.

"Recognized and respected as a youth leader, I received additional acclaim and awards as winner in local and state essay and radio-script writing contests, and as an honor student for four years at Savannah State College, I served as a feature writer and editor-in-chief of the college literary periodical, the *Georgia State Herald.* During my college years, I also served as the president of the college's Little Theater movement and each year won the distinction of being voted the best college actor in a play on campus.

"From 1946 to 1949, I served as a Language Arts teacher at Center High School in Waycross, Georgia, where I also organized and conducted a Black Community Theater. I was influential in bringing Black professional theater companies to Waycross. The Little Theater group put on seasons of plays and musicals including some of my earlier efforts at playwriting.

"My first professional introduction to playwriting, however, came in 1949 when Father Hartke at Catholic University in Washington, D.C. gave me my first scholarship to study theater. The scholarship had come as a result of intercessions of Sister Mary Julie at Rosary College, River Forest, Illinois, who had read a play I had adapted from a short story by Paul Laurence Dunbar.

"It was at Catholic University that my love for theater deepened, and I began to understand theater as an art form, its development, its purpose and tremendous possibilities. My first teacher in playwriting was Walter Kerr who opened up to me a whole new beautiful world.

"When I returned to my teaching at Center High School in Waycross, I became more divided than ever between developing myself as teacher and that of a playwright. After many conferences and soul analyses, I discovered I could combine the two, so I was off to acquire an M.A. in dramatic arts at New York University.

"From 1951 to 1958, with my new degree, I taught speech and drama at West Virginia State College, Southern University, and Tougaloo College. On these campuses, I became well-known as a teacher of speech and composition as well as director, drama coach and playwright. I also planned and helped to organize, direct and coordinate community theater groups in West Virginia, Kentucky, Louisiana, and Mississippi. It was during this time that I also worked with the Committee for Negroes in the Arts and studied with Howard Da Silva and Brett Warren in New York City.

"In 1958, I left Tougaloo to study playwriting under John Gassner at Yale University on a John Hay Whitney Creative Writing Fellowship. During this time, I also studied playwriting with Elmer Rice at New York University. I also became the drama coach for Voices, Inc., a Manhattan-based Black company of professional actors, singers and dancers telling of the Black experience through dramatic art forms.

"In studying my career, one would find a fine intertwining of academia and theater. Like most writers, I, too, want to write 'masterpieces', be recognized and celebrated for them, and classified as a 'great' playwright who increases, through his contribution, the development of understanding and appreciation of the human animal. That same ideal holds for my being an educator. To reach both objectives is the ultimate.

"Presently I am the Director of the Writing Lab at New York City Community College. I hold a Ph.D. in Administration and Supervision from Fordham University, and I am a member of Kappa Delta Pi and Phi Delta Kappa. I am the husband of a lovely wife, Ligia Sanchez Rivers, and the father of three beautiful daughters, Luisa, Liana, Loria, and a handsome son, Leigh."

Mr. Rivers' other plays include: *Seeking; Purple Passages; The Scabs; Mr. Randolph Brown; The Making of a Saint; The Ghosts; Monologue for Black Actors; Black Talk from a Barber Shop; Black English; Bouquet for Lorraine;* the musical, *Spiritual Rock Incident;* and *Madama, a Star,* which had a successful engagement at the Off-Off-Broadway New Heritage Theatre several seasons ago.

Characters:

THE SINGER
ROSA
PERRY
SISTER WATERS
THE DEACON
MISS NANCY
LEROY
MR. CHARLIE
MR. MORGAN

All characters are Black except one, Mr. Charlie.

Scene:

Time: 1932. One summer day. Place: A small farm in South Carolina.

Center left is a one-story wooden shack obliquely facing downstage. The shack is above the yard and contains several steps leading from the yard up to its long porch and center door flanked by two windows. The porch holds many potted plants, a bench for sitting, and other household items. Upstage, a curved skydrop runs the full length of the stage giving the scene depth and providing right and left exits. A tree down right helps to define the acting area in front of the house and makes for a third exit to the road beyond the scene. There's an element of mysticism about the scene, the grounds not being clearly defined as separate from the sky.

The curtain rises on a quiet scene, just before dawn. The Singer's silhouette slowly fades in across the sky. He sings and plays his guitar to the night fading into dawn.

SINGER: *(Slow and lamenting)*
"Mornin comes afore the noon.
. . . Then evenin comes . . .
And night's too soon . . .
Spring of year is like the morn   . . .
. . . And so life goes . .
When a man is born.

Autumn comes,
And winter chills.
The baby laughs . . .
The young man thrills.
Day starts low;

The noon runs high.
Seasons begin
And seasons die . . ."
(Singer makes a horizontal crossing against the sky and disappears beyond the house. A lamp light appears in one of the windows and moves across to the next window. Soon Rosa enters from the house. She stands on the porch looking up and about her when Perry, carrying a farming tool, enters from the house; he stands on the porch beside Rosa. Presently he crosses and exits up stage beyond the skydrop. Rosa waves to him, stands there thinking, returns into the house. Soon the light moves from the window to the next; increases in intensity; shimmers; then goes out. The lights fade up to late morning. The Deacon, Miss Nancy, and Sister Waters, fanning herself, enter slowly and heavily, bringing a vase, quilts, and other items. Rosa comes to the porch)

SISTER WATERS: Good morning, Sister Rosa. *(Rosa returns greetings as Sister Waters puts her vase on the top step. Sympathetically)* I tried to sell your things, but nobody was able to buy them.

MISS NANCY: *(Putting her items down on the top step)* And I tried every house on Main Street, Sister. Folks ain't got no use for them now.

THE DEACON: *(He puts his items on the top step)* I even tried the white folks' churches, Sister. But Sister, as Nancy said there's so little money stirrin nowadays. We did our best.

(Rosa looks down on the items then looks searchingly towards the horizon)

ROSA: M-m-m-m-m. *(Presently)* Thank you all for tryin. *(Picks up the vase, studies it)* I remember Misses Walker wanted to buy this.

MISS NANCY: I especially asked Misses Walker.

ROSA: Once she offered me one hundred dollars for this vase . . . said it was genuine antique.

MISS NANCY: She said she'd bought herself another one.

(Rosa fondles the quilt)

THE DEACON: We did our best, Sister.

ROSA: I'm sure you all did.

THE DEACON: And as you know, we couldn't begin to pay what you is askin for them.

ROSA: *(Nods)* I understand. Thank you all for tryin.

MISS NANCY: We wish we could do more to help.

ROSA: Just pray, dear friends, that I don't falter. I've put my trust in Jesus and—well, thank you all for what you all tried to do.

SISTER WATERS: *(Crosses to Rosa)* I pray for you. *(Rosa squeezes her hand)*

ROSA: God bless you. Just remember—I don't want Perry to learn a word about this. *(They nod)* Now don't let me keep you. I know you all have your own chores to do.

(They nod in agreement and slowly and heavily exit. Rosa studies the articles then takes them into the house. When she comes back to the porch she hears Leroy, who is off, singing: "O Mary Don't You Weep". He enters from the opposite direction carrying his coat thrown across his arm)

LEROY: Hey, Mamma!

ROSA: *(Without exuberance)* Hey, Leroy.

LEROY: *(Sits on the top step. Silence, as he looks about him)* Phew! It must be at least ninety in the shade today. *(Takes his polka dot handkerchief from his hip pocket and wipes his brow)* We sure nuff could use some rain, huh?

ROSA: Guess the Lord seen no reason yet to give it. *(Sits on the bench and takes her pipe and tobacco from her apron pocket. She fills her pipe. Leroy obliquely studies her)*

LEROY: I know one thing for sure though, if this dry spell don't end off soon, not nary a farmer around here is gonna git a thing to yield this year but tomatoes.

ROSA: It haint been too bad . . . I guess . . . for the tomatoes. Perry says we ought to get a right good yield.

LEROY: Maybe so! But it sure aint much good when the market is already over-run with tomatoes, and George Junior says he heard Mr. Medina aint giving but thirty cents now.

ROSA: Thirty cents.

LEROY: Yes, mam, thirty cents!

ROSA: Lord, hush! Perry mightyn as well feed his tomatoes to the swine! What's they offerin in the big market?

LEROY: I don't know for sure, Mamma, but George Junior told Clarence Brown they is all offerin thirty cents.

ROSA: M-m-m-m *(Lights her pipe and smokes)*

LEROY: *(Mops his brow)* Phew! This sure is a hot one, huh? Where's papa?

ROSA: Out on the farm—pickin the last of the tomatoes . . . He'll be headin in toreckly for something to eat!

(Silence)

LEROY: You feelin all right, Mamma?

ROSA: No worse then usual.

(Silence)

LEROY: Sadie told me you all finally heard from Carmen! . . . We thought we oughta write them and ask them to help out a bit.

ROSA: Taint no use to write them.

LEROY: I reckon not. Sadie said Carmen wrote she still wish it was some way she could come back home for a while.

ROSA: *(Smoking her pipe)* That's what she writ . . . For a while at least she said. Said Thomas hadn't yet got no steady work.

LEROY: Can't say that sound too good, do it? He's been outta work for a long time.

ROSA: Perry said that, too—Both me and him has heared every-wheres is as mean as hit can be— It's the depression they calls it.

LEROY: Is papa gonna send for them to come home?

ROSA: What for? . . . And with what? . . . Aint no money here. Might as well starve out there as to comin back home to starve down here. *(Silence)* How's your younguns?

LEROY: All right. Booker Washington was kinda puny for a day or so—cuttin his teeth. I reckon—he's all right now, huh? Sadie said you sent a message you wanted to see me.

ROSA: I do! It's on business . . . I want when you go to town this afternoon to fetch Mr. Morgan out here to see me.

LEROY: You mean Mr. J.P. Morgan on West Bread Street?

ROSA: I do!

LEROY: *(Anxious)* Now, what for, Mamma? Didn't you just go to town last week to see Mr. Morgan?

ROSA: I did! Yes, I did. And I went the week before, and he knows it's for business.

LEROY: But, Mamma, why? Why you wanta—

ROSA: *(Puffing on her pipe)* I wants to see the man on business, Leroy. That's all I'm sayin.

LEROY: Mr. Morgan is a busy man—

ROSA: You just go fetch him and leave the rest to me and him. *(Silence)*

LEROY: *(Troubled)* Lord knows, Sadie and me tried everything we knowed to get hold of some money.

ROSA: Payment on the mortgage is due this month. Them bank folks done writ the second letter they don't aim to wait no longer.

LEROY: Mamma, now twont it be better if you and papa just give up all this strugglin and go on and let Mr. Charlie pay off the mortgage—

ROSA: No! It can't never be better!

LEROY: He did it for the others, Mamma!

ROSA: This piece of land is Perry's. Hit can't never mean to Mr. Charlie what it means to Perry. And I don't mind tellin you, Leroy, the whole notion of him losing it is about to heave the heart out of his chest.

LEROY: It aint like you and papa was givin up the land for keeps. Mr. Charlie could pay off the mortgage like he did for Alex and the others, and each year you and papa could pay back a little of whatever you could. I don't see no harm in it.

ROSA: Twon't but a fool who thinks Alex and them others is ever gonna own their lands again.

LEROY: I don't know about that, Mamma—Alex said—

ROSA: Well, I do! Every year Alex, Bo-Sam, and them others don't pay nothing back but the interest on their lands, and the main loans keeps waitin right there for them to pay hit off, and they'll never be able to pay it off. Poor old Mr. Maxwell died and his widow and poor six children had to move offern that farm less in a month, the old lady being too weak to sharecrop—

LEROY: Well, I sure don't see how you and papa aim to beat that mortgage!

ROSA: We'll beat it. I got a plan.

LEROY: (Studies his mother) Got somethin to do with Mr. Morgan?

ROSA: Never you mind! You jest fetch Mr. Morgan. After all, Perry mortgaged this farm for gettin me to doctors—and to the hospital—

LEROY: Papa don't grudge you nothin he's done for you—

ROSA: —And I don't aim to see him lose this land after all the hard work he done put in it—not on my account—especially when all the doctors and hospital aint done me no good!

LEROY: You's doing all right, Mamma! The doctors told you—It takes time. Don't expect to get well as quick as you want to! There's time for everything, Mamma!

ROSA: Hush, boy! Hush, Leroy! Now you know papa wouldn't like to hear you talk like that, huh? He's done everything—

LEROY: (Concerned) Mamma—

ROSA: Do you hear me, Leroy?

LEROY: (Nods) Yes, mam!

ROSA: If God chose it to be this way—then it'll have to be, I guess—But I don't aim for Perry to lose both me and the land, not at the same time. (Rises) Here comes Perry now—drippin with sweat, poor man!

PERRY: (Entering) Thought I saw Mr. Charlie's car headin this way! (Looks to the road) Musta made a stop! Hey, boy! What's brung you over here afore eatin time? (Chuckles) Lookin for a handout, eh?

LEROY: No, Papa! Mamma told Sadie last night she wanted to see me.

ROSA: (Crosses on porch to fetch a towel; throws towel to Perry) Want him to run an errand in town for me.

PERRY: (Sits. Sighs, mops his brow) This sure is a hot one, eh?

LEROY: I told mamma it must be at least ninety degees under the shade.

PERRY: One of them mean critters is down there at the furnace all right. (Bites a piece of tobacco) How's my grandboys?

LEROY: All right. Booker Washington is cuttin his bottom teeth now—and is gittin harder for Sadie to handle.

PERRY: (Chuckles) Little rascal! (Spits) Saw Al Ehlers at prayer meetin last night and he says the mens is meetin over at his place tomorrow night—about men's day in the church—and about that idea of the cooperative the preacher spoke about last Sunday— Wants to be sure you git over there.

LEROY: Yeah, I know. I seen Al in town day afore yesterday, and he told me then about the meetin. You aimin to go?

PERRY: Depends on how Rosa here is feelin—

ROSA: I'll be all right. Don't stay here and watch over me. Go on over there and figure out when you all can get to puttin them steps up on the church. Sure don't look good—all these months the church has went without steps. *(Deliberately)* I don't know how you all would manage to take a deceased body into the church. *(The two men react quietly)* I spoke to Al about that myself.

LEROY: Stop by for me, and we'll go together.

PERRY: I'll head over there after supper.

MR. CHARLIE: *(Off. Calling in the distance)* Hey there, Perry! Perry—

PERRY: I knowed I saw his car headin this way. *(Rises and calls)* Come on up, Mr. Charlie! Mr. Charlie, come on up!

ROSA: *(Straining to see)* Lord, look at that man! He's go come up here wid all his lies! Sure as I'm born, that man is gonna hang up in hell by the point of his tongue.

PERRY: I told the misses and boy here I thought I seed your car comin up the road.

MR. CHARLIE: *(Off)* Stopped off at Buddy's place!

ROSA: Don't you talk too long, Perry. I got your vittles in there nice and hot!

(Mr. Charlie enters. He wears a soiled white linen suit. He mops his brow)

MR. CHARLIE: I'm willin to bet you all anything old Mayor Jenkins is down there firin the furnace today. This is a mean one, and you've gotta have a mean critter at the furnace.

PERRY: As hot as it is, Mr. Charlie, that furnace must be gittin help from the devil hisself.

(Both Mr. Charlie and Perry laugh)

MR. CHARLIE: We's got to git some rain soon or we is gonna parch away like them magnolia leaves. *(He points to a tree)*

PERRY: Sit down, Mr. Charlie.

MR. CHARLIE: *(Sitting)* Phew! *(Mops his brow)* Rosa, how's that overall misery of yours?

ROSA: *(Sits)* I don't complain none, Mr. Charlie. The good Lord knows how much I can bear.

MR. CHARLIE: Now aint that said jest like a Christian? Rosa, I tell you, I do believe the good Lord is purifyin you for his kingdom. I tell my wife all the time if there's a true-true Christian anywheres around these parts, it's you.

ROSA: I tries to be, Mr. Charlie. I tries my level best.

MR. CHARLIE: And by golly you do succeed. I wouldn't want you prayin agin me, by golly, I'll tell you that!

ROSA: You needn't worry about that. If I can't pray for you, Mr. Charlie, I won't pray against you.

MR. CHARLIE: *(Laughs)* That ought to put any mind at ease, eh, Perry? *(Perry laughs)* I sure don't want you people prayin agin me like you all got to prayin agin Mayor Jenkins.

LEROY: *(Chuckles)* Mayor Jenkins was a wicked man, Mr. Charlie.

MR. CHARLIE: Maybe so . . . but twon't natcherel . . . the way he hauled off and went . . . when you all got to prayin! Twon't natcherel. *(Licks his cigar)* Well, Perry, you ready to do business wid me?

PERRY: What business, Mr. Charlie?

MR. CHARLIE: About this here farm. Now you know what I mean—You and me don't aim to start playin cat and mouse wid each other at this late date, do we? You might as well do business wid me. I saw Leonard over at the bank this mornin and he said taint no question about foreclosin on you.

PERRY: They can't foreclose if I make my payments, Mr. Charlie?

MR. CHARLIE: *(Still licking his cigar)* That's all dependin, aint it, if you's able to make them payments? You aint made none in two months accordin to Leonard. I'm saying, let me make them for you like I did for the other boys. They aint regrettin it none, is they? At least I aint heard no complaints. You'd have a much longer time payin it off to me than you'd have payin it off to the bank. *(Strikes a match to light his cigar)*

PERRY: I told Mr. Leonard last week I'll make up the payment at the end of the month.

MR. CHARLIE: That's what he said you said, but then I asked him—how is it you gonna do it? Seeing as the dry season didn't yield you people out here nothin. *(Strikes another match)*

ROSA: We got enough tomatoes to make the payments, Mr. Charlie.

PERRY: That's right! We got quite a good yield. I reckon with them at sixty-five cents a bushel, we'll be able to pay the bank up to three months on that loan—at least.

MR. CHARLIE: That's only three months! Right after, the fourth and the fifth is coming up. What you aim to do about them?

PERRY: Until I start farmin again, I was thinkin of gittin a job in town like my boy here to sort of help out.

MR. CHARLIE: *(Lights his cigar and puffs at it rapidly)* Perry, I didn't reckon to hear you talk no foolery. There aint no jobs in town, boy, and I'm here to tell you. Why there's more men hangin around town trying to git a job—then there is flies on Lyon's Bakershop's screen door. I don't know whether you people know it or not, but we is having one hell of a depression in the country.

PERRY: Mr. Charlie, I can always make it if I have to.

MR. CHARLIE: You's a farmer, and you aint good at nothin else but farming—Aint Alex and the others told you yet—the big market aint givin but fifteen cents for tomatoes now?

PERRY: Mr. Medina told me sixty-five cents a bushel when I spoke with him the last time.

MR. CHARLIE: That was two weeks ago; the market is overrun now with tomatoes. They aint givin but fifteen cents a bushel to nobody! The white farmers as well as you people out here is gettin the *same* thing.

PERRY: Fifteen cents?

ROSA: We'll give em to the hogs before we sell em for that!

(Mr. Charlie and Rosa stare at each other)

MR. CHARLIE: *(Presently)* I know how you people out here feel. I feel the same way myself. It's a damn shame that, after all, I'm stuck with over one-hundred bushels of tomatoes. I paid my croppers sixty-five cents a bushel each last one of them, and now I gotta sell em for much less in the market. Taint no profit in doin that kind of business. Is there? Besides that, hit don't say nothin about the haulin cost from here to Charleston.

PERRY: If I can't get at least sixty-five cents a bushel for my tomatoes, I don't see how I can raise the money for the bank.

MR. CHARLIE: That's why I'm makin you my offer! You a good man, Perry!

(Silence)

LEROY: Mr. Charlie, if papa was to sign up with you—

ROSA: Perry never said he was signin up with nobody, Leroy!

LEROY: I was only—

ROSA: —With nobody, Leroy!!

MR. CHARLIE: *(Presently)* Leroy, what was you gonna ask me?

LEROY: I was gonna ask you, sir, how much would you give papa for his tomatoes?

MR. CHARLIE: Well—now—Leroy—I'll have to see. *(Takes his pad and pencil from his pocket)*

LEROY: The same as you gave the others—sixty-five cents a bushel?

MR. CHARLIE: Well, now that all depends! *(Begins figuring)*

LEROY: *(Strains to see Mr. Charlie's figuring)* Depends on what, Mr. Charlie?

MR. CHARLIE: On how many bushels I could take from your pa! I've got more tomatoes now than I know what to do with! Perry, I tell you what I'll do. For at least fifty bushels, I'll give you sixty-five cents a bushel and pay you cash. How's that? For the remaindin bushels, I'll give you credit at thirty cents a bushel. You can't beat that no-wheres around here.

LEROY: Seems fair enough to me, Papa!

MR. CHARLIE: Damn sight better than what the bank would do! Besides I oughta git a little somethin out of the deal myself—at least gas money for haulin. I'll keep the innerest the same as the bank's now got it! Perry, what you say to that? Come on, boy, I aint got all day.

(Perry looks to Rosa who shakes her head. Mr. Charlie sees it)

PERRY: I can't make up my mind right yet, Mr. Charlie—

MR. CHARLIE: *(Annoyed)* Whatcha got to make up your mind about? *(Perry looks to Rosa)*

PERRY: *(Presently)* I'll have to let you know.

MR. CHARLIE: Sharecroppin aint the worse thing could happen to *you*. I'm good to my croppers! Ask Alex or any of the other boys.

PERRY: I aint sayin you aint, Mr. Charlie—It's just that—*(He looks to Rosa again. Turns to Mr. Charlie)* I've got to have more time to think through what I've gotta do.

MR. CHARLIE: More time! Jesus Christ—Man—You mean to tell me you aim to let a deal like this go by in search of a buyer? Where's your business sense, Perry? Time keeps movin, boy, and opportunity knocks at a new door each new second.

ROSA: Even God Himself allows us time, Mr. Charlie—

MR. CHARLIE: I'll be damn! *(Looks from Perry to Rosa, who stares him down)* All right, Perry! Take as long as you like—but don't let me get off to Charleston before you make up your mind—and I aim to roll my trucks startin next week.

PERRY: All right, Mr. Charlie! I'll let you know by then!

MR. CHARLIE: Good! *(Wipes his neck. Takes a fresh cigar and begins to lick it)* You all take care of Rosa, here, and Rosa, you pray Perry do the right thing by us all. *(Rosa nods)* Oh, by the way, I hear you fellows are havin a church meetin tomorrow night over at Al Ehler's house. Well, I'm sendin you all a case of Amy's home brew over there. I already told Al about it, and I paid Amy for it, and she'll keep it cool in the well till time you all's meetin. I want all of you fellows over there to think right good of me—and when you all pray, don't pray agin me!

PERRY: *(Chuckles)* We don't aim to do much prayin over there, Mr. Charlie—just talk about our men's day program at the church.

MR. CHARLIE: All right, Perry—but just in case you all do, take care! So long, Rosa! You pray good for all of us! *(Starts, but returns)* By the way, Perry, I heard some of you boys been talkin about formin a cooperative—It taint none of my business, but I guess you all know that's communist talk—and against our American government way of life . . . A few men in town got to whisperin about it. *(A pause)* Just thought I'd tell you. Your preacher mightn of knowed it when he suggested it. Well, until you all make up your minds, I'll mosey on along. Gotta lots of chores fore sunset. *(He exits)*

(Silence)

LEROY: Papa, if I was you—

ROSA: You aint your papa! *(More silence)* Perry, aint you ready for your vittles?

PERRY: Yeah—Rosa. Go on in and fix it.

ROSA: *(Rises)* You stayin, Leroy?

PERRY: No, Mamma. Sadie and the boys is waitin for me.

ROSA: Tell the boys I send love to em.

LEROY: All right . . . I guess Mr. Charlie sure nuff believes we all got together and prayed against Mayor Jenkins.

ROSA: That man is scared cause he knows he's a devil! And as sure as I was born a woman, he aims to git a holt of this land, but he won't do it. I swear on my life he won't git this piece of land!

PERRY: Go on! Don't get yourself fretful!

ROSA: Hit don't need nobody prayin for or against him and his kind. They all done made homes for themselves in hell a long time ago right next to Mayor Jenkins—

PERRY: Fix me somethin to eat.

ROSA: Leroy! You don't forget to do what I told you.

LEROY: No, Mama, I won't.

ROSA: And when you see Cousin Julia and Gus in town, you tell them I said they oughta come out to see me soon if they aim to.

LEROY: All right, Mamma, I'll tell em!

(Rosa exits into the house. Presently Leroy rises and stretches lazily. He studies Perry)

LEROY: You all right, Papa?

PERRY: *(Nods)* It's poor Rosa! It's so hard keepin the truth from her.

LEROY: Papa, she ain't worried about herself. She's worried about you losin this land.

(Perry raises his hand to silence Leroy. They both look towards the door)

PERRY: You mosey on along. I'm all right, son.

LEROY: See you, Papa!

PERRY: Yeah, boy! I'll eat and then take some time out to stroll over to Clarence and the others. See what's happenin about these tomatoes.

LEROY: Yeah, Papa, do that! And if I was you, I'd give some real hard thinkin on what Mr. Charlie is offerin you. After all, mamma don't understand everything. *(After a pause, he exits)*

(Perry sits there thinking. He rises, looks up to the skies. Rosa calls him. He wearily exits into the house. The Singer's silhouette appears on the horizon as a bent farmer hoeing the ground. He sings:)

SINGER:

"This is the land promised to me—
Forty acres to set me free.
This is the land—
This is the land—
This piece of land
Belongs to me!

Work hard, my children, eat the dust.
Work long, my children, and you must—
Break ground, my children with your hand—
But hold on—Hold on to your land!"

(The light fades into an hour later. Perry enters from the house picking his teeth. He crosses and stands looking up at the sky. The Singer's silhouette becomes Perry's shadow reaching across the sky. He sings:)

SINGER:

"Mornin comes afore the noon . . .
. . . Then evenin comes . . .
And night's too soon . . .
End of morn is when he's born,
And so death comes
With the sun at morn.
Laughter cries . . .
And weepin fills the empty quest
A black man makes
Of him that's low
And God on high,
Reasons for why . . .
He was born to die." *(Exits)*

(Perry bites a piece of tobacco and crosses to exit by the way of the road. The lights fade down to a sunset. Rosa enters from the house with a small pail of water to wet her potted plants as the Singer appears on the horizon. When she comes to a dying plant, she pulls it from the soil and turns it over in her hand and clutches it hard against her bosom. She looks to the horizon

to see the silhouette of the Singer who watches. Finally she throws the plant to the ground and exits into the house. The Singer moves slowly across the horizon. Leroy and Mr. Morgan enter from the road. Mr. Morgan fans himself with a paper-card fan. He stands at the foot of the steps while Leroy enters upon the porch and calls)

LEROY: *(Knocking and calling)* Mamma! Mamma, it's me, Leroy with Mr. Morgan.

ROSA: *(From the house)* Comin!

LEROY: Come on up, Mr. Morgan. Have a seat.

MR. MORGAN: In a minute, Mr. Tucker! I get a whiff of cool breeze right here.

LEROY: *(Knocking)* Mamma, come on. You know, Mr. Morgan is a busy man.

ROSA: Yes, I'm comin! *(Enters. Leroy senses something is wrong)*

LEROY: What's wrong, Mamma?

MR. MORGAN: Hydo, Misses Tucker?

ROSA: Right fair in the middlin, Mr. Morgan, thank you. How is Misses Morgan, and your offsprings?

MR. MORGAN: They're all fine, thank you.

ROSA: That's a blessin, I'm sure. Come up, Mr. Morgan, and have a seat. I believe it's cooler here on the porch.

MR. MORGAN: No, Misses Tucker, if you don't mind I rather stand right here. I don't know where that breeze is comin from, but right along here I'm gettin a real coolin-off feelin.

ROSA: Well, then, now you just stay right there, and Leroy will fetch you a chair from the house. Go on, Leroy, get Mr. Morgan a chair.

LEROY: *(Concerned)* Mamma, your eyes is wet from cryin. What you been cryin about, huh?

ROSA: Go on, and do as your ma tells you. *(Leroy goes into the house)* I hear tell the folks in town is havin it mighty hard—just as hard as we is out here on the farms.

MR. MORGAN: It's the depression, Misses Tucker. The worse one this country's ever had—and accordin to the newspapers, it's headin even for worser times.

ROSA: *(Sighs)* Lord, I jest don't understand it.

LEROY: *(Returning with chair)* You don't understand what, Mamma?

ROSA: Well, I don't understand for one thing how this country of ours got itself into this mess in the first place. I jes don't understand why there is so much hungriness and misery about us when there is so much food you can't even sell.

MR. MORGAN: Misses Tucker, that's the way it goes with economics. And like the newspapers point it out—in this country one time we have a boom, and the next time we have a bust. You see, at this time, we're havin a bust.

LEROY: Mamma—

ROSA: Leroy, give Mr. Morgan the chair.

(Leroy crosses down to give the chair to Mr. Morgan)

MR. MORGAN: Thank you kindly, Misses Tucker.

(He sits. Leroy returns to the steps below Rosa)

LEROY: Mamma, if you is painin at all, tell me the truth!

ROSA: *(Looks down at Leroy affectionately)* Son, Mamma is painin every blessed hour of the day.

LEROY: Mamma, do papa know it? Have you told papa? Is that why you've been cryin cause you's painin?

ROSA: *(Touches his head)* Mamma is all right!

LEROY: But you've been cryin, Mamma . . . and that's not like you!

ROSA: After a while, you get used to livin with pains. It's the questions, son, that keeps turnin over in your mind you jest can't seem to get no answer to.

LEROY: What's the question, Mamma? Ask me the question! I'll answer the question, Mamma! What's the question you keep turnin over in your mind? Is that why you sent for Mr. Morgan?

ROSA: *(She gently places her hand across Leroy's mouth)* Only God knows the answer, son. *(She moves away from Leroy)*

MR. MORGAN: Misses Tucker, I don't *think* it's our Christian place to ever ask some kinds of questions. We then come mighty close to blasphemy.

ROSA: The good Book says God's got a reason of some kind for *everything* . . . a reason for all of us being here . . . a reason for some of us being white, and some of us being black . . .

LEROY: Mamma, stop talkin like that! You aint yourself! You want me to call the doctor?

ROSA: Why don't He see fit to let the reasons be made clear to us. Hit don't make no sense—Me being born, you, Perry, Leroy here . . . all of us strugglin to live, strugglin to hold on to a little somethin we can call our very own—and then without havin nary a word to say about it, we have to give it up and go away and be jedged.

LEROY: Mamma, you want me to call papa?—I'm goin—You don't sound right to me.

ROSA: No! *(Stops Leroy)* Aint no doctor can do me no good except Doctor Jesus! *(To the alarmed Leroy)* Oh, you gotta ask if you is a honest woman. Why, God Almighty, did you see fittin to put hatred and malice in the hearts of your children . . . to put this livin things within me . . . *(Holds her abdomen)* that don't serve no aim but to sap the usefulness outta me!

LEROY: *(More alarmed)* Mamma, what you talkin about?

ROSA: *(To God)* Why, God, *why? (To Leroy)* Hit don't make no sense! And all the pushin and shovin and folks starvin and tearin the hearts out of one another. Why?! Didn't Jesus die on the cross to put an end to it all? *(Long silence. She looks down at the frightened Leroy and to the uncomfortable Mr. Morgan)*

MR. MORGAN: Them's mighty powerful and frightenin questions you is askin of God, Misses Tucker!

ROSA: Mighty powerful questions, but you gotta ask them if you is honest, Mr. Morgan.

LEROY: Mamma, I'm gonna call papa!

ROSA: He aint on the place, Leroy! He went over to see Clarence and the others about what they aim to do with their tomatoes. He oughta be gettin back soon. You set down there and hush a while whilst I talk business with Mr. Morgan. *(She goes down to the ground to look over the land)*

(Leroy sits on the top step anxious about Rosa. Mr. Morgan rises when Rosa comes down. Rosa finally takes a deep sigh and turns to Mr. Morgan)

ROSA: Sit down, Mr. Morgan. *(He sits)* Did you figure out the full amount as I told you to?

MR. MORGAN: Misses Tucker, there's plenty of time for us to figure out these things. Aint no sense in hurryin them on.

ROSA: I told you I wanted all that information figured out by the time I sent for you.

LEROY: *(Rises)* Mamma—

ROSA: *(Waves Leroy quiet)* How much you gonna charge me for that gray casket?

MR. MORGAN: *(Takes his paper from his pocket)* Now, Misses Tucker, you—

ROSA: I mean the one with the golden stars. And the family cars? I figured it would take at least three to hold all of my relatives and closest of friends.

LEROY: By God, it aint natcherel, Mamma! It aint natcherel for us to go plannin our own burial.

ROSA: I guess it aint—when you don't know it's comin—you might look like you's hurryin it on— *(Silence)* but when you know, Leroy, I don't see why it haint the natcherelest thing on God's earth to do.

MR. MORGAN: The sickest aint always the nearest to the grave, Misses Tucker.

ROSA: How much, Mr. Morgan?

MR. MORGAN: Well—now—you realize you picked one of the best caskets in the house. That casket by itself at least cost five hundred dollars.

ROSA: That's too much!

MR. MORGAN: But I'm gonna let you have it at three hundred dollars though.

ROSA: And the cars?

MR. MORGAN: Each car—let's see—well, it should cost you—say thirty dollars a car—all together ninety dollars.

ROSA: That's three hundred and ninety dollars. What's for the chimes on the hearst?

MR. MORGAN: Well, now—let me see—the chimes ought to be an additional thirty dollars. But, being it's you, I'll say twenty-five dollars. Now let's see twenty-five dollars for the chimes, plus ninety dollars for the cars, plus three hundred dollars—all total four hundred and fifteen dollars.

ROSA: Make it a round four hundred dollars, Mr. Morgan! Oh, my God! Here comes Perry. Now let's all make out like we was just talkin. You all set and keep quiet.

(Perry enters. He immediately senses something is wrong. Mr. Morgan rises)

PERRY: Howdy everybody?!

MR. MORGAN: Hydo, Mr. Tucker?

PERRY: Howdy, Mr. Morgan? *(Looks from Leroy to Rosa)* What's Mr. Morgan doin out here wid his pad and pencil?

(Leroy turns away)

LEROY: Mamma wouldn't let me fetch you!

PERRY: *(Turns to Rosa, who walks away. Turns to Mr. Morgan, who lowers his head)* Aint somebody's gonna tell me what the buryin man's doin out here on my place? *(Goes to Rosa)*

ROSA: Perry, I sent for him to come here!

PERRY: Is you shuttin me out on something, Rosa? Why? What you want to see Mr. Morgan about?

ROSA: Perry, can't a woman who knows she's gonna die, make the arrangements for her own funeral?

PERRY: Who's dyin?

ROSA: *I'm* dyin! Perry, I'm dyin.

PERRY: Who said anything about you dyin? *(Turns to Leroy)* Boy, did you tell your ma—

LEROY: Not me, Papa! By God, I never mentioned a word!

PERRY: *(To Rosa)* Who told you such an audacious lie, Rosa? Who in heaven's name—

ROSA: Taint no lie, Perry, and if anybody told me, it was you! *(Reads his eyes)* The deep down hurt inside you told me. You told me in everything you did, in everything you said to me—

PERRY: Oh, Good God, have mercy. *(Walks away)*

ROSA: *(Follows him)* Don't you know when you hurt deep you can't hide it from me—Perry, this is Rosa! You's been tryin to hold the truth back ever since the doctor told you months ago.

PERRY: Doctors have been wrong before, Rosa, you know that!

ROSA: This time, the doctors aint wrong! And I know that. You've did your best. You sent me to the hospital and they couldn't do no good! So before I go Perry, I wants to arrange things the way I want them to be . . . I went down last week and picked out the casket I like. I figured with the family we got, we could get by with the three cars. Other church members, I reckon, will donate their wagons and buggies to accommodate those others who wants to follow me to the buryin ground.

(Leroy takes his handkerchief and weeps quietly)

PERRY: Rosa, don't bust my heart wide open! Don't you bust my heart, woman!

ROSA: Leroy, you stop that! Now don't you do that to Perry. *(Goes to Leroy)* This is the time, boy, to give him your strength, not your weakness.

LEROY: Mamma, please—

ROSA: Taint no tears, no nothing's gonna change what's gonna happen—so we might as well build ourselves to bear the truth. *(Crosses to Perry)* You come, Perry, sit down over here. *(She leads Perry to the step)*

(Leroy puts an affectionate arm about his father and sits beside him, weeping quietly)

ROSA: Now, let's see Mr. Morgan, where was we?

MR. MORGAN: We figured the total to be four hundred and fifteen dollars, Misses Tucker.

ROSA: We said four hundred dollars even, Mr. Morgan.

MR. MORGAN: Yes, that's right, four hundred dollars.

ROSA: That's gonna be the cost of my funeral, not a cent over!

MR. MORGAN: If you say!

ROSA: That's what I say! *(She pulls her apron. For a brief silence she watches Perry and Leroy)*

MR. MORGAN: No floral pieces?

ROSA: Don't worry about the flowers. The Sisters and Brothers of the church will see to that. *(Takes policies from her apron pockets)* Now, Mr. Morgan, here is all my life insurance paid up to full. Here's the policy for the Pilgrim's Life, the Metropolitan Life Policy, policy for the Freedom Life—all paid up to full: they should total to two thousand and four hundred dollars.

MR. MORGAN: Yes, um!

ROSA: I'm gonna ask you to make a deal with me. If you don't want to do it, you just say so. I don't want no hemmin and hawin about it, if you can't then I'm gonna send for Mr. Kraft at the Sunshine Undertakers—and I'll make the deal with him!

PERRY: No—

ROSA: My God, Perry don't fight me! *(Above Perry)* Is it a deal, Mr. Morgan?

MR. MORGAN: *(Flustered)* Well, now—Misses Tucker—I don't—

ROSA: *(Sharply)* I don't want no hemmin and hawin, Mr. Morgan! Is it a deal or aint it?

MR. MORGAN: *(More flustered)* Well, I never had no deal like this before. I don't even know if it's legal.

PERRY: It aint legal! It's a sin before God!!! *(Points the way)* You get off my place, Mr. Morgan! *(He starts for Mr. Morgan. Rosa and Leroy struggle to stop him)*

ROSA: Perry, it aint no sin! . . . *(Stops Mr. Morgan who has been edging away. She breaks into tears but aborts them)* And it's legal all right!

MR. MORGAN: How do you know, Misses Tucker? How can you tell?

ROSA: Because it's my life, Mr. Morgan. That's all it's worth. I'm givin it to you in order to save the land!

MR. MORGAN: Misses Tucker, should a piece of land mean so much to you?

PERRY: Mr. Charlie can have this damn land! I don't want it!! *(A silence. Overcome by tears, he walks abruptly away from Leroy who tries to console him, giving the others his back. The others watch his back, seeing him finally gain control)*

ROSA: *(Quietly)* Is it a deal?

MR. MORGAN: *(Finally and quietly)* It's a deal if that's—what you want.

ROSA: Very well then. You go down tomorrow and settle the business with the bank and bring the final papers and the remainders of nine hundred dollars to me—*(They hesitate)* Thank you, Mr. Morgan! You's a good man! *(She shakes his hand and starts for the house. Stops to observe Perry and Leroy)* Leroy, you go home to Sadie and the younguns! Me and Perry wants to be alone . . . for a while.

MR. MORGAN: I'll drop you off, Mr. Tucker!

LEROY: Mamma—

(Rosa moves swiftly and exits into the house)

LEROY: *(After a moment)* Papa, we shoulda known we could *never* keep her from knowing. *(He slowly moves towards the exit)*

(Mr. Morgan crosses to Perry)

MR. MORGAN: You being the man, Mr. Tucker, tell me what to do.

PERRY: *(Lowers his head)* I wish I knowed . . . *(Looks into the sky)* I wish I knowed what to tell you . . .

LEROY: Coming, Mr. Morgan?

PERRY: *(More to himself then to Mr. Morgan)* I wish I knowed.

MR. MORGAN: Mr. Tucker, God help you. I'll go down to the bank first thing in the morning.

(Mr. Morgan exits. Leroy follows. Perry crosses to sit on the step with his head in his hands. The sun sets more. Soon Rosa enters. She's smoking her pipe. She stands there watching Perry)

ROSA: Perry?

PERRY: Yes, Rosa?

ROSA: You vex with me? *(Perry shakes his head)* Don't be.

PERRY: I'm losing you, Rosa . . . What good is the land without you?

ROSA: Well, Perry . . . *(Sits next to him)* for one thing, you won't lose the land to Mr. Charlie! *(Silence)* I reckon—with all the work we put into this land, we have just about paid for it three or more times over . . . and to lose it for a little of nothin—you love this land—you love it like some men love a second woman—*(Silence as the two look over the land)* We've got the grandchildren . . . they ought to have some home place they can return to—there's Carmen and Thomas wantin to come home for a visit . . . and Leroy and his younguns—This land will be a remembrance—We always said every man oughta have a little piece of land to call his own.

PERRY: But, Rosa, to take your life insurance money—

ROSA: This land is our pride . . . *(Puts her arm around his shoulder)* Since I was a little girl, each week we paid on them policies. Before I did, my pa did; and since they air called life insurances they ought to go for helpin life! Don't make no sense that all I'm worth should be put into the ground behind me. *(Silence as she studies Perry)*

PERRY: *(Alarmed)* What's the matter?

ROSA: Perry, do you believe in the hereafter?

PERRY: I do!

ROSA: Do you believe that heaven is as light and coolin as a rain shower on a hot summer day?

PERRY: Yes, Rosa, I believe it.

ROSA: And, do you believe hell is there at the end of eternity in all its bleakness and ugliness for wicked men?

PERRY: What you gittin at, Rosa?

ROSA: Oh, Perry, pray for me! I jest can't git it out of my head and heart—Is God any more fairer to us than the white man?

PERRY: Rosa!

ROSA: Perry, I'm falterin.

PERRY: Now don't talk no more like that!

ROSA: Perry, God mustn't be white—God mustn't be white!

PERRY: God aint got no color at all. God is the spirit of love. Jesus lived and was crucified to teach us to love one another, and he was a white man. *(He holds on to her hands)*

ROSA: Perry, God mustn't be white. *(Holds tightly to Perry. Presently)* I'm feelin all right now, Perry . . . Look at the sun . . . The day's almost gone . . . Tomorrow, a new day, a new life . . . another beginning . . . *(After a long silence she rises)* Come on in, and I'll rub your back for you.

PERRY: I'll come.

ROSA: All right. *(Touches him tenderly)* Don't fret none. I'm all right now. *(She lingers to look off into the sky then exits into the house. The Singer in silhouette, appears on the horizon)*

SINGER: *(As he sings, the light appears in the window. Perry slowly rises and exits into the house)*

"Mornin comes afore the noon . . .
. . . Then evenin comes . . .
And night's too soon . . .
Spring of year is like the morn . . .
. . . And so life goes . . .
When a man is born.

Autumn comes,
And winter chills.
The baby laughs . . .
The young man thrills.
Day starts low;
The noon runs high.
Seasons begin
And seasons die . . ."

(The light in the window goes out. The Singer continues to sing as he slowly moves across the horizon to completely enshroud the stage)

Curtain

William Hauptman

DOMINO COURTS

William Hauptman

When William Hauptman's *Domino Courts* originally opened at the American Place Theatre, New York, in December, 1975, it generated considerable interest among theatregoers and members of the press. According to Terry Curtis Fox, a correspondent for the *Village Voice:* "The theatre has been packed beyond capacity, with good reason. For *Domino Courts*—like *Heat* and *Shearwater,* the two Hauptman plays before it—is a haunting, terrifying, funny, beautiful piece of writing, the kind of play that sticks, naggingly unforgetful, in the nether reaches of the brain.

"Hauptman creates situations which spring from shared cultural myths and expectations. *Domino Courts* is a Dust Bowl gangster movie, a direct descendent of *You Only Live Once* and *They Live by Night* . . . The gangster film is one of the Great American Myths, containing within it the myth of the road, the myth of male companionship, the myth of the moment, not to mention the myth of the movies . . . *Domino Courts* is a dream world of unexplained violence, mysterious loss of power, total vulnerability, and sheer sex—bits of an American landscape hardly limited to the Southwest."

William Hauptman was born in Wichita Falls, Texas. He attended the University of Texas in Austin, and later lived in San Francisco before doing graduate work at the Yale School of Drama. While at Yale, he held fellowships from the Shubert Foundation, the John Golden Foundation and the William Morris Agency.

Before emerging as a playwright, Mr. Hauptman worked as an actor in New York City and at a number of regional theatres.

In 1975, he was the first John Golden Playwright-in-Residence at the Williamstown (Massachusetts) Theatre Festival, where he also taught workshops in acting and playwriting; and in 1976, he was one of four playwrights chosen to receive a CBS Fellowship in Creative Writing at the Yale School of Drama, where his newest work, *The Durango Flash,* will be presented early in 1977.

Shearwater was his initial play to be produced in New York—at the American Place Theatre in 1974. During that same year, *Heat,* was presented by Joseph Papp at the New York Shakespeare Festival Public Theatre, and subsequently, by the Toronto Free Theatre and numerous amateur groups.

The author, who has taught playwriting in the English and Drama Departments at Adelphi College, is presently working on a novel, *Tulsa.*

Author's Note

Domino Courts was inspired by several things: by the prose of Edward Anderson's THIEVES LIKE US, *a forgotten Depression novel that's had two movie versions, by a reunion with some of my oldest friends in a cabin outside of Uvalde, Texas, in 1971, and by a shoebox of old photographs my parents kept in the closet, where I found unfocused sepia-tone snapshots of them standing in front of a car in Tulsa, Oklahoma, in 1939—a brown decade with soft outlines, a time before I was born. It does not take place in the real Oklahoma, nor is it about the real Depression. My hometown is only ten miles South of the Oklahoma border, and as a child in the early Fifties I can remember dust storms that blew so thickly they had to turn on the streetlights at noon. Domino Courts takes place in my imagination; and Oklahoma, because of its physical relation to my hometown, has always been a dusty landscape without realistic detail hanging somewhere above my head.*

Characters:

FLOYD
RONNIE
ROY
FLO

Scene:

A tourist cabin somewhere in Southern Oklahoma in the late 1930s.
Preshow music is heard. The Mills Brothers singing "Paper Doll." As the song plays, the houselights dim; as it ends the houselights go dark and the stage goes black.
Noon. Floyd sitting on the bed, wearing a suit, holding his hat in his hand. His jacket is on the coatrack. Another, identical hat sits on the chair in the center of the room. When the stage brightens Floyd speaks.

FLOYD: The Hot Grease Boys, that's what they used to call us. We thought we were hot grease. You should have seen us in those days, walking in a bank and sticking our guns in their faces and saying hand over your money. Hot Grease. That was before Roy and I split up. When I close my eyes, I can still see us driving down the highway, the centerline disappearing under the hood. I can see us driving at night, headlights shining in our faces and those silver posts going by along the sides of the road. Then they found out who we were. You started seeing our pictures everywhere—in the papers, in the post office. Oklahoma was getting too hot for us; so I retired and Roy drove North. *(Crossing to chair where hat sits)* Wait up, Roy, I shouted, you forgot your hat. But the car was already moving and he couldn't hear me and I watched him vanish in a cloud of dust. That was four years ago. Now Roy's coming back, and I can see the look on his face when I show him I've still got his good hat. *(Floyd's wife, Ronnie, enters. She wears a bathrobe over a bathing suit. She sits at the vanity, ignoring Floyd and starts brushing her hair, looking in the mirror. Floyd doesn't look at her)* I remember the day we busted that bank in Mound City. I remember us on the road. I remember that last hot day, the car moving and me shouting and the car gone. Dust on my good shoes. Hot—hot—oh, we thought we were so hot . . .

(Pause)

RONNIE: Talking to yourself again, Floyd?

FLOYD: I get worked up. They'll be here soon.

RONNIE: I don't know why they couldn't come to our house in town.

FLOYD: It's private out here in the country. Nobody knows our faces out here, we can do what we want.

RONNIE: Nobody knows us in town either.

FLOYD: *(Crossing suddenly to window)* There's a car coming.

RONNIE: It's not them.

FLOYD: It's not slowing down . . . it's gone past. How'd you know?

RONNIE: I always know what's going to happen. Sit down, Floyd, they're not coming yet. *(Floyd sits in chair by window and continues to stare out)* You should go for a swim.

FLOYD: Not me. I'm not going to be standing around without any clothes on when Roy comes. No, sir.

(Pause)

RONNIE: I think you're jealous of Roy. He's still working. You'd like to be famous again.

FLOYD: No. No, he's not that famous now. You never see his name in the papers anymore, not now that we've split up. But when we were together, nobody could stop us. *(Crossing back to the hat on the chair)* I hope you brought your gun along, Roy. We could still show them. What a character you were, you old pisspot! I always said if we were a deck of cards, you'd be the joker. I'm talking about Roy. That's his hat. *(He puts it on, leaving his own hat on the chair)* How do I look?

RONNIE: It looks like your hat.

FLOYD: But this is Roy's hat . . . *(He advances toward her menacingly)*

RONNIE: Let's play dominos.

(Floyd stops instantly; turns and starts unfolding the card table. When he starts talking again, he talks like a hoodlum)

FLOYD: She likes to play dominos. Do you? I've always thought it was a waste of time myself. Cards—that's my game. And bingo. I do like the way the dominos look. There's several versions of dominos. One's called forty-two and another's called moon, and that's how I got to know you, Roy. Yeah. *(He works silently for a moment. Ronnie ignores him. He moves the chair with his hat left in front of bed and positions the card table center stage)* Good old Roy. We both had the same dream when we were boys, didn't we? That's how close we were. We dreamed about the Man in the Moon. I always thought I looked like him. When I was a boy I used to lie awake nights and watch him floating there, outside the window, thinking we both had the same ghostly grin. So does Fred Astaire. Those are the only other people I've ever wanted to be. Good old Roy. We burned up the roads in those days, didn't we? *(Normal voice, crossing to window)* There's another car coming—

RONNIE: It's not them. Sit down, Floyd.

(He sits, instantly. Ronnie drags her chair from the vanity to the table, sits up center and starts setting up a row of dominos. Floyd joins her, bringing the chair he was sitting in and placing it stage left. He drags it very slowly so it scrapes the floor)

FLOYD: That scare you? That loud noise?

RONNIE: No.

FLOYD: *(Sitting; sadly)* I used to scare you when we were first married. That's the trouble, I don't now.

RONNIE: This is making you nervous, isn't it?

FLOYD: What?

RONNIE: Seeing Roy again.

FLOYD: Why should I be nervous? You're the one who should be nervous. You're going to be meeting his new wife, comparing yourself to her. *(Pause)* I just hope he brought his gun along. That scare you?

RONNIE: It's your move.

(He tips over a row of dominos. She starts setting up another one)

FLOYD: Why should I be nervous?

RONNIE: It's been four years. People change.

FLOYD: Not Roy. Some people would, but not him. *(Standing, getting excited)* That's what was so important about the day we stuck up the Mound City Bank. Roy was disguised as Clark Gable. We al-

ways did our jobs disguised as movie stars. He'd drawn a little
moustache on his face with a pencil; he said he only wished his ears
stuck out more. I was disguised as Fred Astaire. I had on my patent
leather shoes and my trousers with the black satin stripe. When he
asked me who I was, and I told him, he said that was all wrong:
Clark Gable and Fred Astaire never made a movie together yet,
and anyway, who ever heard of a dancing stickup team? Then he
looked at me, and he rubbed off that penciled moustache. Let it go,
Floyd, he said. Hell—let's be ourselves. So he shook my hand and I
stopped grinning and we busted that bank as the Oklahoma Hot
Grease Boys, and it went for over four thousand dollars. *(Almost like
a boy)* There's another car coming, can I go look?

RONNIE: You could never go back on the road again, Floyd. Not
now.

FLOYD: You talk about me as if there was something wrong with
me. I'm not old.

RONNIE: I didn't say you were old.

FLOYD: *(Agitated)* There's nothing wrong with me, Ronnie.
Why . . . you talk about me as if I was an alcoholic! *(Laughs loudly)*
Maybe I do want to join up with Roy again. Maybe he feels the
same way. Maybe I brought something along that would make your
blood run cold.

RONNIE: *(Bored)* Did you bring your gun?

FLOYD: That's for me to know and you to find out.

*(Roy appears behind them in the door. Ronnie sees him over Floyd's
shoulder, gasps and points. Roy is dark-haired, handsome, sleek, and
looks apprehensive. He wears a suit almost identical to Floyd's and carries two yellow suitcases like a porter)* Roy . . . *(Roy says nothing. He
just grins)* You old pisspot! *(Roy starts out)* Roy—it's me—Floyd!
Don't you know me? This is my wife Ronnie.

*(Floyd starts toward him. Roy abruptly motions no. He cases the cabin
first, disappearing into the kitchen. Floyd gets his jacket from the coatrack
and puts it on, Ronnie straightens her robe. Roy reappears, every move
alert, and manhandles the suitcases downstage right, taking a long time,
looking around the room. When he speaks, it is almost in a whisper)*

ROY: Everything looks so small now. So small and flat . . .

FLOYD: You don't look any different, Roy!

ROY: The buildings are so much larger up North. That must be
it. But driving down here, things get smaller and smaller. The road
changes. Goes from a turnpike to a blacktop to that narrow little
dirt road outside. When you finally get here, Oklahoma's no bigger
than a tablecloth . . . Your house looks like a dollhouse, Floyd.
Look at that chair! *(He points and laughs. Floyd laughs, then catches*

Roy's eye and stops abruptly) Like to introduce my wife Flo. Flo!
(He crosses and shouts outside door. Nobody appears)
FLOYD: *(Starting towards them)* Those suitcases look heavy—
ROY: *(Crossing quickly back to suitcases)* There's nothing in them.
Nothing but Flo's things and some hotel towels. I can't stop stealing
them . . .
(Pause)
RONNIE: Can we see her?
(Flo's face appears at the door. She is drab and timid)
FLOYD: *(Booming)* Well come in, honey, and let us have a look at
you!
(Flo disappears again)
RONNIE: Floyd, not so loud. *(Flo reappears)* I'm Ronnie.
*(She holds out her arms. Flo steps hesitantly into the cabin, first removing
her hat and wiping her feet. She hands Ronnie flowers. Then they sud-
denly embrace. Floyd backslaps Roy, and Ronnie takes the flowers into the
kitchen)*
FLOYD: This is something! Boy, it's good to see you, Roy!
ROY: Same here.
FLOYD: Hey! You remember the invisible rope? *(They leap apart
downstage, standing facing each other)* We stand on either side of the
road. A car comes along and— *(They pull an imaginary rope taut
between them. Flo gasps)* Can you see it?
FLO: It looks real.
FLOYD: He slams on his brakes, and when he gets out we make
him give us all the money he's got. Go on—try to cross it.
(Flo puts her hands over her eyes and runs through it)
FLO: Oooh.
FLOYD: Go on, Ronnie. Can't you almost feel it?
RONNIE: *(Crossing slowly to rope, smiling)* Yes.
FLOYD: *(Scornfully)* You can't feel it, there's nothing there. *(He
embraces Roy. Ronnie clears dominos from card table and sets tablecloth
and four plates while Flo wanders)* Boy, this is gonna be great. We'll
stay up all night talking about the days of the Hot Grease Boys, the
Mound City Bank, the old invisible rope trick, and our dream
about the moon.
ROY: . . . Dream about the moon.
FLOYD: Sure, you know. Our dream.
ROY: We had a lot of trouble finding this place. *(Looking around,
easing somewhat)* I think you gave us the wrong directions, Floyd.
Maybe not. I didn't dream the town would look so small now. We
almost didn't find it at all . . . Just four houses. That's not much
of a town.

FLOYD: You're not in town, Roy. This is a tourist court.

ROY: No wonder we had so much trouble finding it. Why'd you do that?

RONNIE: Who knows? Floyd wanted to rent a cabin for some reason.

FLOYD: So we could do what we wanted. *(Booming)* So we could make as much noise as we wanted.

ROY: *(Crossing to Ronnie at table)* Floyd wrote me lots about you. I don't know how he got such a good-looking woman.

FLOYD: *(Bringing the remaining chair downstage and trying to get between them)* You haven't changed, Roy. Not a particle.

ROY: Neither have you, horseface.

FLOYD: So tell us about things, about things up North.

ROY: For one thing, I'm thinking about joining a mob.

FLO: *(Picking up a shriveled balloon off end table down right and putting it in her purse)* Somebody had a party . . .*(The others ignore her)*

FLOYD: A mob?

RONNIE: He means a gangster mob, Floyd, like in the movies.

FLOYD: I know that; sounds good.

RONNIE: Floyd. Not so loud.

FLOYD: I might like to get in on that action. Think one of those mobs would consider taking on another country boy?

RONNIE: You don't look right, Floyd. Not for that. *(To Roy)* You are handsome. You've got a profile like the magician in the comic strips. You'd look exactly like him if your hair was blue.

FLOYD: I'll show you your cot.

(Roy stiffens again, grabs suitcases)

ROY: I don't think so, Floyd. Flo and I have got to go straight back. We're just passing through this part of the country.

FLOYD: But . . . We were going to talk. There's a pond in the back so we can swim and I was going to cook us a big supper. You've got to stay.

ROY: *(Starting toward the door)* I've got important things cooking up there, Floyd. *(Flo is standing still, looking out the window)* What are you looking for?

FLO: A chair. So I can . . . sit down.

(She crosses slowly down to the table, looking at Roy, selects the up center chair and sits)

RONNIE: *(Breaking the silence)* Stay as long as you can. I'm dying to hear about things up North.

ROY: All right. But just for a while.

(Roy, Ronnie, and Flo sit around the table; Ronnie stage right, Roy stage left. Floyd doesn't sit, but remains standing upstage right, staring at Roy. Roy sits on Floyd's hat)

RONNIE: Now. I want to hear about the clothes, and Floyd will want to know all about the new model cars.

ROY: I'll make it short. You can get anything you want up North. But you've got to think clear. When I first got there, I was confused. I don't know if I can describe it, but . . . To make a long story very short, I found the right people; started hanging around the right places. In fact, I've got my own night club now. The Panama Club.

RONNIE: It sounds glamorous.

ROY: You should see it. You wouldn't know it if you did. It's shaped like a jungle. I hired a colored band and there's palm trees and all the waiters wear gorilla suits. Nothing up there is what it seems. It's a whole new world. You can be anyone you want. To make a long story short, I've finally found the place where I belong . . . *(Pause)* Floyd? You going to join us? *(Floyd sits in the chair to Flo's left, never taking his eyes off Roy)* So as soon as I join the mob, I'm on my way to the top. I can't say too much more about it, but . . . my head's clear and I've got both feet on the ground. And I'm not coming back to Oklahoma again, because everything's fine now except the old things look small . . . *(Looking around uneasily)* Everywhere I go, everything looks smaller now than I thought it should . . . I guess because now my mind is so large . . . *(He finishes, staring at Floyd)* You're looking good, Floyd. *(Floyd doesn't answer. Everyone looks at the tabletop)* Floyd? What are your plans?

(As he says "plans," Flo coughs so the word is inaudible)

FLOYD: What?

ROY: Your plans.

FLOYD: Ronnie? What are my plans?

RONNIE: He hasn't got any.

(As she says "hasn't got any," Flo coughs so that the words are inaudible. Each time she coughs, they glance at her momentarily)

ROY: What?

RONNIE: He hasn't got any.

(Pause)

FLO: There's a lot of dust in the air down here.

ROY: *(Sharply)* That's not polite, Flo. *(Pause)* You wrote me a postcard saying you had some plans.

FLOYD: I was going to start a café. Ronnie's a good cook—*(As he talks in a low voice, Flo coughs and continues coughing so he is almost inaudible)* We thought we might start a short-order place. You know . . . blue-plate special . . . homemade pies . . . and . . . all that. Ronnie's a good cook. But . . . we gave it up.

ROY: So you don't have any plans? *(Floyd nods his head "yes")* Yes you do or yes you don't? *(Floyd shakes his head "no")* You don't?

(Floyd shakes his head "no") I give up, it's impossible to have a conversation with you. Say what you're trying to say.

FLOYD: You're sitting on my hat.

ROY: Oh. *(He removes the crumpled hat from underneath him and tosses it on the bed. He stands, crosses around the table to Floyd)* You've got to understand, Floyd, the things we did in the old days . . . that was small potatoes. Shotguns and smalltown banks. That was small potatoes. So you never started a café and you don't have any plans. I'm disappointed in you, Floyd. Can't you do anything?

(Floyd suddenly stands and jerks the tablecloth towards him. The dishes clatter to the floor. Silence. They all stare at him)

FLOYD: I thought I could pull it out from under the plates . . . Sorry. I'm all right.

ROY: *(Watching Floyd as he clumsily starts restoring tablecloth and plates)* Sure. You've just been down here in the Dust Bowl too long, Floyd.

(He slaps him on the shoulder. Dust flies out of Floyd's suit. He doesn't see. Roy and Ronnie laugh)

FLOYD: What's so funny?

ROY: Nothing.

FLOYD: Am I doing something wrong?

ROY: No. No, sir.

(He slaps him again, more dust. Roy covers his mouth with his hand)

RONNIE: *(Standing)* Why don't you go for a swim, Floyd?

ROY: Why don't you? Cool off. Flo can go with you, and I'll sit here for a while and get to know your wife.

FLOYD: That sounds like a good idea.

(He goes to the door, takes off jacket and leaves it on the coatrack)

ROY: Flo?

(She joins Floyd at the door without a word. They start out. Floyd stops and turns)

FLOYD: You won't be gone when I get back, will you?

FLO: I'm your hostage. Roy couldn't leave without me, could he?

(She bats her eyes. They exit. Ronnie and Roy are standing facing each other across the table. Silence)

ROY: How low you sunk. I don't believe it. Does he know?

RONNIE: No.

ROY: Four years . . . I wouldn't have thought he was your type.

RONNIE: *(Smoothing tablecloth nervously)* He's not the man he was.

ROY: So I noticed.

RONNIE: He's got some kind of problem. I think he drinks.

ROY: He didn't drink before.

RONNIE: Well, something's wrong with him.

ROY: That's obvious.

RONNIE: Maybe you could help him out. I'd think so much of you, if you could light a fire under him.

ROY: *(Draws back suddenly)* Please! Don't say that.

RONNIE: Why not?

ROY: Just don't *(Smugly)* You should have come with me. You wanted me, but you were afraid of me. So I guess you settled for Floyd out of disappointment.

RONNIE: I never wanted you.

ROY: What do you do now?

RONNIE: Play dominos.

ROY: What a waste. *(As he speaks, Ronnie picks up the plates and puts them in the kitchen. Then she crosses to the vanity, picks up a Flit gun and walks around the room slowly, spraying)* I remember the first time I saw you. I walked in the Comanche Café and there you were, looking great in your white uniform. It was thin as paper so I could almost see through it and you had a pencil stuck behind your ear. And you said, "May I take your order?" *(Grabbing her down left)* You don't fool me. You're Floyd's wife now, but you'd still like to take orders from me, wouldn't you?

RONNIE: Do you really have a night club?

ROY: Hell, yes! *(He lets her go, walks upstage center)* You should see it. A real night spot.

RONNIE: It sounds magic. I wish I could. Before, when I knew you, I always thought something magic was going to happen to me. I had premonitions, thought I could foretell the future. Sometimes I still think I can. I believed in ghosts.

ROY: Yeah.

RONNIE: I thought there was more to the world than just what you can see, I believed someday a ghost story would happen to me. But I never saw one. And I married Floyd, and now I play dominos.

(She walks around the room spraying again)

ROY: Did you have a premonition I was coming?

RONNIE: Yes.

ROY: You know why I left Oklahoma, doll?

RONNIE: You were running from the law.

ROY: They could never have caught me. No, I'd gotten too smart for this place. Didn't I tell you ghost stories were a lot of baloney? Nobody believes in ghosts—not if they're smart. And I was the brains of the Hot Grease Boys. *(She walks away, spraying)* Come back here!

RONNIE: I'm nervous.

ROY: Stand still when I'm talking to you! *(Ronnie freezes)* You've still got a good figure. Still dream of being in the movies?

(She smiles, drops Flit gun on bed. She removes her robe, straightens her shoulders so her breasts rise, and walks across the room stage right, almost in a trance, the robe flung over her shoulder. Then she catches herself and stops)

ROY: Miss!

(She freezes. Roy sits at the card table like a customer. She approaches him like a waitress)

RONNIE: Could I take your order?

ROY: That's more like it. *(Leaning back in chair)* I know a lot of things you don't. I'm smart. *(Pulling her down on his lap)* You see those flies on the ceiling? How do you think they do it?

RONNIE: What?

ROY: Walk on the ceiling. Wouldn't you like to know how?

RONNIE: *(Uncomfortably; trying to get up)* I shouldn't have left the windows open.

ROY: But wouldn't you like to know? Why do you think they can do it and we can't?

RONNIE: Because they're smart?

ROY: *(Grabbing her angrily now, trying to kiss her)* Forget Floyd. Come back up North with me—

RONNIE: What about your wife?

ROY: Forget Flo. Look at me—

RONNIE: No! *(She slaps him. He throws her roughly to the floor)*

ROY: *(Dramatically)* Hell, you don't know what you're missing! I could show you sights you never dreamed of. Picture it: you and me headed North, driving through the night. There's a star hanging over the end of the road, and I point the car at it. I'm driving faster and faster, the closer we get, and I'm telling you things that make your mouth water. Just us and the billboards going past in the dark, and the stars . . . I could show you a star that's shining so hard it sweats . . .

(Roy has found the snaps on his suitcase. It springs open)

RONNIE: What's that?

(He pulls out a black tuxedo)

ROY: That's my soup and fish—for the Panama Club.

RONNIE: You must look handsome in it. Let me see you wearing it.

ROY: *(Crossing to her)* I might do it, doll—if you'll be nice to me. *(Their faces are almost touching)* You have on bright red lipstick . . .

(They kiss. Floyd appears in the doorway. His hair is sopping wet. He has on bathing trunks, his shirt, shoes, and socks, and there is an unlit cigar jammed in his mouth. He takes them in. Their mouths stay glued together. He comes downstage, sits in chair left of table, and speaks loudly:)

FLOYD: Oh, boy. You should try that pond. Boy, do I feel good now. *(Roy and Ronnie have broken apart. Flo appears in the doorway)* That's all I can say. That was a wonderful experience. Soaking in that nice warm pond water . . . I soaked all my troubles out.

FLO: Can we go swimming?

ROY: No.

FLO: I watched Floyd. It looked like fun.

(Floyd strikes a kitchen match, holds it to his cigar)

FLOYD: Sure you don't want to try it, Roy?

ROY: Please! Don't hold that match so close to that table. It could go up in flames, it's only cardboard. *(He lunges forward and blows it out. Everyone stares at him)* Look at Floyd's socks!

(They are fallen down in Floyd's shoes. He points and laughs)

FLOYD: *(Blowing out a cloud of smoke)* You don't know what you're missing until you've soaked in that nice warm pond water. You should both go . . . soak yourselves.

ROY: We're going—

RONNIE: Please stay. It seems like you just got here. *(Stopping him)* Don't leave me now, Roy.

FLO: I'm so hungry I could eat a horse!

FLOYD: Then sit right down, honey. We wouldn't dream of letting you go until you've had your supper. Ronnie? Set the table.

(He pulls back a chair for her. She sits. Ronnie starts restoring the plates and tablecloth)

FLO: Thank God.

FLOYD: No, sir. You deserve to eat at least.

FLO: I didn't want to be impolite, but I was so hungry I thought I was going to faint.

RONNIE: You look sort of pale, honey.

FLO: You don't know. A minute ago when I was standing out there in that hot sun, I thought, Flo, you're going to faint.

FLOYD: No danger of that now, honey. Soup's on. You want a stogie?

FLO: No.

FLOYD: You can have anything you want here, don't be afraid to speak up.

ROY: I'm staying only if Floyd will talk about this situation man-to-man. Will you? *(Floyd nods)* Can you be serious about it?

FLOYD: If you want to.

ROY: You know what I'm talking about? *(Floyd nods)* Then let's get down to it.

FLOYD: Fine, let's talk about it.

(Roy sits)

ROY: You're willing?

FLOYD: It's fine with me, I think it's about time we did.

ROY: All right. Let's get to the point. Ronnie says there's something wrong with you. You've got a serious problem. *(Looking at Ronnie and Flo)* Now I've known Floyd here for a long time, and he's a great guy. But I have noticed this one flaw in Floyd, it's that he—where you going?

(Floyd has crossed and sat on the bed)

FLOYD: You looked at her, I thought you were talking to her.

(Pause)

FLO: We gonna eat now? *(No one answers)* Roy's never told me about you and Ronnie. He never talks about his past; he's always talking about his plans, or the mob. I guess he wanted Oklahoma to surprise me. But now that I met you, I like you. *(To Ronnie)* I'll bet Floyd's a good cook.

ROY: Flo.

FLO: I don't know how to cook. Neither does Roy. We're always saying we're going to learn, but we never have time, we're always on the go.

ROY: Flo.

FLO: I met Roy at the movies.

RONNIE: Sounds romantic.

FLO: He was sitting in the balcony with his feet propped on the seat in front of him. I knew you shouldn't do that. I guess I'm trying to say he had an air of danger about him. I was ushering, so I shone my flashlight in his face and asked him to please stop. He looked so handsome. He asked me to sit down and share his popcorn with him, and I couldn't believe anyone like him would be interested in me—he was so handsome, and I'm so plain.

(Pause)

FLOYD: *(Pointing at a cloud of cigar smoke)* I saw a cloud outside. Now there's one inside. *(Not looking at Roy)* You goin' for a dip, Roy?

ROY: Not now.

FLOYD: You don't like the water, do you, Roy? You're like a cat.

FLO: Maybe we could all go for a dip . . . after we've had lunch.

ROY: No.

FLO: But I want to go, Roy. I want to go for a dip.

ROY: No dip.

FLO: My throat's getting dry again. How about it? We can have a nice home-cooked meal, then the four of us can go for a dip—

ROY: Shut up, Flo!

FLOYD: Don't treat her that way!

ROY: I'm trying to help you solve your problem.

FLOYD: What about *your* problem? *(Roy stiffens, stands)* Shoe's on the other foot now, isn't it? You know what I'm talking about. At least I haven't changed my personality. You're playing a part. Flo doesn't know because she didn't know you before, but you've got another personality now.

(Roy goes to Floyd, grabs the cigar out of his mouth, breaks it and drops it on the floor)

ROY: What's it like?

FLOYD: What?

ROY: This so-called phony personality.

FLOYD: It's something like a fish.

ROY: Why'd you say that?

FLOYD: *(Staring at the fish on the wall)* I don't know. That's just how it strikes me.

ROY: You'd better lay off the booze, Floyd; that's all I've got to say.

FLOYD: Did she tell you I drink? That is a lie. An absolute lie.

FLO: I believe him. I believe Floyd.

ROY: *(Crossing back to table)* Don't you know an alcoholic can't tell the truth?

FLO: Floyd says he's not one, and I believe him.

ROY: Stay out of this, Flo, this is none of your business! He's probably got bottles hidden all over this cabin.

FLOYD: I do not.

ROY: All I can say is, I'm mighty disappointed in you, Floyd.

FLOYD: I am not a drunk!

ROY: Ronnie says you are.

RONNIE: I never caught him at it . . .

ROY: Well, something's wrong with you. You act like you don't know me any more, you talk like you've lost your mind, and you haven't got any plans.

FLOYD: I planned for us to stay up all night reminiscing about our days on the road and all our dreams.

ROY: Don't start that crap again, Floyd! I had no such dream about the moon.

FLOYD: You did!

ROY: I did not!

(Flo faints. Her head smashes down on the tabletop)

RONNIE: She's fainted.

ROY: *(Trying to revive her)* Flo—snap out of it, Flo!

FLO: I thought we were going to eat. I had such high hopes . . .

ROY: We haven't got time for that now.

FLO: I like Floyd. Stop bothering him. Floyd's like me, he says things; he just opens his mouth and they come out . . . but not like he meant. I thought that was why you liked me, Roy. I say funny things and I make you laugh. Like the other day when I was tired and I told you my feet were on their last legs.

ROY: Do we have to talk about this? The important thing is Floyd's problem. Hell, Floyd; I saw it coming a long time ago. You never could have made it up there. That's why I wanted to go it alone. You don't know how much nerve it took. *(Crossing downstage right)* The first night I stayed in a cheap hotel. I'll never forget looking out the window and seeing the searchlights shining in the sky— a new movie premiere or another filling station opening somewhere. Down below there were guys climbing out of taxicabs with beautiful women wearing furs. Nobody in this city ever sleeps, I thought—nobody who I'd want to know.

RONNIE: It sounds just like I dreamed it would. Wonderful.

ROY: I wanted to stay awake, but I couldn't. I kept staring at the brown wallpaper. The carpet was so moth-eaten you got drowsy just looking at it. There was a green stuffed chair and an empty glass and the lampshade was full of dead flies. I knew I wouldn't always be staying in cheap hotels like that, but I felt like if I slept I'd be . . . dirty somehow. I thought, Roy, this is no way to get started. So I did something dangerous to stay alert. I got a box of matches and lay down in bed and lit them one at a time. I knew if I fell asleep while one was burning the bedspread would go up in smoke—hell, the whole hotel would. There's almost nothing that won't burn, you know. I've seen pictures of buildings after they've burned down and there's nothing left but shoes and old springs poking up through the ashes. Once a fire starts it can get out of control so easy, and that's why . . . *(Faint sound of a fly in the room. Roy snatches, catches it in his bare hand)* You've got to stay alert! Sometimes I thought I heard footsteps in the hall—probably bellhops. But it sounded like somebody was looking for me. Don't lose your nerve, I thought. Those guys in the mobs will be looking for you soon enough. That's just your Good Angel. Everything took nerve up there. But if you just stay alert, nothing can go wrong . . .

(Sound of the fly again. He picks up a flyswatter off the vanity and crosses back to the table. Floyd looks slightly confused, his eyes unfocused as if the story has hypnotized him) But you, Floyd, you're drowsy. You live in a dream. Look at you. *(He smacks the flyswatter down on the table. Everyone starts)* Pull yourself together! It's a hard world out there. They don't forgive mistakes. Have you forgotten guns, Floyd? *(He smacks the flyswatter down several more times)* You've got to stay awake. But you—you're hiding from the world down here, living in some kind of soft dream—because you're afraid. You've got to pull yourself together!

(Floyd snatches the tablecloth out from under the plates. Not one falls to the floor. He stands there grinning triumphantly. Flo applauds)

RONNIE: Why don't you put on your soup and fish? Show him how good you look when you walk into your club.

ROY: *(Crossing to suitcases)* I'm going to show you how we do things up North, Floyd. Understand? I'm going to show you how to do things in style.

(He exits)

FLO: Good bread, good meat, good God let's eat! We going to eat now? No.

FLOYD: Do you think I should let Roy talk to me that way? *(Ronnie gets up without answering and goes downstage to the vanity, taking her chair with her; sits and starts brushing her hair. Floyd looks at Flo)* You afraid of Roy? Does he make you nervous? I know, you can't say anything. *(He takes Roy's hat and places it on the floor downstage. Then, while they wait, he sits in the stage left chair, takes a deck of cards out of his pocket and pitches them at the hat. Some of them go in)* I'm Floyd Simms. Roy probably hasn't told you my name. Four years ago I was as famous as him, but now . . . That's how it goes. There's no getting along with him. If you say something he doesn't like, he'll bite your head off. *(Flo gets up when he says this and crosses to the down left end table. She finds a book and starts leafing through it)* I understand. Roy thinks Oklahoma is small potatoes now. He wants to be moving on. Roy's talented, he could always talk to people . . . all sorts of people. I never could. *(Pause)* I'm doing something wrong. I know I'm doing something wrong. Seems like nothing's ever important enough for you, so you let it go. You don't even try. Then there's all the little things that are always happening to you that make you sad. You fall asleep in the afternoon and you don't wake up until after the sun's gone down. There you are in a dark room; you don't know how you got there, and it makes you sad. Or you go to a show but you don't get there until the last feature. At first it's crowded, but then people start leaving. Finally, you're almost alone. And when the lights come on you walk up the aisle real slow, looking over your shoulder at the credits, showing you've got all the time in the world and you're not afraid to be the last one out of there. It makes you sad. *(Flo discovers the book is hollowed out. She lifts out a whiskey bottle. She looks at Floyd, then replaces it and closes the book)* Or you go to a store to buy clothes. You feel pretty good—You feel pretty good—then suddenly here it comes, out of a mirror in the corner, that face you don't recognize at first because you've never seen yourself from that angle before. Then you see it's you and it makes you sad and you walk out of there without buying any clothes. What am I talking about? Something about success, I think . . . Look at my socks. It just makes you sad the way you let things go, because nothing's ever . . . important enough for you. Because you're not. I'm wasting my life. *(To Flo)* One thing: do you think I'm handsome?

FLO: You got a sad face. But it's nice. It's like those pictures you see in the drugstore window. They're yellow and faded from being in the sun for so long, and they look sad. But when you look closer, you see they're really movie stars . . .

(They look at each other. Floyd smiles. Roy appears, wearing the tuxedo. He walks slowly down right to Ronnie; proud, making the final adjustments—straightening tie and cuffs)

ROY: I look great, don't I? Admit it.

RONNIE: *(Standing, circling around him)* Oh, yes. Those trousers. That boiled shirt. Those shiny black shoes.

ROY: Nothing like being well-dressed and ready to face the world. How do you like it?

RONNIE: Won't you look, Floyd? He's just trying to help you.

ROY: You could look like this if you could lick your problems, Floyd. You know your worst enemy is yourself.

FLOYD: I got something for you, Roy. I forgot to give it to you.

ROY: *(Eagerly)* A present?

FLOYD: *(Smiling sadly)* I hid it somewhere in this room.

ROY: Can I have it now?

FLOYD: If you can find it. *(Roy starts looking, under the table, in the vanity. Meanwhile, unnoticed, Floyd takes a black Lone Ranger mask like his from under the bed and places it in the hat he has been pitching cards into. He gives Roy directions)* You're getting warmer. You're getting hot now. Hotter. No—you're cold *(Roy goes into the kitchen, pokes around the shelves)* You're getting warm again.

(Floyd goes to the coatrack and pulls on his pants, ignoring Roy as he ransacks the room. He keeps giving him hints. Roy searches more and more frantically until he has turned the cabin upside down, getting now

hotter and now colder, upsetting the chairs, throwing the covers off the bed, pulling out the vanity drawer and emptying it on the floor. The girls follow him, trying to pick up. When Floyd has gotten his pants on, the room is demolished and Roy has found the mask)

ROY:　Hell, Floyd, I'm touched. Where'd you find this? *(He puts it on)* You know this means a lot to me, don't you, Horseface?

FLOYD:　Sure, you old pisspot!

ROY:　You know it's hard up there in those big cities—and you've got to be the same way if you want to make it. Maybe I've been too hard on you today.

FLOYD:　Nobody liked you up there, did they, Roy?

ROY:　What?

FLOYD:　That's why you came back—you got lonely.

ROY:　Lonely? No—I'm a born loner.

FLOYD:　I see through you now. You came back so I'd look up to you, like in the old days.

ROY:　You're wrong about that, Floyd.

FLOYD:　Be ourselves, you said that day in Mound City. But you're not! You even told me you had the same dream I had, like we were one person.

ROY:　You starting that crap again, Floyd?

FLOYD:　Something was chasing you in the dark, under the moon. You didn't know what, but you woke up in a cold sweat.

ROY:　I don't remember.

FLOYD:　You're lying! You've got to!

ROY:　I never woke up in a cold sweat about anything. Floyd!

FLOYD:　It makes me sad—another thing to make you sad.

ROY:　*(Putting his arm around Floyd patronizingly)* What's happened to you? It's like you died. There was a time I didn't think you were afraid of anything. Look at you now.

FLOYD:　Let go!

ROY:　Don't you think two men can touch each other? What's the matter, you afraid of me too, Floyd? Are you afraid to try?

FLOYD:　All right, go ahead. *(Roy touches him carefully)* Let go of me, you homo! *(He pushes Roy away, snatches up flyswatter off the end table)* Try to screw my wife, will you! *(Flo gasps)* It's true! I saw them!

FLO:　It's not true, is it, Roy?

ROY:　I made a pass at your wife. But she was asking for it.

RONNIE:　*(Ashamed)* He said he wanted me to run away with him, and I believed him. He told me he was going to take me to his night club.

ROY:　You married a tramp, Floyd. If I'd been around I could

have told you. *(Floyd advances with the flyswatter)* You've got to get mighty close to use that. *(He swings, Roy jumps him, forces him to let go of it like you would a gun; throws Floyd down)* I don't scare easy, Floyd.

FLOYD: I didn't scare you with that?

ROY: I don't know the meaning of the word.

FLOYD: *(Pulling gun out of his trouser pocket)* What about this? Hold still, or I'll blow you apart! You're not the only one who can be a tough guy. This puts us on equal ground, doesn't it?

ROY: Is it loaded?

FLOYD: You want to find out? Ronnie?

RONNIE: You wouldn't shoot, Floyd. Not me.

FLOYD: Oh, wouldn't I? Get over there against that wall, both of you. *Move!* *(They do. Floyd lies down casually on the bed, gun still pointing at them, his head propped on one hand)* Now. I'm gonna lie here and watch you spill your guts. Do you feel like pleading for your life, Roy? Ronnie? Would you plead for him? I've been hearing about up North and I've been hearing about your bigshot night club ever since you got here; and now I'm fed up. You're gonna drop this phony personality—or you're gonna die!

FLO: There's no night club!

ROY: Flo!

FLO: Don't, Floyd. You're making a mistake, you can't shoot him!

RONNIE: No night club?

ROY: She's right. It's gone—burned in a horrible fire. I couldn't tell you. It's the worst thing that ever happened to me. *(Rushing on dramatically)* I'll never forget the palm trees and tablecloths burning, and the tinsel on the ceiling and the women's hair. The smoke came boiling down so thick you couldn't see or breathe. Flo and I are the only ones who got out alive. She can tell you—how I pulled her into the kitchen and we crawled into the icebox. When the firemen got us out the next morning, there was nothing left but ashes. So go ahead and shoot, Floyd—I've got nothing left to live for now anyway. But do you know why I really came back down here? I wanted to join up with you again. Like in the old days. Look, Floyd, I know you're still sore about your wife. But don't let her come between us. It could be like it was, Floyd—you know, the two of us, driving in the heat. I can almost see it now. You know, those old days were great . . . *(Suddenly he grabs Ronnie, holds her in front of him as a human shield)* O.K., drop your gun, Floyd; it's a stalemate! Floyd? *(Floyd doesn't react. He advances cautiously on bed, still holding Ronnie in front of him. Floyd is asleep)* You shithead! *(He throws his hat down on the floor and tramples on it)* And that's for your hat!

RONNIE: It's your hat. So—there's no more Panama Club.

FLO: There never was one! You got that from that story you heard about that joint that burned down in Boston, and you so afraid of fire and all you couldn't stop talking about it. *(She lights a match)* The Panama Club was another one of your plans. But you'll never do it. You'll never stay in one place long enough to do anything!

(She backs him out the doorway with the match)

ROY: I'm going for a walk. To . . . clear my head.

(He exits. Flo lights a last match, blows on it, drops it into the ashtray. It doesn't go out. She blows on it and ashes fly all over the table)

FLO: Sorry.

RONNIE: Forget it.

FLO: I know: I'm plain. I'm not good-looking like you. But it seems to me I deserve to eat. *(Ronnie goes tiredly into the kitchen, returns with a piece of bread on a plate, puts it down in front of Flo. She looks at it, then pushes it away)* You were a waitress? *(Ronnie nods)* That's been my problem—restaurants. He likes to eat out, you know. Travel and eat out. I'm so bored with always being on the move, but I'm so afraid I'll lose him. Then when Floyd said that about you and Roy . . .

RONNIE: Yeah.

FLO: You're not to blame. I can't keep him interested. I thought I could, but . . . something's always bursting your balloon.

(She gets up and crosses to the window. Ronnie follows her)

RONNIE: Let's wake up Floyd.

FLO: Why?

RONNIE: He'll know what to do. Floyd?

(He doesn't move)

FLO: Rise and shine, Floyd.

RONNIE: He's out like a light. *(Looking out the window)* It's getting dark outside. Another day almost gone. *(She crosses to the lamp and turns it on. The girls cross toward each other, meeting in the center of the room)* You've got to learn how to deal with men. You know how to dance?

FLO: No.

RONNIE: I'll show you. *(She goes to the radio, turns it on. She and Flo do a brisk two-step downstage right to Bob Wills' "I Had a Dream")* Things are gonna look up for you soon, honey.

FLO: You think so?

RONNIE: I know so. You're a good kid. Maybe I could teach you how to play dominos.

(She turns off the radio and they sit at the table)

FLO: See, it's not the food in restaurants I can't deal with. It's the menu. You've got to order your food by the name on the menu or they won't bring it to you. So if you ask for breakfast, they say, don't you mean The Little Red Hen? You want a steak and they say, oh, you mean the Panhandle T-Bone Platter. You want to cover your head with the tablecloth, but you've got to say it out loud. It gets worse and worse. Bring me your Pittsburger. Bring me your Tater Tots. If there's a number, you can say, bring me the Number Four, thank God. But mostly it's bring me the Chew N' Sip, bring me the Thanksgiving Turkey in the Straw. Bring me a Bromo, I'm sick. There must be more to life.

RONNIE: *(Knocking over a row of dominos)* Yeah.

FLO: A Blue Plate Special—that's what I ask for. Anyone can say they want the Blue Plate Special. You've heard it asked for in the movies. So they bring it, and I eat it even if it's something I don't like. The thing is, it never is anything I like. What I really wanted was a blue plate. By now, it's the only thing I'm hungry for. A nice, blue plate. I want the food I hear them eating on the radio—it sounds so good when they talk with their mouths full. I want the food they eat in movies, the food mice eat in cartoons. I wish I was in a cartoon. *(Voice breaking)* Somebody would hit me on the head and stars would fly out . . .

RONNIE: Don't you think you could talk him into settling down?

FLO: I can give you the answer to that in two words: Im possible.

RONNIE: Don't cry, honey, no man's worth it.

(Roy rushes back in. He stops just inside the door, his back pressed to the wall. He has no pants)

ROY: Don't go out there! There's something out there. Something loose in the bushes; it chased me back here. *(Looks down)* Where's my pants? Flo, go back and get my pants.

FLO: Where are they?

ROY: I know: I left them on a branch. It was a dog—a big dog loose in the bushes. Flo, go out and get my pants. *(She laughs)* That's an order!

FLO: I can't take him seriously. I never knew your legs were so white.

ROY: Somebody's got to. My keys are in them. Flo?

FLO: Why don't you get them yourself if you want them so bad?

ROY: I was down by the pond. For some reason I thought I'd

like to go wading, so I took off my trousers so they wouldn't get wet. There was mud and dead leaves on the bottom. The water was cold. I was wishing I had a light so I could see if there were any fish, and then whatever it was must have heard me; because then something came rushing towards me. Something running through the woods—something on four legs—an animal on the loose. I thought it must be a dog—a mad dog. And I lit out before it could catch me and bite me; lit out so fast I forgot my pants. I ran so hard I felt like I was floating. And the moon was shining down the whole time with this cold grin, like it had nothing to do with me. That's how I ran all the way back here, that mad dog right at my heels.

RONNIE: You sound scared.

ROY: Hell, no—I'm not scared. But how can I walk around here without any pants on?

RONNIE: Pretend you're at a nudist camp.

ROY: But we've got to go. We've got to start back up North. Hit the road.

FLO: We can start tomorrow. Sit down, let's play dominos; Ronnie's showing me how.

ROY: *(Crossing to Ronnie)* You'll get them for me, won't you?

RONNIE: You're making this whole thing up so we'll feel sorry for you, aren't you?

ROY: No! There's something out there.

RONNIE: You'll wake Floyd.

ROY: I tell you, the dog is real.

RONNIE: Like your night club? *(She picks up Flit gun and advances on him)* Why'd you ever have to come back here?

ROY: Ronnie—

(She sprays him in the face)

RONNIE: Siddown!

(Roy hesitates. She pulls back the handle of the Flit gun threateningly; he crosses quickly and sits in the stage right chair. Ronnie then sits in the center chair)

FLO: You cried wolf once too often, Roy.

RONNIE: Now. We've got the whole night ahead of us. Let's tell ghost stories.

FLO: Oh, good. I like being scared.

RONNIE: Let's turn out the lights so it'll be spookier.

FLO: Roy? Turn out the lamp. *(He looks at her uncertainly)* Come on, honey, be polite.

ROY: She can turn it out herself.

FLO: You're closest.

(Roy gets up, goes to the lamp and stops)

ROY: What happens if I do and that dog comes in? *(He goes to the kitchen and gets a rolling pin)* I'll use this to protect myself. *(He crosses back to the lamp)* Here goes.

FLO: Nothing's going to happen, honey.

(He turns off the lamp, Floyd groans, startling Roy, and sits up in bed)

FLOYD: Unnnh. I dreamed it was snowing. I dreamed I was covered with snow . . . *(He looks at Roy)* You still here?

ROY: *(Starting toward him)* Floyd, it's been swell, but we've got to go—

FLO: Come and sit down, honey, I'm not going anywhere.

ROY: I guess . . . we'll stay instead.

(Roy goes back and sits at the table holding his rolling pin. The girls are playing dominos. Without lamplight the stage is bathed in a melancholy bluish glow)

RONNIE: I haven't told ghost stories since I met Floyd. But it seems like tonight ghost stories might be possible. There's one about a drowned girl. That was one of my favorites. *(Standing, taking position up center to create the mood)* You're driving by the lake one night and her ghost stops you. She's got wet hair and she asks you in a real sad voice, "Can I have a ride home?" You don't know she's a ghost yet. So you say yeah, and for some reason she gets in the back seat and you start back to town. You're nervous, and you keep trying to see her in the mirror, because all the way you think you can feel her eyes staring at the back of your head. But when you get to her house, it's gone. *(She stops, thinks hard)* Or it's a haunted house. No.

FLO: Her parents come out and tell you their daughter drowned four years ago.

RONNIE: Yeah.

FLO: I heard that one before. I didn't want to spoil your story.

RONNIE: It was my favorite one. I used to know thousands of ghost stories. Thousands. Now I'm not sure I can remember how any of them end. But wasn't it frightening? Floyd?

FLOYD: How come the lights are out? *(He gets up, goes to the lamp. But instead of turning it on, he notices Roy and stops)* You're half nude, Roy. What for? *(He goes to the kitchen and comes back a moment later with a steak on a plate. He puts it on the table in front of Roy and stands, waiting. Roy looks at everyone. He prods the steak with a fork. It squeaks and he draws back, startled, dropping the fork. He looks up; everyone is smirking at him. Then he puts his head down on the table and begins to sob quietly) (Coldly)* O.K., Roy. You got the part.

(Floyd crosses to the coatrack, puts on jacket, takes a cigar out of the pocket and puts it in his mouth)

FLO: You tell one now, Floyd. I want to hear a real one—about ghosts wearing sheets, with holes for eyes. Haunted houses. About somebody waiting for you by the side of the road, a hitchhiker who glows in the dark.

FLOYD: *(Sitting at table between the girls)* In the old days, Roy and I drove through all those small dark towns at midnight. Not a light burning. And you'd read the signs out loud. City Limits. Spark Garage. Utopia Hardware Store. Gas. Cactus Cafe. Brown Stationary. Gas. City Limits. Airport Motel. Sunset Motel. Gas. Then you're out in the dark again, moving on.

RONNIE: Where does the ghost come in?

FLOYD: Nobody saw you. You felt like a ghost.

ROY: You felt like you were dead. There was nothing to go back to, and nothing ahead but more empty towns like that. So you kept moving. How did I end up back here in Oklahoma? It's the last place I wanted to be. There must be somewhere left to go! *(Suddenly he stands)* There's something under the bed!

FLO: I don't hear anything.

ROY: Listen! *(They do, turning front. Nothing is heard)* Have you got that dog under there, Floyd?

FLOYD: I think you've lost your mind, Roy. I don't have a dog.

ROY: You don't? Don't fool me!

FLOYD: Look for yourself. *(Pause)*

FLO: Let's sing to keep our spirits up.

(Pause. Nobody sings. Nobody looks at anybody else, Ronnie stops playing dominos. When Roy starts singing, she begins again)

ROY: "I'm gonna buy a paper doll that I can call my own . . . and not a . . ." *(He falters and stops. They all look at him. When he starts singing again, they go back to playing dominos)* "I'd rather have a paper doll . . . that I could call my own . . ." *(Silence)* That doesn't sound like me. I'd never have a paper doll.

FLOYD: Like I say, that's your problem. *(He gets up, moves around the table and takes Roy's chair)* Gimme a light, Flo.

(Flo strikes a match and holds it to his cigar)

ROY: I think I'd better have a look under that bed.

FLOYD: You still nervous, Roy? I'll look for you.

ROY: No. I'll do it.

FLOYD: Suit yourself.

(Roy goes over and starts crawling under the bed, upstage)

RONNIE: Sometimes you wonder where it's all gone. I know now I'll never leave Oklahoma. And Floyd and I will never start a café. My ghost story was a failure and I don't think I'll have any more premonitions now. I can't even remember why ghosts should scare you . . . something about the word boo. I'm sticking to dominos. They don't surprise you, but who needs surprises? Dominos is fine from now on. Except for sometimes you think you should walk out the back door and drown yourself in that pond . . .

FLOYD: *(Standing and crossing up to the door, looking out and smoking)* I liked that pond. I was lying on my back, looking up at floating clouds. It felt like I was floating up there in the sky with them . . .

ROY: *(Under bed)* Floyd?

FLOYD: Roy?

ROY: There's nothing under here. You were right. But a while ago I could have sworn you had a vicious dog around here you weren't telling me about.

FLOYD: There's no dog.

ROY: Good. But if there was, you wouldn't let him in here, would you?

FLOYD: Nope.

ROY: Good. *(Pause)* But I think I'll stay under here for a while anyway. Things look pretty good under here. I'm going back up North tomorrow. I'm going alone—as Clark Gable. You know, you're all in a fog. That's what's wrong with you. Your minds aren't clear, like mine. But things look fine under here. And I'm leaving first thing tomorrow. *(Pause)* As soon as Floyd calls off that dog.

RONNIE: In the old days, when I worked at the Comanche Café, everything was good. Then it seemed like one day it was gone. What went wrong?

FLOYD: Wind. That wind started blowing and overnight everything turned into the Dust Bowl. Wind blowing all day long and brown, blowing dust everywhere, so thick you couldn't talk or think. Overnight this country changed. It turned into the worst place in the world. Everything died. Nothing could grow. Nobody had any money. *(Coming back down to sit stage right at the table)* But worse than that, you couldn't think for blowing dust, and trying to finish a sentence was like trying to work a crossword. There was nothing more to do, and it seemed like everyone was killing time, waiting around and coughing, and everything sounded dead, like it does on a record when the music's over and there's nothing to hear but the empty part, just scratches going round . . . and round . . .

FLO: I like it here. I'm never leaving this place again.

(She takes the balloon out of her purse and starts to blow it up)

FLOYD: One thing was good . . . driving. When you were moving down the road, in the heat; and somewhere way out in front of you, you could see that water shining on the road. Those silver puddles where the centerline hits the horizon. They always made me so mad. I drove faster, trying to get there before they dried up. I drove slower, trying to keep them in sight. But before you got there, they were always gone. They were the best thing—and they weren't even real.

FLO: *(Showing him the balloon)* Look, Floyd.

(He grins. They grin at each other, and he pops it with his cigar. Silence)

FLOYD: Only the sound of our guns was real.

(The stage is bathed in a bluish glow. Floyd is looking out, puffing on his cigar, Ronnie and Flo are bent over the table, Roy hidden under the bed. The air is cloudy with smoke. In the distance, a dog barks. The stage darkens slowly)

Curtain

Mordecai Gorelik

THE BIG DAY

Mordecai Gorelik

Mordecai Gorelik, whose play *The Big Day* appears in print for the first time in *The Best Short Plays 1977*, is a prominent American scene designer, author, director and educator. Though born in Russia, Mr. Gorelik grew up in New York where he attended public schools and Pratt Institute. He studied scene design with Robert Edmond Jones, Norman Bel Geddes, and Sergei Soudeikin, three masters of this theatrical art, and in time, Mr. Gorelik was to be linked with his mentors as one of the truly great craftsmen of scenic art.

After completing an apprenticeship painting scenery and working backstage at the Provincetown Playhouse, New York, he designed *King Hunger* for the Players Club, Philadelphia, in 1924. Since then he has created the settings for more than fifty professional productions. Among these: *Processional; Success Story; Little Ol' Boy; Men in White; All Good Americans; Golden Boy; Tortilla Flat; Casey Jones; Thunder Rock; Volpone; All My Sons; Desire Under the Elms; St. Joan; The Flowering Peach;* and *A Hatful of Rain.*

In 1956, Mr. Gorelik supervised the designs of the Comédie Française and the Old Vic Company for their memorable American visits.

As an educator, he has been on the faculty of the American Academy of Dramatic Art, The Drama Workshop of the New School for Social Research, the Biarritz American University (France), University of Toledo (Ohio), University of Hawaii, New York University, Bard College, Brigham Young University, and since 1960 and until recently, was research professor in theatre at Southern Illinois University where he also directed and designed numerous productions.

Mr. Gorelik also was production designer for a number of major films, including: *Days of Glory; None But the Lonely Heart; Our Street; Salt to the Devil;* and the French-made *L' Ennemi publique No.1.*

In addition to *The Big Day,* he is the author of a number of other plays: *Paul Thompson Forever; The Annotated Hamlet; Yes and No; Andrus, or the Vision; The Feast of Unreason;* and the translation of Max Frisch's *The Firebugs,* which has had more than three hundred productions throughout the United States.

His book, *New Theatres for Old,* originally published in 1940, has since become a classic in its field and his writings also have appeared in the *Encyclopedia Britannica* and in dozens of national and international periodicals.

The multi-talented artist served as expert consultant in theatre for the U. S. Military Government in Germany in 1949, and he has been the recipient of many awards including a Theta Alpha Phi Medallion of Honor in 1971, a Guggenheim Fellowship and Rockefeller Foundation Grant for study of the European theatre, and a Fulbright Scholarship to survey the Australian theatre.

Mordecai Gorelik and his wife Loraine presently live in Huntington Beach, California.

Characters:

FERN, *Les's secretary.*
DORIS, *Joe's wife.*
CHET, *a machinist.*
PROUT, *personnel manager.*
RAMSEY, *plant manager.*
DOYLE, *Union business agent.*
LES, *shop supervisor.*
HARRY, *Les's assistant.*
JOE, *a machinist.*
PHOTOGRAPHER

Scene:

Les Palmer's work-office at Ajax Pumps, a branch of Superior Acrylic Industries Corporation. Right of center, a small vestibule next to the hall door. A low railing separates the vestibule from the office proper. Door to Superior offices in the center of the right wall. Door to the machine shop in the left wall.

Filing cabinets, lockers and a blueprint-table against the rear wall. Left stage, Les's desk and telephone. Right stage, Fern's desk and typewriter. Three or four chairs. An office bench in the vestibule. Job-sheets and clip boards hang on the walls. In the rear wall, a narrow, horizontal window above head height, with fluorescent lighting visible behind it.

There is a clatter of machines and the grind of metal on metal; but the noise is muted except when the shop door is open.
Time: The present.

At Rise: Fern is carrying a sheaf of papers from the files to Les's desk. On the way she glances at Doris, who sits motionless on the bench in the vestibule.

FERN: *(Puts down papers. To Doris)* Really, it's like I told you: there's no use waiting. You've been here half the morning—
DORIS: I have time.
FERN: Mr. Palmer's the supervisor here, and he has a lot on his mind. Especially today. He can't have strangers barging in on him. If you wanted to see him you should have made an appointment.
DORIS: He'll talk to me.
FERN: He's a considerate man. *Over*-considerate. I wouldn't presume on that.

DORIS: Don't tell me I'm presuming! Who do you think you are? Mrs. Ajax Pumps? *(She starts for the shop door)*

FERN: *(Blocks her way)* I have my orders, if that's what you mean, and I carry them out. Write Mr. Palmer a note, if you like. *(Doris hesitates)* How will it help if you lose your cool?

(Chet enters, left, with a small, flat crate)

DORIS: No notes. I'll come back. *(Exits)*

CHET: Who was that?

FERN: Somebody with no respect. She wouldn't even say what she wants or who she is. They all try to walk in here—salesmen, busybodies, soreheads—If I let them all get at the company—

CHET: What company?

FERN: What do you mean, "What company"?

CHET: Ajax Pumps or Superior Industries? Since we got taken over, I don't know who's in charge here—Palmer, in this machine shop, or Ramsey and Prout, in the new front office. I get my pay check from Superior, my orders from Ajax—

FERN: All too confusing for your young, weak mind?—I'll unravel it for you, Chet: we're not a little independent outfit any more. Ajax is part of something a whole lot bigger; and speaking for myself, I'm proud to be with a great concern like Superior, which pays my salary and is entitled to the best I have to give.

CHET: And the best is none too good.

FERN: Chet, dear, you're not always funny.

CHET: I guess not.

FERN: Let's see that package.

CHET: For Lester W. Palmer, from "Superior Acrylic Industries, Michigan." What you've been expecting?

FERN: That's it. Take it upstairs and open it where he won't see you. It's a surprise.

CHET: You call that a surprise? It must be one of those framed testimonials they always send. And a gold-plated watch or gold-filled something-or-other always comes with it. *(He goes to the file drawer)*

FERN: You know there's such a thing as sentiment? After all the years Mr. Palmer has been here—

CHET: They'd rather cut out his gizzard.

FERN: *(Stung)* Who told you a thing like that?

CHET: My good woman, everybody knows the front office has been laying for him! Ramsey, the plant manager—Prout, at Personnel—

FERN: If you're going to repeat all the stupid things you hear around the shop—

CHET: Just waiting for him to take one wrong step, and he sure obliged them, this time. The Union business agent is here—

FERN: Is that Mr. Palmer's fault? If you knew him the way I do, if you knew what Ajax Pumps means to him—

CHET: *(Takes out blueprints)* He tries to play both sides, Fern. You think he's so crazy about the guys in the shop? No, sir. He's the supervisor—a top foreman.

FERN: And you're against all foreman.

CHET: Well, I don't stand up and salute. Them and a certain type of shop steward. They breathe down your neck.

FERN: *(Earnestly)* I'll grant you a sneaking little shop steward like Harry Fulton, but all you think of are your own prejudices. You'd get a lot further, Chet, if you had the moral courage to think straight.

CHET: *(Picks up blueprints and the crate)* That depends. Where is further?

FERN: And if you'd stop kidding, for once—

(He twinkles his hand at her and exits, right. Fern goes back to her desk as Ramsey enters with Prout, left. Prout carries a briefcase)

PROUT: *(As they come in)* Palmer's sat on his rump so long his brains have turned to lard. He was warned about that fellow, Nesbit—I told him myself. At a time like this, when we have to know who is with us or against us—

RAMSEY: *(To Fern)* Will you ask Doyle to step in here, Miss Carmine? The Union business agent. You'll find him out there; Mr. Palmer is talking to him.

FERN: Yes, Mr. Ramsey.

RAMSEY: Mr. Prout and I will be using this office for the next half-hour or so. If there's anything you have to do—

FERN: Oh. Yes, sir. *(She exits, left)*

RAMSEY: *(With a glance through the shop door)* Still talking to Doyle. About "Let's everybody be reasonable," you can bet on it. As if there were two sides to this—Superior's and the Union's.—How long has Palmer had that list?

PROUT: Almost four days.

RAMSEY: What in hell did he wait for? If we had put it through at once, we'd have had an accomplished fact by now. Instead of that—

PROUT: Don't think I didn't make it clear. I told him: it's a bad mistake to do it by degrees—you'll get the Union on top of us.

RAMSEY: And he has. "That couldn't happen," he told me, "I know the Union," he said, "It's nothing but a dues-paying club; it won't lift a finger." "Then what are you trying to appease it for?" I asked him. And while he talked, Nesbit got busy.

PROUT: Exactly.

RAMSEY: I know the Union doesn't investigate unless it gets a complaint from a member. But *are* we sure it was Nesbit who made the complaint, George? He's been employed in this shop only three days; the Union wouldn't act that fast.

PROUT: He was in the Shipping Area last month.

RAMSEY: Only a few days there, too.

PROUT: I can't be entirely sure, Ed. Even Harry isn't absolutely sure why the Union started to act up. Doyle is probably the only one who could tell us, but he's a politician—he's not talking. But one thing Harry made perfectly clear to me; it's a different Local since Nesbit transferred into it last month.

RAMSEY: *(As Doyle enters, left)* Well, Mr. Doyle. Seen all you wanted to see? Quite a while since you were here last.—You remember Mr. Prout: Personnel?

PROUT: Please have a seat, Mr. Doyle.

RAMSEY: Please do. Give him that chair, George. *(Doyle sits)* Always a pleasant visit with you, Mr. Doyle.

DOYLE: Same here, and I'm sorry about this. Always enjoyed doing business with Ajax: wages and working conditions right, nothing more than minor complaints—We hoped it would be the same with Superior coming in here.

PROUT: And isn't it?

DOYLE: It was—up to six weeks ago.

RAMSEY: A partial layoff when the economic crisis finally hit us. Something entirely out of our control.

PROUT: The men understood that.

RAMSEY: And we've been grateful for their loyalty.

DOYLE: They tried to help you out, sir. But now you're separating some of them for good.

RAMSEY: Let's have the figures, George.—Mr. Doyle, nobody feels worse about that than we do, here at Superior Industries. But Ajax is only a subsidiary, and the home plant in Michigan is taking a beating. *(Takes sheets from Prout)* Look at these figures. We have a moral obligation to our shareholders, Mr. Doyle. *(Hands over the sheets)* You can see how we're hurting. And we're not the only ones: the whole U.S. economy is in reverse gear. We need a breathing spell to see us through.

DOYLE: Same with our members, Mr. Ramsey. With a sky-high inflation going on—

PROUT: Is Superior Industries responsible for the inflation?

RAMSEY: All right, George. *(Doyle hands back the papers)* Mr. Doyle, give us credit for going about this in a good way. We can't offer more work when there isn't enough to go round. It may be painful, but it's more humane to let some of these fellows go. The sooner they leave us, the sooner they'll find well-paying jobs elsewhere.

DOYLE: Well, now, I have to tell you, Mr. Ramsey; the men don't see it. I wouldn't have thought it possible as late as a month ago, but now they not only won't stand for being cut off—they want a cost-of-living increase. At least thirty per cent, and they'll go to the Labor Board for it.

PROUT: How will it help if they wipe us out? They'll be out in the street or on Welfare.

DOYLE: And not on "well-paying jobs elsewhere"? *(Dryly)* Mr Prout, you can't ask us to support you. If you can't make a go of it, that's your hang-up, isn't it? Not ours. As long as you keep going, it has to be on Union terms.

RAMSEY: And what about loyalty? The Union members' wage scale, these days, is unbelievable: some of them own two cars apiece and send their sons to college. We've given your men continuous work for years, but they owe nothing in return—is that how you see it? .

DOYLE: I'm here to talk business, not moral questions. And if I were, it would cut both ways: the men don't want to lose what they've gained. Whatever they have, they've earned. *(With a change of tone)* I wasn't sent to be tough on Ajax or Superior, you know that, sir. We wish you well and always have, you know that, too. And speaking personally, Mr. Ramsey, I don't make the policy of the Local. There's been a big change there, lately . . . Phone me if you want to negotiate. *(Exits)*

RAMSEY: The honeymoon is over.

PROUT: The s.o.b.! He never talked like that before.

RAMSEY: He's under pressure himself. We've got to act, or else—and fast, too.

PROUT: I'm ready for them, Ed. I can hand out the pink slips myself, this very afternoon if I have to, and cut off all the temporary help. The steadies will back off if they think their own jobs remain safe. Harry's got a good, compact following of the right-minded element in the Local; with his help we've swung the membership before, and we can do it again. At least long enough to quiet things down while we get this complaint taken out and lost some place.

RAMSEY: Provided we impress the men.

PROUT: Right. Throw Nesbit the hell out of this shop—out of the Local, if possible—nail him to the barn door, and there'll be no more loud-mouthing.

RAMSEY: I'm leaving him to you.

PROUT: Right, sir. I'll give him a going-over in front of Palmer.

RAMSEY: There comes Palmer himself. Two birds with one stone. —You're positive about your information on Palmer?

PROUT: Absolutely. I've had Harry check and double-check, here, and Michigan sent me its records.

RAMSEY: Then my mind's made up. Even this Union business will be worth it if we can knock Palmer on the head once and for all. He'll have his showdown today.

PROUT: Today, right when he's getting his testimonial from the head office?

RAMSEY: It's a routine matter with the Corporation, but that's not how he'll see it—he'll have a rush of importance to the head. No, it's got to be done today; it'll be harder tomorrow. Only go easy—give him all the rope he needs.

LES: *(Entering, with Harry, left)* That's all well and good, Harry, but there's no substitute for experience. When I was starting in here— *(Sees Ramsey and Prout at the door, right)* Coming to see me, Ed?

RAMSEY: Later on, Les. *(He and Prout exit)*

LES: Desk men—their company sends them down here to administrate. Conglomerate machinists: they wouldn't know a cam from a bushing. *(Picks up a swipe; cleaning his hands)* They can't fire my mechanics; even my best men won't stay here if they let out any more people—and I can't run a machine shop with chemists. *(Goes to his desk; takes out a box of cigars)* It's my day—hand these out to the boys for me. Best on the market for the price—have some yourself.

HARRY: Yes, sir. *(Turns to go)*

LES: *(Somewhat too casually)* If you see Joe Nesbit out there, Harry, send him in.

HARRY: Yes, sir. He gets cut off tomorrow. He came in on the Union hiring list, a month ago, for three days; and he has three days, now, in the shop, but that's all he's entitled to.

LES: I've been thinking about him. He's a blue-chip machinist and we're short of the more experienced people; I don't see why he can't go on steady.

HARRY: You don't mean that, Mr. Palmer?

LES: He's been out of work a long time, you know that. It explains a lot. He's minded his own business around the shop, so far. A couple of months' steady employment and you'll see him change his whole nature.

HARRY: You believe that, after the way he's carried on around the Local? The Union Executive Board hates his guts, and so do all the regulars.

LES: He called you a company stooge in open meeting—you told me that. Nobody is perfect, Harry. You're running for secretary of the Local; when a man runs for office, he's bound to be sized up and called names.

HARRY: It doesn't matter what he calls me personally. It's what he's done to this company—a firm with a great national reputation. Ever since he checked into the Local he's been on the floor at every meeting, making speeches, agitating—

LES: Let's get this straight, Harry. I'm in charge of hire and fire in this shop. Let Ramsey look out for Superior Industries—I'm looking out for Ajax. What has acrylics got to do with building pumps? Next thing you know we'll be owned by a dairy products company or a fried chicken syndicate! *(With finality)* Either I mean something here or I don't. I'll take the responsibility for Nesbit. And for the rest of the boys, too. I know them all—I've weeded them out for years, getting rid of the ones that wouldn't play ball. Unless they're given no way out—like seeing they're next on the chopping block—they'll never raise a peep.

(Fern enters, right, with flowers)

HARRY: I've given you my opinion.

LES: I appreciate that. It's my big day; let's have good feelings here.—Look in at eleven o'clock, Harry, that's when the ceremony comes off. The publicity man will be here and they're taking pictures.

HARRY: I'm looking forward to it of course, Mr. Palmer. *(Exits, left)*

FERN: *(As the door closes)* He'll be around to the front office in a minute, talking to Mr. Ramsey. Nothing but a shop steward, but he has conferences with the plant manager when your back is turned! He's learned how to butter up Ramsey and Prout; he spreads it on with a trowel, Chet says. *(Les opens a second box of cigars)* Doesn't it bother you?

LES: What for? He looks out for himself, and so do I—we all do. This place is like a merry-go-round, Fern; you jump on and try any way you can to keep your seat. I've seen lots of others get bounced off but I'm still here . . . You think I don't know what they're saying? They say this testimonial is nothing but a put-on; that Ramsey is grooming Harry to take my place—

FERN: And you don't believe it.

LES: I'm Ajax Pumps and Ajax Pumps is me. I was here when

Ajax was nothing but the back of a junkyard. There isn't a machine in the catalog that didn't go through my hands. *(With pride)* I build pumps. What does Ramsey know—how to sign checks? Let him try and budge me—he'll get further trying to shove that stamping press out there with his bare hands.

FERN: It all depends who your friends are, don't you think? Mr. Ramsey's friends are in Michigan.

LES: Sure—he's been sending them reports ever since he's been here: how everything is fine, everything is under control—except me. He wasn't here three weeks before he ran to Nat Webster—Nat was the original owner here—with complaints about me. That was two years ago, after Nat sold Ajax and was made a vice-president of Superior Industries. "I put my bet on Palmer," the old man told him; and Ramsey backed down the way he always does in a pinch. Let him talk, let him make reports . . . *(Waves job-record sheets)* You've been getting these out of the files for me, and they talk louder than anything he can say. There's my record: clean jobs, everything planned, no waste, no stoppages. This whole year Ramsey's been running the plant at a loss, but my department shows a profit.

FERN: You know what I think? I think if a person gets too sure of himself it's the beginning of the end.

LES: *(Lights a cigar, tolerantly)* All right, I'm a dead duck, and you're bringing me flowers.

FERN: I borrowed these from Publicity just for the occasion. *(Goes to the door right)* Don't say you don't like them. They smell better than your cigars.

LES: I like them, Fern, I like them. Don't take my head off.

FERN: *(Calls)* You can come in now, Chet.

(Chet enters, carrying a package and blueprints)

LES: What's he doing in here? I told him to take those prints upstairs.

CHET: I brought them back again. It's cozier here.

FERN: *(To Les)* He was on his way, but I had him uncrate this picture for you. *(Chet removes wrapping)* It came by express today from the head office.

CHET: Congratulations, Mr. Palmer.

LES: Well, well.

FERN: Look what it says: "Faithful employee . devoted service." Hand engraved. You should be proud.

LES: You bet I am.—See those signatures? All the vice-presidents except Mr. Webster; he passed away this year. *(Moved)* Nathan T. Webster—one of the old school; carried a micrometer in his pocket to his dying day. Kept his eye on me from the day I started as a learner, saw me doing my job, day in, day out, cheerful and willing; he recognized me as the kind of man they needed. Twenty years with the company—twenty years today. Do you know how it makes me feel?

CHET: Like you're wondering about your next twenty years.

LES: Stand that picture up there, on the locker. I know how you kid about Ajax Pumps; you think it's something to kid about.

FERN: Quote, by Chet Mayfield: You don't have to be crazy to work here, but it helps; unquote.

LES: *(To Chet)* Get going—take those drawings up to Engineering and give them an argument.

CHET: I don't know what they drew. Whatever it is, it won't pump.

LES: Make up a query sheet first. *(Chet exits, right, with blueprints)* I know who takes him seriously.

FERN: Chet's a machinist, Mr. Palmer. He may be tall, dark and handsome for all I care.

LES: Don't tell me. He's got brains and some backbone, not like the rest of them. What's more I swear he's kissed you a couple of times. Or you him. Right in this office.

FERN: I've crossed off marriage. I was engaged once, to someone. Men are so disappointing, even when you don't ask for much.

LES: What did you ask for?

FERN: Just to be happy.

LES: That isn't much.

FERN: You're laughing at me. *(Goes to the files)* You might as well know it, Mr. Palmer. Chet is leaving.

LES: *(Startled)* Chet? Why would he leave? That's nonsense—he's been getting on fine here. *(Suddenly)* That's what's bothering you—

FERN: I'm free, white and going on thirty. Nothing bothers me, Mr. Palmer. Nothing in the wide world!

LES: I'll talk to Chet. This place is steady for somebody like him, and he knows it. Safe and steady; he could have a job here the rest of his life if he wants it.

FERN: He doesn't want it. *(Controlling herself)* I have to take down the time sheets.

(She exits, left. Les closes the files; turns, finds Doris standing at the partition)

LES: It's you, Doris! I'd been wondering when you'd look me up—

DORIS: And hoping it wouldn't happen . . . Never mind, don't answer me.—You don't seem to believe it's me, the way I look, now—

LES: Is that what the years have done to you?

DORIS: We're going under.

LES: As bad as that?

DORIS: You can't imagine it. The last of our unemployment insurance money used up, and nothing left for rent. We have two kids; they never fill their stomachs. We came back to this town last month because we didn't know where else to turn to any more. Joe's had six day's work here since we came back—it's the first time he's worked in half a year. He doesn't know I'm here talking to you; he wouldn't allow it.

LES: He's a damned crazy fool. Got himself boxed in for fair, and you with him. Just what I knew would happen! *(Goes to his desk)* He never even asked me about work: he came here off the Union hiring list. He saw me in the shop and turned his head away.

DORIS: I haven't room for pride any more, but he'll be that way to the last. Hellish pride!—But you're not going to abuse him in front of me!

LES: All right, all right—

DORIS: You've got to help us, Les.

LES: How?

DORIS: Give him his chance to work. Whatever else he is, he's a good workman. Put him on steady, give us a chance.

LES: He's been working here.

DORIS: Three days each month?

LES: It so happens that it's not a good time to ask that, Doris.

DORIS: It's never a good time to ask a favor.

LES: You don't know the ins and outs of things here. It's a bad time. It isn't that I don't want to help—

DORIS: Only it's not convenient.

LES: If you'll take some money to tide you over—

DORIS: I'm down so far I wouldn't even refuse that. Only how long do you think we can live on handouts? Let him work. I know he's no concern of yours—

LES: I didn't say that, either. You know I'd never say that, after what you've both meant to me . . . Did you think I'd forget about you through all those years of my marriage to the wrong woman?

DORIS: Les—

LES: Don't worry—I'm not going into it. *(Changing, forcefully)* Doris, believe me, I've wanted to keep Joe on. But it's not easy. He worked in another section of the plant last month; he kept his mouth shut, but they knew about him and didn't keep him on. They don't want him here.

DORIS: It's for you to decide in this shop. You're the boss here.

LES: They're crowding me. You don't understand—Ajax Pumps is not the same since it was taken over.

DORIS: Is that how far you've got in all this time—you can't give Joe a job when we're so desperate?

LES: *(Dismayed)* Don't let go like that, Doris. You can't think what it means to me to see you this way.—I'll do my best for you— and him. I promise you. I'll do it right away. Only it'll be a fight. They have a plant manager on my neck, sent down from Superior Industries, and everything is departmentalized: I can't scratch my nose without getting approval in triplicate—*(Fern enters)* Pull your- self together—

FERN: *(To Doris)* So you're here again! *(To Les)* She had no ap- pointment, but she hung around for hours. I told her you were not to be bothered—

LES: That's all right, Fern. It's Mrs. Nesbit. She came in to talk to me about her husband.

DORIS: I'm sorry; I'll go now.

LES: *(Goes with her to the hall door)* Don't worry—you'll hear from me. *(Doris exits. Les turns to Fern)* You're taking a lot on yourself, Fern. Why wouldn't I talk to her? She's up against it; she came to plead for help—

FERN: She walks in here and you fall for her line! That husband of hers—

LES: I can use him steady

FERN: Him? A known troublemaker, everywhere he goes?

LES: That's Harry's opinion.

FERN: Everybody in the office says so. Everybody can't be wrong.

LES: Yes, they can! The man is a crackerjack machinist, born right in this town—

FERN: You know all about him?

LES: His wife just told me. *(Sharply)* You've got the fever too, now! Every lunch hour Ramsey and the other big shots sit around their table at Belardi's Restaurant talking about how the bleeding hearts are letting troublemakers destroy this country; they get so they yell anarchism if they can't find their socks in the morning. A bunch of corporation minds—they don't half believe that junk themselves but they've got you barking up a tree!

FERN: I'm of age. I know what I believe in. *(Sits)* Let me tell *you* something, Mr. Palmer. You ought to stop smoking. If you didn't smoke so much you'd have a clearer mind.

(Prout enters, right)

PROUT: How's the big day going, Les?

LES: Hardly had time to notice.—Have a couple of these on me,

George. *(Lights Prout's cigar)* What about Doyle? What was the upshot?

PROUT: *(Sits)* Not good, Les. They'll drag us before the Labor Board, or throw a picket line around the plant. An old, established firm like Ajax—

LES: It'll blow over if we're half-way reasonable. The only labor troubles we've ever had here was way back when they first began unionizing this shop. The Union's been satisfied ever since; and as old Webster used to say—

PROUT: Let's forget old Webster—he's dead, now. *(Les turns away) You* said the Union would never go as far as it has.

LES: Maybe I did, George; we're all entitled to our margin of mistakes. Your office has made mistakes, too, ordering part-time layoffs while a runaway inflation is going on. Now you want to drop people altogether.

PROUT: Only the newer hands.

LES: We've got orders on our books, George. Who's going to do the apprentice work? Our best machinists? They'll laugh their heads off at you; or worse yet, they'll see the handwriting on the wall and you'll have the Union on your back for fair.—You can sit at your desk and scribble on a piece of paper; but I have to turn out pumps.

PROUT: You're crossing bridges before we get to them. *(Leans back; evenly)* Something I'd like to know, Les. This Joe Nesbit who's working with you—

LES: What about him?

PROUT: Is he one of those you have to keep here? He's just a substitute. And I believe I told you—we dropped him out of our Shipping Department.

LES: I need a good man on the radial drill. He's an expert.

PROUT: Is that your main reason?

LES: What other reason do I need?

PROUT: You're not touchy about this, are you, Les? I only want to make it clear to Ed. *(Gets up)*

LES: When do we have a conference about the Union situation?

PROUT: Who?

LES: You, me and Ed Ramsey.

PROUT: There's none scheduled between you, me and—Ramsey.

LES: He doesn't need my advice any more, is that it?

PROUT: I don't know what's on his mind. *(Pause)* About Nesbit—there are still plenty of good machinists walking the streets; if you need a man for the radial drill you can get one. As long as there's no special reason to keep him—

LES: He fills the bill, as far as I'm concerned.

PROUT: Right. Well, I'll tell Ed your point of view about Nesbit.—This isn't a bad cigar, Les. *(Exits)*

FERN: The merry-go-round is going round, Mr. Palmer.

LES: Let it go round.

FERN: *(Gets up)* I guess I just don't understand you any more, do I? *(Joe enters, left)* Here's your friend, Mr. Palmer. *(Exits, right)*

JOE: Is that a permanent cramp—her nose in the air? Or just whenever she sees me?

LES: She's all right; a little teed off today, that's all.

JOE: *(Casually)* To hell with her. *(Surveys the room)* Flowers—testimonials—

LES: Have a cigar.

JOE: I'm not used to cigars.—What do you want of me, Les? The congratulations of a mere mechanic?

LES: I seem to be the punching bag today. Step up, everybody; you, too. *(Curtly)* I sent for you because I want to help you.

JOE: I didn't ask for your help.

LES: That's right, you didn't. *(Without rancor)* You don't like me, Joe—that's your privilege. But I'm going to tell you just the same, I've stuck my neck out on account of you. Personnel doesn't want you here. That bastard of a Harry has gone around raising an alarm; Ramsey's all steamed up—

JOE: What's all the uproar? They don't have to keep me.

LES: No. And you don't have to work, either. You can go beat your brains out.

JOE: I get along.

LES: Okay, you get along.—Sit down at the other desk and fill this out. *(Hands him a blank form)* It's the employment questionnaire for Personnel. You're starting in the tool room tomorrow morning; there's no seniority problem there. It's a good job; you'll punch the time clock steady from now on. How does that suit you?

JOE: *(With a faint grin)* They want to throw me out, and you're putting me on steady? You know I'm on the blacklist.

LES: Nobody's blacklisted. It's illegal. *(Joe chuckles)* Fill out that form, that's all I'm asking you to do; I'll see that it gets by the front office. I'll tell them the truth about you: you're not organizing any more, you've learned better. I'll even tell them you'll keep quiet around the Union—

JOE: So that's it!

LES: *(Stung)* What do you care what *I* tell them? You can keep your jaws clamped while you're on the job; you can do that much? That's all I ask. —You're in. Go back to your machine, now. Tell Doris the good news when you get home tonight.

JOE: *(Not moving)* Would you mind telling me why you're doing this, Les?

LES: Why shouldn't I do it for you?

JOE: Don't tell me I dreamed everything that's happened. You couldn't hide your hatred of me—not even from the beginning, no matter how you tried. When Doris—

LES: Don't drive nails into me, Joe!

JOE: You couldn't stand me, for a whole list of reasons: because I had more life than you—because I always led, while you followed—

LES: I'm not listening!

(Door left opens and Harry enters)

HARRY: I'm sorry, Mr. Palmer—the detail sheets on the Tri-County job—

LES: They're on Charlie Conroy's bench.

HARRY: Yes, sir. I'll look there again.

LES: Did you want to see me?

HARRY: No, sir, not right now. *(Exits)*

LES: He spies on me; I sit in this office spying on the men.— You don't remember what my job is like: the bootlicking and con-niving. All you know is that I've been riding the gravy train while you've been knocking around every hole and corner. That's all you want to know—

JOE: I've got what's coming to me. Is that what you're working around to, Les? There's no law says I have to listen—

LES: *(With feeling)* You think I'm doing myself a favor looking out for you? I know how you see it—I don't even rate a thank-you. *(Harshly)* Since you bring it up, let me remind you: it was your own fault to start with—and you knew it. When I first came here as a learner you'd already been foreman two years; but everybody knew you couldn't last. You couldn't or wouldn't keep the men in line. Your head was full of idealistic notions that had nothing to do with your job. Then came the walkout—

JOE: And my finish.

LES: The day before the walkout you and I stood outside this shop, talking. You'd never go through a picket line, you said. I pleaded with you. I said, "You're the foreman here, Joe. Where's your common sense?" And what was your answer?

JOE: My answer was to stay home two days running. And on the third day you quit the Union and went up to Webster's office, beg-ging for my job.

LES: They wouldn't have taken you back for a present. Someone was bound to replace you—if not me, then somebody else. I went in and made good—is that something to be ashamed of?

JOE: Of course not. You're in the great tradition, Les. Walk over people till you get there, then do them favors out of the kindness of your heart.

LES: Joe, I believe in lending a hand when I can—"We pass this way but once," as the book says. You say I've always hated you, but you're wrong. I could have been a little jealous once, and it was understandable; but it was never my real feeling.—Sit there; there's something in this locker I want to show you. *(Takes dusty clothes out of the locker)* You know what these are? My old overalls and work shoes; I put them in there the day I became foreman. That was before I got harnessed up here like a goddamn mule— when I was still a raw kid, learning from you. Life was juicy in those days—the sky was bluer and the grass was greener. There were places like Raymond's Joint on the turnpike, where we used to go; the girls, Doris and Emma—we laughed a lot and learned a lot. *(Putting clothes back)* You may not consider it a debt I owe you; but I do.

JOE: What do you owe me?

LES: A thought of something more than this machine shop— industrial democracy, you called it, a better world, not dog-eat-dog . . . Go on hating me if you have to; but you need this job and I want to see you keep it. I have my hands full in this place, and I may be a fool for taking this on, in addition. But what have *you* got to lose? Nothing—not even your opinion of me! *(Quietly)* You baffle me, Joe. It can't be that you're just ornery—I know better. When I replaced you on this job, I was sure you'd boil over. All you said was "That's how things are," and then you simply went away—you and Doris—out of my life . . .

JOE: Yes.

LES: I try not to keep grudges, but I don't think *I* could have been so tolerant. It's gone on bothering me. Especially after all those years of silence, when you learned that Emma had died and you sent me a message. I wanted to tell you how grateful I was, but you'd written from some place unknown. *(Almost pleadingly)* What's made you so frozen, unforgiving and unreasoning except for that one time? What's turned you into an outlaw—and why must Doris and your children have to pay for it?

(A pause, as Joe remains silent. Chet enters with blueprints)

CHET: If you're busy, Mr. Palmer—

(Joe goes slowly to Fern's desk with the questionnaire; picks up a pen)

LES: *(With relief)* It's all right, Chet.

CHET: There's the list, boss. Those Engineering boys with their little pencils—

LES: You're up in the air, too. What for?

CHET: I got blown up by a land mine in Vietnam. Maybe I'll never come down.

LES: Fern says you want to leave here; is that true?

CHET: Why should I hang around when the company is getting ready for a mass layoff? They'll get away with it, too: the Union will let them.

JOE: *(Looks up)* Maybe not this time.

CHET: Sure it'll let them. That's the kind of Local we have. *(Without heat)* I know how you talk, Nesbit: "Stick together and it won't happen." But we've got no Union; all we have is a debating society—you and Harry tearing each other apart at the meetings. And you call that sticking together! I don't know what it's all about and I don't give a damn—I've got a good offer somewhere else.

LES: Look before you leap, Chet.

CHET: Yes, sir, I'm looking.—Meanwhile I'll go see those white-collar boys upstairs. When they draw something we have to build it. I wonder if they know that? *(Exits)*

LES: That's youth for you. Spit and vinegar. He'll find out what machine shops are: they're all alike.

JOE: Some day he'll learn to be part of the Union—that's even more important. *(Puts down pen; gets up)*

LES: Where are you going?

JOE: Back to my machine.—I can't answer this. You'd think they were passing me through the pearly gates instead of the employees' entrance. What'll I write down? That I was a union organizer once, out west? That I've been kicked around from here to hell and gone? That I changed my name half a dozen times to try and hold a job?

LES: Not even a good organizer, were you? Too headstrong—too outspoken—

JOE: I'm not accountable to you.

LES: You're accountable to your wife and kids. Doesn't that trouble you?

JOE: *(After a moment)* It does.

LES: Fill out that form. Leave the rest to me.

JOE: It's no good, Les. The Union's toughening up; that means your front office will cut my throat if they can do it. I've been on my feet at the Local, talking up for a wage hike, fighting the layoffs. Your office knows it; they know everything that goes on—or almost everything.

LES: You're impossible! I fought the layoffs too, didn't I? Anybody can tell you. And I'm still doing it.—Answer that thing any way you can, and I'll accept it.—Remember that little place around the corner—the Grotto? We'll go in there later and hoist a couple of beers to celebrate your job.

JOE: No, Les. You've been warming that chair of yours too long; you can't see that things don't come as easy as sitting down. How much can you do with the front office fighting you? It's all over the shop that they're ready to take you apart. Forget this gesture of yours—it doesn't suit you.

(He starts to exit. Prout enters, right)

PROUT: Just a minute, Nesbit—I want to talk to you.

LES: *(At once)* What for?

PROUT: We have something to ask him, Les.

LES: He doesn't have to answer.

PROUT: I think he does, if he wants to work here. We want to know who complained to the Union about this place.

JOE: I'll answer that. It's none of your business. The charge against the firm is made by the Union, not by any one member.

PROUT: Are you ashamed to admit *you* made it? I thought you pride yourselves on your principles—you and your kind?

(Ramsey enters, right)

JOE: *(Ominously)* What do you mean by "my kind"?

RAMSEY: The hate-America kind.

JOE: Who are you?

LES: Mr. Ramsey, the plant manager. Take it easy, Joe.

JOE: *(Calmly)* So you're Ramsey!—Suppose we talk about *your* kind—church-going, star-spangled jokers who pad their expense accounts—leeches who live off the work of others, fixers who buy off the people's representatives, "patriots" who don't even pay their income taxes if they can help it—

LES: That's enough!

JOE: The kind who tell me to get off the earth—

LES: *(Losing patience)* What sort of talk is that? You had a chance to clear yourself—

RAMSEY: Let him go. He's said enough to hang him.

JOE: Try and hang me, Mr. Ramsey—I have a hard neck. *(Exits, left)*

RAMSEY: Are you satisfied? I couldn't believe my eyes when George showed me his record. A professional agitator! You know he started his career here, in this very shop? He even got to be foreman before they threw him out—

PROUT: He's knocked around the country—a man with a string of aliases. Last year he worked at the plant in Michigan until they caught up with him.

LES: He makes a bad impression if you jump on him that way. He's his own worst enemy—one of those bad-tempered idealists. But he didn't sign that complaint, Ed—I'm sure of it. It's immaterial, anyhow, if the Union backs it up—

RAMSEY: We'll not discuss it any further. I want him fired, and at once, whether he signed a complaint or not. *(Pause)* Do you refuse?

LES: I do.

RAMSEY: *(Quietly)* I had an idea it would come to this, Palmer. This isn't the first time you've set yourself up as absolute in this shop. You've resisted every attempt to make Ajax a part of Superior—because the Corporation means nothing to you, and I, as its representative, mean still less. You've entrenched yourself here; you've built up a little empire with everybody taught to ignore any authority but your own— *(To Prout)* Give him that paper, George. *(Prout puts a legal paper on the desk)* This is a formal statement of Corporation policy on Ajax Pumps. So that there will be no further misunderstanding on employment or wage policies, I want your signature on that paper.

LES: Before I sign anything of the kind I expect to be consulted on it, Mr. Ramsey. I'm a shop supervisor here, not a foreman. *(He crumples up the paper, throws it into the waste basket)* Go ahead and take this up with Michigan. I'll match my department against the rest of this plant any day. I show a profit. What do you show?

RAMSEY: You may show a profit here, because you haven't deducted your share of the gross overhead. You show no percentage profit, which is all that matters. I don't expect you to understand that. But I'll tell you something you *can* understand: I've had enough of your obstruction—from now on I'm running this whole plant, and that includes Ajax Pumps. *(To Prout)* Find Harry. Tell him to give Nesbit his walking papers.

PROUT: Right, sir. *(Exits left)*

RAMSEY: That takes it off your hands.

LES: I don't recognize this firing. Nesbit is on our payroll until I say he's off.

RAMSEY: He's off as of this moment.

LES: *(After a pause)* I quit.

RAMSEY: That's ridiculous. The man's notorious, and you're making an issue of him—

LES: Nobody can take the hire and fire out of my hands. I'm leaving when the whistle blows. *(Goes to locker, starts getting his things together)*

RAMSEY: You can't walk out just like that. You have obligations to this firm.

LES: I have no contract with this firm.

RAMSEY: Nobody's telling you to leave. We're only asking you to recognize that Ajax Pumps is part of something greater.

LES: It's still Ajax Pumps to me—you can explain that to Michigan when they ask you why I left.

RAMSEY: You seem very sure Michigan will be interested.

(Les doesn't answer. Prout comes back with Harry)

PROUT: *(To Ramsey)* Nesbit's getting out of his overalls. If you want Harry for anything else—

RAMSEY: I have some news for you. Palmer has taken it into his head that he wants to terminate here.

PROUT: Well!

RAMSEY: He seems to mean it. He says he's walking out at noon.

(Ramsey and Prout exchange glances. They both turn to look at Harry)

RAMSEY: What do you say, Harry? Can you take over—beginning this afternoon?

HARRY: This afternoon, Mr. Ramsey?

RAMSEY: I know it's very short notice. We're running at top speed, just now.

HARRY: Yes, sir, it's pretty sudden—*(Sweating)* I could get into the swing of things in another week or two—

LES: Not today, Harry? It ought to be easy for a bright boy like you, stepping into another man's shoes. All you need is a little nerve. What of it if you *do* make a mistake or two? Like the time you forgot to drill the oil holes in the Fairmount job and we had to tear out the whole job and bring it back—

HARRY: Give me a chance at it, Mr. Ramsey. I can do it.

RAMSEY: We'll talk to you later, Harry.

(Harry exits, left)

RAMSEY: *(To Les)* You've taken good care he didn't learn the ropes. It's up to you to break him in before you leave. We're entitled to that much loyalty, at least—we've paid for it all these years.

LES: I've given my life for this firm—cracking the whip for you, cutting corners off the payroll, gouging your customers—I couldn't sleep nights; and now you call me disloyal!

RAMSEY: It's my belief that this whole Union trouble started with you—that you put yourself against the layoffs to show we can't run this place without you—

LES: *(Staggered)* That's a contemptible lie!

(Fern enters)

RAMSEY: Michigan will want to know why you want to keep this man Nesbit here; why you've handled him with kid gloves; why you refused point-blank to fire him—

PROUT: And why he wanted to put Nesbit on steady just this morning—even after the Union came down on us—

LES: I told you why!

RAMSEY: Isn't there something you forgot to mention? Hasn't Nesbit been a bosom friend of yours for almost twenty years?

(Pause)

LES: He married a girl I was engaged to. What does that prove?

RAMSEY: Come on, George. *(He and Prout turn to go)*

LES: You think I owe him anything—someone my girl friend married just for spite? *(They stop)* To spite me! It's true Joe Nesbit once was foreman here—that's how we met him, Doris and me. She didn't care anything about him until he was thrown out of here, then she turned right around and blamed me. "I'll stick with Joe until hell freezes over," she said—and that's the last I saw of either of them until he turned up here looking for work.

RAMSEY: You can tell that story to Superior Industries for what it may be worth; only this time there'll be no Nat Webster to validate it for you. George and I have a different testimony: about the way you've been apologizing for management, telling the men it's not *your* fault they're laid off . . . And it doesn't end there: all that talk about industrial democracy, anarchistic claptrap—You and Nesbit, two sides of the same coin!

PROUT: Only Nesbit is aboveboard.

LES: Get out of this office! I've had enough from you both!

RAMSEY: You've been aching for a showdown, Palmer, and you can have it. Leave here whenever you like—now or later. Ready or not, Harry will take charge. And let me warn you: if there are any Union repercussions over Nesbit, it will all be in your lap.—Miss Carmine!

FERN: Yes, sir.

RAMSEY: That paper Mr. Palmer threw into the waste basket a minute ago—if he stays here, I want it signed by him and delivered to me before noon today.

FERN: Yes, sir.

(Ramsey and Prout exit, right. Fern picks the crumpled sheet out of the basket, lays it on Les's desk)

FERN: Is this the paper he means?

LES: They saved up their maneuver for today!

FERN: *(Calmly)* What are you going to do about it?

LES: *(Shuts locker door)* I'll give Ramsey a run for his money— that's what I'll do! That's how they work, the Ramseys and the Prouts—while people like me build machines, they sit behind their desks writing notes, juggling figures; they spin webs just like spiders! The plant is showing a loss—that's why they have to frame me.

FERN: That's a reckless statement, Mr. Palmer. Mr. Ramsey and Mr. Prout are gentlemen, both of them.

LES: Maybe to their mothers! These administrators are all the same from Maine to California; yammering about loyalty and looking out for Number One. And anybody who interferes with their racket is "notorious"!

FERN: Nesbit is a buddy of yours—I heard you admit that yourself.

LES: Is that a crime I committed?

FERN: You ought to be more careful about the sort of accusations you make, Mr. Palmer. You'd do a lot better to show you're against Joe Nesbit and everything he stands for.

LES: How about the accusations you and they make? I didn't know you could be like that, Fern. You give me goose pimples with that talk.

FERN: I can't take it as calmly as you can, Mr. Palmer. I believe in loyalty and gratitude. My brother Clive died fighting for his country while you sat here making a good salary all through the war. *(Exits, right)*

LES: Goose pimples! *(Joe enters, left)* Come on in. You're just the man I want to see.

JOE: Just give me my time slip, will you, Les?

LES: I suppose you think you gave them a high-minded answer!

JOE: The way I answer is nobody's business but my own.

LES: You're wrong! It's my business, too. Ramsey jumped on me after you left. I threatened to quit, and he called me on it.

JOE: You threatened to quit? *(Sobered)* He can't let you do that. He'd have to explain it to the home office.

LES: He thinks all he needs to say is that you're a friend of mine.

JOE: Is that another thing he knows?

LES: He knows it, and he'll use it . . . Just because I wanted to help you—

JOE: I told you I don't want your help.

LES: Doris wanted it. She asked me for it.

JOE: Doris was here? *(Angered)* She had no right to come here!

LES: She had a right to ask for help. *(Bitterly)* Forget it. Ramsey's been looking for any excuse to get me, and the fat was in the fire when I didn't carry out his order. Now that Webster's gone, he thinks he has a clear field . . . But he'll learn different. This is only the beginning: when Michigan hears the truth, like you said—

JOE: It won't do, Les.

LES: What won't do?

JOE: Forget about Michigan. You're not acrylic. You won't get a hearing when they know you've been friendly with someone like me.

LES: That's insane! I'm the opposite of you in every conceivable way—

JOE: Will you listen to me? I worked at Superior Industries in Michigan last fall—you'll find that in my record. That's where all this panic is coming from in the first place—they've got over two thousand employees, and they're leaking in their pants for fear those people will go militant on them. Why should they believe you instead of Ramsey? Superior sent Ramsey down here because they have confidence in him, because he's their kind of administrator. You think he hasn't been writing to them all this time, poisoning their minds against you? And now he'll tell them you've been encouraging the Union, with my help—

LES: And they'll swallow that?

JOE: Did you ever try talking sense to anybody who's afraid of losing his shirt? It's either you or Ramsey, and Ramsey knows them all at the head office. Who do *you* know, now that Webster is dead? If Ramsey can't prove you encouraged this Union action, he'll have no trouble showing you condoned it, at least. One thing is sure: you're not with them, and that's an unforgivable sin . . . I'm not the only one who sticks in their throats; you do, too! You said so! They want you out, and you've given them an excuse. Any stick to beat a dog! *(Grimly)* Better go back and make your peace with Ramsey; ask him to forgive you.—I'd ask him for you, only I doubt if he'll listen to me.

(Pause)

LES: You think I'll go beg Ramsey to forgive me? So I can be a straw boss from now on, passing orders for him? After all my work here?

JOE: You have no choice.

LES: *(Fiercely)* Yes, I have. There are other jobs, by God!

JOE: Other jobs like this one? At the same wages?—The idea appeals to you, I can see that: walking out of here, saying "To hell with them." That feels good—that's a little taste of freedom; you'll kick up your heels for a week or two or three. Then you'll start looking for the kind of job you had, and you won't get it. You'll never have it again. Twenty years in one place, a shop supervisor used to giving orders, not to taking them. You're well into your forties now—that's a good age for bankers. And you walk out of here with a bad report card. Who's going to sponsor you? The men who kicked you out of here? You'll start looking for work—

LES: *(Frightened)* That's your own picture you're painting, not mine!

JOE: Are you sure? You're breaking into a cold sweat, just listening to me talk. What will you do when you're really up against it? When you pound the sidewalks looking for a job, and everywhere you go they whisper, "That's Les Palmer, the dog who bites the hand that feeds him"? If you're lucky you'll be back where you were twenty years ago. If not, you'll get into your overalls and cry with relief if somebody lets you go to work by the day, by the hour—

LES: *(Shouting)* I can do it if I have to!

JOE: *I* can do it. I'm tough, because I've had to do it all my life. But you—you bag of mush! . . . There's only one way to square yourself now—and that's to join the man-hunt! *(Phone rings)* That's for you. Why don't you answer it?

LES: *(Picks up the phone shakily)* Hello! Oh—Mr. Ramsey. I— That's all right . . . *(More relaxed)* We both did, Ed. I have a way of shooting my big mouth off sometimes . . . Naturally . . . I see what you mean about Harry . . . more experience . . . Nesbit? No, he's through. Even told me he doesn't want to stay. *(Pause)* Yes, sir, I have the paper you left. Thank you, Ed. *(Joe laughs. Les hangs up)* I knew he'd weaken. The whole thing was just a flareup. He wants to go on like before—

(He reaches for the crumpled sheet, signs it hastily)

JOE: Not like before. You think they'll forget what happened here today? You'll stay on just to show Harry how to take your place. You know that, but you're shutting your eyes tight, thinking only how much longer you can hang on. Another hour, another minute— *(Hard)* You thought you were building security here, brick by brick. You worried more about this place than your boss did. And somebody like Ramsey raises his voice and you're through for good.

LES: Laugh if you feel like it—but you're the one who makes the big mistakes—not me. You had your chance and you chose the hard way. I don't make mistakes like that—not big ones. Sometimes, like today, I begin to get excited—but I always get cold feet, and that's what keeps me safe. I've spent my whole life playing safe, and I know the game backwards. It's a game you'll never learn.

JOE: Sign my time slip.

LES: *(Signs it)* I tried to help you—don't forget that.

JOE: I'll remember it. Among my souvenirs. *(Getting up)*

LES: You can't go before you promise me something. You're not going to complain to the Local about being fired?

JOE: Why not?

LES: You can't do that, Joe. Ramsey'll hold that against me—he said he would.

JOE: You think I ought to lie to the Local for your sake? Ramsey knew I'd be through here tomorrow night, but he couldn't wait for that. "At once!" he said—and you let him do it. It's a real issue for the Local to fight on.

LES: You're going to drag this whole business into your Union meeting?

JOE: Certainly. That's where it belongs.

(Harry enters with a clip board, left. Seeing Joe and Les together, he starts to back out)

LES: *(Deliberately)* Come on in, Harry—I want to talk to you. Nesbit, here, is making threats: he claims he was wrongfully dismissed. What will the Union do? Take *his* word?

HARRY: *(Looks from Les to Joe, sensing a trap)* You two slugging it out—it's not what I expected.—It'll be up to the Local. If he makes out a case he'll be supported. If not—

(Fern and Chet have entered quietly, left)

LES: What sort of case can he make out, after practically assaulting the plant manager? A gadfly, a subversive and a dangerous malcontent—all the years I've known him!

HARRY: At last we're getting the truth.

JOE: A smidgen of truth in a full load of horseshit. You expect to sell that to the Local? Who's going to buy it?

HARRY: The Ex Board, to start with. They'll call a special meeting to take care of you—and the Union will tear up your working card and throw it in your face.

JOE: We'll see about that when the time comes, Harry. It's a backward Local, that's true: fallen asleep in a dream of prosperity forever; and some of the members haven't liked the way I talk at meetings. But the times are jolting them awake. Nobody wants to be separated from his job in the middle of a raging inflation, and the Union knows I fought this company while you were making excuses for it . . . And the Union's Ex Board has long been used to pulling the Red scare—but they're out of date: that steady diet of red herring has finally turned everyone's stomach.

HARRY: *(Ignores him. To Les)* Have you decided if you're leaving this afternoon, Mr. Palmer? Because if you are, I'd better start on the work sheets.

LES: Rest easy, Harry. I'm not leaving this afternoon—or tomorrow—or the day after. I'm not leaving, period. I'm staying in charge here.

HARRY: You took that up with Mr. Ramsey?

LES: Mr. Ramsey took that up with me.

HARRY: Yes, sir. I was only asking. *(He exits, left)*

LES: That two-faced little bastard! He's not eating me. Not yet.
(He becomes aware of Fern and Chet)

FERN: You fairly took my breath away, Mr. Palmer. I want to congratulate you—

LES: Who asked you two to come in here, in the middle of this?

FERN: I ran into Chet upstairs. I've been trying to make him reconsider staying here. His future—

CHET: What's my future in this place? What I just saw? What'll I turn out to be—a foreman like Les Palmer, brown-nosing all my life? Or a hustler like Harry Fulton? If that's my future, you can have it.

LES: Where do you get the insolence to talk like that? You're not dry behind the ears yet; learn your place!

CHET: *(To Joe)* It hit me all of a sudden, Nesbit—when a pair like Harry and Les put their heads together, none of us is safe.
(Exits, left)

FERN: *(Runs after him)* Chet!

LES: There's no respect any more. Every punk thinks he has the right to wipe his feet on you.

JOE: He doesn't go for your kind of world, that's all.

LES: He'd better learn to live in it. It's his world, too.

JOE: What if he's not sure it's going to last forever? Lately it's been looking very sick.

LES: *(Savagely)* It'll last! You had me scared for a while with that hard-luck picture of yours; you have imagination, I'll say that for you . . . Maybe you're right about this is my end as a supervisor. Well, I'll be foreman, if they'll have me; when a man is older he takes what he can get. And even if I never work again, I still have a small balance in the bank and my home almost all paid for—besides social security and retirement. It may not add up to much, in your opinion, but I have no one to support, and it'll be enough. I was never in a fix like yours, and never will be. *(Changing)* I'm sorry at the way things turned out, Joe. I had to act the way I did, you know that. You'd do the same if you were in my place.

JOE: You're throwing your garbage into my yard. *(As Ramsey enters, right, with Prout and a Photographer)* Here comes your owner.
(He withdraws upstage)

RAMSEY: *(To Photographer)* Ready? Let's go! *(Extends his hand to Les, reads from a mimeographed sheet)* "On this auspicious occasion it is indeed gratifying to honor one who has served Superior Industries and its subsidiary, Ajax Pumps, so faithfully and so well."
(They shake hands formally)

LES: Thank you, sir.

(Harry enters, left, joins the group at a nod from Prout)

RAMSEY: "On behalf of the Superior organization—its officers and shareholders, its supervisors and employees—it is my great privilege to present to you, Lester Woodrow Palmer, in commemoration of your twentieth year with the company, and as a small token of our affection and regard, this gold cigar lighter." *(Presents the lighter)*

PHOTOGRAPHER: Hold it that way, please. Let's see the cigar lighter. Move in closer together, folks. *(Flash)* Just once more. A little more animation— *(Flash)* That will do nicely. Thank you one and all.

RAMSEY: I'll take that signed paper now, Les . . . I'll see you and Harry in the afternoon: we have a lot of work ahead of us on the termination schedule of this department.

(Ramsey and entourage exit, right; Harry exits, left. Joe starts to leave)

LES: Joe! Wait a minute! *(Counts out bills)* I want you to take this money; it's for Doris and the kids, not you. I'll see that they get more if they need it. Only don't keep them and their grief in this small town, where I and others have to see them.

JOE: We're staying right here to fight this out, Les. Shove that money up you-know-where! *(He turns to go)*

LES: You're telling yourself it's your turn at last, is that it? Evening up the score with me—with this place—

JOE: No. Not really.

LES: Rubbing it in that nobody owns you . . . That's true: you're ownerless as a stray dog in the street.—I hang on here because I've got something to hang on to. What have *you* got? The love of a family you've made miserable? The respect of your enemies, who step on your head? The conscience of a pauper? What's brought you to this pass?

JOE: I can't hope to make you understand it, Les. It's the sound of a different drummer.

(He exits, right, Pause. Les starts to light a cigar with his new lighter, as Fern enters, left)

FERN: *(Exclaims)* You have your present, Mr. Palmer! Don't tell me the ceremony is all over!

LES: One, two, just like that.

FERN: Couldn't they have waited? Goodness, how annoying! Now I have to take these flowers back. *(Picks them up)* I tried to talk things out with Chet, but it's useless. It's all for the birds, he says.— You know what I'm beginning to think? He's just another one of those longhairs! And he seemed like such a serious type at bottom!—I'm so relieved you spoke out, Mr. Palmer. It was so impressive the way you stood up to Nesbit! It took moral courage.

(Les tosses down the lighter, his cigar unlit)

FERN: Is something wrong, Mr. Palmer?

LES: A little let down, that's all, Fern, after a big day.

FERN: You smoke too much, Mr. Palmer. You ought to give up smoking. It isn't too hard to stop, if you make your mind up. It only takes a little moral courage. *(She dabs at her eyes)*

Curtain

Stanley Richards

Since the publication of his first collection in 1968, Stanley Richards has become one of our leading editors and play anthologists, earning rare encomiums from the nation's press (the *Writers Guild of America News* described him as "easily the best anthologist of plays in America"), and the admiration of a multitude of devoted readers.

Mr. Richards has edited the following anthologies and series: *The Best Short Plays 1977; The Best Short Plays 1976; The Best Short Plays 1975; The Best Short Plays 1974; The Best Short Plays 1973; The Best Short Plays 1972; The Best Short Plays 1971; The Best Short Plays 1970; The Best Short Plays 1969; The Best Short Plays 1968; Great Musicals of the American Theatre: Volume One; Great Musicals of the American Theatre: Volume Two; America on Stage: Ten Great Plays of American History; Best Plays of the Sixties; Best Mystery and Suspense Plays of the Modern Theatre; 10 Classic Mystery and Suspense Plays of the Modern Theatre* (the latter six, The Fireside Theatre/Literary Guild selections); *The Tony Winners; Best Short Plays of the World Theatre: 1968-1973; Best Short Plays of the World Theatre: 1958-1967; Modern Short Comedies from Broadway* and *London; and Canada on Stage.*

An established playwright as well, he has written twenty-five plays, twelve of which (including *Through a Glass, Darkly; Tunnel of Love; August Heat; Sun Deck; O Distant Land;* and *District of Columbia*) were originally published in earlier volumes of *The Best One-Act Plays* and *The Best Short Plays annuals.*

Journey to Bahia, which he adapted from a prize-winning Brazilian play and film, *O Pagador de Promessas,* premiered at The Berkshire Playhouse, Massachusetts, and later was produced in Washington, D.C., under the auspices of the Brazilian Ambassador and the Brazilian American Cultural Institute. The play also had a successful engagement Off-Broadway during the 1970-1971 season; and in September, 1972, it was performed in a Spanish translation at Lincoln Center. During the summer of 1975, the play was presented at the Edinburgh International Festival in Scotland, after a tour of several British cities.

Mr. Richards' plays have been translated for production and publication abroad into Portuguese, Afrikaans, Dutch, Tagalog, French, German, Korean, Italian and Spanish.

He also has been the New York theatre critic for *Players Magazine* and a frequent contributor to *Playbill, Theatre Arts, The Theatre* and *Actors' Equity Magazine,* among other periodicals.

As an American Theatre Specialist, Mr. Richards was awarded

three successive grants by the U.S. Department of State's International Cultural Exchange Program to teach playwriting and directing in Chile and Brazil. He taught playwriting in Canada for over ten years and in 1966 was appointed Visiting Professor of Drama at the University of Guelph, Ontario. He has produced and directed plays and has lectured extensively on theatre at universities in the United States, Canada and South America.

Mr. Richards, a New York City resident, is now at work on *The Best Short Plays 1978* and a collection of *Great Rock Musicals*.